THE INDIANA 1820 ENUMERATION OF MALES

Compiled by

Mary M. Morgan

The Family History Section Indiana Historical Society

Indianapolis 1988

Library of Congress Cataloging-in-Publication Data

The Indiana 1820 enumeration of males.

   Includes index.
   1. Indiana--Census, 1820. 2. United States--
Census, 4th, 1820. 3. Registers of births, etc.--
Indiana. 4. Indiana--Genealogy. I. Morgan, Mary M.
F525.I53 1988   929'.3772   88-292
ISBN 0-87195-010-3

Copyright 1988 Indiana Historical Society

Copies of this publication may be obtained from the Indiana Historical Society, 315 West Ohio Street, Indianapolis, Indiana 46202.

FOREWORD

Census records are among the most useful of genealogical resources for locating a person in a certain place at a certain time. Pre-1850 enumerations are of less value than those of 1850 and later, due in part to their lack of completeness. Thus parallel records like tax and voter records provide a much needed alternative.

The Indiana enumeration of white male inhabitants over twenty-one years, as it survives, contributes significantly to the body of census-related records. The 1816 Indiana Constitution, Article III, Section 2, required, for legislative apportionment, that the general assembly "in the year eighteen hundred and twenty, and every subsequent term of five years, cause an enumeration to be made of all the white male inhabitants above the age of twenty-one years." The whole of Indiana was divided into thirty-three counties by February 1, 1820. Clerks of the circuit court were to send a record of return to the Secretary of State. Fourteen clerks did, and these records were used to make this publication of the Family History Section, Indiana Historical Society.

Mary M. Morgan, a member of the Family History Section, has generated an extremely accurate transcript of the original returns, now deposited in the Archives Division, Indiana Commission on Public Records. She worked from an enlarged photocopy of the original, copying entries exactly as they were spelled. She verified questionable entries against the original, consulted with others on interpretations of names, and checked names against the 1820 federal census and other contemporary records.

The Indiana 1820 Enumeration of Males provides an additional source for genealogists as a part of the continuing publications program of the Family History Section, Indiana Historical Society, to provide little-used but highly valuable public and private records for those interested in Indiana family history.

John J. Newman, Chair
Family History Section

INTRODUCTION

This compilation was made from a photocopy of the original record. Faded ink, poor writing and poor spelling made some of the names very difficult to read. They were copied as nearly as possible as they appear. No attempt was made to correct obvious errors in spelling. In the records of one county no "i" was dotted nor "t" crossed. Vowels were added, interchanged and omitted. Parts of Monroe and Wayne counties were especially difficult.

Every effort was made to decipher the names. Questionable ones were checked with the original record, the 1820 census and available marriage records. Check every conceivable spelling to find the name you are hunting.

Knox County was listed by township. The spelling of the township names was retained as they appear in the original record.

Perry County listed one name per household followed by an Arabic number to indicate more than one.

The following counties show the date the enumeration was certified:

Gibson	1 Nov 1820	Monroe	20 Oct 1820
Jefferson	4 Nov 1820	Perry	2 Nov 1820
Jennings	23 Oct 1820	Ripley	20 Oct 1820
Knox	13 Nov 1820	Vanderburgh	27 Sep 1820

Abbreviations used:
- m/o   Name entered then marked out
- +   Name appears more than once on that page

CONTENTS

Crawford County	1
Gibson County	4
Jackson County	8
Jefferson County	13
Jennings County	24
Knox County, Vincennes Township	27
Knox County, Widener Township	31
Knox County, Washington Township	31
Knox County, Palmyra Township	32
Knox County, Harrison Township	33
Knox County, Johnston Township	34
Knox County, Decker Township	35
Knox County, Busseron Township	35
Monroe County	36
Orange County	39
Perry County	46
Posey County	49
Ripley County	54
Vanderburgh County	57
Washington County	60
Wayne County	71
Index	77

CRAWFORD COUNTY

ABELL FRANCES
ANDREWS WILLIAM
ALEXANDER WALKER
ALLEN ARCHIBALD
AUBREY THOMAS N
BULLOCK JOHN
BOGARD BENJAMIN
BENTLY WILLIAM
BARKER HENRY
BANNON JOSEPH
BROWN WILLIAM
BROWN JAMES
BARNET WILLIAM
BARNET JAMES
BARROWS THOMAS
MacBRIDE ALLEN
BOWMAN JAMES
BRISCOW WILLIAM
BLACK RICHARD
BLACKBURN EPHRAIM
BASTEN JAMES
BARTEN JOSEPH
BELCHER JESSE
BIELS DAVID
BIELS JOSEPH
BRILEY JAMES
BRILEY ABSOLOM
BIRD MASON
BIRD JONATHON
BESLEY SAMUEL
BABB STEPHEN
BARNS THOMAS
BOGARD JAMES
BOONE WANTLEY
BAILY JOHN
BABB WILLIAM
BELL JOHN
BROWFIELD WILLIAM
BURROWS WILLIAM
BARNET ALEXANDER
CAMPBELL WILLIAM
CANNON JOHN
CRIUTOUS PHILIP
CONDRY JOHN
CAUSBEY JOHN
COAPLAND ANDREW
CAROD JACOB
MacCURRY EDWARD
COAPLAND CHARLES
CHAPEN SAMUEL
COURSE WILLIAM
MacCARTY WILLIAM

CLARK JOHN
CAMPBELL ENOS
CONDRA PHILIP
CREEK WILLIAM
CAMP REUBEN
McCARTY JOHN
MacCARTY ABNER
CLARK JOHN
MacCULLUM JAMES
CAMP CHARLES
CAMP SAM'L
CAMP WILLIAM
DAVIDSON THOMAS
DAVIS THOMAS
DOWN EZEKIEL
DAVIS PETER
DAVIS EVIN
DILLIMO MICHAEL
DEE SAMUEL
EASLY THOMAS
ESLY STEPHEN
EDSOL DANIEL
EVIRAGE ABRAM
FREED JOHN
FORD NOAH
FOLLOWELL JOHN
FROMAN JACOB
FOLLOWELL WILLIAM
FLEMMON THOMAS
FLEMMON DAVID
FLINN JAMES
FRAKES PETER
FLANNERY JOHN
FLANNERY JAMES
FRAKES ALEXANDER
FULLINGWIDER HENRY
FROMAN ABRAHAM
FUNK PETER
FUNK JOSEPH
FUNK JOHN
GREEN HENRY
GLENN JOHN SR
THOMAS GOLDEN L
GOODSON JOHN
GOLDEN EDWARD
GOLMAN JOHN
GRAVES WILLIAM
GOODMAN WILLIAM
GOODMAN JESSE
GRAVES WILLIAM
GLEEN JAMES
GLEEN SAMUEL SR

GLEEN THOMAS
GLEEN SAMUEL JR
GOOLMAN JOHN JR
GRIGGS DAVID
GUEN ISM
GRIMES ROBERT
GILLILAND JOHN
HOYT WILLIAM
HAWKINS DAVID
HART REGUS
HELOBY JACOB
HELBY JOSEPH
HELBY RICHARD
HARVEY MICHAEL SR
HARVEY MICHAEL JR
HAWES JAMES
HALL CORNELIUS
HOLLAND ANTHONY
HOBB ISAAC
HOSKEN NENUR
HALL WILLIAM
HOBBS ABRAHAM
HOBBS NATHAN
HOBACK ANDREW
HOBACK MARQUIS
HOBBS NATHAN
HOLT JOSHUA
HANKS JOSEPH
HUGHS ELEPAT
HUEY BENJAMIN
HOBBS HIRAM
JEWELL JOHN SR
JEWELL JOHN JR
JUSTICE JOHN
JONES DAVID
JONES HOMER
JUSTUS MOSES
JONES GOREG
BLY MESOM
JEWELL WILLIAM
JONES MICHAL
JONES JACOB
MacINTOSH JAMES
KING ALEXANDER
KELMS JAMES SR
KINKAID ANDREW
KINKAND JOSEPH SR
KINKAD JOSEPH JR
KELMS JAMES JR
KELMS ISAAC
KINKAID WILLIAM
KINCAID JOHN

1

CRAWFORD COUNTY

KELLOR JOHN
McKEE WILLIAM
KENDELL YELLY
LUTHER GEORGE
LUTHER PETER
LEWIS JAMES
LAURANCE LANDEN
LAURANCE WASHINGTON
LYNCH JOHN
LYNCH THOMAS
LYNCH JESSE
LYNCH CHARLES
LONGEST CALEB
LONGEST JAMES
LUCAS JOSHUA
LEE JOHN JR
LEE JOHN SR
LEE ABRAHAM
LEVENWORTH SETH M
LEVENWORTH ZEBULON
LEVI SOLOMON
LOVELL REUBEN
LIKINS MARK
LANDERS WILLIAM
BEBY ALLEN
SLATER WILLIAM
MAYFIELD THOMAS
MARTIN EDWARD
MOORE ELISHA
MEATHERS WILLIAM
MORGAN EBENEZER E
MACMAHAN SAMUEL
MORE ROBERT
MUND SAMUEL
MEATHERS JOHN
MacMICKLE PETER
MacMICKLE JACOB
MAY WILLIAM
MUSROVE AQUILER
MILLS WILLIAM
MANSFIELD JAMES
MASON ANDREW
MORROW SAMUEL
MONK MALECHA
MILLER DAVID
MILLER PETER
MILLER HINEY
MacMURTER JOHN
MacMURTER JAMES
MacMURTER WILLIAM
NICHOLSON JOSEPH
NICHOLSON ZACHARIA

NANCE JAMES R
NICHOLSON JOHN
NIGHT ROBERT
NEWKIRK CORNELIUS
OSBURN WILLIAM
OSBURN ROBERT
OSBURN RICHARD
OSBURN SOLOMON
OSBURN JOSEPH
OSBURN JAMES
OBANION BRYANT
OSBURN SAMUEL
OSBURN JOHN
OSBURN JONATHAN
PECKINGPAW PETER
PEARSON WILLIAM
POPE ELIJAH
PECKINGPAW JOHN
MacCARTY NICHOLAS
EDES JOHN
PHIPS JAMES
LEE JESSE
SIMSON DAVID S
MARTIN JAMES D
DAVIDSON DANIEL
TILLER GEORGE
PETER EDWARD G
PAYTON JAMES
PEYTON JOHN
PENNINGTON MOSES
PENNINGTON WILLIAM
PATRICK MASTEN
POSEY A W G
PEARSON REUBEN
POE JEREMIAH
PATRICK BRI
POPE PILGRAM
POTTER WILLIAM
PARR THOMAS
PASUR WILLIAM
PEARSON JAMES
PETTET WILLIAM
PECKANPAW HENRY
RASOR CHRISTIAN
REEL MICHAEL
RICE JACOB
ROBESON ZENO
ROBERTSON THOMAS
RUTH JOHN
RIDDLE GEORGE
RYLE WILLIAM
RYLEE JOHN

ROOS DAVID
ROBERTS WILLIAM
DAVIS JOSEPH
MARTIN JAMES
DAVIS JACOB
CLARK JOHN
DENISON JOHN
RIDDLES BENJAMIN
REAL CLARK
RIDDLE CHARLES
RANDLET JOHN
RIDGE CHARLES
RIDDLE JOHN
RIDDLE JESSE
ROUSE JOHN
ROSS ISAAC
ROUSE JAMES
ROBERTSON STEPHEN
RODEROCK HENRY
ROUSE WILLIAM
RODROCK SOLLEN
RODROCK PETER
RUSH JAMES
HELMS THO'S
REECE JONATHAN
RICHARDS JOHN
MacRAE DANIEL A
MacRAE ALEXANDER B
RIDDLE JAMES
SAVAGE CHAMNESS
SMITH MOSES
SAMUELS ROBERT
SECATT PETER
SCOTT MORT
STURGEON DAVID
RODEROCK - - -
MAESWELL THOMAS
MAESWELL JONATHAN
STEWART BENJAMIN
STURGEON JEREMIAH
STURGEON ROLLY
STURGEON JOHN JR
SPRINGER CHARLES
STURGEON JOHN SR
STROUD THOMAS
JONUR JAMES R S
STONE JOHN
STONE CLEON
STEWART LASARUS
STEWART DAVID
STEVENS JOHN
SANDERS BENJAMIN

CRAWFORD COUNTY

SCOTT ROBERT
SCOTT WILLIAM
SAMUELS WILLIAM
STARR JOHN
SCOTT WM L
SCOTT WILLIAM C
SCOTT JOHN W
SYBERT JOSEPH
SYBERT JOHN
SCHOONOVER DAVID
SANDS ROBERT
SHAW JOHN
SLOAN ARCHIBALD
SNILLING BENJAMIN
SCRUTCHFIELD JESSE
SAMUELS JOHN
SHEPHERD JOHN
SMITH ABRAHAM
SCOTT JOHN R
STARR JOHN J P
STURSON NATHAN
STOVERING DAVID
LISTON JOHN
SAVIN PETER
SHACKLE ABRAHAM
STRAUGHN NATHANIEL
TIBB JOSEPH
TOLLER JESSE
TONEY ALEXANDER
TONEY JOHN
TOWER A BATES
TOWER COTTEN
TIBB JOHN
TUCKER MARTIN H
TUCKER DAVID
TAYLOR DAVID
THOM ALLEN D
TADLACK ELISHA
TADLOCK JEREMIAH
TOTTEN JAMES
TOTTEN LEWIS
UNDERHILL JAMES
UNDERHILL WILLIAM
UNDERHILL JOHN
VAUGHN OBADIAH
VAUGHN JAMES
VANWINKLER JOSEPH
VANWINKLE ABRAHAM
VANMETTER JOHN
VANWINKLE JAMES
VINSON JESSE
WALLACE DAVID

WYMAN GEORGE
WILLIAMS CONSTANT
WATSON WILLIAM
WEDMAN JACOB
WEATHERS SAMUEL
WILLS ANTHONY
MacWILLIAMS JOHN
WOODS JOHN
WALKER ROBERT
WILLIAMS RICHARD
WILLIAMSON THOMAS
WILLIAMSON THOMAS
WILBER WILLIAM P
WISMAN ABRAHAM
WATSON BENJAMIN
WATSON JOHN
WRIGHT CHRISTOPHER
WHITEHEAD ARTHUR
WEATHERS BENJAMIN
WAY SAMUEL
WESTFALL VINSON
WILSON JOHN
WILKS GEORGE H
WILKS HENRY
WILKS SAMUEL
WYMAN LEWIS
WESTFALL SAMUEL
WHITEHILL DAVIS
WHITEHILL WILLIAM W
YATES ROBERT
YATES JOHN
WARFIELD HENRY ESQ
DENFORD JOHN
CANROOD HENRY
ALLEN JOHN
TYLER OLIVER
GOWER WALTER
DAMPILL WM
BROWN JAMES
DENFORD TOBIUS A
FOLLOWELL LINDSEY
SHAVER JONATHAN
GLASS GEORGE
TUCKER WILLIAM
BEBBY ALLEN
PINTOX SAMUEL
COT JOHN
BRACHNEY ELI
HALY RUIR
WHITE RICHARD
LAURANCE ALFORD
BULLINGTON WILLIAM

CAMPBELL WILLIAM H
HALL GARRET
GOTT GLAYSEN
WITMAN WILLIAM
SAMSON DAVID
YATES BENJAMIN
MILLS REUBEN
FLANERY JOHN
HOBACK MARQUES
ESLY STEPHEN
WILSON STEVEN
MacFARLAND ROBERT
GOLDMAN MOSES
MAYFIELD THOMAS
GABHARD HENRY
POTTER JAMES
SAYYEARS LEVY
FOWLER DUDLY
O'BANNION JOSEPH
EVENS ABRAHAM
ROLLAND ANTHONY
HALL WILLIAM
CURRY WILLIAM R
FOLLER RICHARD
WILLIAMS ISAAC
BURROWS JESSE
CARTS EDWARD
BEDWELL JOHN
LINDSEY JOHN
SOUHEAVER VALENTINE
HUFMAN JEROD
LYON TIMOTHY
WOODFORD JULIS
BEARS ANDRUS
LYON BENJAMIN
LOTT WILLIAM
SMITH JOHN
DOVER THOMAS
BENNET JAMES T
RAYMON A
LATHROP SAMUEL
DAVIS ASY
McNIGHT JOHN
SHAFFER DANIEL
LYON JAMES
WEST STEPHEN D
AMOUS WILLIAM
LYON JOEL
WILSON STEWART
WILLIAMS JESSE
THOMSON THOMAS
SMITH WILLIAM

CRAWFORD COUNTY

BLACBURN HUGH
BROWN FREDRICK
NOX FACTOR
THURSTON RICHARD
NUHAL BENJAMIN
COOPER JOHN G
JONES GEORGE
MacGEE JESS
FOLLOWELL MARTIN
BROWN JAMES
JEFFRES ELIAS
GREIGS DAVID
DOVER JACOB
TILLER JOEL

HART JOHN
DUNAN ANDREW
BUCHANON JOHN S
GOWEN WALTER
PORTER JOHN
BROWN BENJAMIN
THOMSON ISAAC
FORD NOAH JR
SAWHEBBER JACOB
DANFORD JOSIAS
HELMS THOMAS
HILORY CHAMNESS
HOLMES THOMAS
MacCARTY NICHOLAS

DAVIDSON DANIEL
JAESON ROBERT
GOTT HASON
WILSON STEWART
GOURDAN MOSES
HAMBLIN JOHN
SAWHEBBER JOHN
ADAM JOHN
JACOBS JOHN
LANNON WILLIAM
WISEMEN JOHN
WESTFALL WILLIAM
LAKE WILLIAM
GRIMES ROBERT
ONNEAL JOHN

GIBSON COUNTY

ADAMS JAMES
ALCORN THOMAS
ALSOP REUBIN
ASH ROBERT
ARCHER THOMAS
AYRES AZERIAH
ASH JAMES
ALDREDGE JOHN
ARCHER WILLIAM
ALEXANDER JOHN
ARBURTHNOT JOHN
ALSOP WILLIAM
ASH THOMAS L
AYRES CHRISTOPHER
AKIN JAMES
ALLON GASHAM
AYRES HENRY
ALLEN CLEMANT
ANDERSON JAMES
ADEASON SETH
ABECRUMLY ALEXANDER
ATHERINGTON HENRY
ADAMS SAMUEL
ARMSTRONG WILLIS
BROWN JOSEPH R
BALDWIN LEMUEL
BURLIN JOHN
BREUNER FREDERICK
BRADING JAMES
BARKER JESSE
BRITTINGHURN WILLIAM
BURNETT ARMSTED

BRARETTON JOHN
BARR JOHN
BROWN GEORGE
BENSON WILLIAM
BARKER WILLIAM
BEARD SAMUEL
BORING ABSOLAM
BRISCOE PHILLIP
BROWN JOHN
BENNETT HEZEKIAH
BULLARD BRYANT
BOWMAN GEORGE
BRAZELTON DAVID B
BOICOURT SAMUEL L
BURNETT JAMES
BLITHE ANDREW
BLACK ROBERT
BULLARD JOHN
BULLARD PETER
BROWN JOHN
BENNETT LEWIS
BRIGHT LEWIS
BORING NICHOLAS
BORING JOHN
BROTHERS DAVID
BROTHERS WILLIAM
BOILES JOHN
BORING GEORGE
BERNETT JOHN
BENSON JOHN
BARTON DAVID
BUCKNER HENRY

BARNOTT JAMES
BARR WILLIAM
BORING JOHN D
BINGHAM WILLIAM
BIDLEMAN SAMUEL
BROWNLEE GEORGE
BAKER WILLIAM
BALDWIN JAMES
BROWN BASEL
BECKS BENJAMIN V
BURTON JOHN
BREEDLOVE JAMES
BORING ABSOLAM
CONGER LEWIS
CROW ROBERT
CROW JAMES JR
CODE GEORGE
CONGER SEBASTON
CULBERSON BENJAMINE
CREEK KILLION
CUNNINGHAM ANDREW
CUNNINGHAM STEWART
CHAMBERS GEORGE
COCKRAM WILLIAM
CALVIN WILLIAM
CHEEK JAMES
CHEEK LEWIS
COCKOM JAMES
COCKOM WILLIAM
CHAPPEL THOMAS
CULBERSON ANDREW
CHITTENDEN HOMER

GIBSON COUNTY

CONNER ROBERT
CROSS FITHUSON
CARLTON WILLIAM
CREEK JACOB
SHARP ABRAHAM
CURRY JAMES R
CLARK ARCHEY
CLARK OBEDIAH
CROW WILLIAM
CHAPMAN THOMAS
COCKRAM JAMES
CUNNINGHAM GEORGE
CHEEK WILLIAM
CROW JOHN
CHITTENDEN WILLIAM
CASCEY JOEL F
CHAMBERS JOSEPH
CURRY HENRY
DUPRIEST JOHN
DECKER JACOB
DECKER LUKE
DAVIS JOHN
DAVIDSON JOSEPH
DAVIDSON ELIJAH
DUNICK WILLIAM B
DECKER ABRAHAM
DAY ROBERT
DECKER NICHOLAS
DAVIS RICHARD
DUNKIN JOSHUA
DAVIS DANIEL
DEFFINDALL PHILLIP
DECKER JOHN
DAVIS SOLOMON
DEVIN ALEXANDER
DAVIS LOVE
DAVIS WILLIAM
DARNELL EPHRAIM
DUPREEST WILLIAM
DUNKIN GREEN
DOWNEY JOHN
DAVIS BENJAMINE
DAVIS JESSE
DAVIS ROBERT C
DICK DAVID
DUFF JOSEPH
DANIEL RICHARD
DEFFINDALL JOSEPH
EMMERSON JESSEE
EMBREE WILLIAM
EMERSON JONATHAN
ELLIOTT ROBERT

EMMERSON RUBIN
EVANS ROBERT M
EVANS JAMES
EDINGLOW SILAS
ENNIS JOHN
FISHER JOHN B
FREDERICK SEBASTIN
FREDERICK PHILLIP
FENNY JAMES
FITZGERAULD JOHNSON
FREDERICK PETER JR
FALLS ROBERT
FITZGERAULD JAMES
FREDERICK MICHAEL
FITZJERAULD JAMES
FORGERSON JOHN
FORBUSH GEORGE
FIELDS ABERHAM
FIELDER JOHN
FINNY SAMUEL
FERGERSON JAMES
FISHER STEPHEN
FISHER PERNELL
FINNY ANDREW
FOSTER WILLIAM P
GULLICK JONATHAN
GORDON SAMUEL
GARDISON JOHN
GAMBERL WILLIAM
GARRETT PRESLY
GARDNON RICHARD
GARTON WILLIAM
GORDON JOHN
GALAWAY DAVID
GAMBORE HENRY
GARRETT HENRY
GAMBERL DAVID
GRANEY THOMAS
GRISSOM THOMAS S
GRIGSBY DEMPLES
GORDON SAMUEL
HALLBROOKS WILLIAM
HALLBROOKS GEORGE
HANKS WILLIAM
HOW ROBERT
HARDY WILLIAM A
HEDESTOOW ALEXANDER
HARVEY ALEXANDER
HANDMAN JOHN
HOPKINS FRANCIS
HAWKINS THOMAS
HUMPHREYS GEORGE SR

HAZELTON DANIEL
HOGER WILFERD
HOGE JAMES W
HARTON GEORGE
HARRINGTON WILLIAM
HARRINGTON CHARLES
HUMPHREYS UNAL
HUMPHREYS JOSEPH
HARBER JOSEPH
HOLCOMB HOSIA
HOGE SAMUEL
HARPER ADAM
HARVEY ANDREW
HARDY LUKE
HUNTER JOHN
HARMON LEWIS
HOLCOMB JOHN
HENSON THOMAS
HALL SAMUEL
HART DAVID
HAWKINS ARTHER
HAWKINS HENRY
HALBROOK DANIEL
JERAULD WILLIAM
JONES CHARLES
JOHNSON JOSEPH
JOHNSON JACOB
JOHNSON JOHN
JOHNSON ALEXANDER
JOHNSON DAVID
JACOBUS JACOB
JACOBUS THOMAS
JOHNSON THOMAS
JORDON LEVI
JORDON LEVI R
JOHNSON JOHN
JOHNSON GEORGE
JONES FELIX
JONES JOHN
JACKSON THOMAS
JONES JAMES W
INGRAM RICHARD
KIRK JOHN
KEY WILLIAM
KIRK RICHARD M
KIRK DANIEL
KEY LANDON
KNOWLES JAMES
KNOWLES PURTYMAN
KNOWLES JESSE
KNOWLES EDY
KIMBALL JESSE

GIBSON COUNTY

KELL JOHN
KIRKWOOD WILLIAM
KNOWLES JESSE
KING DAVID T
KINNER RODIN
KELL MATHEW
KELL ARCHABALD
KIRKMAN JAMES
KING SOLOMON D
KING SAMUEL
KEY THOMAS
KNOWLES JAMES JR
KNOLES DAVID
KITCHEN THOMAS
KITCHEN WILLIAM
KEY WILLIAM SR
KNOLES ELIGAH
LATHOM WILLIAM
FIELDING LUCAS
LAGRANGE ARON
LASTLY JAMES
LUCAS ZACHARIAH
LUCAS OLIVE
LYNN JAMES
LESLY JOHN
LAWDEN THOMAS
LAWSON WILLIAM
LOWELL SAMUEL D
LAMASTERS SIMEON
LEWIS THOMAS
LYNCH EDWARD
MONTGOMERY THOMAS
MONTGOMERY JOHN
MONTGOMERY JAMES
MADDOX JOHN W
MONTGOMERY SAMUEL
MELLBOURN JOHN
McCLURE ROBERT
MONTGOMERY BENJAMINE
MARVEL JOHN
MOSELY ROBERT
MENNIS COLVIN
MAYHALL FOXWORTHY JR
McCLARY JOHN
McCLURE JAMES
McCORMACK WILLIAM
MELBORN DAVID
MORENCE GARRETT
MORENCE SMITH
McGARY ROBERT
McGARY HUGH
McGARY HARRISON

MONTGOMERY JESSE
MARVEL PURTYMAN
MARVEL BENJAMINE
MONTGOMERY JOSEPH
MONTGOMERY WALKER C
MARTIN JAMES
MONTGOMERY SAMUEL
MARVEL ELISHA
MILLER PETER S
MILLBOURN ROBERT
MARSHALL JOHN
MUSICK JOHN
McGUIRE JOHN
MAY BENJAMINE
McCUNE JOHN
MOUNCE THOMAS
MOORE JAMES T
MANIM SYLVESTER
MAYHALL TIMOTHY JR
MONTGOMERY JAMES
MOORE EDWARD
WELLS ASA C
MELTON MICHEL
McKEDDY JAMES
MONTGOMERY JOHN
McINTIRE WILLIAM
McINTIRE JOHN
MILLER WILLIAM
MILLER DAVID
MARTIN THOMAS H
McGEHEE JACOB
McKEDDY STEPHEN
MALONE JOHN
MALONE JAMES
McCLURE JAMES
MUSICK JAMES
MONTGOMERY ROBERT
McGARY JOHN
MARVEL PANTER
McCRARY ROBERT
MILLER JOHN
MANGNAM HENRY
MILLS JAMES
McGRAGER ANDREW
MADISON OLIVER
MONFORD JOHN
MASSEY ALEXANDER
MAGHALL WILLIAM
NEELY JOHN J
NIXON ANDREW
NOWLAND THOMAS
NIXON ABERHAM

OWENS RANDOLPH
OGLESBY JONATHAN
ONEAL HENRY
OSBURN WILLIS C
PEA DANIEL
PRICE WILLIAM
PHILLIPS WILLIAM
PHILLIPS RODY
PRINCE WILLIAM
PHILLIPS CHARLES
PERRY JOSEPH
PARVIN MARK
PERSON WILLIAM
PAROIN WILLIAM
PRICKETT JOHN
PECK JAMES
PETERS WILLIAM
REVIS DANIEL
ROBB JAMES
REVES ISAM
ROBB DAVID
REEL JOHN
ROSBOROUGH JOSEPH
ROBERTS JOHN
ROBERTS JOSEPH
RICHARDS ROLAND B
ROBINSON HUGH
ROULLE GEORGE H
RECKETTS WILLIAM
RADBURN WILLIAM
ROLSTON ANDREW D
REAVIS WILLIAM
REYNOLS EZEKEL
RENNY WILLIAM
RICHEY JOHN
ROBB WILLIAM
REEL FREDERICK
REEL HENRY
ROBINSON WILLIAM
ROBERTS JAMES
ROBERTSON JOHN
ROOKS ELIJAH
ROBB JAMES SR
SLOAN JAMES K
STEWART JAMES
STONE THOMAS
STORMONT ROBERT
LEAT ISAAC
HARDY RICHARD
STARNATURE ANDREW
STEWART WILLIAM
STEPELLOW JOSHUA

GIBSON COUNTY

STOVER ABRAHAM
SHANNON ROBERT
SHARP WILLIAM
STRICKLAND STEPHEN
STRICKLAND ELISHA JR
STEWART WILLIAM
SHARP McCAGAH W
SHARP JAMES
SHARP JOHN
SKELTON JOHN
SHARP THOMAS
SHARP HORATIO
SHARP GEORGE
SHEALDS THOMAS
SPENCER THOMAS
STURGES AUGUSTUS B
SHANNON SAMUEL
SMITH JAMES
SOVERNS JOHN JR
STRAIN ELI
SAMPLE THOMAS
SKELTON WILLIAM
SKELTON JACOB
SPORTSMAN HUGH
SCIDS JOHN
SWANGO JOHN
SIMPSON JOHN
SKELTON JOHN
SPELMAN JAMES
SPELMAN JOHN
SPELMAN SAMUEL
SULIVAN ABLE
SIMPSON ARCHIBALLD
SIMPSON WILLIAM
SHEETS JAMES
STRICKLAND ELISHA
STOCKWELL ROBERT
SPENCER JOHN SR
SHAW WILLIAM
TRIBITT WARTMON
THOMAS SAMUEL
TRUESDELL JOHN N
TWEEDLE ISAAC
TEST NICHOLAS
TOMKINS RICHARD
TERRY JOHN
TEAL ADAM
TERRY WILLIAM
TEEL WILLIAM
THOMAS ISAAC
TAYLOR WILLIAM
TAYLOR JOHN

THURMON JOHNSON F
TAYLOR WILLIAM
TOWNSON ERASTUS
VANDUSON JACOB
VANARSDALL CHRISTOPHER
WOODS PATTERICK
WOODS JOSEPH
WEST NATHANIEL
WOODS JOSEPH L
WARRICK MONTGOMERY
WALTERS WILLIAM
WATERS THOMAS
WATERS JAMES R
WELLS JESSE
WELLS ABRAHAM
WOODS ISAAC
WESTFALL HIRAM
WASSON HIRAM
WOODS JOSEPH
WOODS DAVID
WHEELER JAMES
WILSON WALTER
WILLIAMS ROBERT
WOODS JOHN
WHEELER ROBERT
WHITESETT JOSEPH
WOOD VINCENT
WHITESETT JOHN
WHITESETT JAMES
WEST THOMAS L
WISEMON ROBERT
WOOLF PETER
WILLIAMSON JOHN
WELLS JONATHAN
WELLS WILLIAM
WALDEN JAMES
WEST JAMES
WOODS WILLIAM P
WOODS SAMUEL
WHEELER CHAS
WALTERS ENOCH
WHEELER DAYTON
WHEELER CLAYTON
WHEELER SAMUEL
WILKS JOSEPH
WHEELER JAMES B
WALTERS STEPHEN
YOUNGMAN JOHN
ZIMMERMAN SAMUEL
ROBERTSON JOHN
DIFFINDALL SIMON
SCANTLING JAMES

CAPEHART THOMAS
FREDERICK DANIEL
CALDWELL JOHN
BLACK ROBERT
PHILLIPS JOHN
IVA JAMES
PAINE PATERICK
GRISSOM JOHN W
SMITH RALPH
STUART ABEL
HEDGPETH ISAAC
LEACH JOHN
McNEAL DANIEL
THOMPSON ROBERT
KEY JOHN
CRISS MICHEL
STUART WILLIAM M
McFETERIDGE SAMUEL
DANIEL WILLIAM
SADLER J D
JARAULD EDWARD G
TRUSDELL SAMUEL
SPENCER JOHN
FORDHAM ELIAS H
BUTLER THOMAS
BUTLER NELSON
HENSON JOHN
FOSTER AMASA D
BRAZELTON JACOB
RIPPY WILLIAM
MINNIS MITCHEL
OGLESBY DAVID
MINNIS THOMAS
BROWNLEE HUGH
BROWNLEE JAMES
TOWNSON WINTON
TOWNSON ELI
TRIBBY JOHN
LINDY FREDERICK
SUMNON JOHN
MUSICK ASA
McCRARY THOMAS
SUMNOR JOSEPH
HANKS NICHOLAS A
MONTGOMERY HUSTON
HUNTER JOHN
LEACH WM
STAPELTON JOSEPH
SAPELTON FREDERICK
RAGSDELL FREDERICK
COVELL JOHN
CROSS CHARLES

7

GIBSON COUNTY

MITCHUR STEPHAN
JONES LEVI
BILLUE JAMES
COX ARON
CROWLEY KENELUS
CROWLEY JAMES
JERDON OVER R
HOWCHIN JESSE
HOWCHIN WILLIAM
CREEK ISAAC
CREEK KILLON JR
HUNTER HENRY
FORBUS JOHN
GREEN THOMAS
HINTON WALKER
HAMELTON JOSHUA
HUNTER HARRY
JOHNSON THOMAS
PERSON NEWSON
NEWSON WILLIAM

NUTON CHARLES P
OVERTON BENJAMINE
PERCE CHARLES
HUMPHREY GEORGE
McCUNE JOHN
MONTGOMERY RUSSELL
McDONELL JOHN A
MONTGOMERY HUGH
MULLOY MALONE
MULERY WILLIAM
MULERY JEREMIAH
MANNING JOSEPH
MOORE JAMES
POWE BENJAMINE
PETERS GODFREY
POTTER THOMAS
RODNEY DAVID
RICHEY JOSEPH
CHAMBERS JOHN
HOWE WILLIAM

DAVIS DANIEL
BROWNLEE JOHN
GRIGGS HUGH
VANDIKE JOSEPH
STACKHOUSE STASEA
ROBERTSON BENNETT
RUMBLE FREDERICK
SCOTT JOHN
SCOTT SAMUEL T
STRICKLAND ARON
SIMPSON WILLIAM
SMITH DAVID
STILWELL DAVID
SMITH JOHN
STEWART JOHN
WELLS JOHN
WELLS JAMES
RUTLEDGE ABSOLOM
RICHEY GIDEON
SMITH DAVID

JACKSON COUNTY

GRAHAM WM
DUNHAM JESSE
EWING THO'S
CRAIG ALEX'R C
SHOEMAKER LEONARD C
McGEE JA'S SR
McGEE JA'S JR
ROGERS HENRY
BEEM RICHARD
CRAIG JOHN
PECK DANIEL
VANDAVEAR CHARLES
WOOD DANIEL
AULSIK JOHN
LANNING JOSEPH
ROGERS LEWIS
BEEM MICHAEL SR
BEEM MICHAEL JR
HANNEN BARTHOLIMIUS
HANNEN JOHN
BUNNEL FRANCISS
BUNNEL REUBEN
BUNNEL JESSE
MORRISON WM C
MIRRIT EDWARD
KINWORTHY THO'S SR

KINWORTHY THO'S JR
TABOUR WM
TABOUR JESSE
RICHARDS ZADOCK
FINLEY HUGH SR
ROBERTSON WM
HITE THO'S
ROBERTSON JOHN
ROBERTSON ANDREW
ROBERTSON GEORGE
HAMILTON JOE
HAMELTON JOHN
CRABB CHARLES
DAY ELIAS
HENSLEY RICHARDSON SR
HENSLEY RICHARDSON JR
COLYER RICHARD
OWENS JA'S
OWENS DAN'L
BOAS HENRY JR
BOAS HENRY SR
HUTCHENSON JA'S
TULLES JOHN
BABBIT CHARLES
LASSER THO'S
McKINNEY JOHN

JARVIS HENRY
KINDRED DAVID
McGEE JOHN
JACKMAN VINCENT
JACKSON MILLINGTON
HENDERSON DAVID
BURCHIM SAM'L JR
BURCHIM JOHN
BUTTON JESSE
BROWN NATHANIEL
THOMPSON JOHN
THOMPSON JA'S
BOTTOMS THO'S
SHOEMAKER JOHN
JACOBS EDWARD G
DOWDEN WM
GRIESMIER HENRY
HOLMES SOLOMON
SLADE SAM'L
ROMJUE JOHN
HONNALL ISAAC
HONNAL JOHN
EMSPON JOHN
EMSPON RICHARD
DOWDEN JA'S
SHIPMAN JA'S

JACKSON COUNTY

McCOY DAN'L SR
McCOY DAN'L JR
SHIPMAN NICHOLAS
SHIPMAN JOHN
HOLMES ROBERT
BLACKWOOD JA'S
JUDA JOHN J
DOWDEN ZACHARIAH
DOWDEN ZEPHANIAH
WALKER OBADIAH
SAGE JOHN
KINDLE THO'S
SUMMERS JOHN
SUMMERS WM
EVANS JESSE
LYSTER CORNELIUS
LYSTER PETER
LYSTER FRANCISS
ALEXANDER REUBEN
CARTER McKINNEY
CORD JOHN
PAWNELL JOSEPH
SEWELL PETER
HANKINS LEWIS
KINDLE HENRY
COPELAND JA'S
COPELAND HUGH
ISAMINGER GEORGE SR
ISAMINGER GEORGE JR
ROGERS JA'S
ROGERS AQUILLA SR
ROGERS AQUILLA JR
BERKEY HENRY
BERKEY CHRISTIAN
ROGERS BENJAMIN
HUFFMAN BENJAMIN
STEALY JACOB
COTNEY JA'S
COTNEY PHENEHAS
ROWLAND JESSE
CLOAK JOHN
WORREN JOEL
COTNEY ARCHABALD
HILL WM
TUELL JESSE
BURGE ISAAC
PARKS JOHN
BRAMAN JA'S
BEATTY WM A
CONGLETON WM
McTAGERTT JA'S
BURCHEM SAM'L JR

ROGERS AQUILLA W
GRAHAM JONATHAN
DENNY HENRY
MORING WALTER
NATION ISAAC
TRIMBLE WM
CONNELLY LEMUEL
PRATHER DAVID
PRATHER JOHN
STRAIN WM
MARMON FRANCESS
PHAROW WM
NICHELSON SAM'L
NICHELSON THO'S
DRAPER BENJAMIN
WHITE JOSIAH
DRAPER PETER
LITTEN JOHN
FORTNER FORD
BEDLE LUTHER
BAILY HENRY
McCRARY WM
PORTER GEORGE K
HUTTO WM
PRIME JOHN
PRIME NATHAN
CROSS CHESTER
SOLSBURY JOHN
SCOTT WM
MORLAND JOHN
ARBUCCLE JOHN
ARBUCCLE THO'S
BRIGES JOHN
GALASPY ROBERT
GALASPY GEORGE
RUDDICK THO'S
LITTON HIRAM
COX JESSE
GLASSON WM
LITTON CALIB
SOLOMAN HENRY
HAMELTON ADAM
BLAND BENJAMIN
NEWBY JOSEPH
LOVE JOHN
HOWEL WM
NEWBY ROBERT
GRAHAM JEREMIAH
STEPHENS DAVID
ADAMSON SIMON
HERENDON ELLIOTT
BAILEY HENRY m\o

GRAY SAMPSON
ELLIOTT CALIB
DRAPER JESSE
DICKSON JESSE
WRIGHT SMITH
SPRING JOHN
SHEPHERD PETER
SHEPHERD ABRAHAM
SHEPHERD ELI
FENTRESS EDWARD SR
FENTRESS EDWARD JR
FENTRESS PHOROAH
FENTRESS JA'S
GOSSETT WILLIAMSON
GOSSETT JOHN
JONES GEORGE
WHITSON JOHN
BLISS JA'S
DOUGLESS MARTIN
COX BENJAMIN
NEWBY GABRIEL
CESTER JOHN
GLOSSEN WM
MARSHELL WM
MARSHELL SIMON
STEPENS HORACE
DEE DANIEL
WHITE CRIDEN
SLADE JAMES
SPARKS JAMES
BRIAN ANDERSON
OGLESBURY THO'S
SHICK SAM'L
BECKEHAMMER JOHN
WALTERS ABNER
STEPHENS JONATHAN
MEDE JA'S
JONES JEREMIAH
WORREN GABRIEL L
BROYLES CHARLES
BROYLES JA'S
BROYLES WM
MILSAP BILLY
OGLESBY WM
DAVIS ELIAS
GREEN NATHANIEL
GREEN McCALLEN
DICKSON THOMAS
MERRIMA LEWIS
CINNONS SILAS
CINNS AARON
HOOPINGGARNER JOHN

JACKSON COUNTY

SULLIVAN JA'S
FLINN JOHN
FLINN WM of JACOB
FLINN MATHEW
FLINN AARON
CAMBERS WM
MATHIS JA'S
ANDERSON JA'S
CURRY WM
GRAY WILY
CURRY ELIJAH
MILLS JOHN F
WOODEN WM
DODDS ANDREW
OWENS WALTER
SCOTT JOHN
ZOLMAN ADAM
JOHNSON JOSEPH
GOFF JOSHUA
BROWN WM
WIDDLE THO'S
CINDY WM
WILY JA'S
CALLIHAN JESSE
JOHNSON RICHARD
ELKINS WM
KING THO'S
JOHNSON JOSEPH
JOHNSON DANIEL
JOHNSON WM
JOHNSON DAVID
STEPHENS FRANCISS
ARTHUR ELIAS
WINCLES JEREMIAH
MATLEY HUGH
GRANTHAM JOEL
ALLEN JOSEPH
THOMPSON McKEE
RIBBLE JOHN
WHITE DAVID SR
NEWBY GABRIEL SR
SWARUNGIN THO'S V
BROOKS WM m/o
BROOKS JOSEPH
BAKER RICHARD
McPHERSON ANGOS
HAND AARON
McAFEE JA'S
HOLLAND ANDREW B
TULLIS JONATHAN
TULLIS IZRA
TULLIS JOHN

LOVE RICHARD
ELY GEORGE
DUNHAM WM
WALDRON DANIEL
ELLIS SETH
JONES JA'S
MURPHY SAM'L
GLOVER ASA
DEVENISH STEPHEN
EWING WM H
HAY JOHN D
RUGGLES WM B
GRANT DAN'L
GRANT JA'S
BURGE ROBERT
HAROLD ELISHA
BENTON DAVID
BENTON WALTER
BENTON HENRY
TURK THO'S
YOUNG REUBEN
KRISS HIRAM
KRISS GEORGE
WEATHERS ROBERT
WEATHERS JOHN
SHATTO NICHOLAS
COCKESHAM WM
WILLIAMS ANDERSON
SMALLWOOD GEORGE
HICKS WM
VOSHELL WM
St CLEAR THOMAS
WHITEHEAD AMOS
HAMMON OLIVER
HOLEMAN WM
WILSON BENJAMIN
SHIPMAN STEPHEN
CHAPMAN JOHN
SMITH ARASTUS
MURPHY JOHN
COLT ARASTUS
SCOTT RAWLEY
MARSHELL WM
WHITE JONATHAN D
PERRY JOHN
HOWARD ALEX'D
GOLD AUSTIN
SEALY MORRIS
SPRING LEVIN
MAPES JOHN
WINKLER JOHN
BURR DAVID

STANLEY SAM'L
JACOBS JOHN
KELLY JACOB
DARLING WM
HANNON JA'S
ELLIOTT FRANCISS
ELLIOTT JOHN
BEACHER ALVA
BEACHER THO'S
GRIFFITH GEORGE
GARDINER STEPHN
RICH JOSEPH
GORE FREDARICK
FINLEY HUGH
FINLEY ABLE SR
NEWLAND WM
FINLEY ABLE JR
CLARK SAM'L
WHITE JOHN
IRELAND JONATHAN
ALLISON JAMES JR
AMMON RUPHAS
ALLISON JA'S SR
DOTY JOHN SR
DOTY JOHN JR
CHINNETH ABRAHAM
McKINLEY JA'S
MILLER ABRAHAM
WEATHERS ISAAC
WILSON JOHN F
PARTLOW WM
BUCKHANNON WM
DICKENSON JA'S
SMITH HENRY
JOHNSON PETER
JOHNSON JA'S
WOODMANSEE GABRIEL
WOODMANSEE JA'S
DEAN JOSEPH
HORNEDA ISAIAH
SULLENDER WALLACE
SPRINGER JOHN H
TAYLOR JOHN
WHITSON THO'S
WYMER WM
NELSON SAM'L
GRAHAM JA'S
SIMS JA'S
PRATHER THO'S
PRATHER ELISHA
SIERS ALEX'R
SIERS WM

JACKSON COUNTY

- WOODMANSEE JA'S
- WHITE JOSEPH
- HANNA JOSEPH
- BROTHER RANSSEL
- TALTON JOHN
- BRANAMON ABRAHAM
- KINDRED JOHN
- WEDDLE EDWARD
- KINDRED BARTHOLEMEW
- KINDRED EDWARD
- CARUTHERS WM
- WELLS JACOB
- HATTON JOHN
- BUTLER JOHN
- STEAR JAMES
- EWALT JOHN
- PRATHER THOMAS
- STANLEY WM
- WILLIAMS NOTLEY
- WALKER DAVID
- WALKER EDWARD
- WILLIAMS WM
- LAYLON WM
- WOOD MOSES G
- McAFEE JOHN
- MILLER ADAM
- HOLMES WM
- HOLMES BENJAMIN
- OGLE WM
- WEDDLE DAN'L
- JACKSON MATHIAS
- HOUSTEN WM
- GOSS JOSEPH
- GOSS FREDARICK
- WHITCONACK JOHN
- BOONE JOEL
- HOUSTEN LEONARD JR
- CARR THOMAS
- HOUSTEN LEONARD SR
- PHELPS ASAHEL
- PHELPS GEORGE A
- TALBERT EDWARD
- BROWN JA'S
- VANDERVORT JOHN
- BRIAN JAS'S
- GOFOUTH WM
- FLINN WM SR
- FLINN WM JR
- - - - GUTHRIE
- WHITE DAVID
- FLINN JACOB
- TAGGERT JA'S
- GUTHRIE HUGH
- HENDERSON WM
- HENDERSON ROBERT
- FLINN ROBERT
- NEWKIRK BENJAMIN
- NEWKIRK HENRY
- SPARKS MOSES
- SPARK HENRY
- FLINN GEORGE
- SPARKS STEPHEN
- HOOVER JOHN
- HOOVER ABRAHAM
- CUMMINS MAJOR
- RICHARDS GEORGE
- RICHARDS GABRIEL
- DICKSON WM SR
- DICKSON WM JR
- HOOPINGGARNER JACOB
- HOOPINGGARNER CONRAD
- NEWKIRK ISAA
- WEDDEL JOHN
- MILSAP ROBERT
- MULLIS JACOB
- LACY NAHAMIAII
- McCAGG ROBERT
- WILLIS NOAH C
- WELSH STEPHEN S SR
- HUFF ABRAHAM SR
- HUFF ABRAHAM JR
- MAY JOHN
- SMITH THO'S
- BOAS GEORGE
- BLAND JOHN
- BLAND THO'S
- BLAND WM
- BLAND MOSES
- MILLER BRISON
- FINNEY JOSEPH
- JOHNSON ANDREW
- BROOKS WM
- ROGERS PHILIP
- HOLMES FORGUS
- WINN JAMES
- CROUCHER DAVID
- BLAND ABEL SR
- ROGERS JEREMIAH SR
- BLAND ABEL JR
- WORMON WILSON
- EDWARDS DAVID
- SMITH WM
- MONAY JA'S
- BUSH JOSIAH
- EDWARDS WM
- EDWARDS ELI
- CHILCOT JOHN
- ASPON WM
- HARTLEY JOHN
- DOW JOHN
- SPERGEON JOHN
- SPEAR JOHN
- KELLY JOHN
- JONES JA'S
- KILYEN MICHAEL
- BRADLEY WM
- WEATHEMAN SIMON
- KELLY DAVID
- LUPTON DAVIS
- YOUNG THO'S
- SOWDER JONATHAN
- TANNER MATHEW
- STILWELL WESTLEY
- BROWEN JOHN
- SMITH ISAAC
- KELLER ABRAHAM
- HARRISON DAVID
- BOFFMAN JACOB
- SHOMON SAM'L
- WHEELER ELANTHAN
- DAVENPORT WM
- HOLEMAN ISAAC JR
- HOLEMAN AARON
- CRABB JA'S S
- CRABB EDWARD
- CARR JONATHAN
- SPENCER JA'S
- THRELDKELD - - -
- SHOUS JOHN
- SHOUS LEWIS
- STEPHENSON GEORGE
- HARTLEY STILMAN
- HARTLEY JOSEPH
- BURGETT GEORGE
- THOMAS JOHN
- THOMAS JONAHTAN
- THOMAS JOHN
- THOMAS JA'S
- THOMPSON WM
- THOMPSON JA'S
- EDWARDS JA'S
- HARMON JOHN
- LINK JOHN
- HUBBARD PETER
- INNIS WM
- HARRIS JOHN

JACKSON COUNTY

CARR HENRY
CRANE JONAS
CRANE JABEZ
CRANE DAVID
CRANE JABEZ O
CRANE OBADIAH M
KITCHELL ASA
CODY DAVID
CRANE ASA
HARLOW JOSHUA
HARLOW RICHARD
WADKINS JONATHAN
KRISS NICHOLAS
RYNOT JA'S
TIFNEA JOHN
OWEN WM
MOONEY WM
OWEN GEORGE W
PARKER ABSALOM
BROWN JOHN
HAMPTON JONATHAN
HAMPTON JOHN
LUCAS CALIB
HAMPTON JA'S
MARMIN THO'S
CRIDER JOHN
SMITH JOHN
HARDWICK THO'S
HILL WM
WINKLER THO'S
SMITH WM
CORN WM
ABLE POLLARD
SULLIVAN PATRICK
EMMONS JESSE
RENNO JA'S
BROWN HUGH
BROWN SAM'L
BROWN JA'S
SULLIVAN WM
LAKEN DANIEL
MARMIN JOSEPH
BELDING AARON
DAVINPORT JESSE
SALMON JACOB
KESTER JACOB
SHIELDS JA'S
SHIELDS WM
BALDWIN JACOB
BALDWIN JOHN
FISLER JESSE
MOONEY JA'S

GARNER WYATT
HORN FREDARICK
PARMER JOHN
BROWN JA'S
JACKSON LAMANUEL
DEWIT BARNET
MOORE JOHN
LANE JOHN
LANE EDWARD
JONES WM
PATTERSON WM SR
PATTERSON WM JR
PATTERSON DAVID
HOLEMAN ISAAC
HALE DAN
SCOTT ISAAC
HUBBLE BENJAMIN
DOUGLAS CYRUS
WHEDEN SAM'L
McCORMACK JOHN SR
McCORMACK JOHN JR
McCORMACK JA'S
BLOSS DORMON
HAMMON JOHN
HAMMON ARASTUS
MASON ANSALAM
WHEELER HEZAKIAH
WHEELER JA'S
DAVIS ZACHARIAH
ENNIS ARCHABALD E
SANDERS BENJAMIN
STRAIN THO'S M
TUELL REASON
MOORE WM SR
MOORE WM JR
DAVIS JOHN
BRIGHTMAN GEORGE
PERRY WM
SMITH JA'S
BROWN JOSEPH
FISLER JACOB
BROADSTREAT THO'S
APPLEGATE HESAKIAH
BELDING AARON O
RUSSELL JA'S
RUSSELL WM
YEARY HENRY O
FISLER JOHN
FISLER JOSEPH
CARTER TRAVIS
CARTER JOB
CARTER BENJAMIN

BLAIR JOHN
BLAIR JA'S
HUSTON JOHN
WORREN MOSES
DOBSON JOHN
HOPKINS HENRY
BRINER PETER
BRINER PHILIP
HENDRIX JOHN
DUDLEY JA'S
HOSTON JA'S
CARR SAM'L
KELLER ABRAHAM
KELLER ISAAC
KELLER GEORGE
KELLER ISAAC
KELLER EDWARD
SHOEMAKER JAMES
COX WM
COX NATHAN
HIATT JOSEPH
HIATT JACOB
WHITE CALEB
MOORE JOSHUA
GUYER HENRY
RUDDICK SOLOMON SR
RUDDICK WM
HOLEMAN MOSES
DRAPER NATHAN
GUYER SAM'L
NEWBY THO'S
STEPHEN JOHN
OALDS ELIJAH
KEITH DANIEL
MARSH JAHU
STORM THO'S
WRIGHT JONATHAN L
WRIGHT THESON
COFFIN BARNABAS
STANFIELD SAM'L
STANFIELD JOHN
SWINNEY JOHN
THOMPSON GEORGE
THOMPSON RICHARD
SWINNEY NATHAN
COX ENOCH
COX HARMON
MOFFET SOLOMON
COX WM SR
MORRIS DEMPSY
CHOWNER JOHN S
ALBERTSON THO'S

JACKSON COUNTY

MARSHELL JOHN
MARSHELL ISAAC
RIDDICK OLOMON
RUDDICK MORDICA
NEEDHAM ISAAC
PARISHAW JA'S
MORRIS JACOB
THORNTON SAM'L
THORNTON ABNER
THORNTON LEVI
BROWN ISAIAH
CAVENDER JOHN
LOCKMAN JOHN
BROOKS WM
SOLOMON DAN'L
POTTER LEMUEL
NEWBY NATHANIEL
NEWBY NATHAN
COX STEPHEN
RUCKER REUBEN
FINLEY JOHN
HOLMES BENJAMIN
WILSON JOHN A
McCOY STEPHEN
HOLMES FRANCISS
COX SOLOMON
KIRKPATRICK ANDREW
RIBBLE WM
BOTTOMS WM
RUTHERFORD LARKIN
ROGERS RICHARD
HARRIS JACOB
HARRIS THO'S
SPAHAM THO'S
EMPSON PETER

JEFFERSON COUNTY

DEREE SAMUEL
BONTE CORNELIUS
ECCLES JOHN
ECCLES SAMUEL
ECCLES BAZEL
COSSE JESSE
GUTHRIE WILLIAM
WILDMAN JOHN
WILDMAN JAMES
BOWEN J H
HERRING JOHN
DONNER GEORGE
DONNER TOPIAS
LEE A
BROOKS W
SMITH BAMA
HOPPER MOSES
HOPPER JAMES
GILMORE LUTHER
HARRIS DANIEL
DONNER JACOB
JACKSON GIDEON
CURTES ARNOLD
CUSTES JESSE
CUSTES WILLIAM
M'MULLEN ARCHIBALD
HUMPHREYS CORNELIUS
DENNY CHRISTOPHER
DEMAREE SAMUEL
DEVORE BENJ
HENRY JOHN
JAMISON THOMAS
JAMISON THOS SR
HUMPHREYS SAMUEL
LAME JOSEPH
LAME CALEB
HORTON JOHN
BIRD THOS
AGINS J
HENIGAN JOHN
HOOT JOHN
IRWIN THOS B
BRAMWELL JOHN
IRVIN ROBT
SCONCE ROBT
PATTON HEZEKIAH E
BACKSTER JAS
BACKSTER DANIEL
ROBINSON SAMUEL
CASTER ISAAC
HOPPER SMALLWOOD
STEEL HUGH
STEEL JOSEPH
BANEE ROBT
BANE SAML
REDDEN THOS
COX ASAS
COX HENRY
COX JOHN
DAYLEY E O
LALYERS J D
M'MILLEN DANIEL
VENTIONER JAS
CLINES LEVI SR
LEWIS THOS
BAILEY JOSEPH
WISE JAS
SULLIVAN DANIEL
IRWIN JAMES
MILES EVAN
MILES JESSE
ROBINS WM
PENN EPHRAIM
CALVERT MARTIN W
STEWART I/J
SMITH BARNE B
HUMPHREYS LOVE S
CLINE JOHN
CLINE LEVI
BONDURANT NOAH
CHRISTY ISAAC
M'COY JOHN
M'COY GEORGE
YOST ISAAC
SMITH JOHN
DONNER JOHN
HILL JOSEPH
BARTON ROSWELL
STOUT HEZEKIAH
FEATHERS STEPHEN
GLASGOW SAMUEL
FRANCIS JOHN SR
FRANCIS JOHN
FRANCIS WALTER
NEEDUM WM
THOMAS ELIAS
CHAPMAN ROBERT
BLAN JAMES
M'CLELLEN WM
WILLIAMS REMEMBRANCE
WILLIAMS ROBT
WILLIAMS GARRET

JEFFERSON COUNTY

GUTRY RICHARD	WEATHERFORD HARDIN	LAUGHRIDGE GEORGE
GUTRY JOHN	WEATHERFORD JAMES	LAUGHRIDGE WILLIAM
BOON WILLIS	LITTLEJOHN JOHN	LAUGHRIDGE SAMUEL
RITCHIE JAMES	LITTLEJOHN LEMUEL	LEE GERSHAM
RITCHIE WILLIAM	COOK WILLIAM	M'CARTNEY ENOCH
ANDERSON WILLIAM	COOK JOHN	ETHERINGTON JOSEPH
ALEXANDER JAMES	SIMPERS AMOS	CONNER LEWIS
MARSHALL JOHN	COX CHRISTOPHER	ROBB JAMES
KING JOHN	MITCHELL R B	WARFIELD JOHN
KING GEORGE SR	MITCHELL THOS	WARFIELD JERARD
KING GEORGE	MITCHELL ROBT	VALLALEE ROBT
CHAMBERS ANTHONY	CLA JAMES m/o	GORDON WM
KIRKLAND JAMES	BRADY CHARLES	CAPLINGER SAMUEL
LINDLEY OLIVER	RIDDLE JACOB	CAPLINGER ADAM
LINDLEY LEMON	DARINGER JACOB	WILLIAMS EDWARD
MAPES JAMES	MITCHEL JOHN	WILLIAMS MOSES
SYLVESTER GEORGE	TALBOTT DANIEL	WILLIAMS PHILIP
FITCH-PATRICK J	YOUNG HEZEKIAH	BATES ALFRED
FENTON BART.	BENNEFIELD WILLIAM	WILLIAMS J
GOODALE WILLIAM	HYATT GIDEON	COX RUSSEL
GILMORE LUTHER	COPELIN SAMUEL	COFFMAN JACOB
ALLISON JAMES	COPELIN THOS	WILSON RICHARD
HOPPER WILLIAM	COPELIN JAMES	MARTON JAMES
ROBINS WILLIAM	HERRING FIELDING	LOTT ABNER
CHRISTY ISAAC	HERRING PRESTON	WILSON JOHN
SPRILLER WILLIAM	HERRING BARTLETT	HILLIS EBENESAR
MARQUES ROBT	LEWIS ABRAHAM	GORDON JAMES
BOOTH JOHN	LOTT JOHN	RYKER GERARDUS
STORM PETER	LOTT JOHN JR	DUFIELD WILLIAM
PROTHERO WILLIAM	LOTT ELIJAH	RYKER SAMUEL
LOTT JAS	LOTT JESSE	DANIELS JOHN
DUVAUL CHARLES	JONES DAVID	SYLVESTER SAMUEL
DUVAUL LOT	JONES DAVID JR	RYKER JOHN
DUVAUL NOAH	M'COY MOSES	SMOCK G
GREEN JOHN	BERRY JAMES	WOODFILL SAMUEL
MIRES GEORGE	MINOR JOHN	WOODFILL GRABRIEL
RYKER JOHN	SMITH W M	WOODFILL DANIEL
SHAVER JOHN	M'CROSKY JOHN L	WOODFILL DANIEL JR
BENEFIELD GEORGE SR	HINTON THOMAS	GORDON GOERGE
BENEFIELD GEORGE	WILLHITE ECHILLOS	M'COY SAMUEL
WARD DANIEL	WILLHITE JOHN	GORDON GEORGE JR
ROB JAMES	DAVIS THOS	HUGHS PETER
WEST JOHN	OXSHEAR M	WATERMAN JOHN
M'CLELLEN ROBT	CORALE SAMUEL	HARRIS AUGUSTUS
BERGEN CHRISTOPHER	SMITH HENRY	ALDRIGE DENNIS
BERGEN GEORGE	DEVORE D	INGALS EBENEZER
CAMPBELL JAMES	HALL WM	SHEPHARD H
CONNER LEWIS m/o	HALL JOHN	BARTON ROBT
M'CARTNEY JONATHAN	HALL ZACHARIAH	DUGAN SAMUEL
M'INTAUSH JOSEPH	PHILIPS ROBT	KENNEDY ROBT
GOLY DAVID	PHILIPS PRESTLEY	MILTON ALLEN
WEATHERFORD JOHN	JAMISON ALEX	MILTON JOHN

JEFFERSON COUNTY

MARSHALL THOS	FITCH ELIAS	BROOKS WILEY
DUFIELD WILLIAM	RUDE NOAH	M'KAY URIAH
BRADSHAW PLEASANT	AKINS WILLIAM	WINDSOR THOS
CAVET THOS	JOHNSON ELISHA	BARR JOHN
KENNED JOHN	HOLMES GEORGE	JACKSON JOHN
MARQUES JOHN	TOTTON ARCH	LARIMORE DANIEL
LEE ANDREW	MILLER JOHN	FOX SHUBAL
TRAVES J	MILLER SAMUEL	TRUMAN HOMER
SHIRLE JOHN	HOLMES GEORGE	ROTHBURN THOS
COPE DAVID	M'KAY ABRAHAM	LAUGHRIDGE JOHN
LITTLEJOHN WILLIAM	ONEAL JAMES	LAUGHRIDGE WM
FUNK JOHN	MANVILLE NICHOLAS	CONNER LEWIS
LEAVIT B C	HOWARD ISAAC	DECK JAMES
SHEARMAN BENNONCE	LEE JOSEPH	TATE JOHN
SHEARMAN ELISHA	WILCAL FRANCIS	WEATHERSPOON WILLIAM
AKINS REUBEN	WILCAL WM	WEATHERSPOON DAVID
GORHAM SILAS F	WILCAL JNO	WEATHERSPOON - - -
BANDY JOHN	WILCAL JOHN JR	BROWN JOHN
BANTA JOHN	HELMS ABR.	DOW WM
MORTON ANDREW	HELMS G	DOW WILLIAM
MULLEN EDWARD	HELMS ISAAC	TAYLOR THOMAS
OBRINE JAMES	HELMS JOHN	HENDRICKSON WM
KINKADE JAMES	SHORT JACOB	GRANT CALIN
ONEAL WILLIAM	COBB WM	STEWART JOHN
WASHER SOLOMON	RIDDLE J	McGREGER ALEX'R
WASHER SOLOMON JR	LEE NATHAN	JACKSON JOHN
SHORT ISAAC	PERSON WM	WELCH SAMUEL
WASHER ALEX'R	LEE JOHN	JAMISON ROBT
VANDENBURGH JOHN	COX SAMUEL	GRAY ROBT
BARTLE JOHN	WILLIAMSON W	MORTON ANDREW
GARRET JAMES	HENRY J	MORTON JAMES
BUCKHANNON WILSON	REATHERFORD JOHN	MORTON JOHN
GRIFFIN JOHN	BRUMBARGER JACOB	MORTON WILLIAM
HOWE LEVI	BRUMBARGER JOHN	SPENCER C K
HOWE LEVI JR	GRIMES STEPHEN	ELLIAS STEPHEN
EMMERSON BENJ	WINDSOR WM	ELLIS JOSEPH
WERT JACOB	REATHERFORD STEPHEN	NILES JOSEPH
WERT JER	REATHERFORD SHELTON	SKEEN JONATHAN
WEET ISAAC	NEAL JESE	BEEBE TIMOTHY
WERT REUBEN	NEAL DANIEL	BEEBE DUDLEY
STEPHENS SAMUEL	VAINHAM NEHEMIAH	BEEBE SYLVESTER
STEPHENS JACOB	VANHORN B	BEEBE FREDERICK
SALYERS HENRY	ROGERS GEORGE	PULLIUM ROBERT
WASHER STEPHEN	LANHAM JOHN	COX JOHN
WASHER STEPHEN JR	SHORT ELISHA	TAGUE JOSEPH
HUMBLE JOSEPH	INGALS CHESTER	M'QUESTON WM
HANKINS JOSEPH	INGALS CHESTER	HORTON JAMES
HANKINS ABSOLEN	BUNDIAN LEE	ALLCORN JOHN
HANKINS WM	BROOKS M	BAKER WM
BARKER WM	BROOKS HUMPHREY	CAMPBELL JOHN
EDEN ELIAS	BROOKS NOAH	CAMPBELL WM
WALLACE JOHN	NEAL JOHN	CAMPBELL JAMES

JEFFERSON COUNTY

BENNEFIELD GEORGE
ROBERTS JOHN
BUCKHANNON WM
DUNLOPE JOHN
ASDALE ROBT
COX JOHN
HARPER GEORGE
HARPER J
FAVOURS THOS
MEDISK GERARDUS
ROTHBUN S
M'CARTNEY G B
M'CARTNEY COY
GOW PETER
MOORE JOHN
BESHEARS REASON
M'GREGAR THOS
SKINNER S
VAINHAM NEHEMIAH
BROOKS JOHN
HEATH SAMUEL
HEATH WM
BROOKS SAMUEL
HUTCHINSON DANIEL
WILKINS JER
JACKSON THOMAS
JACKSON JAMES
CLOUD ISHAM
JACKSON SAMUEL
JACKSON JAMES
DANNER JOHN
TRAVES JAMES
AMES AARON
NEAL JOHN
LAW STEPHEN
CAMPBELL JOHN
VON THOS
DANNER D
DANNER JOSEPH
M'KAY DAVID
LOVE JOHN
SLATER S
SLATER PHILIP
SLATER FREDERICK
OSBORN PETER
BALDIN SAMUEL
DEMENT JOHN
DEMEN WM
WATERS JOHN
YOUNG MOSES
M'KAY JOHN
KEEL JOHN

M'KAY ROBERT
M'KAY ALLEN
WALKER JOHN
WALKER ALFRED
WALKER JOHN JR
ALDREDGE WM
M'KAY GEORGE
HILLIS DAVID
KINNEY HIRAM
McCOLLOUGH JAMES B
TAYLOR THOMAS
OWENS GEORGE C
MILLER BENJAMIN
PARK JAMES
HEANING GEORGE
SHANNON JOHN
HAY WILLIAM
MARTIN WILLIAM
ANDERSON JOHN
McMILLAN JOHN
SWAN JOHN
TAYLOR ROBERT
MATTHEWS JAMES
McLAIN SAMUEL
McLAIN JOHN
PATTERSON JAMES
WATSON WILLIAM
BROWN JAMES
ANDERSON JAMES
THOMPSON ALEX
MAXWELL SAMUEL C
BICKERSON JESSE
SCOTT JAMES
ALEXANDER W R
DUNN WILLIAM
HENDERSON C A
MITCHELL WILLIAM P
MAXWELL EDWARD
MOUNTS AMOS C
M'CASLON JOHN
SNODGRASS SAMUEL
DINWIDDIE ALEX'R
HUFFORDE GEORGE
McCAMON GEORGE
BAILEY SETH
TRIMBLE ROBERT
ROSS JAMES
CAVATT JOHN
DORAN JOHN
WILLHAITE POSHUA
HAMMON JONATHAN
MAXWELL JOHN

CAMPBELL JOHN
LOWRY THOS
M'DONALD ROBERT
SMITH PETER
RICHARDSON JOHN
KING DANIEL
COGHILL MATTHEW
SPELLER WILLIAM
HARTWELL EPHRAIM
TWADDLE JAMES
DRUGGAN JOSIAH
SHANNON GEORGE
SMITH BENJAMIN
CURRIE ROBERT
ANDERSON THOMAS
ANDERSON JOHN
PARKS WILLIAM
CHISM JOHN
McMILLEN JAMES
STEVENS EMOR
LUPER SAMUEL
IRVIN JOHN
HANING WILLIAM
PARK ALEX'R
PATTERSON SAMUEL
HELM JAMES
JONES THOMAS
ARBUCKLE JOHN
FIELD WILLIAM
CUMINGORE DANIEL
HOLLENBECK ANDREW
HOAGLAND HENRY
FIELD JOHN
DAVIDSON ALEXANDER
HOLLENBECK JOHN
MINELA JOHN
SPADER BERGEN
CRAWFORD DAVID
ANDERSON WILLIAM
PAYNE JOHN
REDDENBAUGH FREDERICK
WELLS SAMUEL
WELLS WILLIAM
McCUNE JOSEPH
MAIDEN ANDREW
RITCHIE ADAM
BLACKFORD ISAIAH
CRAWFORD WILLIAM
REDDENBAUGH GEORGE
LOWREY JAMES
SNOW SAMUEL
CRAWFORD JOHN

JEFFERSON COUNTY

McCONNELL WILLIAM
HULICK SAMUEL
REDDENBAUGH SAMUEL
REDDENBAUGH FREDERICK
REDDENBAUGH PHILLIP
MILLS AMOS
STUCKER HENRY
GUDGILL ISAAC
STUCKER SAMUEL
VARVILL ABRAHAM
SNIDER JOHN
GUDGIL NATHAN
ANDERSON JAMES
STUCKER JOHN
SAMPLES JACOB
PHILLIPS JOSHUA
McCLELEN JAMES
ACRE THO'S
GUDGEL NATHAN
GUDGEL STEPHEN
EDDINGTON THO'S
WALKER JOHN
PATTERSON JOHN
DOTY EPHRAIM
HASTE WILLIAM
ORNOLD JOSEPH
McCASLON JOHN
SNODGRASS HUGH
DICKERSON JOHN
REID FREDERICK
MONTGOMERY WILLIAM
HILL ABEL
BURCH SELBY
ELDRIDGE LEVI
LOWDEN JAMES
HUTTSELL JACOB
BROWNSLON JACOB
DITSLER JOHN
McDOUGLE JAMES
FIN JACOB
STUCKER JACOB
CAMPBELL LAW'E
LORING DAVID
SEBREE JAMES
ALLEN WILLIAM
COLLINS AMOS
RAY WILLIAM
NICHOLSON THO'S
BARRY ROBERT
STUCKER JACOB JR
RADEY JOHN
McCLELEN RICHARD

STUCKER WILLIAM
WEST JOHN T
WARRELL JOSHUA
McKINLEY JAMES
STUCKER JOHN
SMOCK JEREMIAH
SARGENT NELSON
MIKESELL PETER
KISTLER JOHN
BORDEN GAIL
FINCOAT THO'S
VANNORMAN AARON
BEAR HENRY
HENDERSON WILLIAM
BARNETT BYRUM
MONROE CHARLES
HAVEN DAVID
DONALDS JAMES W
VANNORMAN DANIEL
SPEER DANIEL
HOPKINS RICHARD
HAMDEN JOHN D
FRIEND JOSEPH
ARNETT SAMUEL
BAILEY AARON
MONROE GEORGE
PORTER AARON
HILL JOHN
DOUTHIT JOSE
McKINLEY SAMUEL
WEST JOHN
WEST JAMES
McNEW ZEDEKIAH
MIKSELL JACOB
KESTLER FREDERICK
STUCKER MICHAEL
McCLELEN JAMES
SMITH OSWALD
McKINLEY JOHN
CONSLEY THOS
CARTER THOS
SHED LUTHER
STEPLES JAMES
GORE LEVI
SLOUN JOHN
COLLINS AMOS
COLEMAN JOHN
GALAHER THOS
CAIN JACOB
HUBBARD RICHARD
JONES JAMES
DAVIS THOMAS

CROTHERS JOHN
DAVIDSON THOMAS
DAVIDSON THOMAS SR
WOODS JAMES
SMITH SOLOMON
WILSON BENJAMIN
SMITH JOHN B
CLOYD JAMES
MAXWELL WILLIAM
McCLUNG SAMUEL
McCLUNG JOHN
MINGS AARON
MARQUES GEORGE
BUTLER JONATHAN
McCASLAND WILLIAM
WHEATLY JOSEPH
CORNELISON MOSES
LYNN HUGH
DUNGAN JOHN
RAMSEY JOHN
RAMSEY THO'S
RAMSEY LEVI
RAMSEY BENJAMIN
PURDIN JOHN
ROBINSON RUSSELL
GALUSHA AZABAH
THICKSTEN ISAAC
THICKSTEN WILLIAM
SWINDLER SAMUEL
BLANKENSHIP JAMES
GREEN LOVREIGN
WHITESIDES WILLIAM
WILSON MOSES
WOOD JOHN
MARSHALL ROBERT
TILFORD ALEX
WILEY JOSEPH
CHITWOOD AMOS
CHITWOOD JAMES
ROWAND ALEX'R
CANDSEY CALEB
CHAMBERS WILLIAM
STEPHENS ISAAC
SABERN JOHN
SMITH JAMES
JACKSON GEORGE
McGILL JAMES
WEAVER ADAM
CRESWELL JOHN
CRESWELL JOHN
RYKER JACOB S
WALLS ARTHER

JEFFERSON COUNTY

- DAVIS THOS
- MONROE RANDALL
- CURRELL JOHN
- CARREL BARTHOLOMEW
- RYKER SAMUEL S
- SMOCK PETER
- WHEAT ABRAHAM
- GADDES JAMES
- HOUGLAND MARY
- CARREL HENRY
- MONROE AUSBURN
- DAVIS SOLOMON
- WOODBURN ROBERT
- ARBUCKLE NATHAN
- JENNINGS OSIAH
- REID THO'S
- AMOS JOHN
- ROBINSON JOHN
- HOADLAND AARON
- McNUTT ALEX
- WHEAT DAVID
- MONTGOMERY ALEX
- JONES ISAAC
- ANDERSON JAMES
- WILSON ALEX'R
- MONTGOMERY ARCHIBALD
- ANDERSON ALEX'R
- MONROE FELIX
- ANDERSON JOHN
- DAVIS BENJAMIN
- GERDON JOSEPH
- OWENS THOMAS
- CUNNINGHAM JAMES D
- SLOUGHTER JER
- CURRY DAVID
- MONROE ROBERT
- HILER JOSEPH
- WEAVER MICHAEL
- TILFORD SAMUEL
- MONROE MICHAEL
- ANDERSON WILLIAM
- CHAMBERS ALEX'R
- THICKSTON ABRAHAM
- BLANKENSHIP ISOM
- McCURRY ABRAHAM
- JACKSON JAMES
- LATIMORE DANIEL
- RICH AMOS
- LOGO CALEB
- WATSON ANDREW
- FOSTER GABRIEL
- LITTLE JOHN
- SOUDERS ABRAHAM
- McCARTNEY JAMES
- ROSEBERRY THOS
- ROSEBERRY GEORGE
- LEMON JAMES
- WALTON JOHN
- TRUMBO JACOB
- CAMPBELL GEORGE
- RUBURN WILLIAM
- WILSON GEORGE
- STEWARD DAVID
- BLAKE GEORGE
- WHITESETT WILLIAM
- RUTLEDGE JACOB
- WILSON PATRICK
- WILSON WILLIAM
- JONES JOHN
- TROUTMAN ADAM
- CARPENTER JACOB
- AMMONS THOMAS
- WILSON ALEX'R
- McCRORY SAMUEL
- THOMAS EVANS SR
- TANNIHILL ZACHERIAH
- HUTCHISON NATHANIEL
- FLEMING JOHN
- COGWELL LEONARD
- EDWARDS NANCY
- YOUNG ANDREW
- McKAY JAMES
- KENNEDY JOSEPH
- EDDLEMAN DANIEL
- OFFICER WILLIAM
- CERNS WILLIAM
- FORD ROBERT
- MAGNESS PERRY G
- PROCTER MOSES
- TERRILL ACHILLES
- CRAVENS JOHN
- CRAVENS WILLIAM
- DUFFY JOHN
- BARNES LEONARD
- BUSLINGAME WILLIAM
- FITCH JOHN
- JACKSON JAMES R
- CRISMAN JACOB
- SWEET ELIAS
- MONROE ARTHUR
- TWADDLE JOHN
- SWEET ABRAHAM
- SWEET ISAAC
- WATHERTON DAVID
- JACKSON THO'S
- BAILY JOHN
- BAILY SAMUEL
- DRYDEN JOHN
- LAW JOEL
- HINDS FRANCIS
- WHITE SAMUEL
- TOOLE LAURENCE
- BOYD BENJAMIN
- CHAMBERS AVERY
- STAPLES NATHANIEL
- GRUDGEL JOHN
- GASAWAY THO'S
- LEWIS JACOB
- McCAMANT JOHN
- SMITH RITCHIE
- BLAKE LEWIS
- ROBINSON MIDDLETON
- McCRORY JOHN
- SMITH ROBERT
- WILSON MOSES
- DEPUTY JOSHUA
- BARNS REUBEN
- WILKENSON JOHN
- JOHNSON JAMES
- DIXON HENRY
- THOMPSON ELISHA
- WATSON JAMES
- HAWKINS WILLIAM C
- WELLS JOHN
- WELLS LEVI
- MILLER ROBERT
- QUIER DAVID
- WINCHESTER JOHN
- WALTON ISAAC
- WALTON ABRAHAM
- McCLANAHAN ROBERT
- PHILLIPS ZEKIEL
- PHILLIPS JOHN
- WHITESITT SAMUEL
- ROBINSON ELIAS
- NAY BENNET
- SAGE JESSE
- ALEXANDER WILLIAM
- HAYS SAMUEL
- FUEL SPENCER
- LOGAN EZEKIEL
- ABBOT JOHN
- KYLE JAMES
- HARRISON ROBERT
- WILDMAN JOSEPH
- LATHROP ISAAC

JEFFERSON COUNTY

WILDMAN BENJAMIN	SHREWSBERRY BENJAMIN	MARSHALL DANIEL
LAYTON WILLIAM	SPANN JESSE	McCOY GEORGE
HALL DAVID	BRADGELEY JOHN	PENN EPHRAIM
CRAWFORD JAMES	NELSON JAMES	HILLIS JAMES
WILKING JAMES	CHAMBERS JAMES	McKAY ROBERT
PATTON JOHN M	BROWN WILLIAM	SLATER PHILLIP
VANTER JESSE	NELSON DANIEL H	McKAY JAMES
CARREL JOHN	HUTCHISON SOLOMON	McKAY WILLIAM
CARREL JOHN	HUTCHISON EBENEZER	TUTTLE WILLIAM
GRAY JESSE	GREEN ABRAHAM	WEED STEPHEN P
STEPHENS JOHN	SPRAGUE HOSEA	COMLEY ABSOLOM
BRANHAM LINSFIELD	PARSON NATHANIEL	GATES WILLIAM
BRONTON JOSEPH	SAGE JOHN	BLACKMORE DAWSON
VANTER JAMES	SAGE WILLIAM	BURTON GEORGE
STRIBLING THOMAS T	MUNSON ALANSON	LEMENTON ROBERT
NOBLE THOMAS	ADMINES JESSE	FURGUSSON JOHN
JONES THOMAS	EBLEN MICHAEL	HALL ROBERT W
WHITE ABROSE	CRAWFORD WILLIAM	LOGAN GEORGE
DUFFY ANDREW	HENSLEY JOSEPH	PULLIAM M J
BASSETT ELISHA	UNDERWOOD JACOB	HILLS JOHN
SULLIVAN WILLIS	CRAWFORD ISAAC	McKAY DAVID
ARMSTRONG LANTY F	UNDERWOOD JOHN	SLEVIN JOHN
LONG WILLIAM	CAIN PETER	AMBY JOHN
HUDSON THOMAS	UNDERWOOD SALENA	BURNHAM CALVIN
PEARCY ROBERT	PURDEN CHARLES	ACKINS REUBEN
KELLY SAMUEL	DUFFY JAMES	THOMAS JOHN
KELLY JOHN	MILLER HENRY	CRAWFORD THOMAS
NEAVILL GEORGE	BRANHAM ROBERT	WILSON NATHANIEL
COCHRAN ANDREW	WILKINSON JOSHUA	RITCHIE JOHN
COCHRAN FRANCES	WILSON SOLOMON	WILSON JAS
KINNEAR MICHAEL	BARBER T	BRISBIN JOHN
COCHRAN JOHN	COPE DAVID	COTTON ROBERT
KINNEAR CAMPBELL	KINNEAR ROBERT	ATKINSON JOSHUA
VANHORN BANJAMIN	HUMPHREY SAMUEL	COPE JONAHTAN
COBB THO'S	COX ER	TRAVIS JAMES
MEDLY JAMES	GUTHRIE RICHARD	CUSTER WILLIAM
LONG ABRAHAM	CLOYAR HENRY	MARQUES JOHN
McKAY THOMAS	BROWN WILLIAM P	RHOADS JACOB
McKAY BARBARY	LOMIS OLIVER	DONNAH GEORGE
FUEL MASON	HALL WILLIAM	ROBINSON DANIEL
KELLY ABRAHAM	BICE JOHN	LAME JOSEPH
WRIGHT LEVI	PHILLIPS ROBERT	SUTTON DAVID
RECTOR H P	JONES DAVID	WALKER JA'S
RECTOR JOHN	HILLIS MATTHEW	HYATT MISHACK
RECTOR DANIEL	PAUL JOHN of P	REYNOLDS S L
MURPHY WILLIAM	GRIFFIN RALPH	CRAWFORD JAMES M
HUGHES THO'S	STOGSDILL DANIEL	GLOVER THO'S
CHINOUETH JAMES	HARTSOCK JAMES	MINOR ROBERT
DANFORD WILLIAM	WOODFILL JOHN	RYAN ROBERT
HAYS JAMES	TROXELL JOSEPH	JOHNSON HUGH
ALLEN MOSES	SIPE FREDERICK	WELLS ASA
DAVIS AMOS	MEDDEAK EMANUEL	WEST WILLIAM

JEFFERSON COUNTY

MONCRIEF WILSON
HEATH BENJAMIN
JOHNSON SAMUEL
MEWHERTER W P
TAYLOR DUDLEY
BURNS JAMES
HARBERT ROBERT
MONCRIEF ABNER
OLOUGHLIN PRESILLA
JOHNSON WILLIAM
JOHNSON CHARLES
SHARTEEN SAMUEL
RITCHIE WILLIAM P
HARLAND WILLIAM
JEWELL JAMES
SMITH HENRY
WALLACE NATHANIEL
PATTON HOUSTON
SMITH DANIEL
RODGERS ROBERT
McCALL JAMES
INGALLS ABRAHAM
HARKINS GEORGE
CHENOWETH THOMAS
BENSON JOHN
BADGELY ANTHONY
FENTON BARTHOLOMEW
RIGHT LEVI
WILSON SAMUEL
MILLET WILLIAM
WILLIAMS THOMAS
ROLLINSON AARON
CULBERTSON CHARLES
JOHNSON WILLIAM
SPAUN JOHN
ARMSTRONG THOMAS
NORTON JOHN
WARD SAMUEL
KINNEAR JOHN
HIBNER JOSEPH
HIBNER JAMES
MALEK DAVID
THOM SAMUEL
SMITH ASA
BROWN WILLIAM
BADGLEY BENJAMIN
COX JOHN
WAY MARTIN
WAY ORA
McCASLON RICHARD
McKINLEY SAMUEL
WILKEY SAMUEL

CRALE SAM'L
MITCHELL JAMES B
COPE JESSE
HAMILTON WALKER
COPE WILLIAM
WILSON JOHN
LAME CALEB
COPELIN WM
COPELIN JOHN
GOUNT NICHOLAS
LITTLEJOHN JAMES
HUMBLE JOSIAH
ELLIOTT ROBERT
McNULTY JOSEPH
BAXTER DANIEL
HORTON JAMES
SMOCK SAMUEL
JACKSON JOSHUA
SMITHEE JOHN
RYKER JOHN
LEDGERWOOD SAMUEL
DEMAREE DANIEL
WOODFILL ANDREW
REED THO'S N
MAYFIELD SOUTHERLAND
WEST REUBEN
RITCHIE JAMES
RYKER J G
MARSHALL JOHN
McCLELEN ROBERT
ROBINS G R
CALVERT M W
MOORE WILLIAM
RYKER PETER
SPENCER CHARLES R
CAMPBELL JAMES
VALELY ROBERT
BUNDON LEANDER
WHILKELL WILLIAM
McKAY URIAH
WHELKEL JOHN
PRYOR NICHOLAS M
SMOCK JACOB
LEE NATHAN
BENEFIELD WILLIAM B
HARTWELL EPHRAIM
GRANT WILLIAM
SILVESTER LEVI P
DONNER JOHN
ALLEN JOHN
LONCE JAMES
JAMISON ROBERT

WOODFILL JOHN
MARQUES GEORGE
COX RUSSEL
BAKER WILLIAM
REA JAMES
HUGHEY PETER
LAMARR ISAAC
MORRIS ROBERT
WILSON WILLIAM
BRADSHAW PLEASANT
DUGAN SAMUEL
DUFIELD WILLIAM
VANCLEAVE PETER
CUSTER RUEL
McCLELEN JOHN
BROWN PATRICK
BROWN JAMES
RUTLEDGE J
GLOVER JAMES
RANDALL JOHN
GALE ISAAC
GALE RUFUS
SAWYER DAVID
SAWYER MOSES
SAWYER HIRAM
JACKSON WILLIAM
RYKER SAMUEL J
M'CURDY WILLIAM
LANIER J F D
POLLOCK J D
THOMAS WM F
TALBOTT R C
SULLIVAN JER
SULLIVAN THO'S
ROBINSON WILLIAM
BRANETT FELIX
BACKMAN E
DORSEY SAMUEL
PATTERSON JOHN
RUNION SAMUEL
BROWN THO'S H
CROSS SAMUEL T
MEEK JOHN
CRAVENS ROBERT
HITE ABRAHAM
KENT DAVID
BENTON EDWIN
VANDAVIER NICHOLAS
DOUGLAS ASHEL
COCHRAN JAMES
SMITH L
JUDSON MICH

JEFFERSON COUNTY

TAYLOR JOSEPH	CUNNINGHAM PHILIP	BROWN JOHN K
WILSON DAVID	COLWELL BENJ	COMSTOCK BATSFORD
PATTERSON J	GAVIT MARCUS	BONER HENRY
GIBSON JOHN	PAUL JOHN	BRIGS JOHN
SHORT GEORGE	HENDRICKS WILLIAM	ALBY PETER
MURPHY JOHN	BENTLEY BASEL B	WHEEDEN STEPHEN
FRICK FREDERICK	CUSHAW JOHN	HUFF ORSON E
KIKENDALL JOHN	HUNT JOHN	YOUMANS JOHN
KIKENDALL SAMUEL	DOYLE JACOB G	WHITES RICHARD
EATON SOLOMON	VAIL THOS	WHITES THO'S
EATON T W	GROVES BENJAMIN	WALLACE JAMES
WILSON JAMES	GROVES N D	LAWRENCE NATHANIEL
COWDEN JAMES	BELDING G H	SHANNON HENRY
HOWES JOHN	ANDREWS STEPHEN	GLORE JACOB
WILSON JOSEPH	PURDIE RICHARD	RAMSEY THOMAS
BECK STEPHEN	HOLMS S	CLOSE SAMUEL
HAYS JAMES	RUSSEL J	HELDRITH HENRY
M'CALROY ENOS	HAMILTON WILLIAM	BOSWELL JOHN
M'CALEB HENRY S	HAMILTON SAMUEL	KYLE JOHN
OLMSTED SAMUEL	CULMARY JAMES	M'INTIRE JOHN
SIMPSON ALEX'N	COMSTOCK DANIEL	OSBORN ISAAC G
M'GEE JOSEPH	SAMPLE ROBT	RUCKLE CHARLES
MEAD JOSIAH	GUIN JOHN	ROSS JAMES
KING VICTOR	HICKS JAMES	MILLER SAMUEL
ARION COPELAND J L	SMITH JOHN	BAKER ESRA
LEONARD L R	HILL JAMES	MARTIN GEORGE
LEONARD G W	ABBOTT MICHAEL	SULLIVAN WILLIAM C
BENNETT BROOK	JEWELL JOHN	KIRK JOHN
OGLESBY JOSEPH	HUNT NATHANIEL	KIRK MOSES
STOCKWELL CYRUS	BORIOURT THOMAS	KIRK ADAM
DOUGLASS THO'S	HEMPHILL PETER	SERING JOHN
HIBBARD TRUMAN	EPPERSON WILLIAM	GROVER JER.
LATTE WM	EPPERSON JAMES	BROWN JAMES
DOUGLAS AMZI	BARKER DAVID	BLOOMER JOHN R
MEEL A A	ROADS SAMUEL	SHANNON WILLIAM
McCULLAUGH JOHN	HANEY JOHN	DURT RICHARD
McCULLAUGH THOMAS	GRAHAM JAMES	WERE HUGH
LUND JOHN	BIGLER DAVID	BUTLER ANDREW
NEW JOHN B	WILSON JACOB	DEVEROUGH RICH'D
PRINCE JOHN	STRICKLAND JOSEPH	KEYTON JAMES
SHEETS JOHN	FELL MAHLON	HYNES PETER
SHEETS GEORGE	MACINTIRE JOHN	M'NULTY JOHN
WHORTON WILLIAM	KENNEDY ALEXANDER	JEANNERETT P
MORRIS WALTER B	NICKEBOCKER HENRY	BACKMAN LEWIS
BANTZ GEOGE W	GOLDSBY WILLIAM	REED L W
BANTZ WILLIAM	GHOLSON FREDERICK	WESTGATE J B
KYLE FREDERICK	HAMILTON JAMES	M'KINLEY SAMUEL
COLLINS ANDREW	GREEN GEORGE	TUCKER JOSHUA
PALMER NATHANIEL B	INGRAM JAMES	WALLACE WILLIAM
WHITNEY JACOB	GORSUCK JOHN	WALLACE JAMES
PUGH JOHN	BINDER SAMUEL	LODGE JOHN
GAVIT JOHN	DAWS L	STAPP MILTON

JEFFERSON COUNTY

STAPP SILAS
CARPENTER WILLIAM
DEARBORN RICHARD
KEEN SAMUEL
VAIL JENNINGS
NEWBERRY JOHN
STONE JOHN W
CRITS HENRY
WATTS HOWARD
HEATH JOHN
DUPUY B
STERRITT JAMES
PARK M
CANBY I T
M'CLURE DAVID
KING JOHN
JEFFRIES C G
COFFMAN JOHN
COFFMAN JACOB
COFFMAN GEORGE
COFFMAN PHILIP
DORSEY JOHN
M'VICKER JAMES E
KEYS JOHN
BAYLEY S NATHAN
RIDDLE JOHN
DAY SAMUEL
SMITH ELIHU
KEATON JAMES
WOODWARD CHARLES
HENDRICKS JOHN
TAYLOR GAMALIEL
BAIRD ROBERT
SHEETS LEWIS
THOM WILLIAM W
COTTON JAMES C
MEEK ROBERT
WITHAM GIDEON
POWELL WILLIAM
STEPHENS SAMUEL
HAUGHBOY JACOB
DILLON ROBT
ENOS W C
KENT CARLTON
BRADLEY ISAAC
KOONS JOHN
WEST JACOB
JAQUESS JOHN
JAQUESS JOHN JR
NICHUM JOSEPH
ROWSER MARTIN
EVERHART JOHN

EVERHART WILLIAM
BUCHMAN DAVID
CAIN JOHN
SEELEY STEPHEN I
ROBERTS WILLIAM
WALKER LEWALLEN F
BARNETT CHARLES W
BROWN WILLIAM
SEARLE THOS C
WIRE THO'S
EBLEN JOSHUA
WHITE JAMES
RISTINE JAMES
WOODWARD HENRY
JOHNSON L/I
ROACH JOHN
REED A G
KING ALEX'R
VICKERS BENJ
GOLD EDMAN
FLEMING ROBT
HOUSTON SAMUEL
GAGEBY JOHN
DONNALDSON EBENEZER
SYLVESTER LEVI P
WIT B
HATCHET PLENA
DELONG AMASA
PEARSON E
NEWMAN ADAM
BROOKS NOR
BEAR CHRISTIAN
FUGIT JESSE
SHERMAN NATHANIEL
WALKER JOHN
KISER JACOB
BURNS JAS
INGRAM JAMES
CAMPBELL ALEX'R
CAMPBELL JOSEPH
HENDERSON ANDREW
DAVIS BENJAMIN
SULLIVAN ARYAN
SPENCER JOHN
KELLY CORNELIUS
HEATH MARTIN
HAMILTON WILLIAM
GUTHRIE JOHN
CLAXON CASSIUS
BUTNER ISAAC
BEBEE DUDLY
HALL ZACHARIAH

HELMS ABRAHAM
WILLHOITE JOHN H
MATTHEWS JOHN
McCARTNEY ENOCH
ELLIS STEPHEN
MITCHELL JOHN M
MINOR BEBE O
PATTON MATHEW
WAGNER GEORGE
McCARTNEY NICHOLAS
CHAMBERS ISAAC
BAXTER JAMES
IRWIN THOS B
MILES EVAN
WEATHERFORD HARDEN
RYKER SAMUEL
BRADA CHARLES
MARQUES EBENEZER
HEATON DAVID
BRALY JOHN
ROBINSON DANIEL
HENDERSON ANDREW
ELLIOTT WILLIAM
MARQUES SAMUEL
LEVITT BANJAMIN
FOSTER A
THORNTON JOBE
RIPLEY WILLIAM P
BUCHANAN JOHN
CLEMINGS WILLIAM
DICK JAMES
BRASHEARS REASON
MORTON JOHN
KEENE DAVID
POSTON LEVI
LEE ANDREW
KENNEDY JOHN
BRIGHT DAVID G
HEATH JOHN
COWAN JAMES
MAXWELL B E
FIX WILLIAM
FIX JACOB
STUCKER JACOB
VANNORMAN D
ADAMS L
MONROE WM
HILL JOSEPH
WEST DANIEL
BAILEY J
CONSLEY SAM'L
SMITH JAS

JEFFERSON COUNTY

CURRIE JAMES	LATTY WILLIAM	BRUSTER JAMES
KISTTER MANUEL	MINER THOS	CROWLEY MATHEW
STUCKER JOHN	MAPES JOS	M'CASLAND WILLIAM D
WALKER WM	CONLEY HENRY	NORRIS SAMUEL
WALKER J	SCONEE ROBT	DUNGAN NATHAN
TAYLOR THOS	MELTON JOHN	DUNGAN SAMUEL
TAYLOR JOHUA	BROWN JOHN	MEDLEY JOHN
HILL JOSEPH	HASETT JOSEPH	MARSHALL THOS
STUCKER ANDREW	GALE ELMON	TILFORD WILLIAM
BURNHAM JOSIAH	SAWYER LEIR	CHITWOOD JOSHUA
MONROE WILLIAM	GEER J C	CONDREY CLABORN
CRAWFORD JAS	SAWYER HIRAM	BURNSIDES JOHN
DIXON JOHN	M'CURDY WM	DAVIS HANDY T
WILSON JOSEPH	COLIER JAMES	JENNINGS SHERROD
BRISBEN JAMES	MITCHELL THOS	WRIGHT HORACE
HULICK ISAAC	PATTON JAMES	ANDERSON WILLIAM
HULICK ABRAHAM	WILSON WILLIAM	CUNNINGHAM ANDREW P
HIGGINS ABRAHAM	WILSON WILLIAM	WEAVER PETER
HULICK ISAAC	WOODFILL GABRIEL	ANDERSON JAMES
HICKS DAVID	TAYLOR DAVID	ROSS WILLIAM
FIELD JOHN	WOODFILL DANIEL	TAYLOR ROBT
SHANNON GEORGE	COX J	TAYLOR CRANSON
SHANNON THOS	COFFMAN JACOB	SWAN JOHN
SMITH SAM'L	WILLIAMS JOSEPH	SWAN THOS
SMITH JAS	WILLIAMS MOSES	SWAN ANDREW
LAME JOESPH	WOODFILL JOHN	HAINING JAMES
ARNALD JOHN	HALL SQUIRE	THOMPSON ROBT
M'KINSEY ALEX'R	M'CLELLEN JOHN	GUN JAMES
PATTON JAMES	ABBOTT JOHN	M'LAIN JOHN
FOX ROBT	ATHRON JETHREN	TULL JOSEPH
ROGERS JOHN	ATHRON WILLIAM	SWEET JOBE
BRANHAM EBIN	ALLEN WILLIAM	DRYDEN THOMAS
THORNTON JOSEPH	ALLEN JOSIAH	LOWELL JONATHAN
ORTON JEREMIAH	BEACHBOARD WM	LOWELL JONATHAN
SMOCK J R	DANSEY JOHN	LINDSAY JOSHUA
JACKSON ALIJAH	UNDERWOOD JAMES	LEWIS SWEAR
JACKSON DRURA	UNDERWOOD JAMES JR	SAW WILLIS
STODDARD RUSSEL	UNDERWOOD COLBY	LITTLEJOHN JOSEPH
SAYERS JOHN m/o	STEWART WM	FORBUS JOHN
ELEWELL DAVID	STEWART JOHN	WILSON WILLIAM
CAMPBELL JOHN S	ALLEN JOHN	JARVIS JAMES
WAKELAND WILLIAM C	JAMESON ALEX'R	THOMPSON LARUE
CATLAND EBENESAR	MORRISON ROBT	TOBIAS TOBIAS
BURNS EDWARD	HINTON THOS	DIXON JOHN
HAMILTON SAMUEL	ECHOLS JOSEPH	DIXON JOHN
HAMILTON WILLIAM	GULION WILLIAM	THOMSON GEORGE
MAY JOHN	MORRIS ARCHIBALD	MONROE WILLIAM
COTLAND EBENESAR	SMITH HENRY SR	BLANKENSHIP WILLIAM
ARNOLD JOSEPH	CLOYD JAMES	SETTLE HENRY
ARNOLD JOHN	M'CLUNG LYLE	FUEL NATHANIEL
BICKERSON LAMBERT W	WHEATLEY WILLIAM	ROSEBERRY JOHN
VILES JOSEPH	HOPKINS JOHN	CAMPBELL JOHN

JEFFERSON COUNTY

WILLSON ANDREW
LITTLEJOHN JOSEPH
TANNAHILL JAMES
HAMMOND JAMES
HAWS REUBEN
TERREL WILLIAM
CRAVENS BENJAMIN
WELLS SAMUEL
SAGE WILLIAM
HUDSON PETER B
LATHROP SILAS
LATHROP SIMON
DOUGTHTY SIMPSON
LOWRING RICHARD
HOLEMAN RICHARD
M'KAY THOS

M'KAY JOHN
M'KAY ANGUS
SHAIK ROSS
HUGHES WILLIAM
SPAIN MOSES
SMITH HENRY
HUTCHINSON EBENESOR
WALTON COMFORT
WALTON DANIEL
WALTON EUPHRATES
WILLINGTON JOHN P
CAIN CHRISTOPHER
UNDERSWOOD BENJAMIN
SYPES I
COLIER I T
FLARHERTY PATRICK

CARY WILLIAM
GRIFFIN JOHN
MEDLEY JOHN
BURTON THOS
M'CAMMON JAMES
M'CAMMON ARCHIBALD
M'KINLEY L
M'KINLEY SAM'L
FERGUSON WASHINGTON
POGUE WILLIAM
POGUE JOHN
VANDAVER JACOB
SMITH SAMUEL
SALYERS GEORGE
RITCHIE ADAM JR
COWEN JOHN

JENNINGS COUNTY

ANDREWS JOSIAH
ARBUCKEL MATHAN
ADAMS SAMUEL
ADAMS DAVID
ADAMS ALLEXANDER
AGELL JAMES
ANDERSON GEORGE
BROMWELL WILLIAM C
BURNS JOHN
BRANHAM JOHN
BONER JOHN
BUTLER JAMES
BUTLER CHANCY
BUTLER JOEL
BOYLE GEORGE
BUTLER JOEL SR
BARRETT JONATHAN
BARRETT ABRAHAM
BOYLE JOHN
BANFIELD JOHN
BARNUM BARNEY
BARRONS FREDRICK
BUTLER THOMAS
BUTLER JOHN
BRANDON EBENZOR
BRANDON JOHN
BRANDON MOSES
BAKER MORRIS
BAKER JOEL
BAKER WILLIAM

BAKER PELEY
BULLOCK WILLIAM A
BLANKINSHIP ISEAH
BAKER ELIGAH
BARNS DAVID
BARGE WILLIAM
BUNDY MILES
BROWN JAMES
BUCKELS JAMES
BUCKELS WILLIAM
BURCH WILLIAM
BRIDGES JOHN
BENNET JOHN
BENNET ROBERT
BENNET WILLIAM
BORRELL JOHN
BALLARD JOHN
BLANKENSHIP LEWIS
BALLARD URIAS
BIGGS JOSEPH
BRONGHER JACOB
BRANFIELD THOMAS
BENNET SAMUEL
BOSS JOHN
BARR HENRY
BROWN MOSES
BUMGARDNER GEORGE
BLANCHARD ROSWELL
BROWN BENJAMIN
BARANY JOHN

BROWN HERMAN J
BRACKEN JOHN
BARNES JOHN
BRACKEY SAMUEL
CARNEY JOHN
CURTIS WILLIAM
CARNEY PLEASANT
CERN JOSEPH
CAMPBELL ALLEN
CAMPBELL DAVID
CAMPBELL SAMUEL
CLARK BANJAMIN W
CLARK WILLIAM
COMSTACK JOHN
CUTLER LENARD
CHECE SETH
CHECE ASA
CONNER WILLIBY
CHEIVER JOSHUA C
CHANDLER DANIEL
CHANDLER BRADDOCK
CHANDLER ALFORD
CHANDLER WILLIS
CALLICOT WILLIAM
CALLIHAM JOHN
CAMPBELL FRANCES
CAMPBELL JOHN
CARLEY RICHARD
CUNNARD HENRY
CRERY JOHN

JENNINGS COUNTY

CHAPMAN   JAMES
CHANBERS   JOHN   SR
CHIMLEY   JOHN
CARSON   WALTER
CARSON   WALTER   JR
CARSON   FELIX   W
CARSON   WILLIAM
CARSON   DANIEL
CARSON   JAMES
CLARK   JOHN
CHAMBERS   JOHN   JR
CHAMBERS   ALLEXANDER
CARLEY   ELIGAH
CONNER   PHILLIP
CLOVER   CURNELUS
CLINES   NICHOLAS
COONFIELD   JOHN
CRANSE   WILLIAM
CHEIREU   ABNER   H
CRUSAN   THOMAS
CURTIS   FREDRICK
CURTIS   FREDRICK   A
DOLF   STEPHEN
DAVIS   NATHANIEL
DAVIS   PENUEL
DOBBINS   JOHN
DENNY   FEILDEN
DAVIS   SEPTEMUS
DENSLOW   JOHN
DENSLOW   CHAPMAN
DURBINE   AMUS
DENLOW   JOHN
DAVIS   ELIGAH
DAVIS   JONATHAN
DAVIS   JAMES
DENNIN   JAMES
ELIOTT   ALLEX'R   McCLURE
EVERLING   GEORGE
ERLE   JACOB
ERLE   JAMES
EDWARDS   JOHN
EASMAN   NATHANIEL
EASMAN   SOLOMON   R
EDMESTER   JOSEPH
ENGLISH   JOSEPH
ELLIOTT   WILLIAM
ELLIOTT   JONSTON
ELLIOTT   DAVID
ELLIOTT   ROBERT
EASMAN   NATHAN
ELLIOTT   JAMES
EENS   ENOCH

FOWLER   JOSHUA
FINNEY   ROBERT
FRESURE   BENGAMIN
FRANCIS   WILLIAM
FOWLER   JAMES
FINCH   WILLIAM   S/L
FRENCH   ZEPHNIAH
FRENCH   HARRIS
FREEMAN   STEPEN
FERRON   ISAAC
GRIFFIN   BENGAMIN
GRIFFIN   THOMAS
GRINSTEAD   JOHN
GREEN   JOSEPH
GREEN   JAMES
GATTES   JOHN
GREHAM   THOMAS   JR
GREHAM   WILLIAM
GREHAM   SAMUEL   S
GREHAM   JAMES
GREHAM   JAMES   SR
GREHAM   THOMAS
GREHAM   LEWIS
GEAR   JOHN   C
GALLOWAY   ELIHU
GUINEY   CHARLES
GRAY   WILLIAM
GRANT   WILLIAM   A
HALE   GEORGE
HOBBS   JAMES
HOLTON   ALLEXANDER
HUGHS   JOHN
HILTON   JAMES
HAMPTON   JAMES
HOBBS   JOSHUA   W
HARTWELL   WILLIAM
HARTWELL   WILLIAN   JR
HUGHS   JAMES
HICKLIN   WILLIAM
HICKLIN   JOHN
HICKLIN   JOHN   L
HUGHEY   JOSEPH
HOPKINS   JOHN
BENDOW   JOHN
HOPKINS   SAMUEL
HOPKINS   DAVID
HOPKINS   THOMAS
HUDSON   ANNIAS
HILL   THOMAS   JR
HILL   THOMAS   SR
HALL   ISAAC   JR
HALL   ISAAC   SR

HALL   ABNER
HOLLENSHEAD   BENNONI
HURLBUT   LEWIS
HURLBUT   CELEP
HOLLISTER   JOHN   W
HUTCHINS   DANIEL   A
HARMAN   GEORGE
HOWLET   WILLIAM
HUGHS   SAMUEL
HUGHS   DANISTON
HANNAH   JOHN
HEDRICK   ABRAM
HERRINGTON   JOSEPH
HARKINS   JOHN
JUSTICE   PETER
JONES   LEWIS
JAMES   THOMAS
JAMES   JOHN
JEFFERS   FRANCIS
JONSTON   JESSE
JOHNS   JOHN
KELLY   JOHN
KIMBERLY   ZENES
KELLER   ADAM
KELLION   JOHN
KIRTLEY   ABREHAM
KING   JOHN
KYSOR   JOHN
KEETH   SAMUEL   A
KEETH   JAMES
KIA   PHILLIP
KINDER   PETER
KNAP   JOHN
KNAP   AMUS
KNAP   DANIEL
KNAP   JOHN   W
KYZER   JOHN
KYZER   FREDERICK
KYZER   WILLIAM
LEWIS   ALLEXANDER
LONDEN   NATHAN
LATTIMORE   JOHN
LEE   RICHARD
LOCKWOOD   JOHN
LOCKWOOD   JAMES
LOCKWOOD   SETH
LANSON   STEPHENSON
LETT   ISHEM
LOWRY   ROBERT
LARD   SAMUEL
LAWRENCE   JACK   H
MEEK   BAZEL

JENNINGS COUNTY

MEEK SAMUEL
MEEK DAVID
MEEK JEREMIAH
MEEK RICHARD
MONCRIEF CELEPH
McMANNAMY HIRAM
MARTAIN WILLIAM N
MEEK NATHAN
MEEK JEREMIAH JR
McKEEHAN JOHN
McKEEHAN GEORGE
MUNSON HIRAM
MOUNTS JOSHUA
MOUNTS JOSEPH
MINTON JACOB
MINTON WILLIAM
MIDCAP JOHN
McOLLISTER DAVID
MERL SETH
McASLON GEORGE
McLOUGHLIN JOHN M
McLOUGHLIN JOSEPH
MIDCIF URIAH
MITCHEL JAMES
MILLER JOHN S
MILLER JOHN
MCARTY NICHOLAS
MEEK DANIEL
MEEK JOSEPH
MEEK WILLIAM
MEEK NATHANIEL
MCURRY JACOB
MOSS JOHN
MCRACKEN VIRGIL
MIRES JOHN
MATHERS JOHN
MILLIM RICHARD
McLEY DAVID
MUSELMAN DANIEL
MCOLLISTER MATHEW
MANEY JACOB
NEWTON JOSEPH
NEWTON LEWETHER
NEWTON REUBEN
NEWTON DANIEL
NEEDHAM JOHN
NOLTON STEPHEN
NOLTON JOSHUA
NOLTON EPRAIM
NORTHWAY JAMES F
NEEL MOSES
NEEL JOHN

NEWKIRK PETER
O'LOCKLEY JOHN
OWNS BRICKET
O'DANIEL SETEN
PAGGET WILLIAM
PALMER JOSHUA
REITHER WILLIAM
PAYBODY EZRA F
PENDLETON ROBERT
PENDLETON DAVID
POPPLE SIMEON
POWERS NEHEMIAH
POTTER JOHN B
PERRY RANSOM
POOL EPRAIM
POOL JOSEPH
PEOPLES HECTOR
PRITCHARD JOHN JR
PRITCHARD JOHN SR
PENNIC ALLEXANDER
POWERS GEORGE
PERDUE RICHARD
PHELPS ARONOUS
PHELPS SETH
PLYMET JOHN
PATTERSON ROBERT
PORTER - - -
PARKER JOSHUA
PETTES SAMUEL
PLYMET SERVICE
RHODS JOHN
RUSSEL JOHN
RUSSEL ROBERT
RAMSEY WILLIAM
ROBISON STEPHEN
RUSSEL ROBERT JR
RICH JUSTICE
RICH ISEAH
ROSS JAMES
ROBERTS JOHN
ROBERTS ALBERT
ROGERS JOHN
ROBISON NATHAN
ROBESON SAMUEL
RUSSEL WILLIAM
REED JOHN
ROSEBERRY THOMAS
RICHEY THOMAS
ROWLEY MILLER
RIGS JOHN
ROGERS JOHN
ROBISON HENRY

RANSOM ROBINS
RENNOCK ALLEXANDER
STOTT RICHART
STOTT WILLIAM F
STOTT JAMES
STORRY THOMAS
STRIBLING WILLIS
STRIBLING GEORGE
SANDFORD WILLIAM
SANFORD GIGION
STITES JOHN
SKINNER ASE
SKINNER DANNIEL
STROWDERD FILON
STIDMAN JAMES
SHELLEDY GEORGE
SHELLEDY EPRAIM
SAGE MORGAN
SWEET GEORGE
SCOTT THOMAS
St CLEAR HENRY
SHEPERD JAMES
SHEPERD JOSHUA
SHEPERD WILLIAM
SAWYERS HIRAM
SAWYERS LEVY
SULLIVAN NOAH
SMITH THOMAS
SMITH WILLIAM
SHIELDS WILLIAM
SHIELDS SAMUEL
SHIELDS JAMES
SHIELDS WILLIAM JR
SMITH GEORGE M
SHEETS MARTAIN
SUTTON JOHN
STILLWELL JOHN
SOPHER HENRY L
SHELLEDY GEORGE
SHELLADY EDWARD
VAWTER ACHILLIS
VAWTER JOHN
VANSIL JOHN
VANDOREN JABIS
VINCENT RICHARD
VANARCLE EB
VANCE JOHN
THOMAS EVEN
THOMAS BOOTH
THOMAS JAMES
TOWLER ROBERT
THORN WILLIAM

JENNINGS COUNTY

- THOMPSON ROBERT
- THREALKILL MOSES
- TRUMAN JOSEPH
- TURKIHISOR LEONARD
- TERLL EDMAN
- THOMPSON GEORGE
- THOMAS ELIGAH
- THOMAS JOHN
- THOMPSON ELIHUE
- TWEEDY PATRICK
- TOBY SAMMUEL
- THOMAS FREEMAN
- WARNER SAMUEL
- WATSON JULIAS
- WOOD MARTAIN M
- WHITE EDWARD
- WOODS WILLIAM
- WAGONER LEWIS
- WALKER JOHN
- WALKER WILLIAM
- WATSON ROBERT
- WILSON ROBERT
- WILSON ALLEXANDER
- WILSON JOHN
- WILSON MOSES
- WICOFF JAMES
- WATSON ROBERT SR
- WAGGONER JOHN H
- WILSON JOHN
- WHITESIDE JOHN
- WINCHEL JOHN
- WILKISON BENNIGAH
- WILSON SAMUEL JR
- WILSON SAMUEL
- WILKISON ROBERT
- WOOD ELIAS
- WILLIAMS SAMUEL
- WOODWARD CHESLEY
- WHITTIN JOB
- WILKY HIRAM
- HIERS - - -
- HALE LEMUEL
- CORNS EDWARD
- STUBINS HARRIS
- SMITH - - -
- TOWNSOND JOHN
- SHIELDS ROBERT
- JOHNSTON JAMES W
- BACKEY SAMUEL

KNOX COUNTY   VINCENNES TOWNSHIP

- PARKE BENJAMIN
- SERRA VINCENTS
- REED JOHN
- HENRY WILLIAM
- ARMSPAW EACH LEONARD
- WILLIS JAMES ABRAHAM
- TOMPKINS SYLVENIS
- OSTEN DANIEL
- PRICE RICHARD P
- CARSONS WILLIAM
- BONNAR WILLIAM
- HANAWAY AMOS
- CROWSMAN JOSIAH
- FEILEY JAMES
- COOPER CHARLES
- MOFFITT JAMES T
- MOFFITT WALTER
- TUCKER CHARLES
- PATTERSON JOHN
- COLLINS DAVID
- IRVIN JAMES
- WHEELER HENRY D
- BLANEY DANIEL T
- BRIGGS GEORGE H
- DONIVAN JEREMIAH
- WILLARD TITUS B
- YEOMAN PETTER
- DOUGTHERTY HENRY
- PARKESON JAMES
- SMITH NICHOLAS
- ROSS LEWIS
- ROSS MATHIAS
- PARR SAMUEL
- SPARKS RICHARD
- CETCHIM WILLIAM
- COLLINS SAMUEL
- WELLMAN BARNABUS
- HOOPE ISAAC
- BROCKAW HENRY
- PEARSON MOSES B
- MARTIN JOHN B
- DAVISON SAMUEL
- MONTGOMERY RICHARD
- KICTLAND AARON F
- LEE SAMUEL JOHN
- WEBB EZRA
- HALEY JOSIAH
- BERON HENRY
- MOORE EDWARD
- WILLARD PETTER
- ROBISON FRANCIS
- SPEARS STEPHEN
- HAIRBACK HENRY
- ALBERT MARTIN
- McDONALD GEORGE
- FARRINGTON JAMES
- BABCOCK PELAGE
- MORRISON JOHN
- COATS ERASTUS
- McCALLON WILLIAM
- HOLLOWELL LEVI
- MICHAEL CONSEDDER
- CLARK ORINGE
- FELLOW WILLIS
- BURRUAW JOHN BT
- BABBETT STEPHEN
- JELBA JOHN
- SWIFT SETH
- CHATTSEY JOHN
- CHATTSEY BENJAMIN
- DEWYER CHARLES
- MEREAW HENRY
- PEARSON THOMAS
- SHELBY JOHN
- GREENAUGH WILLIAM
- REDMAN GEORGE
- FELLOW WILLIS JR
- FELLOW HART
- FLETCHER GEORGE
- WHITNEY JAMES
- LATURE JOHN BT
- HARRISON SIMMS C
- LOW JACOB
- BELL WILLIAM
- WHELPLOY DAVID
- MORFOND JOSIAH T
- BABER HENRY B
- BOBERTS HARVEY
- ROBERTS RANSEM G
- BROULLETT MICHAEL

KNOX COUNTY   VINCENNES TOWNSHIP

- RUSHERVILL ANTOINE
- BUNTIN ROBERT SR
- BUNTIN ROBERT JR
- BRADLY VALENTINE I
- JOHNSTON GEN. W
- SMITH CHARLES
- SAYRE DEMICE
- SAYRE JAMES
- BOUDINOTT ELISHUA
- BLACKMAN NATHANIEL
- McGIFFEN JOHN
- BARR SAMUEL H
- BUCKEN EDMOND
- PROCTOR AMOS
- BONTEN STEPHEN
- CUNNINGHAM JOHN
- NICHOLAS EZRA
- CORBERN NATHANIEL
- TRUESDALE WILLIAM
- WHITSEY ISAAC N
- SHULER LAURANCE S
- ASH PATRICK
- NOLEN HENRY
- SMITH GEORGE SR
- ROBERTS JOHN
- ROSS JOHN
- TOMLINSON SAMUEL
- TODD JOHN N
- YOUCE JOSEPH
- SMITH JAMES
- SMITH WILLIAM C
- WOOD JEREMIAH
- WOLBERTON JOHN D
- JAQUESS GEORGE F
- MONK SIMON
- REILEY JOHN C
- REILEY MARTIN
- SHEIRER ADAM
- DUNN JOHN
- DRAKE ALEXANDER
- DRAKE SAMUEL
- FISHER PALMER
- SMITH GEORGE
- HOFF ISAAC
- DANIEL MERCER
- DANIEL WILLIAM
- SERANTEN I G
- HALE TEMPLE
- BEAMAN CARTER
- MONGIN M
- HAY JOHN D
- VANDEVENTER WILLIAM C
- ONLOY BENJAMIN
- BREADING WILLIAM E
- KAUSTLER JOHN
- WISE SAMUEL
- BODDOLETT ALBERT
- BOOTHIS WILLIAM
- HENDERSON - - -
- JOHNSTON HOMER
- JUCTION JOSEPH
- RUNALD JOHN M
- COLMAN JEREMIAH
- CHATFEY AUSTIN B
- ADAMS JOHN
- SWANK WILLIAM
- CONROUGH MICHAEL
- GODARE JOHN
- SHAPAUR AMBROISE
- LINDSEY WILLIAM SR
- LeMEMORE JOHN BT
- SICKMAN FREDERICK
- BAILY JOHN SR
- BAILY JOHN JR
- BAILY THOMAS
- COBB EBENEZER
- LINDSLEY A B
- BONO JOHN BT
- MERRY CORNELIOUS
- CARY ANTHONY
- RAMORE PEIRRE
- PERYEA PAUL
- MYRES JOHN
- WHITE THOMAS
- WHITE CHARLES
- TEEPLES JOHN
- STOUT ELISHUA
- CREELY GEROME
- BRUNNER JOHN
- BRUNNER ABRAHAM
- BRUNNER ISAAC
- BURGOY FRANCIS
- CUNNINGHAM FRANCIS
- SHULLER PETTER
- HOOP ISAAC
- ELDER WILLIAM
- BOLUE PETTER
- FOYLES JAMES
- DOTY JONATHAN
- PIGEON PATRICK
- GLASSEY MICHAEL
- CARTER ELEAZER B
- MIEURE WILLIAM
- MERROW HENRY
- AVLIGNE LAUREAU
- PROCTOR WILLIAM
- FAFOYE LAMBARE
- BUCKSTON E
- GARNER PHINES
- NICHOLAS - - -
- COURANITON JAMES
- BLAKE THOMAS H
- ABERTE WILLIAM
- WOOD EARL
- WILLIAMS - - -
- JONES ISAAC
- SHABLOTT BURNOW
- DUPREE LEWIS
- TACIEA FRANCIS
- PECOR ALEXIS
- LUNGO LEWEY
- LEVESON ANTOINE
- TRUSDALL FRANCIS
- DUBOIS MICHAEL
- GREMORE FRANCIS
- TERPAN LEWIS
- LATREMORE BT
- LAPLANT JOSEPN BONYEA
- GONZALES SIMON
- NABB JAMES
- REILEY OWEN
- ROBISON MARTIN
- JONES LEVEN
- BORWAY LOMBAR
- BORWAY JOHN
- RACINE PIERRE
- OYOTTE JOSEPH
- St ANTOINE FRANCIS
- SISCOW WILLIAM
- SISCOW MICHAEL
- GRIFFIN IRA
- HUNTER ROBERT
- WEATHERS WILLIAM
- GEREW LEVEY
- BEAMEN LYONS
- CORNIA FRANCIS
- COMPOW ENIAC
- BARROW JOSEPH
- JACKERY SCOTT
- DUBOIS AKINS
- CARDINAL JOSEPH
- BARNETT MARK
- GREATER FREDERICK
- ALMY SENICA
- EARLY JOHN D
- PULAM ZACHIRAH

KNOX COUNTY   VINCENNES TOWNSHIP

- LINDSEY WILLIAM JR
- BUTTLER JOHN
- SMITH MECHAEL
- REILEY DAVID B
- BROWN MANNUSHA
- WATSON FREDERICK
- FISHER ALEXANDER
- BRIGG WILLIAM
- REIBLE HENRY
- COCHRAN JEREMIAH
- BRADY JOHN
- McCALL JAMES B
- HART DAVID
- PRINCE WILLIAM
- FISHER CHARLES
- ELDER J ELI
- REYNOLDS ROBERT
- BONNER DAVID
- JACOBS SAMUEL
- JACOBS JAMES
- COULTER JOHN
- LeROY ALEXIS
- DEXON FRANCIS
- McKLLERORY ARCHIBALD
- GAULT WILLIAM
- MORRISON MATHIAS
- COLEMAN ISAAC
- MOORE JOHN
- SMITH PHILLIP
- ROBISON THOMAS
- SEVINEA PIERRE
- GODARE ANDREW
- COMPOW MICHAEL
- COMPOW ANTOINE
- KEREY ZADON
- MALLENEY ANTOINE
- GREENAUGH DEVORICK
- WALKER WILLIAM W
- ELOXANDER JOHN
- ROSEMAN JOSEPH
- ROSEMAN THOMAS
- McNEE ELIAS
- NYSWONGER JOSEPH
- CYAN ABRAHAM
- BUTLER NELSON
- HICKES WILLIAM
- WALKER ISAAC
- PECKHAM LEWIS
- ROME A S D
- ALMY PHILLIP
- HOIL GEORGE
- BATSON JONATHAN
- DECKER HIRAM
- TROMBLEY STEPHEN
- KUYKENDALL JACOB
- GEATER CHRISTIAN
- LANDER LEVI
- CORNIEA AMBROIS
- DEDWAIRE CHARLES
- BUSHEY VITAL
- PAGE WILLIAM
- PAGE DOMENICE
- BOYERYON NICHOLAS
- DENOE TOUSANT
- DABYEAN ANDREW
- LADERUTE LEWIS
- DENION LEWIS
- ERNEA JOSEPH
- ERNEA LEWIS
- CORNIEA ANTOINE
- GAMLIN PEIRRE
- BUSHOY JOSEPH
- UNO JOSEPH
- MATHENY JOSIAH
- SHARKEY BATEAST
- BLACK JOHN
- FULLETION JOHN
- DELIELE JOHN
- DELUNIOW JOSEPH
- GOODMAN JOHN BT
- VILNAVE JOHN BT
- HARRINGTON JOHN
- HARRINGTON DANIEL
- ALLEN JOSEPH
- JOHNSTON PRESLEY
- JOHNSTON WILLIAM
- JOHNSTON WESTLEY
- SNAPP ABRAHAM F
- SNAPP ABRAHAM
- BOLO MABB
- KNOX GEORGE
- JACOBS DANIEL
- WELL AUGUST
- ROSS BRITMAN
- ROSS RUSSELL
- THOMPSON SIRAS
- HODGENS JAMES
- HODGENS WILLIAM
- BROWN ELISHUA
- DEVENDALL SIMON
- SMITH BASTION
- CONAWAY SAMUEL
- SMALL JOHN
- SMALL THOMAS
- BROWN SAMUEL
- BROWN PETTER
- SMITH SILAS
- CARUTHERS SAMUEL
- CHRISE JACOB
- WATKINS STEPHEN
- SHSHLOR WILLIAM
- MOORE SAMUEL
- POOL PETTER
- BROULLETT PIERRE
- CARDINAL NICHOLAS
- MALLERY HIRAM
- M'COULAUGH JOHN
- BURK JOHN
- SCOTT JAMES
- SCOTT THOMAS
- LEE SAMUEL
- KIRK HENRY D
- SCOTT JOHN
- SCOTT GEORGE
- BRIGGS IZREAL
- SHORES JOSEPH
- MILLER SAMUEL
- EMMERSON SAMUEL
- HOLMS JOSIAH L
- McCLURE JOHN
- BOILES CHAS ALLEN
- COLLINS JOHN
- LUSTER JOHN
- BARIONS ERICK
- SCOTT SAMUEL T
- ARMSTRONG ANDREW
- CARIGHT JOHN
- GALSPIA PATRICK
- BROWN SAMUEL
- STAPSSOX LEWIS
- FULLINGTON WILLIAM C
- THRAILKILL JAMES
- DAVIS GEORGE
- VIGO FRANCIS
- EWING JOHN
- GARDENOR ANDREW
- EWING NATHANIEL
- EWING GEORGE
- SULLIVAN GEORGE R C
- CALL JACOB
- DILWOURTH SAMUEL
- LASSELL HYACINTH
- BRUNNER SAMUEL
- SPARKS JOHN
- SPARKS MARTIN
- CECHUM WILLIAM

KNOX COUNTY   VINCENNES TOWNSHIP

COLLINS SAMUEL	McOMMACE GEORGE	DELENIA JOSEPH
BRUCKLEBANK JOHN	REEDER ELISHUA	DELENIA LEWEY JR
- - - EATON	ROADES JOSEPH	DELENIA PAINE JR
BROXKAW HENRY	TAYLOR GABRIEL	RUSECOW FRANCIS
REILEY JOSIAH	HOLSCAW WILLIAM	COMPANIOTTO PIERRE
BUSHEY FRANCIS	DEVENDALL JOHN	FONTANY JOHN BT
BUSHEY LAURISH	COLLINS JEREMIAH	GROMORE CHARLES
EDWARDS LEWIS B	SIMPSON PATRICK	MALLOTT PEIRCE
ALMY HUMPHRY	LAMOUNT JOHN HENRY	BUSHING JOHN BT
OSBOURN JOHN W	BADOLOTT JOHN	MALLETT FRANCES
THOMPSON CHARLES	BADOLOTT JAMES	BOURDELOW RAME
TILINGHURST CHARLES H	BADOLOTT SIDENNY	BOURDELOW PIERRE
POLSTEWEIGHT SAMUEL	EWING GEORGE SR	MALLETT LEVEY
THOMPSON WILLIAM	LATURE PIERRE	RAVOLETTE ANTOINE
MALLETT FRANCIS	HOLLEY TRUEMAN	RAVOLETTE LEWEY
SMITH SOLOMAN	NICHALAW AMBROIS	RUSHERVILLE JOHN BT
BLAKCBURN THOMAS	PETIT ANTOINE	GODARE FRANCIS
HOLMAN RICHARD	GAMBEN TUCATE	LAPLANT JOHN BT
MIEURE JOHN	LEPLANT PIERCE	BONO FRANCIS
MEDFORD LEWIS	COMPOW NICHOLAS	LAPLANT JOHN BT JR
MARNEY JOHN	ROQUESS SAMUEL	CABBASHE PEIRRE
GAMBLIN USTAS	GEROME ANTOINE	BARBO FRANCIS
RAVERSON JOHN	HERKOY PIERRE	DELLENICO JOHN BT
RECINE JOHN	BOURDELOW ENIAS	DELLENICO FRANCIS
ELDSWORTH JAMES	RUNO JOSEPH	TOUCKOY FRANCIS
THOMPSON FRANCIS	LEFAVE ANTOINE	NORO GABRIAL
HAIRBACK HENRY	LEFAVE JOSEPH	DANIOU TOUSANT
THORNTON BENJAMIN	COMPOW MICHAEL	DELELE CHARLES
BURCH WILLIAM	THORN SAMUEL	CHAPPORE AUGUST
LEE JOHN	GORDEN GEORGE	RACINE JOSEPH
TARDICE FRANCIS	NOLEN HENRY	SYOUSCE GOEMAS
BIRYEAR FRANCIS	LEWIS - - -	CREELY CHARLES
BOLO FRANCIS	STEWART JAMES	DONEY ANTHONY
HAMELL HUGH	PITCHER JOHN SR	RAVOLETT FRANCIS
PATTERSON ARTHUR	PITCHER JOHN JR	RACINE PEIRRE
JOHNSTON JOHN	CHATTBURN JOHN	DELLENIEA LESCAU
JOHNSTON JAMES	DONELLY DAVID	BORRWAY LAMBAIR
HAND CHARLES	COULTER THOMAS	BORRWAY JOHN MARY
McCURE ARCHIBALD	St ANTOINE PIERRE	BOYEAU LEWEY
McCURE JOHN	St ANTOINE VITAL	BOYEAU GABRIEL
McCURE CHARLES	RUBY PETTER	MITTE JOSEPH SR
WREIGHT WILLIAM	HARDISON - - -	MITTE JOSEPH JR
WREIGHT JACOB	ZEDOR AUGUST	MITTE PEIRRE
PRICKETT JAMES	CARDINAL MADORE	COMPANIOTTE JOSEPH
MARTIN HENRY	LUNGO FRANCIS	SHABBOTT JOHN BT
COONS JOSEPH	MALLETT AMBROISE	RACINE ANDREW
MORGAN CHARLES	LANSREANE JOHN	DAKMAN FRANCIS XAVIER
MORGAN SCHLUSS	DOE ZEMEDO	FERRARI ANDREW
MORGAN DAVID	LORANT FRANCIS	BOWLES MATHIAS C
DURELL STEPHEN B	SHALLOTT BARNEAU	BROOKS WILLIAM SR
DURELL STEPHEN	DELENIA LEWEY SR	BROOKS WILLIAM JR
DURELL JOHN	DELENIA PEINE SR	BROOKS ANDERSON

KNOX COUNTY   WASHINGTON TOWNSHIP

- HOLLINGSWORTH   PETTER
- HOLLINGSWORTH   THOMAS
- LARTERS   GEORGE
- NEAL   JAMES
- THOMAS   JOSEPH
- BRISCE   WILLIAM
- JOHNSTON   ROBERT
- ALTON   JOHN
- ROBERTS   NOAH
- POSEY   RICHARD
- CHANSLER   ISAAC
- CHANSLER   JESSE
- FELTON   JOHN
- FAIRHUST   SAMUEL
- FAIRHUST   WILSON
- PURCELL   WILLIAM
- SHAFER   THORNTON
- SCROGGANS   JOSEPH
- CORRELL   ANDREW
- CIBBIT   WILLIAM
- REDENOUR   HENRY
- HOLMES   WILLIAM
- HOLMES   JOHN A
- GARRETT   WILLIAM
- WEAVER   JOHN
- HARPER   THOMAS
- HOLLINGSWORTH   WILLIAM
- HOLLINGSWORTH   DANIEL
- CROSBY   JOHN
- BENEDICT   JOHN
- CROSBY   LEONARD
- IRELAND   JOHN
- HOWARD   WILLIAM
- YOUNG   JOHN
- TIMMS   JAMES
- HOWARD   JOHN
- DURHAM   JOHN
- PRACE   WILLIAM
- WILLIAMS   GEORGE
- COOK   JACOB
- COCHRAN   BENJAMIN
- CROOKS   MICHAEL
- THOMPSON   SAMUEL
- MANNING   SAMUEL
- CADDY   JOHN
- ROACH   OWEN
- CRUM   PHILLIP
- BALTHIS   JOHN C
- BALTHIS   GEORGE
- KYLE   JAMES
- McLURE   THOMAS
- HOLLINGSWORTH   THOMAS
- MCLURE   JOHN
- MCLURE   CHARLES
- RUBY   PETTER
- HARPER   JACOB
- GREEN   JOHN
- OWEN   THOMAS
- EMMERSON   THOMAS
- EMMERSON   JOHN
- COLLINS   JEREMIAH
- ASHBY   NOAH
- McKEE   JOHN
- HUMMER   WILLIAM
- ELLIOTT   JOHN
- ELLIOTT   WILLIAM
- ELLIOTT   JAMES
- ELLIOTT   ROBERT
- McDONALD   WILLIAM
- POMROY   GEORGE
- PALMER   THOMAS
- MCLURE   DANIEL   SR
- MCLURE   DANIEL   JR
- BTEAST   FRANCIS
- PORTER   WILLIAM
- HUNCUTT   WILLIAM
- MEDLY   JOHN

KNOX COUNTY   PALMYRA TOWNSHIP

- SMITH   DANIEL
- SMITH   MINER
- WESTFALL   ISAAC
- SMITH   MOSES
- SMITH   JOHN
- WHICUM   JESSE
- FINLEY   JOHN
- WELTON   JONATHAN
- WELTON   JAMES
- BICKEL   ISRAEL
- WELTON   JOHN
- WHITAKER   EDWARD
- WARD   HIRAM
- HOGUE   ZEBULON
- McLURE   GEORGE
- PURCELL   NOAH
- McLURE   JOHN
- RAPER   WILLIAM
- VANKIRK   JOHN
- HOGUE   JOHN
- BARNARD   RICHARD
- SNIDOR   DAVID
- PURCELL   JOHN
- PURCELL   ANDREW
- PURCELL   JAMES
- SIMPSON   GEORGE
- ALTON   JOHN   SR
- ALTON   JOSEPH
- ALTON   JAMES
- ALTON   BENJAMIN
- LANGTON   SAMUEL
- WARNER   JACOB
- KUYKENDALL   JACOB
- WALLACE   HERMAN
- LANGTON   DANIEL
- COCHRAN   GLASS
- JOHNSTON   SAMUEL O
- GILLMORE   ROBERT
- HOGUE   JOSEPH
- BENNETT   JAMES W
- PARKER   JOHN
- PARKER   BAZEL
- SNIDER   DAVID W
- SNIDER   DAVID
- SNIDER   WILLIAM
- HERRAL   ISAAC
- BRNHUST   SELVISTER
- PETTERSON   JOHN
- ROSS   MARTIN
- HOLLINGSWORTH   JOSEPH
- BAIRD   THOMAS
- BAIRD   ARCHIBALD
- JOHNSTON   HUGH
- JOHNSTON   WILLIAM
- MAXEDON   JOHN
- McDONALD   JOHN   SR
- McDONALD   JOHN   JR
- McDONALD   JAMES
- BROWN   DAVID
- VANKIRK   JOSEPH

KNOX COUNTY   VINCENNES TOWNSHIP

MOORE   ALEXANDER
MOORE   SAMUEL
FORD   WILLIAM

LAW   JOHN
ELSON   ISAAC C

HAGEN   THEODORE
THOMAS   JONATHAN

KNOX COUNTY   WIDENER TOWNSHIP

MEDLEY   JOHN
COX   JESSE
DUTY   RICHARD
CHAMBERS SAMUEL
CHAMBERS ALEXANDER
LEMMON   ROBERT
LEMMON   DAVID
LEMMON   GABRIAL
LEMMON   SAMUEL
COX   JONATHAN
PIEATY   THOMAS
HOLLINGSWORTH   LEVI
BIDDEC   ALLEN
HOLLINGSWORTH   JESSEY
CHAMBERS DAVID
CHAMBERS JOHN
MORRIS   WILLIAM
CHAMBERS JAMES
CHAMBERS LEVI
LINDSEY JAMES

LINDSEY SAMUEL
POLKE   CHARLES   SR
POLKE   CHARLES   JR
POLKE   WILLIAM
NORMAN   SAMUEL
CHAMBERS JOSEPH
KEATH   JOHN
STORM   DANIEL
LEMMON   JOHN
KEATH   WILLIAM
LEMMON   WILLIAM
KEATH   JACOB
SMITH   ROBERT
MILLER   ABRAHAM
WILLES   JOSEPH
SHANNON ALEXANDER
KOFFMAN SAMUEL
WIDENER JOHN
HOUSE   JOHN

DEAN   JOSEPH
STARNER MICHAEL
COX   SAMUEL
PADGETT JONATHAN
BAILEY   ROBERT
ROBINS   JOHN
BROWN   JOHN
SCOMP   SAMUEL
SCOMP   HENRY S
REEVES   ALLEN
PURDUE   FURGAS
JOURNEY WILLIAM
JOHNSTON THOMAS
DUN   ROBERT
PRICE   WILLIAM
HARRISON WILLIAM   SR
HARRISON WILLIAM   JR
JERRELL ELI
JERRELL WILLIAM

KNOX COUNTY   WASHINGTON TOWNSHIP

CROOKS   JACOB
MILLER   ABRAHAM
DOUNS   JOHN
BENUM   JOHN
MELTON   THOMAS
GALLAND ABLE
HOPKINS DAVID
HOPKINS JOHN
HOPKINS JAMES
WILSON   WILLIAM L
MEDLEY   JAMES
PURDUE   EDWARD
PURDUE   JESSEY
PATRICK JOHN F
PATRICK OBEDIAH F
BECKNELL MUMFORD
BECKNELL McGAJAH

BECKNELL ALFRED
BECKNELL JOHN
HULEN   WYETT
HULEN   AMBROSE
HULEN   THOMAS
GOODMAN BARTLETT
ASBY   BARTLETT
ROMINE   ISAAC
COX   JESSEY
JERRELL JAMES
MEDLEY   SAMUEL
MEDLEY   JOHN
HULEN   JOHN
WALKER   ISAAC
TIMMS   JOSEPH
GOODMAN JOHN   SR
GOODMAN JOHN

DUNN   SAMUEL
MORRIS   JOHN
DUNN   JOSEPH
CLARK   WILLIAM A
SIMPSON JOHN
McCONAHAY DAVID
WILLIS   JOSEPH
STUART   JESSE
STUART   ECOBUD
McCORD   ASA
McCORD   WILLIAM   SR
McCORD   GEORGE
McCORD   WILLIAM
PACE   WILLIAM
HOLLINGSWORTH   BARNARD
ELLIOTT LEVI
HOLLINGSWORTH   JOHN

KNOX COUNTY   PALMYRA TOWNSHIP

LAW JOHN SR	STEEN JOHN	MEAD ISREAL
RISLEY DAVID	JONES ISAAC	FAIRHUST JOHN
RISLEY JAMES	HARDEN SION	HOUSE BURKETT
RISLEY JOHN	JONES SETH	COCHREAL ENODS
WELTON DAVID	MILLER PHILLIP	McNUTT ARCHIBALD
RODARMELL JOHN	SHANER GEORGE	MORGAN ZADIOCH
HERRELL JOHN	TOWNSEND WILLIAM	THORN ABSOLUM
LILLIE JAMES	KUYKENDALL JOSEPH	ELLIOTT JOHN
RICHEY JOHN	ROBERSON ABNER	WESTNER DAVID
TREECE DANIEL	ROBERSON HARMAN	HARRISS WILLIAM
CHAMBERLEN JONATHON	BOND JOSEPH	EDDY CHARLES
CHAMBERLEN ASA	COLLINS JOHN	HORNBACK NATHAN
WESTFALL THOMAS	COLLINS DAVID	SEATON FRANCIS
WESTFALL ABRAHAM	COLLINS JOSEPH	COCHRAN JOHN
STEEN RICHARD	FEASLE JOHN	HERRELL WILLILAM
STEEN JAMES		

KNOX COUNTY   HARRISON TOWNSHIP

BAKER NATHANIEL	TEVERBAUGH SOLOMON	COURTNEY HENRY
BARKER ISAAC	LINDER ISAAC	LETZER JOHN SR
JORDAN THOMAS	BROOCK JOHN	LETZER JOHN JR
ROLENS MOSES	SCABHORN JACOB	ADAMS SAMUEL
BEDELL ELIAS	SCABHORN JOHN	ADAMS THOMAS
BEDELL WILLIAM	LONG URIAH	CLAYCOMB FREDERICK
BADGER WILLIAM	HAYES JOHN	COLLINS WILLIAM
SODEN WILLIAM	RISLEY JAMES	ADAMS JOHN
SODEN JACOB	KNOX WILLIAM	MYRES JACOB
SELBY WILLIAM	THORN JACOB	MYRES FREDERICK
JOHNSTON JOSUA	WILLMORE JOSEPH	WILLIAMS JOSEPH
FARIS THOMAS	WILLMORE JACOB	NEAL WALTER
JOHNSTON RUBEN	PANCAKE JACOB	BEDELL ELIAS
THORN ASA	GAMBLE WILLIAM	SUMMETT HENRY
SHAW HUGH	GAMBLE JOSEPH	LIKE ADAM
SNIDER LEONARD	REEL JOHN	SHEATS JOHN
SNIDER JOHN	PATTERSON WILLIAM	HOLDERMAN JOHN
BOND JOSHUA	BALDING JOSEPH	CLAYCOMB ADAM
MIEURE RICHARD	JUNKINS WILLIAM	RAY DAVID
BASS WILLIAM	JUNKINS JAMES	STORK JOHN
TAGUE JACOB	THIXTON JOHN	STORK JACOB
McCOMB WILLIAM	McCOY ROBERT	FUGATE SAMUEL
SLAUGHTER PHILLIP	McCOY JOHN	BONNER JAMES
THOMAS JESSE	GOLDMAN GEORGE	WEBB DAVID
TEVERBAUGH NINROD	BOWERS GEORGE	GILLMORE EPHRAIM
TEVERBAUGH JACOB	GOLDMAN MARTIN	DELLINGER THOMAS
SULLIVAN JOHN	PARTLE HENRY	DELLINGER JOSEPH
SAMPSON WILLIAM	JONES ISAAC	DELLINGER WILLIAM
WEASE PHILLIP	WELTON WILLIAM	DELLINGER CHRISTOPHER
WEASE JOHN	LETZER SAMUEL	WESTFALL ABRAHAM

KNOX COUNTY   HARRISON TOWNSHIP

- THORN MICHAEL
- THORN JOSHUA
- McGOWEN PATRICK
- HARBEN JOHN
- GARROTT GEORGE
- ANDREWS WILLIAM
- ANDREWS JAMES
- BLACKBELL PETTER
- ADAMS AMOS
- ADAMS SAMUEL
- HARRISON - - -
- FLOWER WILLIAM

- FLINN DANIEL
- LATIMORE THOMAS
- BARKMAN JOHN
- REUMINGOR JOHN
- BARKMAN HENRY
- HORTON JOHN S
- BECKES BENJIMIN V
- CORNWELL GEORGE
- BAITH JOHN
- REEL DAVID SR
- REEL DAVID JR
- REEL GODFREY

- THORN JAMES
- DOUTHARD SOLOMON
- HUFFMAN JOHM
- HARTLEY JOHN
- OWENS THOMAS
- LEECH GEORGE SR
- LEECH GEORGE JR
- LEECH FRANCIS
- WOOD JOSEPH
- COOK JOHN
- COLEGROVE GEORGE

KNOX COUNTY   JOHNSTON TOWNSHIP

- MEAL FREDERICK
- MEAL ISAAC
- WARREN STEPHEN
- HARDYSON HARDY
- KIRK WILLIAM
- SMITH ISAAC
- THORN CHARLES
- SPAIN ARCHIBALD
- SAMPSON BENJAMIN
- MARTIN HENRY
- WILSON JOHN
- WILSON ABRAHAM
- WILSON EDWARD
- CATT MICHAEL
- JONES JOHN S
- CATT JOB
- MORGAN THOMAS
- MORGAN JOSEPH
- MORGAN RANDEL
- CATT GEORGE
- DECKER ABRAHAM
- CATT THOMAS
- DEVORE JOHN
- FREDERICK SEBASTIAN
- JOHNSTON ROBERT

- DECKER LUKE
- MINOR WILLIAM
- SHEPPARD WILLIAM
- CARTRIGHT PETTER
- STOUT JOSIAH
- PEA JACOB
- PEA JOHN
- CATT PHILLIP
- SPAID DANIEL
- CARY PEIRRE
- TURNER JESSEY
- MINOR JAMES
- BURNEY ROBERT
- PURCELL ANDREW
- PURCELL JOHN
- PRICE SAMUEL
- WILSON SAMUEL N
- CURRY ANDREW
- LANE SAMUEL
- MAYES JEREMIAH
- MAYES JAMES
- MAYES WILLIAM
- MAYES ELIJAH
- JOURDAN THOMAS
- CALL MOSES

- WELLUM SAMUEL
- AUSTIN JOSEPH
- CORY DAVID
- CORY JOSEPH
- PETTICE DAVID
- BROOK JEREMIAH
- BURT JOHN
- PETTICE JOHN
- AUSTIN DANIEL
- AUSTIN THOMAS
- McGUIRE CHARLES
- MURFIN JOHN
- TAYLOR DAVID
- EDWARDS JAMES
- MICHAEL FRANCIS
- MICHAEL JOSEPH
- MICHAEL JOHN
- BAKER JOHN
- MEAL CHARLES
- JOHNSTON THOMAS
- BILDERBACK JOHN
- CHAMBERS THOMAS
- FREDERICK PETTER
- GLASS THOMAS

KNOX COUNTY DECKER TOWNSHIP

REILEY PHILLIP
VANGORDEN JAMES
PURCELL ADAM
HARNESS NATHANIEL
DECKER ISAAC T
CROOCK DAVID
CROOCK GEORGE
BANIER JOHN
PURCELL ISAAC
ANTHONY HIRAM
PURCELL JAMES
STANLY EDWARD
CUNNINGHAM JOSEPH
CUNNINGHAM JOHN
WARTH ROBERT
JOHNSTON JOSEPH
DECKER DANIEL
KUYKENDALL NATHANIEL
KUYKENDALL GEORGE
VANGORDEN FOFARINE

DECKER ISAAC
GLASPEY JOHN
HARNESS ADAM
McNEELY JEREMIAH
KUYKENDALL ABRAHAM
PEARSON JOHN
PEARSON CHATWELL
HARNESS MICHAEL
DOLOHAN DANIEL
DOLOHAN MILES
BROWNING JOSEPH
BROWNING MARSHALL
KELLY THOMAS
PUTNAM HOWARD
BAINER PETTER
WOODHOUSE HENRY
RAMSEY AQUILLA
RAMSEY WILLIAM H
HANKS PETTER
TRULOCK THOMAS

CRUM COONROID
BUSH WARREN
PLOUGH NIM
SELBY LINGE
KELLY HENRY
HAZELTON JAMES
PLOUGH SAMUEL
PLOUGH SIMON
PLOUGH JACOB
PLOUGH ISAAC
DOLOHAN JOHN
SATTERLY JOHN
RAMSEY ALLEN
RAMSEY AARON
ANTHIS JOHN
IRVIN JOHN
ANTHIS JACOB
ANTHIS FRANCIS
PURCELL JONATHAN

KNOX COUNTY BUSSERON TOWNSHIP

BLETHING DANIEL
FRANCIS JAMES
ALLEN CHARLES
JAMES JOSIAH
DUCKWORTH NATHANIEL
JAMES JAMES
DENNY JOHN
CUNNINGHAM ALXANDER
GARDENER JOHN I
HOWARD WILLIAM
DUCKWORTH WILLIAM
HOGG JOHN SR
GREENFIELD JAMES
CURRY JOHN
CURRY WILLIAM
SWANK RICHARD
TREADO ROBERT
HEATH WILLIAM
SWAN JOHN
CHAPLE JOHN
SHERK JACOB
RUGER DAVID
McCARTHY JOHN
WATSON JAMES
WATSON THOMAS

HICKLON JAMES
HUNT TUNOSS
HARBAND MOSLEY
SUMMERS CALEB
BELLINGS INCREAS
HICKLEN JONATHAN
PEOPLES JOHN
McCURE SAMUEL KY
BAMFORD MOSES
LUDINGTON HARVEY
STEVENS IZREA
LILLIE DAVID
LILLIE ROBERT
CASE ABRAHAM
FREEMAN GARBIAL
LUDINGTON HORICE
WOODEN AMOS
JUSTICE DANIEL
LIGHT JOHN
OCKLETREE JOHN
CLARK GEORGE
ROLER JACOB
HILL JOHN
SULLENGER RUBEN
SHEPARD WILLIAM D

HARPER GEORGE
McHONEY WILLIAM
MICHAM ARCHIBALD
BATES ISACHOR
JOHNSTON JOSEPH
DAVIS WILLIAM
DAVIS JESSE
MEAD JAMES
PRICE DAVID
LEGIER JESSEY
GALLAGHER ADAM
LEGIER GEORGE
MEIGS JOHN
DOUGLAS WIILLIAM
HOPKINS JAMES
BOYLS JOHN
MILLER BENJAMIN
WISMAN FREDERICK
GILL ROBERT
McKUHAR ALEX'R
GALLAGHER WILLIAM
KNOX WILLIAM
KNOX WILLIAM JR
KNOX BENJAMIN
DANIELS CHANEY

KNOX COUNTY   BUSSERON TOWNSHIP

SQUIRE AMOS
NEWMAN THOMAS
AUTRIGHT FERDOMON

CRANE JOSEPH
FOWLER CHESTER
WEST JOHN

McCLELAND SAMUEL
MILLER HENRY

MONROE COUNTY

ALSOP JOHN
ANDERSON GEORGE JR
ANDERSON GEORGE
ANDERSON ROBERT
ANDERSON WILLIAM T
ARMSTRONG DAVID
ARMSTRONG HAWES
ALISON JOHN G
ARCHER EDWARD
ARCHER JOHN
ARNOLD BENJAMIN
ANDERSON DANIEL
ADAMSON DAVID
ADAMS GEORGE
ANDERSON GEORGE
ARMSTRONG ALEXANDER
ARMSTRONG JOHN
ARMSTRONG EDWARD
ABEL PETER
ANDERSON ISAAC
ADAMSON ABRAHAM
ADAMSON MORDECAI
ANDREW JAMES
ALEXANDER ZEBULON
ABRAHAM THOMAS
ARTHUR JOSEPH
ALEXANDER JOHN
ATWOOD JAMES B
BAKER JOSIAS
BOONE WILLIAM
BARKER THOMAS
BURTON JOHN
BLOOMFIELD SAMUEL
BOUGH JOSEPH
BURNS JESSE
BOWEN ISAAC
BAYLEY HENRY
BAYLEY THOMAS
BAYLEY CHESLEY
BAYLEY JAMES
BERRY WILLIAM
BLAIR ENOS
BORELAND EDWARD

BRIENT JAMES
BRUMMET JAMES I
BRUMMET JAMES II
BRUMMET JAMES III
BRUMMET PIERSON
BUTCHER SOLOMON
BUTCHER DANIEL
BRUMMET BANNER
BRUMMET GEORGE
BATES JACOB
BLAIN ABNER
BREEDER RICHARD
BUCKANON ALEXANDER
BERRY JOHN
BRUNER JOSEPH
BURTON WILLIAM
BURKET HENRY
BALES EDWARD
BUCKANON JAMES
BALES JAMES I
BARNES JOHN
BRACHEN JOSEPH
BURCH JOHN
BALES JAMES II
BOURLAND JAMES
BOURLAND JOHN
BROWN JAMES
BUSKIRK MICHAEL
BLAIN ROBERT
BATTERTON HENRY
BATTERTON PETER
BATTERTON WILLIAM
BARLOW SAMUEL K
BERRY JOSEPH
BROWN MATHEW
BOHANON NATHAN
BROWN WILLIAM B
BROWN WILLIAM
COX JOSEPH
CHUME JOHN
CLARWATERS JACOB
CHANCEY WILLIAM
CORR HUGH

CHAMBERS DAVID
COX AMOS
CHRISTIE JOSEPH
CUTTER JOHN
COVERDALE PERRY
COFFMAN ABRAHAM
COFFMAN SOLOMON
COFFMAN NICHOLAS
CLARK NATHANIEL
CLARWATERS REUBEN
CRANE JAMES
CHOUDOIN SAMUEL
CLINDINEN JOSIAH
CLAREWATERS DAVID
CHANDLER BENJAMIN
CHANDLER JAMES
CHANCE TILMAN
CHANCE DANIEL
CHANCE PURNEL
CHAMBERS DAVID
CONNERS MATHEW
CHAMBERS ANTHONY
CHAMBERS JOHN
CURL DUDLEY
CURL WILLIAM
CURL JAMES
CRAIG WILLIAM
CLARK JACOB
CHESNUT JACOB
CHAMBERS THOMAS
CARTER BAYLEY
CLARK ROBERT
CRUMB JOHN
COLLINS JOHN
CLARK JAMES W
DICKENS PEMBERTON
DICKENS JAMES
DICKENS WILSON
DICKENS JOHN
DUNNING THOMAS
DUKE EPHRAIM
DUNNING SAMUEL
DUKES ROBERT S

36

MONROE COUNTY

DARNIELLE ISAAC
DAVIS JOHN
DUNNING JAMES
DOLLARHIDE ABSALOM
DILL ABNER
DYER WILLIAM
DRAIN CHARLES
DAVIDSON JAMES
DOLLARHIDE JOHN
DOWNS DAVID
DYER EZEKIEL
DIX ZACKARES
DUSKIN WILLIAM
DUTTON JOHN
DUFFIELD THOMAS
DEVOIR NICHOLAS
DODD SAMUEL
EDMOND WILLIAM JR
ELLIOT SAMUEL
ESLINGER CHRISTIAN
EWING BARTIS
EDWARDS WRIGHT
ELLIOT SAMUEL
ELLIOT EDWARD
EVANS ABNER
EVANS WILLIAM B
ESLINGER JOHN
EDWARDS HENRY
ELLIOT ELIJAH
FARLOW GEORGE
FULLEN RUEBIN
FRY BENJAMIN
FULLER DARLING
FULLER JAMES
FARES ISAAC
FLENOR NICHOLAS
FULLEN JOHN
FRANKLIN JOHN
FREELAND BENJAMIN
FITTSGERALD JOHN
FULLER JOHN
FOSTER JOHN
GOODWIN JOHN
GOODMAN GEORGE
GROVES GEORGE
GRAHAM ROBINSON
GARRET GIBSON
GIBBS JAMES
GASTON THOMAS
GASTON ANSON
GRIMES DAVID
GIVENS JOHN A

GOYER GEORGE
GRIMES THOMAS
GRIMES STEPHEN
GOODWIN SETH
GOODWIN ELIAS
GILBERT JOSEPH
GILBERT JONATHAN
GARDNER JOHN
GOSNEL ADAM
GOSS EPHRAIM
GOSS GEORGE
GILLESPIE ISAAC
GRIFFITH JOHN
GOODWIN WILLIAM
GREEN SOLOMON
GREEN JOSEPH
GREEN JAMES
GIBSON BARNEY
GILLAM DRURY
GRIMES THOMAS
HOPKINS LEMUEL
HURTSOCK DANIEL
HAYS WILLIS
HUMPHRY HARRIS
HUZZY THOMAS
HANLEY WILLIAM G
HENSON COONROD
HAMILTON WILLLAM
HOGELAN JOHN
HALE JOHN
HALE JAMES
HAVENS STEPHEN
HILL WILLIAM
HENLY WILLIAM
HEDRICK GEORGE
HARTSOCK SAMUEL
HENDERSON JOHN
HAUN JAMES
HALL FRANCIS
HODGES PHILIP
HALE JAMES
HARIMON SAMUEL
HARDISTER SAMUEL
HARDIN WILLIAM
HOWE JOSHUA O
HOUTS JOHN
HALL EDWARD
HEADY THOMAS
HICKMAN FRANCIS
HILL THOMAS
HERRICK ANSEL
HAMILTON ROBERT

HAZELET WILLIAM
HAWORTH JOHN
HAZELET SAMUEL
HIGHT JOHN
HAUGH PHILIP
HANCOCK THOMAS
HICKS MOSES
HOWEL JOSIAH
HOWEL JONATHAN
JULIAN WILLIAM
INYARD SILAS
ILIFF RICHARD
JACKSON WILLIAM
JACKSON WILLIAM JR
JOHNSON GEORGE W
JENKINS JOHN M
JENKINS THOMAS
JACKSON WILLIAM B
JOHNSON JOSHUA
JACKSON LEWIS
JACKSON JOHN
JOHNSON ALEXANDER
JONES WILLIAM
JAMES JOSEPH
JAMES JAMES
KIRKHAM HENRY
KEYS JOHN
KILLOUGH DAVID
KETCHUM JOHN
KNIGHTEN JESSE W
KING WILLIAM
KNUCKLES DAVID
KUTCH JOHN
KARNS ADAM
KILK JAMES
KOONS GASPER
KIRKENDALE HENRY
KELLY GEORGE
LOWE JACOB B
LITTEREL THOMAS
LOOMY TAYLOR
LINDSEY NICHOLAS
LEBO JOSIAH
LEBO JACOB
LEBO ISAAC
LEE THOMAS
LEE ELI
LUCAS JOSHUA H
LOWE WILLIAM
LATHAM JOHN
LITTELL ABRAHAM
LOCKMAN THOMAS

MONROE COUNTY

LOCKMAN CHARLES	MILSAPS JAMES	RAWLINS RODERICK
LINDSAY VINCENT	McKINNEY JOHN	RICHARDSON JOSEPH
LATHAM JOHN JR	MCRUE JOHN	RHOADS LEWIS
LUCAS GEORGE	MOORE JESSE	RIDGE BENJAMIN
LONG HIRAM	MOORE JOHN III	RAWLINS DANIEL
LAKE JOEL	MAY JOHN	REEVES JOSEPH
LUCAS THOMAS	MCPUR JOHN	RHOADS WILSON W
LAKE JOHN	MAY JOHN II	RAYBORN DAVID
LAKE ROBERT	McCANE ANDREW	ROGERS JONATHAN
LOUDER CALEB	McCANE WILLIAM	RAINS JONATHAN
LOUDER JOSEPH	MACY GAMALIEL	RITCHY GEORGE
LAIKY SIMON	MOOREHEAD - - -	RAY WILLIAM
LUCAS SOLOMAN	NICHOLS JONATHAN	ROBINSON AMOS
MITCHEL JAMES	NOEL LEWIS	RAWLEY EVANS
MERCER JOHN II	NEWCOMB WILLIAM	REDIX GEORGE
MAHALA JOHN	NEWTON WILLIAM	ROGERS DAVID
MOORE ELIJAH	NEWBY EDMOND	ROGERS ISAAC
MASON THOMAS	NAIL WILLIAM	RICHMOND WILLIAM
MOORE HENRY	OSBORN JOHN	SWEENEY BENJAMIN
MATTOCK WILLIAM	OWENS ALEXANDER	SHARP GEORGE
McKAN WILLIAM	OWENS JOHN II	SNODDY WILLIAM
MOORE JOHN	OWENS JOHN	STOUT DANIEL
MOORE ARCHIBALD	PHILIPS JOHN	SUMPTER ISOM
MOORE THOMAS	PARKS GEORGE	SMITH ADDISON
MOORE WILLIAM	PARKS GEORGE II	SEARS JOHN
MURPHY ALEXANDER	PARKS WILLIAM	SMITH ANDREW
MORGAN ELIJAH	PATTERSON JOHN	SEDGWICK JOHN
MORGAN SOLOMON	PAWLEY ISAAC	SMITH JOHN C
MORGAN ABSALOM	PECK JACOB	SANDY JEREMIAH
MAY WILLIAM	PECK ISAAC	SANDY THOMAS
MAYFIELD LEROY	PERISHO JOSEPH	SMITH JOHN
McCULLOUGH DAVID	PARKS BENJAMIN	SCOTT SAMUEL
MANNERS JAMES	PARKS JAMES	SCOTT SAMUEL
MAXWELL DAVID H	POUGH WILLIAM	SCOTT DAVID
MOORE JOSEPH	PARISHO JOHN	SEAK STEPHEN P
MOLL ABRAHAM	PRUETT COLEMAN	SLUCOMB JAMES
MOLL ABRAHAM JR	PHILIPS EDMOND	SWIFT JOHN
MATLOCK JAMES	PHILIPS JOSEPH	SMITH JOHN II
McCOLLOUGH WM D	PETTICOURT BOSWELL	SMITH JOSEPH
MILLARD BENJAMIN	PAWLY ABRAHAM	SECRETS MCPUR
McCOY DAVID	PHILIPS SOLOMAN	SECRETS BEESON
MURPHY JOHN	PARSON JAMES J	SMITH DUDLEY C
MOORE NELSON	POTTER THOMAS	SHANK JACOB
MATLOCK DAVID	PARSONS JAMES	STONE ELLIS
McHOLLAND DAVID	PIERCE JAMES	SNODGRASS WILLIAM
MATLOCK JOHN	PATRICK WILLIAM	SHELL HENRY
MILLIKIN WILLIAM	POTTER DUKE	SYMMS ALEXANDER
MILLIKIN JACOB	PRUETT AMSTED	SYMMS NICHOLAS
McALLISTER HENRY	PRUETT WILLIAM	SHIELDS ROBERT
MOORE SAMUEL	PAN HIRYM	SHIELDS JOHN
MYERS NOBLE J	ROGERS ISAAC	STERN ARTHUR
McKINNEY JAMES	ROGERS SAMUEL	SWISS HENRY

MONROE COUNTY

SHELL JOHN
STEVENS LEWIS
STERNS ISAAC
SMITH WILLIAM
SMITH JOHN III
SHERK JOHN
SHIELDS ARCHIBALD
SADDLER JOHN
STORM JAMES
STORM JOHN
SEARS REUBIN
SMOTHERS JOHN
SUMMERS ENOCH
SHAW THOMAS
SNOWDEN DAVID
STOUT AARON
SHIP EASTON
SNYDER MASKET
SEARS JACOB
SEARS DAVID
SILLERS JOHN F
SONNEVILLE WILLIAM
ROSS WILLIAM
TARKENTON JESSE
THORNBURG THOMAS
TARR JAMES
THOMSON JOHN
THOMSON JAMES
TEAGUE DAVID
THOMAS HENRY
TROTTER JAMES
TARKINTIN SILVANUS
TEAGUE WILLIAM

TRUSTY WILLIAM
THACKER AUSTIN
THACKER DAVID
TEBITS EBENZER
WRIGHT CALEB
WILSON THOMAS
WAMPLER HENRY
WOODS JAMES
WILLIAMS ZACHARIAH
WALDEN LEWIS
WHINNAND GEORGE
WRIGHT JOHN
WRIGHT JESSE
WRIGHT JAMES
WOODARD BARDET
WHITSON WESLEY
WARD GRANVILLE
WARNOCK JAMES
WARNER GEORGE
WHITE JOHN
WILSON JOHN
WALDEN ABEDNNGA
WOOD JOHN
WOOD HENRY
WHEELER JOHN
WRIGHT JOSIAH
WILLIAMS MOSES
WILLIAMS JONATHAN
WHISNAND JOHN
WYATT JONATHAN
WALDEN JESSE
WOODARD SILAS
WILLIAMS ISAAC

WRIGHT RICHARD
WYMN WILLIAM
WOODEN SOMOMON
WRIGHT JOHN II
WRIGHT WILLIAM
WRIGHT PHILBERT
WRIGHT PETER
ZINK DAVID
ZINK JACOB
ARTHUR JOHN
ABRAHAM BOSWELL
ADAMSON JONATHAN
CONNELLY ARTHUR
HARRIS RHOADIS
- - - MASON
- - - RUSSELL
JOHNSON JOHN
YOUNG JOSEPH
SHIN JOEL
ARTHUR - - -
RUSH - - -
FRANKHUSM - - -
KING THOMAS
BUSKIRK ISAAC
BUSKIRK JOHN
BUSKIRK JAMES
MAY SILVANUS
CHRISTIE ANDREW
CHRISTIE - - -
CHRISTIE RICHARD
CLARK JOHN W
COFFEE WILLIAM

ORANGE COUNTY

RILEY EDWARD
RILEY ISAAC
WHITMAN JOHN
EASTRIDGE JOHN
HAINED JONATHAN
CASH JEREMIAH
CONNELL WILLIAM
FARRIS GIDEON
BELCHER JAMES
ANDERSON SPEAIR
BROADWELL HENRY
EASTRIDGE ISAAC
VANCE CHRISTOPHER

LASHBROOKS JOHN
FLICK CHRISTOPHER
ANDIE JOHN
KING JOHN B
FLOYD JONATHAN
HOBSON JACOB
COX THOMAS
RILEY WILLIAM
ROADS WILLIAM
RILEY ABRAHAM
LEWIS WILLIAM
BETHEL CLOUD T
RETHERFORD MARK

STANDRIDGE AARON
PITMAN LEWIS
WILSON JOHN
WOODS MARK D
WILLIAMS ABSOLAM
KENDALL WILLIAM
ALLEN LEWIS
McDONALD CLEMENT
CANTRILL DUKE
PINNICK NATHAN
PANTER DAVID
GLEN SAMUEL
HOLLOWELL JESSE

ORANGE COUNTY

BROOKS MIKAJAH
SNIDER SIMON
REYNOLDS WILLIAM
FRENCH GEORGE
CHASE JAMES
ELROD STEPHEN
WILSON WILLIAM
BLAND THOMAS
PURCEL JESSE
IRVINE WILLIAM
BRIANT WILLIAM
LOCKHART WILLIAM
ALDERSON MOSES
WALLS WILLIAM
UNDERWOOD JAMES
HAZLEWOOD JOSIAH
HENDERSON JAMES
MARTS JOHN
STEWARD JOHN
FREEMAN DANIEL JR
KERBY JOEL
KIMBROE JAMES
DENBO JAMES
MANLY JOHN R
ATKINSON THOMAS SR
ATKINSON THOMAS JR
SPEAR MOSES
SORIDER JACOB
FOSTER DRURY
FRENCH SAMUEL
HUNT JAMES
MAGNER JOHN
BROWN ALEXANDER
KING JAMES
CRUM HENRY
RIGNEY JOHN
ALSPAUW DAVID
PETERS JOHN
WOLF PETER
DUNCAN JOHN
SANDERS THOMAS
HOLLOWELL JOHN
HOLLOWELL THOMAS
BENGAMAN CHRISTIAN
McMAHAN JAMES
SPALDING GEORGE W
PHILIPS ELBERT
TUNGATE DENNIS
COOK JOHN
MAXWELL JAMES
SUTHERLIN PHILIP
SUTHERLIN CHARLES

SUTHERLIN WILLIAM
COOPER JONATHAN
HILL JOSEPH
WELLS STEPHEN
FREEMAN DANIEL
ORTEN JOHN Z
FAULKNER WILLIAM
LINDLEY WILLIAM SR
WILSON JAMES
LINDLEY JAMES
LINDLEY WILLIAM JR
LINDLEY DAVID
LINDLEY JONATHAN
FREEMAN BENJAMIN
FREEMAN JOHN
FREEMAN ABSOLAM
MAXWELL JOSEPH
WARRELL SAMUEL
SELF THOMAS
MILLACE EDWARD
KEITH ALEXANDER
PICKENS JAMES
BURT ASA
MILIGAN JONATHAN
HOBSON JOHN
ELROD ROBERT
RAWLEIGH JOHN B
DOWNS CHARLES
SPALDING LEWIS
BOOTHE WADE
GLOVER URIAH
GLOVER JONAH
SHIRLEY JACOB
SCARLET JOHN
SHIELDS JAMES
HUNT DANIEL
HUNT NOAH
CANTRILL JOHN
MOORE EDWARD
MAXWELL JAMES
OSBURN JONATHAN
SHIELDS JAMES SR
SHIELDS SAMUEL
SHIELDS JACOB
EDWARDS RICHARD
DIXON JACOB
COBB SAMUEL
COBB HENRY
TRIMBLE MOSES
PEARSON ISAAC
HOLMES HUGH
HOLMES JAMES

MONARCH GEORGE
MITTON JAMES
LYNCH CLETON
LYNCH JACKSON
SCANLAND JOHN
DANNER JOSEPH
MUNDLE ANDREW
BRACKENRIDGE THOMAS
WADSWORTH THOMAS
HUDLIN DAVID
FREEMAN THOMPSON
STONE WILLIAM
LINDLEY WILLIAM
COWHERD WILLIS
COWHERD THOMAS
BRITON JOHN
SPARLAIN GEORGE
SPARLAIN ARCHIBALD
SPARLAIN EDWARD
McCOY GEORGE
LINDLEY RUBEN
McCOY JAMES
STARKS THOMAS
LINDLEY THOMAS T
McCOLM GREER
STINNETT WILLIAM
GREEN GRAVENON
HOLSCLAW RICHARD
HILL WILLIAM
MURRY JOHN
WELLS PETER
DIXON JOHN
LAWERS JOHN
BUSICK GABRAEL
FIELDS BENGAMIN
STRANGE WILLIAM
MARIS GEORGE
McKERN LUKE
WELLS ISAAC
PICKARD JOHN
PARSONS ROBERT
STRANGE JOHN
TOWEL DANIEL
WAY ANTHONY
SPOONER FREDERICK
SPOONER CALVIN
RORABACK JOHN
CAMPBELL ROBERT
CAMPBELL SAMUEL
KINNEY JOHN
CARTER JOSHUA
WALLACE ALEXANDER

ORANGE COUNTY

ZEABRISKY HENRY
MULLEN JOHN
HARNES JOHN
GLOVER STEPHEN
KEIDY ABRAHAM
HARKMAN DANIEL
STANDIFORD WILLIAM
SANDERS JACOB
WRIGHT JONATHAN
CLAYTON JAMES
BELCHER JAMES
INGRUM GEORGE
SMITH WILLIAM
FISHER ZELEK
SHERER RUBEN
CROWNOVER DANIEL
KIRK JOHN
WILSON SAMUEL
HEAD GEORGE
SUTHARD BURTON
GREY JOHN SR
GREY JOHN JR
FREEMAN WILLIAM
MILLACE NICKERSON
KIRKMAN WILLIAM
ELROD JOHN
KERR THOMAS J
McGEE HENRY
McGEE ELIJAH
McGEE ELISHA
NEILL ARTHUR
NEILL NOBLE
PILES PETER
McKINNEY ALEXANDER
TURNER JULIUS
PICKENS JOHN
INMAN THOMAS
SHIRLEY CHARLES
BOSORE GEORGE
McCRAKEN ROBERT
EDWARDS THOMAS
ARMSTRONG FELIX
FINDLEY SAMUEL
DOWNING JAMES
DOLTON WILLIAM R
DOLTON SAMUEL
DOLTON JAMES
PINKLEY BENGAMIN
SMITH JOHN A
MONROE JAMES
VEARS JOHN
KNIGHT ROBERT

LOCK THOMAS
SCOTT JOHN
SEWEL JOHN
NEILL JAMES
WATSON PEDIGO
PICKLE FREDERICK
FERGUSON JOHN
GRIFFITH WILLIAM C
JOHNSTON LEVI
McCOY JOHN
LANKFORD MEAN
SCARLET JOHN
SUTHERLIN SAMPSON
MILIGAN SAMUEL
SANDERS JOHN
GRIFFITH RICHARD
GRIFFITH JOHN B
BLEVINS WARREN
SUTHERLIN FENDEL
SUTHERLIN WILLIAM
HOLMES JOSEPH
ELROD JACOB
ELROD JOHN
SANDERS JOSEPH
SANDERS WRIGHT
IDINGS DAVID
SIMMS JESSE
BERRY WILLIAM G
CROW JOHN
WILSON JOHN
LEE CLEMENT
INGRUM WILLIAM
FAIT HENRY
CUTSINGER JACOB
BRIANT JOHN
ROBERTS SHADRACK
LEWIS JOHN
TEAGARDEN BAZIL
TEEGARDEN JOHN
SEARS JOHN B
LEE SPENCER
LEE ANDRE
MOYRES MOSES
WEBB BENGAMIN
DOLTAN BRADLEY
WOOD FRANCIS
WEEKS JOSEPH
HOLLEWELL HENRY
MASON JACOB
LINDLEY JONATHAN
CHAMBERS SAMUEL
FREEMAN JOSHUA

DENNY SIMON
DENNY JOHN
CLEVELAND EZER
HARNED WILLIAM
HARNED THOMAS
FREEMAN JOHN
FOWLER JACOB
CALLEMS JOHN
FOWLER WILLIAM
LOMAX JONATHAN
WILSON JASPER
McDONALD WILLIAM
WILSON ANDREW
LOW SAMUEL
SANDERSON ROBERT
McCRACKEN JOHN
HETHER WILLIAM
HETHER JOSEPH
JONES SAMUEL
DAVIS RANSOM
FISHER THADEUS
VORIS GARRETT
VORIS ABRAHAM
WOLF HENRY
LEATHER JONATHAN
MAXWELL WILLIAM
STOUT JONATHAN
TORR JOHN
WILSON PATON
RIGGS MOSES
HADLEY JOSHUA
MCNARY HUGH
MCNARY ALEXANDER
TRUEBLOOD WILLIAM
TRUEBLOOD JOSIAH
TRUEBLOOD JOSEPH
BURGESS MASON
NICHOLS NATHAN
COPELIN THOMAS
NEWSOME WILLIS
JONES JONATHAN
JONES JAMES
DITTEMORE THOMAS
DIXON CARNTON
DISHAN JAMES
WELLS WILLIAM
DONE EBENEZER
McCRACKEN ROBERT
HIATTE EVEN
BOSLEY ABRAHAM
LINDLEY ZACHARIAS
CAVE THOMAS

ORANGE COUNTY

JOHNSTON MICHAEL
MOORE JOHN
ELLIS DANIEL
MATTHERS MOSES
HADLY JAMES
HADLY ELI
McCRACKEN WILLIAM
BAILS WILLIAM
LEWIS SAMUEL
LEWIS JOHN SR
BEACHAMP JOHN
SMITH JESSE
DARROCH DANIEL
BRAXTON THOMAS
MARIS THOMAS
KIRBY ALEXANDER
VEST NATHANIEL
DILLARD JOHN
GRIGSBY WILLIAM
KIRBY EDWARD
TINDALL WILLIAM
JARVIS EDWARD
DAUGHERTY JOHN
DAUGHERTY HENRY
KELSEY ELIAS
McCONNALL JOHN
DUNCAN RUBEN
COLLINS JAMES
VICKERS EDWARD
COULD JOHN
MILLER MACHAEL
MILLER ADAM
PATTON WILLIAM G
FIELDS JOHN
BRIANT EDWARD
MARTIN JESSE
MARTIN GREEN
MARTIN HIRAM
SHIRLEY HENRY
COOK WILLIAM
ROD THOMAS
HENSON JOHN
SCARLET SAMUEL SR
SCARLETT SAMUEL JR
ANDERSON NOAH
GARWOOD JOSEPH
DAUGHERTY GEORGE
PINNICK JAMES SR
PINNICK JAMES
PINNICK ISAAC
MOORE EDWARD
ALLEN DANIEL

BUCKNER HALEY
LEONARD THOMAS
KERSEY STEPHEN
WELLS ZACHARIAS
FLETCHER WILLIAM
BREEZE JOHN
ATKINSON JAMES
WILLIAMS JOHN
FARLOW JOSEPH
WELLS JONATHAN
BURGER JOHN
LINDLEY OWEN
UNDERWOOD BENGAMIN
CAMERON STEPHEN
CARTER NATHANIEL
HOLIDAY ROBERT
ELLISON JOSEPH
WELLS NATHAN
WELLS JOSEPH SR
LINDLEY OWEN SR
SMITH HENRY
DUNCAN FLEMING
DAWSON DANIEL
DAWSON DANIEL JR
MORRIS WASHINGTON
MARIS AARON
BOONE HEZEKIAH
DUNCAN GEORGE JR
LINDLEY THOMAS GENT
DAUGHERTY JOHN
BENSON NATHAN
BENSON SAMUEL
NEWSOME DAVID
BROOKS GEORGE R
GRISSOM JOHN
ROBBINS DANIEL
GIFFORD LEVI BR
GIFFORD LEVI JR
DILLING ANDREW
BRAY EDWARD
BREEZE ROBERT
BREEZE ROBERT JR
BROWN DAVID S
PETERS GEORGE
LUKIN JOEL
LUKIN EPHRAIM
LEE WILLIAM
TROOP JOHN
DONE JONATHAN
DONE JOHN
GREYHAM BURRELL
THOMAS STEPHEN

HACKNEY JOHN
STOUT JOHN
ATKINSON JOHN
STALLENS STEPHEN
LINE JOAB
DAVIS ADAM
CRAIG JONATHAN
BAKER DANIEL
HADLEY JOHN
HADLEY THOMAS
PIERCE PHILIP C
YOUNG SAMPOSON
DAVIS JOSEPH
HAMMONS LEWIS
CONNER JONSEY
PIERCE ELIJAH
CANTRILL ABRAHAM
WILLIAMS LEWIS
WILLIAMS THOMAS
YOUNG WHITTER
WILLIAMS DAVID
GUERKIN JOHN
HART JOHN
HART McKENZIE
OVERLAIN JOHN
BLEDSOE PTOLEMY
ALLEN JOHN
STALCUP JOHN
MAXEDON ROBERT
AGANS WILLIAM
MAXEDON THOMAS JR
NEILY WILLIAM B
WOLFINTON JOHN
MORRIS WILLIAM
MORRIS JAMES
MORRIS ALEXANDER
LANDMAN DANIEL
LANDMAN TRISTRAM
THOMAS LEWIS SR
THOMAS LEWIS JR
HERCKABA LEWIS
BUNDY GIDEON
DAVIS JOEL
LINDLEY THOMAS
LINDLEY DAVID
CROW JAMES
LINDLEY JAMES
LINDLEY THOMAS
MURRY THOMAS
CHAMPBELL JOHN
GIVENS ELISHA
TOWEL JESSE

ORANGE COUNTY

RUBOTTOM JOSEPH
WOODRUFF ANDREW
MOSES ADAM
CHAMPBELL ADLAI
PORTER CHRISTOPHER
BROTHERS JOSHUA
BROTHERS WILSON
BROTHERS ABNER
BROTHERS WILLIAM
OSBURN ENOCH
SMITH JESSE
CONN JOSEPH
TAYLOR JOHN
SORRELS REDMAN
PORTER JAMES
PAINE AARON
PAINE ADAM
MARTIN RUBEN
REYNOLDS JEREMIAH
CHASTEEN WILLIAM
ROBBINS JOSHUA
ROBBINS ABEL
McBROOM DAVID
McBROOM EVAN
WILSON JAMES
BEDSTER JOHN
ALLIGUE JILES
MYERS SOLOMON
VERMILLION JAMES
STEWARD JOHN
JAMES RICHARD
HOLLET SAMUEL
SUMNER WILLIAM
PIFER MICHAEL
PIFER JOHN
BYRAM LEWIS
WOODS NATHAN
DONE DAVID
SMITH ALLEN
PEARSON JOSEPH
SEWEL THOMAS
HOLBERT SETH
MOCK GEORGE
JACKSON JOSEPH
BECK JAMES
DEMOSS ANDREW
WILSON JOSEPH SR
WILSON JOSEPH JR
DONNELL JAMES
CRABTREE WILLIAM
RAYBURN CORNELIUS
FERSITHE DENMARK

HODGES GEORGE
McDONALD ALEXANDER
HOBSON NATHAN
DUNCAN WILLIAM
WAY ABEL
TATE THOMAS
BLAKE WILLOBY
DAVIS DANIEL
GUNN JOHN
EDWARDS THOMAS
WOODS SAMUEL
TONEY STEPHEN
CHATHAM JOHN
MAXWELL JOHN
VONTREASE WILLIAM
VONTREASE JACOB
LINDLEY THOMAS
BLAND FRANCIS
BLAND WILLIAM
FREEMAN SAMUEL
MAXWELL WILLIAM
SANDERS HENRY
MAXWELL WILLIAM
SANDERS HENRY SR
TORREY PATON
TODD JOHN
CALLEMS GILBERT
SCOTT ISAAC
QUINATT CHARLES
HUDELSON DAVID
OSMEN WILLLAM
DILLERY RICHARD
WITSMAN JACOB
PICKET JOHN
WAY JOSEPH
MOSS BENGAMIN
LUTHERIN JOHN
KIRKMAN JOHN
FISHER NOAH
RITENBACK STEPHEN
MARIS JOHN
HOBSON STEPHEN
HAGERMAN JOHN
GARVEY JOHN
COLVIN LEWIS
LAYBOLD JOHN
LAYBOLD JOHN SR
NEWLIN WILLIAM
NEWLIN JONATHAN
DITTO SHADRACK
LYNCH JOHN
LYNCH THOMAS

LYNCH WILLIAM
BRAY ABIJAH
BLAND HENRY
TOMLINSON JAMES
TOMLINSON JOSEPH
BRAY JOHN
HOLLIDAY JACOB
HOLLIDAY HENRY
COCHRAN WILLIAM
DIXON SIMON
QUAKENBUSH PETER
McVAY WILLILAM
McVAY EDWARD
BRADY THORNTON
BOYD ARCHIBALD
HILL CHRISTOPHER
DAVIS JOHN H
DAVIS BARNABAS
MODE JOHN
MOORE JOHN
BEARD ADAM
COPPLE JOHN
HICKS DEMSY
FERGUSON THOMAS
ALLEN ARCHIBALD
GLEN ISAAC B
CANE CORNELIUS
HOPKINS STEPHEN
EVANS JOHN
WEATHERS JOHN
HENSON JEREMIAH
BULLINGTON ROBERT
BULLINGTON BENGAMIN
EVANS STROUD
RODEN ALLEN
STROUD JOHN
JONES HENRY
NICHOLS JOSEPH
WEATHERS JOSEPH
EDES THOMAS
RUSSELL WILLIAM
RUSSELL WILLIAM JR
POTTER BENGAMIN
TADLOCK ALEXANDER
McGEE SAMUEL
WEAVER MICHAEL
AGAN WILLIAM
FOX GEORGE
STROUD ISHAM
FANCHER BENJAMIN
STALCUP WILLIAM
STALCUP SAMUEL

ORANGE COUNTY

RUSSELL GEORGE
STALCUP PETER SR
STALCUP PETER JR
STALCUP HENRY
FINCH JAMES
FINCH JAMES JR
FINCH HADEN
BRACKNEY HUDSON
STALCUP STEPHEN
BRUCE THOMAS
HICKS HIRAM
HOBSON BALEY
BINGAMAN PETER
BINGAMAN JOHN
MOORE DAVID
SANDERS RICHARD
GRIFFITH JOHN
HOLLOWELL JONATHAN
HIDE BENGAMIN
DICKENS JAMES
GRIFFETH WILLIAM
CHAMNESS AARON
BRAY HENRY
HENLY DANIEL
WHITE LEONARD M
STROYERS LEWIS
SONGERS ABRAHAM
SONGER FREDERICK
NEIL ARCHIBALD
WHITEHEAD JOHN
SULLINGER THOMAS
ROBERTS JOHN
SMITH JACOB
MAY FRANCIS
McGREW JOSEPH
SMITH JAMES
JONES ALLEN
MARTIN ROBERT
MARTIN SAMUEL
VANDEVIER JOHN SR
VANDEVIER JOHN
COLCLASHER JACOB
COLCLASHER JOHN
COLCLASHER ABRAHAM
WARDEN WILLIAM
THURMOND DAVID
THURMOND HIRAM
VANDEVEER JOEL
VANDEVEER GEORGE
WOLF JOHN
WHITE WILLIAM
MONTGOMERY ROBERT

CURRY JAMES
ALLGOOD PRESLEY
CLARK ROBERT
CLEMENTS THOMAS
GRIGSBY JOHN
ELLIOTT ZIMRIE
STRANGE CORNWELL
CORNWELL JAMES
OSBURN ABRAHAM
MOSES TOBIAS
MOSES JEREMIAH
MOBLEY EDWARD
JONES EVAN
NICHOLS JOSHUA
LEFLER DAVID
RICHARDSON RICHARD
McGAUHY ARCHIBALD
COOPER JOHN SR
COOPER JOHN JR
COOPER JACOB
SMITH JOHN
TOWEL JOHN
SHIELDS JOHN
SHIELDS ROBERT
CHADWELL DUFF
KING CORNELIUS
KING JOHN
WILLIAMS WILLIAM
HINTON GEORGE
RIGNEY WILLIAM
RIGNEY MARTIN
RIGNEY ISAAC
POTTER BENGAMIN
CONKLIN ZEDEKIAH
MOORE SILAS
WIBLE SAMUEL
LYND SAMUEL
BAKER WILLIAM
MURPHY JAMES
HOLLOWELL SMITHSON
HOLLOWELL NATHAN
BAILEY EDWARD
WILLIAMS JOHN R
VANCLEAVE JOHN
KING CORNELIUS SR
VANCLEAVE BENGAMINE
LEZENBY JERY
DUNCAN GEORGE SR
DILLARD WILLIAM
LYND JAMES
HAMPTON STEPHEN
PERIGO DANIEL

VEACH BENGAMIN
JOHNSTON ALEXANDER
WALKER ANDREW
McKINNEY ALEXANDER
WHITE JOSEPH
McCOY WILLIAM
McPHETERS ALEXANDER
REED WILLIAM
POUNDS JOSEPH
POUNDS MARTIN
McKINNEY DAVID
McKINNY JOHN
CARR WILLIAM
HICKS WILLIAM
INGRUM ANDREW
BRIDGEWATERS LEVI
BRIDGEWATERS JOSEPH
BRIDGEWATERS ELIAS
PORTER NICHOLAS B
KENDALL THORNTON
HOFFERT JACOB
FITSPATRICK JAMES
FITZPATRICK HENRY
MILLER JACOB
WASTNER JACOB
NIDEFFER JOHN
VANVRANKEN JOHN
FREED JOHN
FREED MARTIN
LEATHERMAN CHRISTIAN
HOLSTETLER CHRISTIAN
HOLSTETLER DAVID
LEATHERMAN JOHN
WITTY WILLIAM
EDWARDS ISAAC
GROSS JOHN
GROSS HIRAM
COOK JACOB
WILSON JOHN
WILSON JEREMIAH
MILLER ANTHONY
MOODY ALEXANDER
CRAWFORD JOSEPH
LAW DANIEL
ALLEN JOSEPH
CONDRA JACOB
KERR MICHAEL
HAMILTON JOHN
McCAFFEE SIMON
LAYMASTER ABRAHAM
MOYERS JOHN
MILLS RICHARD

ORANGE COUNTY

FINDLEY JESSE
DENNY ZACHARIA
DENNY MARDICA
HOLSTETLER JOSEPH
BAILEY JUSTICE
KEEDY JOHN
MAXWELL JAMES
MAXWELL WILLIAM
CUTSINGER MARTIN
LEE JOHN
LEE CLEMENT
SMITH THOMAS S
FULFER JOSEPH
CHANEY CHARLES
INGRAM WILLIAM
HANES SAMUEL
FULFER ABRAHAM
REED WILLIAM
GLOVER URIAH SR
GLOVER CHARLES
JACKMAN VINCENT
RILEY EZEKIEL
POI JAMES
FINLEY DAVID
HOWARD JAMES
HOWARD WILSON
MAXWELL THOMAS
EDWARDS MEREDITH
REED ROBERT
REED ELIAS
BAKER FREDRICK
BAKER JOHN
PUYER GEORGE
McCLANE ROBERT
LEWIS JOHN M
LEWIS DAVID F
MOSS BENGAMIN
MARTIN ISAAC
KEMIKAEL WILLIAM
VORIS JACOB
MAGILL ZACHARIAH
COOPER JOHN
COOPER WILLIAM
JOHNSTON DAVID
JOHNSTON MARTIN
WARRELL ROBERT
HENDRICKS ISAAC
JOHNSTON JAMES
GLOVER JOHN
REED DAVID
REED JOSHUA
HINTON THOMAS

PHILIPS THOMAS
DAUGHERTY JOHN
BROOKS WILLIAM
GUYNER JAMES
SMITH HUMPHREY
JOHNSTON DAVID
JOHNSTON JOHN
DAUGHERTY ROBERT
MAHAN PETER
MOORE WILLIAM
TURGATE JEREMIAH
TUNGATE WILLIAM
TUNGATE JOHN
McDANIEL ALEXANDER
DENNY JAMES
WEIR LINDSEY
McCUMBER LEVI
VANDIVEER THOMAS
CLARK JAMES
DISHON JACOB
DIXON JOHN
PENNICK JOHN
WELLMAN JOHN
PHILIPS GEORGE
PHILIPS DAVID
PHILIPS WILLIAM
TINDALL THOMAS
FARRIS JOHN
WOLFINGTON JAMES
WOLFINGTON ABRAHAM
WOLFINTON GEORGE
RODEN JAMES
McMURRY JAMES
BELCHER JOHN
WALLS MANLOW
GRIER RICHARD
JACOBS ELISHA
MILLER WILLIAM
HUNT WILLIAM
TAYLOR CLETEN
TAYLOR SAMUEL
WISE JACOB
HAZLEWOOD MEREDITH
NICHOLS MARTIN
CHARLES JOEL
MOBLEY ELIAS
CHARLES AZER
RUSH ELIJAH
GILES THOMAS
EDWARDS PETER
HAZLEWOOD RUBEN
WARSON JOHN

MULLENS CHARLES
MULLENS JONATHAN
MULLENS WILLIAM
HOLLIDAY SAMUEL
HOLLIDAY ABRAHAM
BRENER GEORGE
ROBBINS NATHANIEL
MAVETY MICHAEL
PECK JOSEPH H
RHODES WILLIAM
PIERCE ELEAZER SR
PIERCE ELEAZER JR
BROWN JOHN
WILSON NATHANIEL
GILL JOHN
SHAW JOHN
COFFIN THOMAS
TUCKER THOMAS L
MEACHAM ISAAC
TRUEBLOOD MARK
SUTTON JAMES
CLENDENIN JOHN G
CULTON JAMES
DONE EPHRAIM
DEAN HALLET B
SPOONER WILLIAM
CHAPMAN THOMAS F
PEARSON JAMES
DEWEY CHARLES
PORTER JOHN R
COWHERD HENRY
STEPHENS THOMAS
ATHENS JOSEPH
GOLDY WILLIAM
HENDRICKS HENRY
CARSON ABRAHAM
REEDY JAMES
McFALL BARNABUS
STEPHENS JACOB SR
STEPHENS JACOB JR
FAIRCHILD THOMAS
WHEELER EBENEZER
HOGGATT WILLIAM
TAYLOR WILLIAM
STEPHENS HENRY
MEKIM NATHANIEL
BLANCHARD ENOCH
LEONARD JAMES
REYNOLDS WILLIAM
BARR JOHN
PARKS ROBERT
PARKS WILLLAM

ORANGE COUNTY

PARKS JOHN
McKINGHT ROGER
McKINGHT CHRISTOPHER
DEPEW ELIJAH
DEPEW ISAAC
MOORE JOHN

BRAXTON JONATHAN
DICKERSON JAMES
COLLINS CHARLES
MORRIS MATTHEW
LEFLER DAVID

JENKINGS JOHN
JENKINGS WESTLEY
SULLIVAN NOAH
WALKER BENGAMIN B
EASTRIDGE JAMES

PERRY COUNTY

FINTCH PHILIP
KEPLER JACOB 2
KEPLER JACOB
BRIGHTMAN WM D
CANNOR TARRENCE
FAITH JOHN
MOSELY ROBERT
OENS STEPHEN
HILL JAMES
LOGSTON JOHN
LANNAN GEORGE
TERRY THOMAS
MACOMSON ANDREW
WILLIAMSON JOSEPH
POWEL THOMAS
POWEL SAMUEL
CUNNINGHAM ALEXANDER
RAMSEY ALEXANDER
MILLER JOHN
RAE WILLIAM
MAIN DAVID
SHRINCLE MICHAEL
GALY DAVID
ROYAL WILLIAM
DEWITT ELISHA
ARTMAN JOHN
HINTON DANIEL
BOILS SIMON
MOCK DANIEL
MOCK WILLIAM
JARBO PETER
GILLILAND JOHN
SHRINGER JOHN
HARDON JOHN
BOMAN WM
QUICK JESSE
CAMRON SAMUEL
BARBRE PETER 2
BARLAW SAMUEL
SANDAGE THOMAS

KINDER DAVID
WILLCOX ISAAC
RICHARDSON JONATHAN
RICHARDSON LARKIN
CUMMINGS THOMAS
ALLIN JOHN
FITZGERALD THOMAS 2
ANDERSON SAMUEL
ASKINS EDWARD
ALVEY THOMAS G
ALVEY JOHN B
ANSON MONTGOMERY
ALLEN DAVID
ALVEY HENERY
ARCHABALD JOHN
ANKERMAN ANDREW
BURNS SOLOMON
BOTTINGHOUSE JOSEPH
BARBRE JESSE
BORER VALINTINE 3
BEST JOHN
BLACK SAMUEL
BARKER MOSES
BALDWIN THOMAS
BOLING JAMES
BLAIN JAMES 3
BALDWIN WILLIAM
BARBRE ELI 2
BUTLER ABEL
BARGER ABRAHAM
BUTLER SILAS
BRAUGH JOHN
CASSON TAFFEE
COLLARS JOHN
CAMMERN IGNATIOUS
CHESSER WILLIAM
CUMMINGS EPHRAIGM
CUMMINGS JOHN 2
CUMMINGS WILLIAM
CASSADAY JOHN

CONNOR DADE
CUMMINGS URIAH
CONNOR SAMUEL
CRIST JOHN
CONNOR WILLIAM
CLACOMB JOHN
CLAYCOMB GEORGE
CONNOR TARRENCE
CLARK ROBERT
COOPPER JOHN
CUNNINGHAM ARON
CART JOHN
CANE JOSIAH
CAFFEE WILLIAM
CROKER JESSE
COX WILLIAM
CONNOR JOHN
CONNOR TARENCE
CUMMINGS ELI
CUMMINGS JOSIAH
CONNOR TARENCE
CRETCHELOW JAMES 2
DODSON JOHN 2
DAVIS RICHARD
DRINKWATER THOMAS
DRINKWATER HENERY
DRINKWATER PAUL
DRAPER GIDEON
DAVIS JOHN
DAVIS THEODORUS
DUNBAR JAMES
DEEN STEPHEN
DAVIS JACOB
DEEN RICHARD 2
DUNN JOHN
DEEN WILLIAM
DAUGHERTY JESSE 2
EWING GEORGE JR
EWING GEORGE SR
ESLIH SAMUEL

PERRY COUNTY

ELDRIDG JOHN
EWING JOHN
ESSARY JONATHAN
EWING ROBERT
FINTCH ABRAHAM
FITSGERALD ARON
FIGGINS GEORGE
FRAIKES JOHN
FAITH JOHN
FITZGERALD THOMAS
FIMISE WILLIAM
FORD JOHN
GROVES DAVID
GARDNER ROBERT
GREGORY DAVID
GILLILAND ROBERT
GOAD GABRIEL 2
GILBERT WILLIAM
GRIMES SAMUEL
GRIMES LENARD
GLEN ADAM
GREATHOUSE ISAAC 2
GREEN ANTHONY
GREEN JESSE 3
GREENWOOD WILLIAM
HILL JOAB
HARGUESS JOHN
HESLEY JOHN 3
HILL HENRY
HILL ROBERT
HENDRICKS DANIEL
HIGHLEY ABRAHAM 2
HALL JESSE
HUSTON ROBERT
HIDE ANSIL
HIX WILLIAM
HUFF RUBEN
HARNES NATHANIEL
HEADY ELIAS
HUFF JESSE
HADDEN SAMUEL
HAWKEE ARTHER
HOWERD CHARLES
HIGHFIELD WILLIAM
HUSTED CALIB
BEARDSLEY JOHN
HORTON ANTHONY
VAUGHN BENJAMIN 3
LATTIMORE ELISHA 2
McCONALD PATRICK
IRVIN ROBERT
COMBS WILLIAM

FALKINBERRY JAMES
IRVIN ROBERT
IRVIN DANIEL
IRVIN SAMUEL
IRVIN JAMES
INLAW JOHN
AMUEL JASON
JOHNSON JOHN 2
JASSON JOHN
JENNINGS EDMOND
KINDER JOHN
KINDER PETER
KINDER DAVID
LITSY ANTHONY
LINDSEY NATHAN
LAKE JESSE
LION STEPHEN
JARBO RICHARD
JARBO HENRY
JARBO JOHN
JARBO JOSHUA
JONES WILLIAM
KUIDER GEORGE
KNIESS JOHN
LACY TIMOTHY
LETHERLAND JOHN 3
LANNON JAMES
LANNON JAMES JR
LANNON JOHN
LAMB EZRA
LAMB ISRAL
McMAHAN ALEXANDER
MILLER JOHN
McFARLING DANIEL
MILLER JOHN
MILLER JOHN 3
MILLER ADAM
LAMB WILLIAM
LARANCE OLIVER
LITTLE JOHN
MATINGLEY THOMAS
MILER CHARLES
McCOY JOHN
MILLER JOHN
MALORY ELEMUEL
NILES MOSES B 2
PRATER HENERY
PECKINGPAUGH PETER
PECKINGPAUGH JOHN
PIATTA AUSTIN
POTTS RICHARD F L
MABERY JOHN

MILLER ALEXANDER 2
MAYHO JOHN
MASON JAMES
MORGAN LAMBETH
MAIN SAMUEL
MAIN RILEY
MARTAIN JESSE
McADAMS DANIEL 2
McCOTHIN DANIEL
MITCHEL WILLIAM
MARTIN ELEMUEL
MORGAIN SAMUEL
MOREL JOHN
MARTAIN JOHN
McCRUM JOHN
MURPHY ABRAHAM
NILES ROBERT
PHILIPS JOHN H
POLK CHARLES 3
PERSON DAVID
PERSON JOHN
POLK THOMAS
PARKERSON WILLIAM
POLK EDMON
PURSINGER BENJAMIN
POLK CHARLES
QUICK DAVID
ROSS CHARLES
RILEY JAMES
ROE JOSEPH
ROBERTSON GEORGE
ROUNDEN ABRAHAM
RIAN DANIEL
RICHARDSON THOMAS
RICHARDSON THOMAS JR
REYNOLDS RUBEN
RODESS THOMAS
ROADES HENERY
ROBERTSON PETER
RIGGS JOHN
RICHARDSON EBENEZER
RICHARDSON AMOS
ROSECRANTY RICHARD
SIMMS ARAD
SPRINGER JOSEPH
SPERS WILLLAM
WEBB ASA
WHITE JOSEPH
WHEELER JAMES
WHEELER THOMAS
WEATHERHOLT WILLIAM
WEATHERHOLT HENERY

PERRY COUNTY

WEATHERHOLT JACOB
WEATHERHOLT JOHN
WHEALTEY ARTHER
WISE HART JOHN
WILLARD HENERY
VANDIVER THOMAS
VANWINCLE ALEXANDER 2
VANWINCLE JAMES
WILLIAMS JOHN
WALKER PHILIP
WALKER ELISHA
WILLIAMS JAMES
VAUGHAN WAIT
VANPETT THOMAS P
VANWINCLE ISAAC
STEPHENSON JOHN
SAP ELIAS
STANCIL WILLIAM
SPRIGGS DAVID S
SMITH ASHFORD
SMITH ROBERT
SHOEMAKER ADAM
THOMSON JOHN
TITCHNER MOSES
TOBIN JOSEPH
TOBIN THOMAS
TERRY JOHN 2
TERRY ELISHA
THOMAS WILLIAM
TINDAL WILLIAM
TOBIN GEORGE
TAYLOR DANIEL
THOMPSON IGNATIOUS 2
TAYLOR WILLIAM
TROOT ABRAHAM
TURNER JOSEPH
THOMAS LEWIS
TAYLOR WILLIAM
TRENARY BENJAMIN
THRASHER THOMAS
LATTIMORE ELISHA
GREGORY JOHN
BERDSLEY JOHN

REES EPRAIGM
McCONOLD PATRICK
TAYLOR SILAS
COAL ROBERT
GODFREY WILLIAM
SHOEMAKER STEPHEN
SHOEMAKER JOHN
SHOEMAKER JOHN JR
STEPLETON JOHN
SMITH BENJAMIN
STEPLETON ISAM
STOCKS JOHN
SANDWITCH THOMAS
BOLING JOHN
BOLING WILLIAM
BOLIN ELET
ROLIN THOMAS
BRISTAW JAMES
HENDRICKS JAMES
GILBERT WILLIAM
SHERLY WILLIAM
MASH RITE 2
MASH DAVID
BOYD ANDREW
IRISH SMITEN
MILLER DANIEL
MILLER SAMUEL
FARRIS JOHN
JAMISON SAMUEL
UMPHRY WILLIAM
GOAD HALY
SULLERS JOHN
PARKER JESTIS
SULLERS JOHN
HAZLE RICHARD
JAMISON JAMES
MILER JOHN
ALUSON JAMES
HADEN GEORGE
ADAMS PRATER
POLK CHARLES
LAMB DORASTUS

HOUSE WILLIAM
WILSON JAMES
FINTCH WILLIAM
NOYS JONATHAN
MALOY MOSES
DONLY JOHN
LASHER JACOB
LITTLE SHUBY
RICKS JOHN W
STONEMETS CASPER
CAR ELI
WRIGHT JOSEPH 6
DANIEL PETER 2
DANIEL JOHN
GRIMES D D 2
PARKERSON WILLIAM
ATHERLON ISRAEL
WARDEN SAMUEL
ELDRIDG JOHN
BRISTOW JOHN
STEPHENSON STEPHEN
LAMB JOHN D 2
JENNINGS EDMAN 3
PHILIPS JOHN H
EASON HARMIN 2
HENDERSON JAMES 2
SOUTHARD WILLIAM
FULLER ARCHABALD 2
MAIN MICHA
MAIN JOHN
BEERS DAVID S
YORK JOHN
BUTLER ABEL
GOODRIDG SAMUEL E
BLAIN JOHN 2
LAMB WILLIAM
DEEVER MILES
TRIGER SOLOMON
MILLS SAMUEL
PHILIP ROBERT 2
SPRINGER GEORGE
TAYLOR WILLIAM

POSEY COUNTY

GRADDEY JOHN
CARTWRIGHT REDDICK
CARTWRIGHT SAM'L
VARNER JACOB
BELL DAVID
DEPOISTER JOHN
DOWNING TIMOTHY
CRUNK JOHN
SMITH ALLEN
SMITH THO'S
MILLS ALEXANDER
CROSS JAMES
M'DANIEL JAMES
NELSON JAMES SR
EATON MORGAN
ASHLEY JOHN
ROBERSON JAMES
MINARD SAM'L J
PRICHARD HERMON
HATFIELD JAMES
LACY JOHN
LEVITT IGNATIOUS
LEVITT NOAH
LEVITT JAMES
ROGERS ALEXANDER
HILL WM
TAYLOR JAMES
COX ALSOLOM
STALLINGS MOSES
HOBBS NEHEMIAH
BRIARS FRANCIS
NESLER SOLOMON SR
LEWALLEN MASHACK
OVERTON RICHARD
SMITH ROB'T B
WILBORN J Y
CRABREEE WM
ACUFF JOHN
ACUFF JOHN D
ACUFF HOGAN
WILLIAMS WILLIAM
ERVIN WM
ROBB JAMES
WALLER JOHN
PATTON WM
LEAVIT DAVID
VANDERVER CHARLES
HARDIN ABRAHAM
THOMAS MEEKS
WAY JAMES
EWING AARON
BOGARD JACOB

EWINGS MOSES
DURLEY ARTHUR SR
DURLEY ARTHUR JR
DURLEY JAMES
MILLER GEORGE
CRABTREE WM SR
CRABTREE JOHN
COX JOHN JR
ROBESON JOHN
COX JOHN SR
ALMON THO'S SR
ALMON THO'S JR
HOLMAN TANDY
PRICE WM
GILBREATH ANDREW
HARRIS RICHARD
ALLEN ROBERT
TAYLOR JACOB
JOHNSON JOSEPH
WILLIAMS JESSEE
GREEN JOSEPH
MOOREHEAD JOHN
WHITACKER JACOB
COOPER JOHN
BLACK WM JR
MEDDERS THO'S W
DERUMPLE SAM'L
STURGES JOSEPH
MARTIN MARTIN
BRITTEN JESSE
BRITTEN MARKES
JEARDIN THO'S
CAULSTEN JAMES
CALDWELL JAMES
HARMON SAM'L
HARDIN NICHOLAS
BARRETT GEORGE
HERREN JOHN
WILLIAMS JOHN
WILLIAMS DANIEL
PRICE GILLESON
PRICE LARKEN
DAVIS WM
HERREN EPHRAM
PARKS SAM'L
NEAL MEEKS
PRICE JOHN SR
PRICE JOHN JR
PRICE FREDERICK
RACHELS J BOSWELL
FLINN THO'S
CARNEY WM

CARNER JOHN
CARNER DAVID
READER SIMON
COX JONATHAN
WAID ZACHARIAH
GORTNEY THO'S
WIGGINS THERON
CALVIN JAMES
COX FURNEYFOLD
KITE EZEKIEL
NUSAM JOSEPH
STALLINGS WRIGHT
STALLINGS HENERY
WILSON LEWIS
WILSON DAVID
WILSON ROBERT
PURSELL CHARLES
JAMES SAM'L JR
DYER JOHN
DOWNEN JOSIAH
DOWNEN DAVID
DOCKINGS JESSE
CHERRY WM
WINEMILLER JAMES
DUNN BERRY
STEPHENS WM
STEPHENS THO'S M
BROWN WM
CARSON HAMILTON
STULL LAWRENCE
STULL GEORGE
CASSELBURY THO'S E
M'COY DAVID
CASSELBERY PAUL
DENNY ROBERT
SAMPPLES JOHN
WILLIAMS WM
M'COWN WM
SHULL GEORGE
SHULL PHILIP
LOVE WM
DOWNS URLANDOW
WILLIAMS JOHN
TROWBRIDGE WM
BLUNT THEOFFILUS
WILLIAMS SAWYER
DICKSON JAMES
CULLY THO'S
WILLLIAMS ELEANAH
BEAN STEPHEN
BEAN WM
RECTOR FREDERICK C

POSEY COUNTY

BARTER WM
BARTER RICHARD
BREEZE JAMES
GOODLETT MOSES
SWIFT JAMES W
ALREDGE HENERY
TEMPLETON THO'S
ANIKLE BARNABAS
EDWARDS RICHARD
THOMAS DAVID
JONES DAVID
CULLY SAM'L
DUCKWORTH WM JR
BIRD JOHN
HENSON SAM'L
MILLS FELIN
STEPHENS JOHN
LAIN JAMES
SEVERS GEORGE
WEAR WM
LITLE JAMES
ALREDGE AARON SR
DUCKWORTH THO'S
DUCKWORTH WM SR
ALREDGE WM JR
WILSON JOHN
WEAR JOHN
ALREDGE JOHN SR
MOFFETT WM
MOFFETT ALEXANDER
ALREDGE RHEUBEN
ALREDGE EZEKIEL
ALREDGE PASSON
GILL SAM'L
BRADLEY JOHN
HOVEY ABIEL
HAMILTON JOHN
JENKINS SAM'L
NESLER JOHN
RATLEY GREEN
ANNIBLE BRUMLY
HAMILTON FRANCIS
HARGRAVES EZEKIEL
BLACK WM
HARGRAVENES THO'S
BLACK THO'S
ROBESON JOHN
DONNELSON JOHN
TODD HUGH
ROBESON HENERY
BACON AARON
JONES CHARLES

MILLS DAVID A
DUCKWORTH JOHN JR
ALREDGE WM
ALREDGE SAM'L JR
ALREDGE ELIJAH
ROW SAM'L
ROW JACOB
ROW GEORGE
ASHWORTH JOHN
HENCHELL JOHN
HERSHMAN GEORGE
BROADHEAD THO'S
SLATER JAMES
NAIL JOHN
FRENCH DORRES
M'FADIN JOHN
M'FADIN JAMES JR
DANIELS JOHN
DANIELS WM
BROADHEAD WM
STEPHENS EDWARD
WELBORN JOHN
HAYNS DANIEL
M'MAHEN MARTIN
BLACK THO'S P
KENNADY SAM'L
FRENCH JAMES
YORK SHUBEL
FRENCH RALPH
FRENCH DORRES
GREATHOUSE JOHN L
M'DANIEL DAVID
GREATHOUSE DAVID
GREATHOUSE DANIEL
AMICK PHILIP
TEPPERS ROB'T C
ASHWORTH CHRISTOPHER
BACON EDMON
DONNELSON JOHN
DONNELSON DAVID D
YORK JONES
WALKER JOHN
WALKER VINCE
SELF BRADLEY
SEVERS JACOB
HOOVER DANIEL
CURTICE JOSHUWAY
DEVENPORT CHARLES
YORK WM
ASHWORTH NATHAN
FRENCH FELEN
JONES SAM'L

BAKER JOHN
MILLER NATHANIEL
JONES NICHOLAS
ADDAMS CHARLES
GREGERY JOHN
GARRISON ABRAHAM
GARISON ELIJAH
DICKSON JOHN
DICKSON WM
DICKSON DAVID
MILLER THO'S
DICKSON JAMES
HOOVER DAVID
MOORE JAMES
ROBESON JEREMIAH
AYRES NATHANIEL
CLARK WM
CLATON ROB'T
MILLER JOHN
ABBITT NATHAN
HILL CHARLES
TYLER ASEY
WILLILAMS HENRY
GRADY THO'S
OBRIAN JOHN I
CONLEN JAMES
CURTIN DANIEL
ASHWORTH JOHN SR
KENNADA DAVID
WEST THO'S
ROBESON MOSES
ROBESON ARCHY
ROBESON JOSEPH
M'DANIEL JOHN
HUFF ELIJAH
ALBRIGHT WM
ALBRIGHT ADDAM
ALBRIGHT JOHN
KIVIT GEORGE
PEAL JOHN
PEAL THO'S
DUCKWORTH EZEKILL
MONSEY NATHANIEL
M'FADIN ANDREW JR
BRADLEY DAVID
BLACK JOHN
BURLESON AARON
M'FADIN ROLEY
M'FADIN JAMES SR
CURTICE JASHUWAY
GIVINS CHARLES C
DURKEE ASIEL

50

POSEY COUNTY

- DUNN ROB'T
- DUNN JAMES
- DUNN JOHN
- M'FADIN ANDREW SR
- HOLEMAN BENNETT
- MOSS BENEIAH
- AKINS JOSEPH
- TODD WM
- PHILIPS ELISHA
- PHILIPS EBENEZER
- MOORE JAMES
- BLACK JAMES
- POWEL ABRAHAM
- JAMES SAM'L
- DRAKE JAMES P
- BARTIN THO'S
- KENOSH ANTHONY
- MERICA JACOB
- BOMAN JOHN
- STALLINGS JOHN
- WALDEN DAVID
- LYNN DANIEL
- INMAN THO'S
- SNAY JOHN
- SPOLDING JOSPEH
- ROBERTS ELIAS
- HENDRY JOHN
- JONES AMOS J
- DUCKSWORTH GEORGE
- RUDOLPH ALLEN
- TODD ROBERT
- BATTSMON PETER
- WHITE SAM'L
- MOORE HUGH
- BARTON JOHN
- BARTON DANIEL
- OSBORN LEMUEL
- ANDREWS ANSON S
- BARTON WM
- MARTIN JOHN
- COLVIN MOSES
- COLVIN LUTHER
- BARTON ALEXANDER
- BARTON WILLES
- RIDENOWER JOHN
- RIDENOWER DAVID
- BOHANNON JAMES
- CORNELUS ELIHU
- DUFF DANIEL
- HUTCHESON WM
- STEPHENS THO'S W
- WHEELER JAMES
- GIVINS THO'S
- GIVINS WM
- SNOVELL FREDERICK K
- COLMON NATHANIEL
- WALLS EBENEZZER
- BOZARTH JAMES
- LOWRY THO'S
- NOWEL JOHN
- LITCHSINGER LEONARD
- SIMMONS CHARLES
- HACKET EPHRAIM
- MILLER THOMAS SR
- GRAVES JOHN
- GILBERT SAMPSON
- PHILIPS JOHN
- ELLESON CHARLES
- YORK SAM'L SR
- YORK ELI
- KIVIT HENERY
- ELLESON HUGH
- GOOD JOHN
- GOOD GEORGE
- GOOD PETER
- GOOD THO'S
- EDMONS HENERY
- WINDER DANIEL
- ALREDGE SAM'L SR
- ALREDGE AARON JR
- KIVIT PETER
- HAYNS JOHN
- JONES ABRAHAM
- COONSE JOHN
- JOHNSON RICHARD
- COOK WM
- FINCH YELVINGTON
- TRAFFORD EDWARD
- NESLER CHRIS'PHR SR
- NESLER CHRIST'R JR
- FOWLER RAWLEY
- JAMES ISAAC
- BATTELL CHARLES J
- PARISH LEVI
- M'FADIN SQUIRE
- KEES EDWARD E
- ALLEN WM
- COX JOHN SR
- COFFER HORRATIO
- HOOD JACOB
- COLVIN JOBE
- CARSON JOHN
- COLVIN JOBE JR
- BOIL WM
- CLEVELAND JOHN
- MOORE JOHN W
- BARTON SAM'L
- MURFEY JAMES
- ELKENS JOSIAH
- FERREE ISRAEL
- GARISON DANIEL
- SCOTT WM
- M'KINNES GEORGE
- HOLLSELL REZIN
- CAVENS JESSEE
- CARTRIGHT NEUTON
- PRICE JOSEPH
- WADE JOSHUWAY
- HUGHES PARLEY
- UNDERWOOD JOSIAH
- CAMPBELL AJACKS
- CAMPBELL ABNER
- WALKER HUGH
- WALKER JAMES
- WALKER JOHN
- GAIL JOHN
- ANDERSON JAMES
- ROGERS WM
- PITTS GIDEON
- GILBERT THO'S
- HARISON WISE
- SPALDING THO'S
- BAKEN ELIJAH
- PEYTON GILBERT
- RISING ASELL
- FAREWELL JOHN
- CASEY WM SR
- CASEY WM JR
- CASEY HENREY
- CASEY GEORGE
- MILLS JESSEE
- ELKINS SHADERICK
- NETTLETON ISAAC S
- BRASS JAMES J
- NETTLETON WM
- DUNBAR JOHN
- MOUTRY JAMES
- DOWNEY WM SR
- DOWNEY WM R JR
- HIMAN ALEXANDER
- MEANS WM
- ALEXANDER JOHN
- ALEXANDER JAMES
- ALEXANDER WM
- CAMPBELL DANIEL
- ATTIZER ELIAS

POSEY COUNTY

OSMORE NATHAN
RANDOLPH ROBERT
CLARK WARNER
PRUSTON N
GREENWOOD ABRAHAM
WHITE GEORGE
REED RICHARD
NASH JESSEE
NASH JOHN
DOWNEY JAMES
BALDEN WM W
LEWIS EVANS
WINEMILLER CONROD
WINEMILLER JACOB SR
WINEMILLER JACOB JR
INMAN SANDY
GARVAS ALEXANDER
BUTLER WILSON
BARTMAS JOHN
GILBERT THO'S
ELISON FINLEY
HATFIELD WM
STALLINGS WILSON
STALLINGS WM
STALLINGS JULIUS
BLACK EZEKIL
LEVETT THO'S
NELSON WM
SIMPSON JOHN
HOPSON WM
GRANT WIAT
PENNYPACKER WM
COATS BENJAMINE
SALTSMAN JOHN JR
SALTSMAN MICHAEL
SALTSMAN JOHN SR
SALTSMAN DANIEL
SALTSMAN ANDREW
RANKIN JAMES
BROWN JOHN
MORRES WM
MORRES THO'S
SKIVER ALEXANDER
STALLINGS JOHN
BLIZZARD WM
HOLCOB BENJAMIN
McCONNEL JOHN
EATON WM
DOWNEY WM
M'CONNEL ROB'T
WILLIAMS ENOCH
WILLIAMS GEORGE

WILLIAMS DANN
CARTER BENJAMIN
LITTELL JACOB
LEWIS AARON
CAHILL WM
CAHILL ELISON
BRADLEY ELIJAH
ROBESON JOSEPH
ROBESON JONATHAN
FOREUM JOHN
BOHANNON WILEY
WHITE GEORGE L
DEPOSITER JOHN
GARRIS JOSEPH SR
COX ABSOLOM
ASHLEY THO'S
ROBESON ISAAM
BORAN EZEKIEL
HARMON WM
DOWNEY JOHN
JOHNSON SAMPSON
GARRIS JOSEPH JR
LEWIS JOHN
WHITWORTH JOSEPH S
BRITTON WM
BRITTON NATHAN
COLVIN JOHN
SEVERS JAMES
JEFFERS JAMES S
CURTICE WILLIAM
MOONE BARNETT
WEST DANIEL
COLVIN NATHAN
HEDDY THO'S
FILLINGIM ENOCH
BUTLER JOHN
KELLER JACOB
BUTLER JAMES
LOVE JOHN
RUSSELL JOHN
RUSSELL WM
OLIVER JOHN SR
OLIVER JOHN JR
ARMSTRONG ELSBURY
CARTER JOHN
CARTER ELDRIDGE
USURY JOHN
MORRES ELISHA
FRANCE JOHN
FOSTER SAMUEL
WILLIAMS RUFUS
FOSTER WM

RICKET RICHARD
SILMAN BENJAMINE
PARRETT ROBERT
DUTY WM
CARPENTER SAM'L
McCOLLON STEPHEN
STEWART JOHN
WILLIAM JOHN
PHILIPS JOHN JR
DUKES ROB'T
DUKES EZEKIEL
ELKINS JOSHUWAY
JENTRY DAVID
GHARRIS SHARP
HAYS GEORGE
DODGE WM
M'COLLUM ISAAC
M'COLLUM DANIEL
MARCUS WM SR
MARCUS WM JR
MARCUS JAMES
NEAL JOHN
FOISTER BENJAMINE
LOW GEORGE
THOMSON JAMES
SMITH GEORGE
BOYLE JOHN
JOHNSON JOHN
SMILEY DAVID
BENSON DAVID
GRIGSBY TOLEVER
HARRES CHARLES
SUFFIELD EPHRAIM
WHITING CHARLES
TITTETT JOBE
KINNERLY ISAAC
NESBITT JAMES
JONES ENOCH
INDIOUT JOHN H
ESTES THO'S
ESTES WM
ESTES BARTLEY
ENDICOTT THO'S SR
ENDICOTT AARON
MULLEN WM
INDICUTT JOSEPH
ENDICUTT JESSE
MILLER SAMUEL
EATON THOMAS
EATON JOHN
EATON STEPHEN
EATON MORGAN

52

POSEY COUNTY

EATON GEORGE
DUTY MATTHEW
MEDDER AARON
ROBESON GEORGE
DOWNEY PETER
DOWNEY ALEXANDER
DOWNEY WM SR
ROBERTS HARDING
CAVITT ANDREW
CULLY JOSEPH
HALL AARON
MOORE AARON
MOORE JAMES SR
DREW LANGSTON
BENNETT JAMES
BENNETT JOHN
BENNETT LEGNO
BENNETT JOESPH
FLETCHER THO'S
DEFURR LEANDER
ROBB ELI
ROBB DAVID
M'CLURE THO'S
M'CLURE JOHN
OVERTON JOSHUWAY
AIGNER FREDERICK JR
CAVINS REZIN
DUCKWORTH JAMES
PATTERSON SAM'L
BATES JESSE
ERVIN SAM'L
ERVIN JAMES
RAGER JACOB
AIGNER FREDERICK SR
AUTERIETH ENGELHARD
AUTERIETH FERDINANT
AUTERIETH CHRISTIAN
BECKER JACOB
BECKER PHILIP
BENTEL GEORGE SR
BENTEL GEORGE JR
BENTEL ARNOLD
BENTEL ISRAEL
BRAUN FREDERICK
BONNET FRANZ
BONNET JOHN
BAMESBARGER JOHN
BENZENHEFER JACOB
BLANK FRANZ
BESSON JOHN
BENZENHEFER MICHAEL
BEIPER GEORGE

BEIPER ROMANUS
BEIPER BOSSILIUS
BAUER GEORGE
BAUER JACOB
BUHLER FREDERICK
BAUER CHRIS'N
BOEHM CONROD
BOEHM EUSEBUIS
BENTZ GEORGE
CONZELMAN GEORGE
DOUT JOHN
DINGLER JACOB
DURR JACOB SR
DURR FRAMPERT
DURR JACOB JR
DIETERLE MARTEN
EHMAN JACOB
GANTER JACOB
FRANK GEORGE
FEUCHT MICHAEL
FORSCHNER GEORGE
FORSCHNER MICHAEL
GAGER ADDAM
GAGER JACOB
GOTTERWA JOSEPH
GOETZ JOSEPH
HAUFLER TOBIAS
HAUFLER MICHAEL
HAINK GEORGE
HERRMAN JOHN
HERRMAN GEORGE
HARTMAN HENRY
HINGER WM
HENNING HILARUS
HOERNLY JOHN
HOERNLY JOSEPH
HUNN JOHN
FOUNG ADAM
KUNTZ JOHN
KURTZ FREDERICK
KRANTER DAVID
KURTZ JACOB
KOENIG DAVID
KEPPLER GEORGE
KEPPLER FLORIAN
KLEIN MATHEW
KLEIN JACOB
KLINGENSTEIN FREDERICK
KLINGENSTEIN ERHARD
KNODEL ALBERT
KNODEL CONROD
KNODEL GEORGE SR

KNODEL GEORGE JR
KRAIL JACOB
KREHMER MELCHION
KANT DAVID
LENTZ DANIEL
LANG CHRIS'T
LAUPHLE JACOB
BAKER JOHN L
BAKER ROMELIUS L/S
LAUPPLE DAVID
LAUPPLE FREDERICK
LENZ DAVID
LENZ ISRAEL
LEUCHT CHRIS'T SR
LEUCHT CHRIS'T JR
LEUCHT ANDREW
NACHTRUL FREDERICK
NACHTRUL ADDAM
NACHTRUL JOSHEWAY
MAHLE LENARD
MILLER CHRISTOPHER
OCHSTREICHER CHRIST'R
OCHSTREICHER ANDREW
PLESSING MICHAEL
RAPP GEORGE
RAPP FRED'K
REIPP JOHN
RALL MARTIN
RUHLE GEORGE
RUSH CHRISTIAN
RICHARD JOHN
SOOPER DAVID
SOOPER JACOB
SCHNABEL JOHN
SCHEEL FREDARICK
SCHEEL LORENZ
SCHANBACHER JACOB
STAHL JOHN
STILZ JACOB
STILZ EDWARD
STUMP JOHN
SPENGLER JACOB
SCHOLLE JACOB
SCHOLLE MATTHEW
SCHOLLE HELPERT
SHULE ADDAM
SMITH GEORGE SR
SMITH WM
SMITH GEORGE JR
SMITH AUGUST
STROHEKER CHRISTIAN
STROHEKER CHRISTOPHER

POSEY COUNTY

SPIDEL   MATTHEW
SEREBER   PETER
SERERIBER   LEWIS
SERIBER   JOHN
SERIBER   JACOB
SERIBER   ADAM
TROMPETER   JOHN
TROMPETER   GILBERT
VETTE   PHILO
VESTER   GEORGE
VEIHMEIER   MICHAEL
VEIHMEIER   JOHN
VAIHENGER   ANGULIUS
VAIHENGER   SEBASTIAN
VAIHENGER   JACOB
WEINGASTNER   FREDERICK
WEINGASTNER   CLEMENTS
WEINGASTNER   GEORGE
WEINGASTNER   MICHAEL
WEINGASTNER   WALRATH
WAGENER   GEORGE
WEIDENBACH   MATTHEW
WOLF   SOLOMON
WOHLGEMUTH   JACOB
WOEHRLY   THO'S

WOEHRLY   JACOB
WALDMAN   CHRISTIAN
WEBER   CHRISTOPHER
ZIMMERMON   NATHAN
ZIMMERMON   JACOB
ZUNDEL   PINODUS
ZUNDEL   JACOB
PFIEF   FREDERICK
SCHAAL   GEORGE
SCHAAL   PHILEMON
BENZINGER   CONROD
BLUHM   JOHN
DICK   JOHN
EKINSBARGER   FREDERICK
ENLELE   JOHN
FRITZ   MICHAEL
FEKHAMNER   GEORGE
GUTBROADT   PETER
HAGMEIER   LEWIS
HAINLEE   PHILIP
KAPPEL   JOHN
KNODEL   CHRISTOPHER
KNAPPER   ANTON
KURTZ   GEORGE   SR
KURTZ   GEORGE   JR

MULLER   DAVID
MEK   SALASTUS
MOESS   GEORGE
ROSSDAN   PETER
RUFF   REGORI
RUFF   ALBRECHT
RUFF   DAVID
SPATH   JOHN
SCHANBACHER   MICHAEL
SILVER   TOBIAS
SCHNEKENBURGER   GEORGE
ZELLER   FREDERICK
HOPKINS   JOHN
JERDIN   ELIJAH
THOMAS   JAMES
KESTER   GEORGE
KESTER   SOLOMAN
JAQUESH   JONATHAN
JAQUISH   GARISON
GAIL   REASKIN
HENSON   JOHN
HENSON   ABSOLOM
HENSON   JONATHAN
FENNIR   THO'S

RIPLEY COUNTY

HENRY   PETER
FISHER   PHILIP
FISHER   HENRY
BREMAN   JESSE
BREMAN   JAMES
BREMAN   JONATHAN
MONTGOMERY   JOSEPH
MONTGOMERY   JAMES
WILSON   WILLIAM
SCOTT   WILLIAM
DEAN   ROBERT
CRANAHAM   ROBERT
HICKMAN   JOHN
HICKMAN   - - -
HICKS   ELERY
BORDEN   JOHN
PECKHAM   ARNOLD
HUGGINS   ADOLPHUS
CRANE   EDWARD
LOOMIS   JAMES
TALMAN   DAVID

TALMAN   STEPHEN
TALMAN   EPHRAIM
SMITH   ZEPHANIAH
McCLURE   WILLIAM
WILSON   JOB
STEWARD   AMOS
HILL   MOSES G
O'NEIL   JOHN
NEVILLS   - - -
NICHISON   ABIJAH
CARDNER   ANDREW
HENDRICKS   DAVID
HUBBELL   JOHN
HUBBELL   HENRY
ROBISON   NATHAN
HINER   JOHN
BOOHAR   DANIEL
EATON   JAMES
PHELPS   ARONAH
PHELPS   SETH
WILKISON   BENAJAH

LYON   ANDREW
WHITE   JAMES
BELT   HENRY
BELT   JOHN
BELT   ASBURY
PORTER   CHARLES
SMILEY   WILLIAM
REEVES   JOHN
ANDERSON   JAMES
DOOLY   JAMES
DOOLY   WILLIAM
BENHAM   JAMES
WILSON   JAMES
McCULLOUGH   JAMES
McCULLOUGH   DAVID
McCULLOUGH   JOHN   JR
OVERTURF   JACOB
DITCH   HENRY
BONTY   JACOB
BONTY   HENRY
ROBERTS   EDWARD

RIPLEY COUNTY

LEWIS THOMAS
CHRISTIE JAMES
HAMILTON JAMES
HAMILTON HENRY
BUCHANAN WILSON
DAVID CHARLES
SHAFER JOHN
DAVID ATWELL
BUCHANAN WILLIAM
BUCHANAN WILLIAM H
BUCHANAN WILLIAM B
WHITHAM JAMES
WHITHAM BENJAMIN
WHITHAM JOHN
HAVENS JOHN
PRYOR JOHN A
REED JOHN M
RITCHIE JOHN
WRIGHT DARLING
SALYERD WILLIAM B
SALYERD JEREMIAH
MAY RICHARD
MAY JOHN
STEVENS BENJAMIN
NELSON SAMUEL
BUNTIN HUGH
SALYERS GEORGE
NELSON JOSEPH
NELSON CHARLES
McCOY THOMAS
SREEVES JONATHAN
BUCHANAN DAVID
VOYLES WILLIAM
WHITTICHKER JAMES
WHITTICHKER THOMAS
WHITTICHKER JOHN
HYATT SHADRACH
BREWER ENOCH
ELLIS ROGER
WHITTICHKER ANDREW
KIPHART CHARLES
KIPHART PHILIP
HARRIS JESSE
HARRIS JOSEPH
MYERS LEWIS
MOORE HUGH
BURCHFIELD JEREMIAH
CURRIE JAMES
BASSETT THOMAS
SMITH JAMES
PARR ISAAC
RUNNER DAVID

YOUNG IRA
MYERS HENRY
McINTOSH JOSEPH
GOLA DAVID
OWEN BENJAMIN
SAFLY THOMAS
GULLY ELIAS
DUMMAREE JOHN
COMER JOHN
STEVENS SAMUEL
STEWARD ISAIAH
WATERS THOMAS
DERINGER JOSEPH
OVERTURF MARTIN
BASSET WILLIAM
HUETT JACOB
WHICHER STEPHEN
CRAIG MERIT S
HUNTER JOHN
OVERTURF CONRAD
BENTLEY JOSEPH
SHEONE WILLIAM
FOX DANIEL A B C
LINDSAY JOHN
KEELER HERMAN
GOODRICH CARMY
HAMILTON BENJAMIN
WOODWORTH CALEB
LEWIS JOHN
LEWIS HUGHY
SHEPARD WALTER
SHEPARD RUSSELL
SHEPARD WHEELER
SHEPARD JONAS
BROWN PARKER
DIMICK ADOLPHUS
DIMICK CORDIAL
TOWNSEND ROBERT
TOWNSEND ABIEL
WEBSTER SAMUEL
WEBSTER CYRUS
WEBSTER GEORGE B
WEBSTER NATHANIEL
SILSON WILLIAM
WAUMAN ELIJAH
WAUMAN CHRISTOPHER
PURCELL JOHN
WATSON JEREMIAH
CURRAN THOMAS
STEWARD ALEX'R W
PURCELL BENJAMIN
LIVINGSTON GEORGE

MONGER JEHIEL
STONE WILLIAM S
GOFF SAMPSON
STOCKWELL JOSEPHUS
KEELEE THOMAS
BOYCE JAMES
MUIR JAMES
THOMAS GEORGE
THOMAS HENRY JR
THOMAS HENRY SR
JOHNSON MARK
STEVENS SOLOMON
STEVENS JAMES
STEVENS ISAAC
LOGSTON THOMAS
ANDREWS LUMAN
COLLINS GEORGE
SCOTT DANIEL
BURKE WILLIAM
PURCELL SAMUEL
McCLANE CHARLES
McCLANE JOHN
DAVIS JOHN
DAVIS THOMAS
DAVIS JAMES
PURCELL MOSES
WILSON JAMES
PELSOLL BENJAMIN
JOHNSON JOHN
JOHNSON WILLIAM
JOHNSON ROSWEL
WATSON EBER
WILKISON JOHN
BOYCE WILLIAM
LEWIS WILLIAM
MITCHELL SAMUEL
COOKSON ANDREW
SCOTT MOSES
STEWARD JOHN
HENSHAW HENRY
PENETENT JOHN
BOZARD WILLIAM
CASTATOR MICHAEL
STEWART WILLIAM
GILHAM JOHN
BLAIR BEVERLY
KENNET SAMUEL
BURCHFIELD ROBERT
BURCHFIELD THOMAS
WEATHERBY JAMES
CLEM CHRISTOPHER
SWISSER GEORGE

RIPLEY COUNTY

MORSE WILLIAM	TALBOTT RICHARD	BOSWELL JOHN
DOWER GEORGE	RAY JOHN	RANEY JACOB
DOWERS AZARIAH	RAY ROBERT	CRAIG JOSEPH
PREBLE TEPHEN	PATTON HUSTON	ROWAN JOHN
JOLLY WILLIAM	BROWN BENJAMIN	HARRIS NATHAN
RYAN ELIJAH	WESLEY JAMES	JOHNS JOHN
RYAN GEORGE	CLARK JOSEPH	WREN WILLIAM
LUCCAT WILLIAM JR	CLARK JAMES	HUSE CALEB
MARTIN HUTSON	COLLINS THOMAS	ESK JAMES
BOATMAN HENRY	COLLINS GARTER	GOWENS STEPHEN
ROBERTS JACOB	COLLINS WILLIAM	McDOWEL MARTIN
ROBERTS GEORGE	YOUNG PETER SR	EVANS SOLOMON
O'NEIL HENRY	YOUNG PETER JR	WATTS MASON
O'NEIL JAMES	YOUNG DAVID	CRISLEY M
O'NEIL JOHN	YOUNG GEORGE	DINGLE JEDEDIAH
RYAN JOHN	STORMS CONRAD	DAWKINS WILLIAM
WILSON HENRY	YATES JOHN	BAKER THOMAS
WILSON JAMES	YATES WILLIAM	LIPPARD WILLIAM
WILSON EPHRAIM	HANN EPHRAIM	LIPPARD JOHN
WILSON JESSE	McDOWEL JOHN	LIPPARD HENRY
PLATTER HENRY	McDOWEL JAMES	LIPPARD MOSES
RADLEY JAMES	HUGHES WILLIAM	LIPPARD WILLIAM JR
SMITH SAMUEL	HUGHES HENRY	BRIDGES JOHN
HODGES SAMUEL	KIRBY JOHN SR	WEBSTER (HOGAN) SAMUEL
HODGES RICHARD	KIRBY JOHN JR	CARR AMES
HODGES WILLIAM	KING JAMES	TISA JOHN
COLE SAMUEL	COLE JESSE	INYARD JOSEPH
BLAIR RICHARD	COLE JEREMIAH	HAMILTON WILLIAM
JOHNSON GEORGE	COLE CHARLES	GRIMES JOHN
KING SIDNEY	BROWN BARTLET	WICHARD JOSEPH
ALLEN MONTGOMERY	WILEY ZECHARIAH SR	SUTTON REUBEN
CRETH ROBERT	WILEY ZECHARIAH JR	HARPER EZEKIEL
NORRIS HEZEKIAH	WILEY WILLIAM	SCOTT ANDREW
MOOR JOHN	WILEY AQUILLA	AUSTIN THISON
MARTIN JOHN	WAGGONER GEORGE	AUSTIN STEPHEN
ALLEN BALAS	McCLASKY JAMES	PALMER THOMAS
PACKER JESSE	SAUNDERS JOHN	THOMAS MYERS
SMITH SAMUEL S	SAMPSON CALEB	CARBOUGH ABRAM
NELAS GEORGE	STIPES JOSEPH	WALLACE DAVID
CAMPBELL JOHN	ADAM WILLIAM	WILGAND GEORGE
SHAW SAMUEL	WILLIAMS JASPER SR	WILLIAMS JOHN
SHAW HAMILTON	WILLIAMS JASPER JR	HINER THOMAS
SHAW JAMES	WILLIAMS ELU	McDANIEL DANIEL
DICKEY HAMILTON	WILLIAMS OTHO	CARR THOMAS
DICKEY GEORGE	WILLIAMS WILLIAM	McKETTRICK JOHN
WOOLEY DANIEL	WILLIAMS DANIEL	GOUCHER SAMUEL
McGUIRE JESSE	WILLIAMS AMOS	ISGRIGG DANIEL
LANDON HUGH	WILLIAMS RICHARD	ISGRIGG STEPHEN
RAY SILAS	HAMILTON WILLIAM	SHOCKLEY JOSHUA
DICKERSON JAMES	YATES ABRHAM	HAWLEY ZALMON
TALBOTT JEREMIAH	RAY MATTHEW	RECHUM JUSHENE
TALBOTT ABRAHAM	KIRBY JOEL	DOUCHY SAMUEL

RIPLEY COUNTY

MESSINGER - - -
BROWN   JOSHUA
BROWN   JOHN
KEENE   DANIEL
SPENCER MR   SR
SPENCER RANSOM
HARDEN   DAVID SR
HARDEN   DAVID JR
SUMMER   CALEB SR
SUMMER   CALEB JR
RANSON   TIMOTHY SR
RANSON   TIMOTHY JR

RANSON   ELISHA
DENNISON TIMOTHY
INMAN   JOHN
INMAN   STEPHEN
FARMER   HILCHAM
FARMER   FREDERICK
FARMER   MR SR
ANDERSON JOHN
ANDERSON ISAAC
NIGHT   SAMUEL
CARPENTER MR
CRITCHELL MOSES

BLACKMAN MR
WILKISON JOHN
WATSON   EBER
SAILOR   JACOB
VANZEL   WILLIAM
CARNES   WILLIAM
BENSONS CHARLES
FELLOWS EDMONS
FELLOWS - - -
DURANT   CORNELIUS
SPENCER MATTHEW
YEARNS   JOHN

VANDERBURGH COUNTY

KINNE   WILLIAM
CHRISENHALL SAMUEL
CHRISENHALL WM
CALENDAR ISAAC
GRATEHOUSE WM
ROGER   BURKET
ROGER   LEWIS
LONG   NICHOLAS
LONG   REUBEN
SHAUFNER JOHN
JONES   JONATHAN
LESTER   ANDREW
BANER   FREDERICK
ROGER   LEWIS
FARNAER ISAAC
MAREQUART ADAM
DUNN   JOHN
McDOWELL JOSEPH M
CASEY   JOSEPH
ANTHONY JAMES
ANTHONY JOHN
STAZER   FREDERICK
SIRKLE   ANDREW
SPRINKLE GEORGE
CAST   GEORGE
SIRKLE   LEWIS
EDMOND   GEORGE
HOOKEN   WM
STONER   JOHN
EDMOND   JOHN
WOOD   A
BARKER   AB'N
HOPKINS EDWARD
HOPKINS STEPHEN

MALLARD GEORGE
INWOOD   WM
WARD   THOMAS
RING   JAMES
SCOTT   SAMUEL
HALL   WM
CARLISLE RICHARD
PECK   WM
WHALER   JOSEPH
HORNBY   WM
RUSSEL   JAMES
SLOW   JOHN
HENNING ARNOLD
MAXBERRY A
COMPTON KENNETH
EVANS   RICHARD
COMBS   WM
ERSKINE JOHN
ERSKINE ANDREW
ERSKINE THOMAS
GORMAN   PATRICK
WHEELER RICHARD
BALSOVER JOHN
BALSOVER JA'S
OLDS   DANIEL
DUKES   JOHN
ELSWORTH ARON
DURPHY   ELISHA
PARKER   GEORGE
LANE   JESSE
LANE   JOSEPH
LANE   JOHN
BURNET   WM
AKIN   DAVID

HAMILTON JOHN R
PARKER   JOHN
SHERWOOD ELI
McCALISTER ARCHIBALD
BARNET   HUMPHREY
LICKAS   JOHN
KNIGHT   ISAAC
FAIRCHILD WALTER
GIBSON   ROBERT
WHITE   WM
McCALISTER JOSEPH
McCALISTER JESSE
KELSEY   AMBRON
MARSH   FRANKLIN
TRANCEWAY JOSEPH
TRANCEWAY ABRAM
KNIGHT   DAVID
VAN   ABSOLOM
YOUNG   NATHAN
KIMBALL NATHAN
SHOULTS GEORGE
WHETSTONE DAVID
JACKSON JOHN
SMITH   WM
WHETSTONE HENRY
STANFIELD ASHLEY
HOOKER   THOMAS
HOOKER   THOMAS JR
ONEAL   JOHN
CHANDLER JOHN G
WARNER   WM W
WARNER   WM
WARNER   ALAIRSON
MORGAN   PETALIAH

57

VANDERBURGH COUNTY

PEARCE EARL
TAYLOR NOAH
LEWIS SIMON
BOARDMAN SYLVESTER
McCLAIN MATTHEW
TAYLOR WM
HOPKINS REUBEN
SMITH H
RICHARDSON JA'S H
WININGH MOSES
WEBB JOHN
FULLER PORTER
BOWERS SHELDRAN
COPES WM
COX JOSEPH
COX JAMES
AYRES ISAAC
TRAFTON WM
FAIRCHILD ALPHEA J
FAIRCHILD ISAAC
McDONALD DANIEL
SHAW JOHN W
SHORLAND E H
CLARK AMOS
ANNABLE SAMUEL
HARRISON ELISHA
CHANDLER H B
BAKER JOHN S
ZIMMERMAN JACOB
CALDWELL NATH
MARALLEE JOHN
STINSON JAMES
MILLS WM JR
PADELFORD JOSEPH
CHUTE DANIEL
PHAR V K
CHANDLER L
KEENE SAMUEL B
GOLDSMITH DANIEL L
GOODLETT J R E
WARNER ALFRED O
BROWN JOHN
HALE NATHAN
HUND AMAYEN
AVERRY D
THOMPSON JOHN
LEWIS WM
CONNER JOHN
McGAREY HUGH
ROBINSON JAMES
CONNER JOHN JR
WATKINS JAMES E

BOIES JA'S A
POTTER JOHN
CLARK WILLARD J
BAKER E R
McGAREY WM R
DUNHAM JOHN M
HARRIS JOAB
WILSON DAVID
McKNITT WM
PAXTON JOHN A
ELLIOTT JAMES
JOLLY STEPHEN
CANFIELD SAMUEL
ARMSTRONG ROBERT
GORDON GEORGE
PRITCHET PRESLEY
LAMPHEAR HYNSEN
STEEL SAMUEL
BEACH JOHN
STEVENS VANCE
SATTERLEE GIDEON
TEMPLETON JAMES
ROWLEY NATHAN
FOSTER WM A
BENTLEY JAMES
MINCHINGTON E H
THORNTON JOHN
STANLEY THOMAS
CURRY ROBERT
ANDERSON THOMAS
GRIFFIN HIRAM
SPEARS STEBEN
SCRIBNER IRA
PARKER SILAS
JACKSON TIMOTHY
ALLEN DANIEL C
TOOL DANIEL
COOK JACOB
SAUNDERS JOHN S
WOOD ANSEL
DIVINE THOMAS
WILLIAMS HARVEY
VANHORN RALPH
JACOBS GEORGE W
TOWNER ELIJAH
BOLING MICHAEL
WOOD LUKE
MOREHOUSE JAY
BARBER HENRY
OLMSTED WM
NEAGLEY DAVID
SHAVER JOHN

SHAVER PETER
WRIGHT JOHN
HARRISON ZEPHANIAH
HARRISON DAVID
HARRISON JOHN
HARRISON BAILES
COMSTOCK ASA
TORQUE JAMES
KIRKPATRICK JOHN
KIRKPATRICK D
HOLLOWAY JESSE
THOMPSON HENRY
FITZGERALD MORRISON
FITZGERALD WM
FITZGERALD ARCH'B
FITZGERALD JOHN
CURTIS REUBEN
SATTERLIE ELISHA
SATTERLIE ASA
SATTERLIE ABEL
HUTCHINS WM
SULLIVAN ANDREW
MILLER PETER
DAVIS BENJAMIN
STERN DAVID
MILLER JOSEPH
TYLER JOHN
TYLER JOSEPH
TYLER THOMAS
TYLER GEORGE
HARRISON JOHN JR
CODY JOHN
WATERS ELIJAH
CHAPMAN WM
CHAPMAN JOSEPH
McCOY JAMES
HILL EDWARD
STINSON JOHN B
PUTMAN HAZEAL
McKINZER MUTNER
MELVIN JAMES
MELVIN JOHN
FAIRCHILD ALPHEAS JR
FAIRCHILD SETH
FAIRCHILD ZERA
FAIRCHILD ELAM
FAIRCHILD ORMAND
FAIRCHILD JONATHAN
GILLETT ARKIMUS
GOLDEN JONATHAN
WILSON WM
WAGNOR WM

VANDERBURGH COUNTY

BARKER FRANK
JOHNSON JAMES
JOHNSON WM
ROBERTSON JAMES
HUTCHINSON JAMES
LAMMA JAMES
SAUNDERS JEFFREY
SAUNDERS EZEKIEL
SAUNDERS DAVID
HAMMONWAY JOHN
KING JA'S
ANNICE JACOB
MILLER DANIEL
PENDLETON CHARLES
SHEGAW JOHN D
BINKET JOHN
SLOVER JAMES
WARREN MATTHEW
WARREN JOHN
WARREN LEVY
WARREN WM
WARREN ALEXANDER
HENSON DAVID
HENSON JESSE
HENSON JOHN
CHAPMAN WM JR
BRYANT WALTER
McNEW BENJAMIN
CHASE JOSEPH
NATTE JOHN
BRYANT JOHN
BRYANT WM
BRYANT JOHN JR
LIVINGSTON JOHN
McNEELY ALEXANDER
McNEELY DAVID
RODGERS RANDOLPH
RODGERS WM
HOPSON JESSE
RENSHAW AB'M
ALLEN ISAAC
WILLIAMS JOHN
TAYLER JAMES
ROSE JOSEPH
ROSE DANIEL
ROSE JOSHUA
McCRAVEY JOHN
McCRAREY JAMES
WILLIAMS LEWIS
CATER WM
MARTIN JAMES
MARTIN THOMAS

DAVIS URIAH
ARMSTRONG JOHN
ARMSTRONG KIRBY
ARMSTRONG JOHN JR
ALLEN ROBERT
SELSON MAJOR
CALVERT PATRICK
CATER JOSEPH
GOTHARD ISAAC
BROOMFIELD DAVID
PREWITT MOSES
EWING HENRY
McGRIDER EZEKIEL
EWING WM
SALSBERRY THOMAS
BENSON WM
KITCHEN JOHN S
BOLING JOHN
McNEW ZADOCH
PATTEN JAMES
KELLEY SAMUEL
GERRARD SAMUEL
RITCHIE SIMPSON
MARTIN CHARLES
TAYLOR SAMUEL
JUDKINS JESSE
JUDKINS DAVID
DUNHAM HUXFORD
HIGGINS ELI H
RAMSEY GEORGE
FERREL JOHN
PAUL MARSHFIELD
PAUL SAMUEL
PAUL CYRUS
McCAULEY HENREY
McCAULEY JOEL
THOMPSON WM
COOK THOMAS
COOK EMMORY
SMITH JOSEPH W
BLEVINS WM
CATTIN DANIEL
GOSS JONATHAN
LINKWYLER GEORGE
LINKWYLER PETER
ROSE THOMAS
ROSE BENJAMIN
KELHORN THOMAS
DOUGHERTY JOSEPH
PATTERSON WM
ADYLOTT PARKER
GIBSON JULIUS

GIBSON JOHN
GILLMORE JOHN W
SAUNDERS DAVID
SHAW WM
HAMPTON WM
KENT DAVID
KENNERLEY EVERTON
WHETSTONE MATTHIAS
STEVENS JOSHUA
WAGGONER HENRY
BALDWIN JOSEPH
BALDWIN ALONSON
BURTIS JESSE
McCLANAHAN JOHN
McCLANAHAN JAMES
JOHNSON CHARLES M
HILLYAR JAMES
HILLYAR JOHN
HILLYAR ALEXANDER
HILLYAR WM
HEWMAN PETER
KINGSBERRY BENJAMIN
MAIDLOW JAMES
MAIDLOW JAMES JR
MAIDLOW EDWARD
TRUSTER GEORGE
TERREL CHARLES
HORNBROOK SANDERS
POTTS GEORGE
PEARCE JOHN JR
LOCKE CHRISTOPHER
PEARCE THOMAS
DUNK SAMUEL
DUNK CHARLES
PEDLEY JOHN
WILLIS WM
MANSELL SAMUEL
CAWSON JAMES
INGLE JOHN
McCAIN JOHN
MOORE T
WORSHAM DANIEL
JOHNSTON JOHN
GRAHAM ANDREW
YOUNG SAMUEL
WILLETT JAMES
SMITH WILLIAM
SMITH JOHN
PORTER ANDREW
ROBERTSON ANTHONY
SWAIN ANTHONY
SPORTSMAN JAMES
PEARSON JOSEPH

WASHINGTON COUNTY

McNIGHT JOHN SR	DOUGLASS WILLIAM	WELLER MATTHIAS
McNIGHT WILLIAM SR	JOHNSON JEHU	COFFEE JOHN H
McNIGHT JOHN JR	BOWERS SOLOMON	HINKLE ANTHONY
McNIGHT ROBERT R	WOOD GEORGE	JONES ISAAC
McNIGHT WILLIAM JR	COOPER EDMUND	FARABEE JOHN
THOMPSON THOMAS SR	COOPER ROBERT	HURST WILLIAM SR
THOMPSON ROGER	COCHRAN JAMES	PARR ARTHUR
THOMPSON MOSES	ERVIN ROBERT	PARR JOHN
THOMPSON JOHN SR	GORDON AARON	PARR MORGAN
THOMPSON THOMAS JR	MORRIS ARON	KILLYAN DANIEL
THOMPSON JOHN JR	MORRIS JEHOSHAPHAT	HURST WILLIAM JR
THOMPSON JAMES SR	PEWED THOMAS	ANDERSON ALEXANDER
THOMPSON ROBERT	TATLOCK AARON	STOCKER GEORGE
THOMPSON JOSEPH	TATLOCK MILES	LOW JAMES
THOMPSON WILLIAM SR	TATLOCK CHALKLEY	PRINGLE JAMES
THOMPSON JAMES JR	McCOY MALACHI	COOMBS JOEL
THOMPSON CARY	NEWBY JOSHUA	CONAWAY JOHN
ROBINSON WILLIAM	TATLOCK JOSHUA	McLALLEN MOSES
ROBINSON ROBERT	TATLOCK BENJAMIN	POUGHMAN JOHN
ROBINSON JOHN JR	TATLOCK DEMSEY	ROSE EDWARD W
ROBINSON JOHN SR	MOORE JOSEPH	McLALLEN CHRISTOPHER
HUSTON ALEXANDER	MOORE SAMUEL	COGSWELL WARNER
HUSTON JAMES B	MILROY SAMUEL	ROSE ELISHA JR
CAREY JACOB	CAMPBELL WILLIAM	ROSE ELISHA SR
BRAWFORD JOHN	FOUTS DAVID	BARKER STEPHEN
JONES PHILIP	KENNEDY WILLIAM	McGILL JOHN
LOCKWOOD RICHARD	TATLOCK JAMES	CREAMER SIMEON
CARMAN ELIJAH	DEWEBER JOHN	MULL TOBIAS
ALLEN JOSEPH	PRITCHARD REES	BROWN JOHN
COOK ASHER	PARR ENOCH	SPURGIN JOSEPH
HAMILTON JOHN	RODMAN JAMES	SPURGIN JOSIAH
DUNLAP JOHN	HERRON WILLIAM	MORGAN ISAAC
DUNLAP STEPHEN S	HUSTON SAMUEL	MILROY JAMES
GARRETT HENRY	McLAUGHLIN JOHN	HARLAND JAMES
LEMMON ROBERT	McMANNIS JOHN	WRIGHT NOAH
RAYHILL MATTHEW	GARRETT JACOB	WILSON JAMES S
BOYER TIMOTHY	GARRETT AMBROSE	TRUEBLOOD WILLIAM
GREEN JAMES	MARKWELL JOHN	TRUEBLOOD ABLE
BISHOP PRESTON	BABCOCK ORLOW	BLANKENBAKER SAMUEL
HODGES ALLEN	NELSON GEORGE	NEWLON JOHN
CHAMBERS WILLIAM	VANMETER WILLIAM	DAVIS HENRY
DEWITT JOHN	WILSON JOHN	DAVIS JESSE
SIMS JOHN	MITCHEL JOHN	McALLISTER ZACHARIAH
SEATON SAMUEL	MERRELL JOAB	SWIM ELIJAH
OLDS JARED	HARTLEY JAMES	FISHER JACOB
BUNDY CHRISTOPHER	HARTLEY WILLIAM	WEAR DAVID
WEAR GEORGE	HARTLEY SAMUEL	ROSE SAMUEL
ROCK ROBERT	JOHNS THOMAS	NEWTON WILLIAM
WEAR ARCHABALD	OLDS DANIEL	HAGAN GEORGE
WEAR JOHN	GARRETT ISAAC	WILSON JOHN
MITCHEL THOMAS	COOPER JOEL	WORREL ISAAC
HARROD THOMAS	HODGES THOMAS	RODOLPH MICHAEL

WASHINGTON COUNTY

GRAY SAMUEL
ALVIS DAVID
SUMMY PETER
GREER GEORGE
GREER JAMES
GOSS JOHN
MORRIS RICHARD
MORRIS LEWIS S
MORRIS JOHN G
MORRIS JOHN
LOCKHART WALTER
STANDLEY THOMAS
STANDLEY ROBERT H
DAY RICHARD
SCOTT ARCHALAUS
GLASBROOK WILLIAM
DAVIS NEWEL
SMILY JOHN
SMILY HUGH
DEWALT HENRY
FULMER HENRY
DUNN JOSEPH
McCOSKEY JAMES
HEATON WASHINGTON
THORNBURGH AMOS
CARISS SIMON
DENNY DAVID
DENNY WILLIAM
WRIGHT WILLIAM
DUFFIELD WILLIAM
DENNY ELISHA
DENNY SAMUEL
DENNY JAMES
KEMP GODLOVE
HEATON WILLIAM
WOOD JOHN
JOHNSON JOSEPH J
PRINCE JACOB
LAMB SIMEON
GREEN ROBERT
ALBERTSON BENJAMIN
LITTLE ALEXANDER
HOBBS WILLIAM
WHITE JAMES
COSAND BENJAMIN
LAMB ERIC
MANAGH THOMAS
ALBERTSON JOSHUA
ARNOLD JOHN
SMITH EPHRAIM
PITTS ANDREW
PITTS THOMAS

PITTS SAMUEL
CAUBLE ADAM SR
CAUBLE PETER
CAUBLE ADAM JR
PERSONS ABLE
CARNS DAVID
HICK WILLIAM
HARRISON CHRISTOPHER
ALBEERTSON ELIAS
HARBIN EDWARD V
CHARLES RISDON
RITTER MOSES
COOPER JOHN
McFARLAND PETER
CAREY WILLIAM
PHILIPS BENJAMIN
CHASE ISAAC
WHITE JAMES
HUFF JOHN
GAILARD EDWARD
ROLLEY ELIJAH
PATRICK EBENEZAR
PATRICK MATTHEW
HENDERSON JOHN G
REED JESSE
CURREY JOHN
BOOTH BEEBEE
NEWBY MICAH
WOOLFINGTON JOHN
LYON JONATHAN
WILEY JOHN
McCULLOUGH JOHN
KENNEDY JAMES
KIMBLE NATHANIEL
McINTIRE THOMAS L
HOWLAND AMOS N
COFFIN STEPHEN
BAKER MICHAEL
LEWIS JOHN
LEWIS WILLIAM
RIBBLE ADAM
RIBBLE SAMUEL
SCOTT OLLEY
REDUS SAMUEL
THOMAS ISAAC
THOMAS JAMES
CARVIN EDWARD
BRADLEY BURR
McMAHAN JOHN
PRATHER BASEL
McBROWN JOHN
LANDRUM THOMAS

MITINGER GEORGE
GREENAWALT JOHN
MALOTT ELI W
LYON ZACHARIAH
HIGGINS JAMES R
NORRIS EDWARD
HOGGETT JOSEPH
BAIRD WILLIAM
FRIDLEY JOHN
PICKSTEY JOHN H
ROWLAND JEREMIAH
DUFFEY JOSEPH
BRAMAN GEORGE
WILKASON SAMUEL
FERGUSON JAMES
CHAPMAN JOHN
LINDLEY WILLIAM
ROWLAND WILLIAM
HARRISON NICHOLAS
JENKINS JOSEPH
TRUEBLOOD JOSEPH
GARRETT CALEB
WOOD MATTHEW
JACKSON SAMUEL
WAUGHTEL FREDERICK
ZIGLER PHILIP
RODMAN WILLIAM
KENNEDY ELIJAH
KENNEDY NORVAL
FOOTS WILLIAM
CLARK JOHN E
GRAHAM JAMES
WHITE SAMUEL
McPHETERS HUGH
WHITE CYRUS
KINGSBERRY JOHN
FENNING THOMAS
NIXON JOSEPH
HOBBS ELISHA
TRUEBLOOD NATHAN
COX JOHN
DRAPER JOSEPH
HARNARD JOHN
LINDLEY THOMAS
LINDLEY SAMUEL
LINDLEY WILLIAM
CHAMBERS JOHN
OVERMAN JOHN
TRUEBLOOD JOSHUA
TRUEBLOOD JAMES JR
HENLEY JORDON
TRUEBLOOD JAMES SR

WASHINGTON COUNTY

PARKER BENJAMIN
THOMPSON LEVI
SAINT THOMAS
HENBY SILVANIS
HENBY JESSE
MUNDEN LEVI
THORNTON HENRY
WOODY LEWIS
OVERMAN JAMES
TAYLOR SAMUEL
SIMMONS JEHOSHAPHAT
McCOY WILLIS
TRUEBLOOD CALEB
BOGUE MARK
BOGUE JESSE
BOGUE NATHAN
BOGUE AARON
FLEENER FREDERICK
JOHNSON FRANCIS
JOHNSON ARCHABALD
JOHNSON HENRY
FLEENER ABRAHAM
CUNNINGHAM ANDERSON
DAVIS JAMES
SPURGIN WILLIAM
CALLAWAY MICAJAH
McCRACKEN HENRY
THOMPSON WILLIAM
GILCREASE WILLIAM
SCOTT BENJAMIN
CUNNINGHAM ELIJAH
NICHOLSON BENJAMIN
GILCREASE ROBERT
SLUDER ISAAC
CARTER HENRY
CARMACK ALLEN
GRANTHAM JESSE
PAIN MILO
FLEENOR JOHN
CARTOR JOHN
HANCOCK WILLIAM
POTTORFF MARTIN
GRANTHAM MOSES
CROW LEWIS.
STUTSMAN ISAAC
YOUNG JAMES
HODGEN WILLIAM
HODGEN JOSEPH
HODGEN NATHAN
REYMAN JOSEPH
REYMAN JACOB B
LAUGHLIN JOHN

LAUGHLIN ALEXANDER
HITCHCOCK WILLIAM
WILSON HENRY
TILFORD ROBERT
ARMFIELD JONATHAN
WEIR ANDREW
GILBERT JOHN
HENDERSON SAMUEL
ALBERTSON NATHAN
MONDON LEVI
BROCK GEORGE
GORDON WILLIAM
GORDON ISAAC
NIXON FOSLER
MORRIS SAMUEL
DAVIS GEORGE
GEORGE DAVID
FRABER HENRY
BRANAMAN CHRISTIAN
GILES JOHN
RUSSEL CURTUS
RUSSEL THOMAS
BROWN JOEL
BROWN WILLIAM
CHANLER WILLIAM SR
CHANLER WILLIAM JR
CHANLER ISAAC
WRIGHT LEVI
BREWER BENJAMIN
KNUCKLES ROBERT
RING PHILIP
MYERS GEORGE A
MYERS DAVID
SINK PETER SR
SINK DANIEL
HELLER DEWALT
WEAVER JOHN
BARNET JOHN
KELLER ANDREW
NIE JACOB
ALBERTSON ELIAS
NEALEY JAMES
LAMB ROBERT
LAMB JOEL
LAMB WILLIAM
BASS ARTHUR
COX JACOB
YOUNG JOSEPH
GOODEN SAMUEL
BUNDY ABRAHAM
HOLLOWELL THOMAS
SPOON CHRISTIAN

GRANTHAM MOSES
GRANTHAM JOSEPH
OVERMAN BENJAMIN
HAWN JACOB
KINYAN JOHN
BARNET JACOB
POTTORFF JOHN
FULK MARTIN
HARVEY JOHN
BARNET ADAM
TAYLOR JOHN
LEWELLING SHEDERICK
NIDIVER FREDERICK
BUBBARD NICHOLAS
BROCK GEORGE JR
NIXON ZACHARIAH
MORRIS BENONI
BROWN JOHN
HUNT ISAIAH
BOULTONHOUSE JOHN
GEI JOHN
LINN JOSEPH
McNEW RICHARD
ALLEN JAMES
HARBISON JAMES
GLAZEBROOK JULIUS
RIBBLE JOHN
GHASKINS JOHN
MITCHEL THOMAS
CLARK ROBERT JR
CLARK ROBERT SR
CLARK JEREMIAH
McHORNEY BERNARD H
RIRKISER CHRISTOPHER
CLARK RICHARD
CURTIGHT RALPH
COFFIN JAMES
BARNET JETHRO
THORNBURGH BENJAMIN
LEFEVER ABRAHAM
HOOVER DAVID
RICHARDSON ARTHUR
RICHARDSON IVY
OVERMAN ELI
MULPHERD JOSEPH
RANSBARGER GEROGE
SIMPSON JOHN
WADE MERREDA
DENNIS ROBERT SR
DENNIS DAVID
DENNIS ROBERT JR
RIBBLE JOSEPH

WASHINGTON COUNTY

MOURNIN DAVID
JOHNSON AARON
HOOVER JACOB JOHN
McCRUTCHEN JACOB
WOOD JOHN
GLAZEBROOK CLIFT
FOUTS NOEL
SHULL JOSEPH
McCLINTIC ROBERT
WRIGHT ELI
RAZOR ABRAHAM
THORNBERRY JOSEPH
AMINON WILLIAM
MORIN BARNARD
MORIN WILLIAM
ALBERTSON JOHN
COOLEY EDWARD
COOLEY THOMAS
KNUCKLES CHARLES
BREWER JOHN
DRISKEL WILLIAM
ARMSTRONG BENONI
WILLIS JACOB
DENNY JOHN
STOVER ABRAHAM
YATES WILLIAM
PIERSON JACOB
MONACLE GEORGE
JONES ROBERT
HITT JESSE
MONACLE PETER SR
YOUNG NICHOLAS
YOUNG HENRY
HINDELL JACOB
NAGGLE PETER
MAHON ANDREW
SPRINGER JOSEPH
MORRIS STEPHIN
MAHONNEY JAMES B
FISHER JAMES B
STOCKER ELI
DRAPER THOMAS
DRAPER PETER
DRAPER WILLIAM
MASEY ISAAC
STARBUCK GEORGE
COFFIN MARMADUKE
COFFIN MATTHEW
EVANS THOMAS
EVANS WILLIAM
EVANS ROBERT
WRIGHT PHILBERT

WRIGHT EVINS
SHORT GEORGE
PRINCE GODFRAY
WALLS HEZEKIAH
MABOUGH JACOB H
HAMILTON BENJAMIN
HAMILTON JAMES
STOCKER JONATHAN
PIGEON BENJAMIN
RING SOLOMON
CARTER CHARLES
DENNEY THOMAS
DENNEY ISAAC
DENNEY WESTLEY
CHAMBERS NATHANIEL
NICHOLSON SAMUEL
COFFIN NATHANIEL
LAWRENCE OLIVER
SMITH NATHAN
WINSLOW JOHN W
WINSLOW JAMES
MEWBY BENJAMIN
OVERMAN HENRY
WILLIAMS JAMES
WILLIAMS MICAJAH
ARNOLD WILLIAM
McKINNEY PETER SR
McKINNEY RANE
McKINNEY PETER JR
JONES CADWALLADER
WATSON JACOB
WATSON SOLOMON
ROBISON MATTHEW
MORGAN WILLIS
GOODSON JOSEPH
MIZE JOSEPH
LIGGIT WILLIAM
LUMLEY WILLIAM
HOUSH GEORGE
CRISTY SAMUEL
BLAKE KENNETH A
MABOUGH MICHAEL H
ALTSTATT JOHN
LONG JOSEPH
ALTSTATT DANIEL
MOLLICOTT JOHN
HOUSH ANDREW
PERRY WILLIAM
SCAGGS JOHN
SCAGGS ZACHARIAH
PRUETT GEORGE
DePAUW JOHN

DePAUW CHARLES
DePAUW BONAPARTE
RANSOM ISAAC
NIELD DANN
FOSTER WILLIAM
FOSTER JOHN
HOUSH ADAM
PRESTON GEORGE
HOUSH THOMAS
PICKETT JEREMIAH
HUFFMAN FELIX
SIMPSON GEORGE
MILLER PRICE
HINKLE NATHAN
HINKLE SAMUEL
PRICE DERASTUS
GOLDSBY EDWARD
GOLDSBY JOHN
TROW GEORGE D
JOHNSON JAMES
PURSEL WILLIAM
JOHNSON WILFORD
GEORGE JAMES T
RUNNELS EDWARD
BURNET JOHN
HEFNER JOSEPH
ADAMS BENJAMIN
ADAMS JAMES
PURSEL WILLIAM
MYERS DAVID
COLLINS JOHN
SANDERS SIMEON
MILLER MORDICAI
GOLDSBY BRIGS M
DAWSON JAMES
PURSEL REUBEN
GOLDSBY GEORGE
GENTLE WILLIAM
HORNER JOHN
GARDNER EPHRAIM
BRANSON BRISCO D
RUNNELS RICHARD
CHAMBERS WILLIAM
McCLASKEY ISAAC
McCLELLAND JAMES
ELLISON ROBERT
LOWDEN ROBERT
RING MICHAEL
ELLIOTT WILLIAM
GORDON HOWARD
NICHOLSON JAMES B
NICHOLSON LARKIN

WASHINGTON COUNTY

GILCREASE JAMES
DUNCAN CHARLES
DOWNING MICHAEL
BLACKFORD ANTHONY
COFFIN WILLIAM
BROWN WILLIAM
CRITTENDON HENRY
McCLASKEY JOHN
LOGAN EZEHIEL
LOGAN WILLIAM
SMITH WILLIAM
JAMISON GARRETT
JAMISON ALEXANDER
HATTABOUGH GEORGE JR
HATTABOUGH GEORGE SR
HATTABOUGH JACOB
HATTABOUGH PHILIP
HATTABOUGH MARTIN B
WESTON THOMAS
SINK JACOB
LANE WILLIAM
EARLEY JOHN
MONACLE JOHN
ELLISON JAMES
WESTON JOSEPH
MIRE REUBEN
WILSON ALEXANDER
PURSINGER LUKE
MAY REUBEN
FIPPIN ANDREW
ELLIOTT ROBERT
REED WILLIAM G
REED ISAIAH
WILSON JOHN
WILSON CHARLES
WILSON WILLIAM
WILSON WASHINGTON
WILSON HARMON
WILSON JAMES
CARTER JAMES
HEAD ANTHONY
McINTIRE JOHN
McINTIRE WILLIAM
HERRINGTON EZEKIEL
MARKS WILLIAM SR
MARKS WILLIAM
CRACRAFT JAMES
RINKER LEVI
BRANAMAN JACOB
RINKER GEORGE
RHUE ABRAHAM
BOWERS JOHN

RICE DINSEY
McNEELY DAVID
WORLEY FREDERICK
ACRES JESSE
ACRES STEPHEN
ACRES THOMAS
NICHOLSON WILLIAM
McDANNEL JAMES
NEWKIRK RICHARD
LITTLE JOHN
NICHOLSON PETER
NICHOLSON ELIJAH
SANDERS WILLIAM
LOWE ABSOLOM
LOWE THOMAS
MENDENHALL JACOB
WILLIAMS JOHN
STANDLEY JESSE SR
STANDLEY JESSE JR
MERRIDETH JOHN
ROBISON JOHN
COX JEHU
BOND JOHN
MERRIDETH JAMES
MASTERS WILLIAM
MASTERS JAMES
JACKSON THOMAS
NEWBY FRANCIS
SANDY WILLIAM
VEST SAMUEL
PROW CHRISTIAN JR
PROW JOHN
PROW ADAM
PROW CHRISTIAN SR
SPEAKS THOMAS
HOLLER ZACHARIAH
HOLLER JOHN
SPENCER JOHN
SPENCER ROBERT
SELLS WILLIAM
TIPPIN JOHN
TIPPIN GEORGE SR
TIPPIN WILLIAM
TIPPIN GEORGE
BUSH SAMUEL
TIPPIN THOMAS
ROBISON BOOTHE
SPENCER JAMES K
BONTY JACOB
LUCAS JOHN
ROBISON DRURY
WILLIAMS WILLIAM

HOLESAPPLE GEORGE
GREEN THOMAS
DRISKILL ELIJAH
CORNET WILLIAM
McNEELY ROBERT
ROWLAND JOHN
STIGGERWAULT PETER SR
STIGGERWAULT PETER JR
STIGGERWAULT JOHN
SMITH NICHOLAS
VEST JOHN J
KYTE HOSTA
GASKINS JAMES
WEBSTER NICHOLAS
GRAHAM JOHN
KENNEDY ALPHRED
VINEYARD JESSE
SHEPHARD MILES
GHARKINS WILLIAM
RAMSEY JOHN
DRISKILL ELIJAH
WALLACE FLOWRY
MILSAPS MOSES
MILSAPS ROBERT
PADGETT NATHAN
HODGES JOHN
BROWN WILLIAM
NICHOLSON WILLIAM
WHEELER JESSE
WHEELER JAMES
BECK JAMES
GROVES PETER
SHALLOWS DANIEL
LITTLE JEHU SR
LITTLE ADONIJAH
LITTLE RICHARD
MAUZEY GEORGE
FIPS WILLIAM
NICHOLSON THOMAS
FORDYCE CYRUS
PLOUGHMAN HENRY
GRIFFETH BARTLEY
GRIFFETH WILLIAM
GRIFFETH LUKE
LANGDON THOMAS G
GORDON WILLIAM
GORDON HUGH
ZARING PHILIP
VAUGHN ISAAC
HUBBARD JOHN
MOUNTS MATHIAS
STILL MURPHEY D

WASHINGTON COUNTY

GRAHAM HUGH
COOLEY ANUNAH
COOLEY JAMES
POWERS JOSHUA
COOLEY ADONIJAH
RICHARDS MICHAEL
COOLEY JOHN
LANGDON PHILIP
OWENS DAVID
HAWN HENRY
BLUNT SAMUEL
RIDER GEORGE
HARBOLT HENRY
PIERSON MOSES B
GILLESPIE WILLIAM
STOOTSMAN ABRAHAM
COOPER WILSON
CROCKET JOHN
TALBOT JOHN
HUCKLEBERRY PETER
MOUNTS WILLIAM
GARRIOTT WILLIAM
GARRIOTT SIMEON
MOUNT THOMAS
HOGGET PHILIP
HOGGET NATHAN
HOGGET JOSEPH
HOGGET ABNER
MARRS JAMES
JOHNSON RANSON
RATTS HENRY
CARTER JEDDIAH
COOLEY JOHN
MULLINIX ELISHA
HAYS JOSHUA JR
WOOD DANIEL
HAYS JOSHUA SR
GUIE ROBERT
WOOD ABRAHAM
KEYT JOHN
KEYT JESSE
BECK PHILIP
STAGLEY JOHN
HARMON DANIEL
BECK GEORGE SR
HUFMAN PHILIP
BECK ANDREW
BECK JACOB
BECK GEORGE JR
BECK JOHN
DAVIS LEVI
DAVIS VALENTINE

RATTS GODFROY
WRIGHT ELIJAH
BROTHERTON JOHN
BROTHERTON ZACHAUS
GILSTRAP RICHARD
GILSTRAP WILLIAM
GILSTRAP DAVID
MOSS WILLIAM
CANTREL WILLIAM
LEWIS JOHN
SHEETS JACOB
SELLS JOHN
KENNEDY JAMES
SMITH NICHOLAS W
BISHOP GEORGE
BISHOP MICHAEL
CLARK MASTEN G
TULLEY RICHARD
THOMPSON THOMAS
RIDICE AARON
VOYLES ABLE
VOYLES THOMAS
VOYLES MOSES
TOWNSEND SILAS
PARKEY JACOB
SELLS WILLIAM
LEE JAMES
LEE WILLIAM
HOWARD THOMAS
HOWARD ROBERT
TOWNSEND WILLIAM
RALSTON GAVIN
ROBINSON JOHN SR
ROBINSON ROBERT
ROBINSON BERRISFORD
ROBINSON WILLIAM
CROCKET WILLIAM
McKINNEY COLLINS
ROBINSON JAMES
WILCOX AARON
WILCOX DAVID
WILCOX ISAAC
BUREY CHARLES
HENDRICKS WILLIAM
MARRS CHRISTOPHER
SHORT JOHN
BILDERBACK DANIEL
WRIGHT JOHN
FOSSEY JOHN
FOSSEY THOMAS
FOSSEY ROBERT
WRIGHT LEVI

WRIGHT AMOS
GILSTRAP PETER
HYND ISRAEL
SINK PETER
PURLEE JACOB
BRITT NELSON
HUFF GABRIEL
HUDDLESTON SAMUEL
HUDDLESTON IRAM
HUDDLESTON JOB
VOYLES DAVID
VOYLES ROLEN
VOYLES JOSEPH
COWEN MILES
VOYLES DANIEL
HARMON MATTHIAS
HARMON GEORGE
WYNN ISAAC
KELLY ABRAHAM
McKINNEY ARCHABALD
CATTRON VALENTINE
BOWLES ISAAC
BOWLES WILLIAM A
DEAN ELIAS
CATLIN THEODORE
ARMSTRONG JOSEPH
ARMSTRONG ROBERT
JACK SAMUEL
ROYCE FREDERICK
SANDY HENRY
AKINS ANDREW
ROYCE GABRIEL
DITTAMORE JOHN
DITTAMORE MICHAEL
DITTAMORE ADAM
McPHETERS JOHN
McPHETERS JOHN W
HUNTER EDWARDS C
DOOLEY THOMPSON
BROWN JOSEPH
PORTER JOSEPH
JACKSON JOHN
JACKSON WILLIAM
LARGEANT WILLIAM
SWENEY WILLIAM
STUCKER PHILIP
TODD WILLIAM
CASTLE GEORGE
ROBERTS JOHN
BUSEY SAMUEL
MARTIN JOHN
HEADRICH DAVID

WASHINGTON COUNTY

MARTIN NIMOROD
MARTIN SAMUEL
MARTIN JOSEPH
MARSHALL JAMES
WAYMAN EDMUND
SMITH JOHN
SUTTON HENRY
MARTIN JOSEPH JR
MARTIN JAMES
MARTIN ENOCH
MARTIN JAMES JR
STANDAFORD AQUILLA
ELROD JOHN
LUCKENBILL HENRY SR
FRASIER ABMEN
LUCKENBILL HENRY JR
FICUS ADAM
FISCUS PETER
FISCUS HENRY
FULCH ANDREW
FULCH JOSEPH
FISCUS FREDERICK SR
FULCH LEONARD
FLETCHER JOHN
PRINCE DAVID
NEAL JOHN
DAVIS BENJAMIN
ALEXANDER THOMAS
JOHNSON JOSEPH P
GREEN JOSEPH
STEWART SAMUEL
STEWART WILLIAM
SHEETS ANDREW
SHEETS FREDERICK
PHILIPS ABRAHAM
ADAMS FRANCIS
STARR BENJAMIN
STARR SAMUEL
OWENS ENOS
BAKER SAMUEL
BAKER VALENTINE
STRAIN JOHN
STRAIN ROBERT
STRAIN BARNET
WATTS WILLIAM
WATTS JOHN
WATTS BENJAMIN
HAMILTON ARCHABALD
McDADE WILLIAM
BISHOP WILLIAM
BISHOP GEORGE
BUSH JOHN

BILLOPS ROBERT
BROWN WILLIAM
SHEPHERD WILLIAM SR
SHEPHERD REUBEN
SHEPHERD THOMAS
FISCUS FREDERICK SR
CAPELEY GEORGE
GREEN WILLIAM
LANNEN JEREMIAH
THOMAS ENOCH
WYMAN HENRY SR
WYMAN LEONARD
ELROD STEPHEN
BUSH JOSEPH
BUSH DANIEL
WYMAN HENRY JR
WYMAN FREDERICK
MILLER JACOB
SMITH NICHOLAS
SMITH JAMES
OVERTON DANDRIDGE
MARTIN JOHN JR
PAYNE JOHN
MARTIN WILLIAM
HAYNES ANIEL
SHOEMAKER DANIEL
CHAPMAN WILLIAM
BLACKMAN SAMUEL
BLACKMAN THOMAS
MARTIN ABNER
MARTIN JAMES H
CRIM JESSE
STOVER JOHN
McCLURE MATTHEW
GRIMES DANIEL
SHEPHERD JOHN
GLOSSER FREDERICK
SHULTS PHILIP
SCOTT ROBERT
CALLAHAN THOMAS
URMY JACOB
GREER JOHN H
GREER JAMES
PHILIPS FREDERICK
EDDINGTON JOHN
MORCKERT GEORGE
SINK JACOB
HIESTAND JOHN
YOUNG JACOB SR
YOUNG JACOB JR
BEKER JOHN
BOSS FREDERICK

BOSS PHILIP
LUCKENBILL PHILIP
EASTER GEORGE SR
EASTER GEORGE JR
JOHNSON JOHN
WAGGONER GEORGE
WELLS BENJAMIN
WELLS JOSEPH
WELLS WILLIAM
HIGHNOTE HIRAM
FLETCHER VERDAMAN
SHULTS CHRISTIAN
MEDLEE JOSEPH M
HIGHNOTE PHILIP
MITCHEL ELIJAH
MARSH CYRUS J
BYRELEY JACOB
SECHAISE JACOB
HARMON MOSES
EVANS ROBERT
SCOTT DAVID
SCOTT ROBERT
MOTSINGER JACOB
MOTSINGER DAVID
WATTS ALEXANDER
MOTSINGER GEORGE
MANS WILLIAM
MONACLE CHRISTOPHER
MONACLE PETER JR
CARLTON WILLIAM
NEAL JAMES
HEDRICK JACOB
NEWTON JOHN
MAMS SAMUEL
HUMPHREY JAMES
BEALER THOMAS
DOWLAND WILLIAM
GRIFFETH JOSEPH
HAMMERSLEY JAMES
DIXON OZEY
PORTER BENJAMIN
HUGHS JESSE
HUGHS JAMES
WELCH WILLIAM
BROCK LEWIS
BROCK JESSE
SCOTT WILLIAM
SCOTT JOHN
ROBERTS LEWIS
PHIPPS SAMPSON
RICHARDS WILLIAM
VEST SAMUEL SR

WASHINGTON COUNTY

FLEMING JAMES
VEST WILLIAM SR
VEST WILLIAM JR
GRIFFETH HORATIO
JEAN WESTLEY
ROBERTS JOHN
GRIFFETH JAMES
THOMPSON JOSHUA
THOMPSON JOSEPH
ARMS REUBEN
HARRISON THOMAS
STEEL ELI
JENKINS NATHANIEL
BORDEN JONATHAN
MATHER ABNER
CAULKINS JOEL
WHEELER EBENEZER S
BARNARD REWEL
BARNARD SAMUEL JR
ALVORD JAMES
BARNARD SAMUEL SR
BARNARD JOHN
LAMBERT DAVID
ANDREWS SILAS
LEMMON MATTHIAS
LOW SAMUEL
CROSS ELI
HAMMERSLY JAMES SR
HAMMER HUGH
BISHOP SAMUEL
WINTERS TIMOTHY
GRIGGS GEORGE
WILLFONG MICHAEL
SCRITCHFIELD ARTHUR
SCRITCHFIELD ABSALOM
WIRE THOMAS
FERGUSON STEWART
HENDERSON ROBERT
MURPHY JAMES
HORMELL JACOB
HORMELL FREDERICK
LONGMIRE GEORGE
DOLTON JOHN
FARIS JOSHUA
BREDON WILLIAM
PELTON JAMES
HARVEY ROBERT
HARVEY MARMADUKE
HARVEY WILLIAM
HAMMERSLEY ABRAHAM
HEADLEY SAMUEL
WAERS THOMAS

JENKS WELCOME
STURDAVANT JAMES
RAWSON DANIEL
RAWSON ANSON
RAWSON HORRACE
CRISS CHRISTIAN
CHILD EZRA
WILCOX ASHER
CHASE WILLIAM J
MACBEE SAMUEL
CASY JOHN
TRINDLE ALEXANDER
WOODRUFF GAD
LEMMON THOMAS
HARRIS NATHANIEL
DAVIS EZRA
STACY ABRAM
KENNEDY JOHN
HARRIS MICAJAH
CARR ELISHA
CASE JOSEPH
MATTHEW SIMON
MATTHEW NATHAN
CASE WILLIAM
MILLER JONATHAN
JACKMAN DANIEL D
LESTOR EBENEZER
NOGGLE DAVID
CARR ELIJAH
GAMMON JAMES
SMITH JOHN B
SCRITCHFIELD NATHANIEL
SCRITCHFIELD JAMES
SEBRISKEY ABRAHAM
FREED JOSEPH
FREED JOHN
McCULLOUGH MOSES
WIRE JOHN
WALKER AARON
SMITH CHRISTOPHER
GOULD JOHN SR
GOULD JOHN JR
GOULD ADOLPHUS
HUMPHREY WILLIAM
WELCH GEORGE
REED JOSEPH
HUMPHREY JOHN
WALKER ROBERT
McKINNEY ALEXANDER
BRUCE NATHANIEL
BRUCE ELIJAH
CROTTS VALENTINE

WILSON THOMAS
CROUCH AARON
HADON THOMAS
LUCAS JESSE
PEW JOHN
GURLOR JOHN
CROW JOHN
CROUCH JOHN
RICHARDSON THOMAS
SCOTT HARMON
BROWN THOMAS
RUSH BENJAMIN
RICHARDS JACOB
MOORE JOHN SR
MOORE JOHN JR
GIBBENS JAMES
BROWN MICHAEL
MOTSINGER JACOB
SOUDERS CHRISTIAN
SOUDERS JACOB
CROW JOSHUA
WILLIAMS WILEY
HURST JOHN
BULL WILLIAM
WIATT ALLEN
HARBART JOSEPH B
ATKINS ROBERT
DUDLEY RANSOM
DUDLEY JAMES
LOWE FREDERICK
ALLEN ELKENER
ELLIOTT JOSEPH
ELLIOTT JOHN
DEALY JAMES
CARTER JEDDIAH
TESH JOHN
TESH JACOB
LOUGHHUNN HENRY
WORRELL JOHN C
BROCK JOHN
RICHARDSON DANIEL
RICHARDSON JOHN
ARBUCKLE JAMES
OLDS WILLIAM
JOHNSON HENRY
KNIGHT ANDREW
COFFIN LIBNI JR
COFFIN LIBNI SR
CLOUD JOSEPH
WOODARD JONAH
GRACE WILLIAM
GRACE JESSE

WASHINGTON COUNTY

HOLLAND WILLIAM
BUNCH DAVID
BOGLE JAMES
RENNICK HENRY
ROSE JAMES S
BUTCHER JOHN
SMALL SAMUEL
BUTCHER DAVID
WELLS DAVID
WELLS RICHARD
WOODARD JAMES
STORK ABRAHAM
McCRARY WILLIAM
FRAKES JOHN
GUIE ABSALOM
WEAVER JEREMIAH
POPE WILLIAM
ELGIN JESSE
SMALLWOOD ELIJAH
FISHER PETER SR
FISHER HENRY
FISHER JOHN
WALL RICHARD
FISHER PETER JR
SMALLWOOD SAMUEL
BRIDGEWATER DAVID
CARR ELIJAH
COLLINS JOHN
HARRIS THOMAS
RANDLE JOHN
HARRIS JESSE
FOSTER BARTLEY
KENNEDY REUBEN
KENNEDY JAMES
GREEN JOHN
HARRIS JOHN
MEEK SAMUEL
HAYS SAMUEL
ELGIN JESSE JR
ELGIN JOHN
HAYS MOSES
WESTFALL JACOB
WESTFALL ALI
BRIAN WILLIAM
FINLEY HARVEY
HARRIS JOHAH
RICHARSON THOMAS
HARRIS WILLIAM
WELLS WILLIAM
LOVELESS RICHARD
SCOTT JOHN SR
WARE THOMAS

McGREW CHARLES
MARTS JACOB
ASHTON ELIAKIM
WILLIAMS CHARLES
CRAGE JOHN SR
CRAGE JOHN JR
CRAGE THOMAS
SCOTT JOHN C
McGREW JOHN
WEAR WILLIAM
VANCLEAVE SQUIRE
McKINNEY JAMES
ROLLINS GEORGE
GARVEY JOHN
WILLIAMS WILLIAM
MANAHAN JOHN
STARK STEPHEN
STARK WILLIAM
STARK ELISHA
CLARK ABSALOM
STARK LEONARD
WADKINS JESSE
STARK JACOB
SHASTEEN RANEY
RUBISON COLZA
STARK WILLIAM
SHASTEEN ABSALOM
MITCHEL ROBERT
MITCHEL JONATHAN
SWENEY MORDECIA
McCAMEL JAMES
SAPP JOHN
SAPP THOMAS
HOKE HENRY JR
PICKLER JOHN
PICKLER JAMES
GASKINS SAMUEL
HENRY PHILIP
LEE WILLIAM SR
LEE WILLIAM JR
LEE MITCHEL
VANCE DAVID
SMITH JAMES
GREEN PETER
YORK JOSHUA
CHANEY JOHN
GALDBREATH SAMUEL
GRACE RUSSEL
GRACE WILLIAM JR
HOKE HENRY SR
HOKE GEORGE
McGREW JOHN

POTTORFF ANDREW
PATTERSON KENNEDY
CRAWFORD GEORGE
CRAWFORD JAMES
MANNING WILLIAM
HOKE CORNELIUS
MODLIN MARK
STEPHENSON BENJAMIN
SHASTEEN WILLIAM
MODLIN NATHAN
SHASTEEN BERNARD
SHASTEEN DANIEL
SHASTEEN JAMES
SNIDER JOHN
STOCKWELL WILLIAM
MODLIN JAMES
RUBISON RICHARD
MANNIN JAMES
POLLARD ELISHA
EDWARDS GRIFFETH
MURPHY DANIEL
BROWN WILLIAM
CLARK BANESTER
CLARK WILLIAM
RIFE ABRAHAM
COLIER JOHN
COLIER HESEKIAH
COLIER JAMES
LOCKHART WILLIAM
LOCKHART JOSEPH
LOCKHART JOHN
HUNGATE JOHN
SMITH ROBERT
JONES DAVID
PAVEY SAMUEL
MYERS JACOB F
PULLIAM BLAN B
STILTS MOSES
JONES HANBERRY
PULLIAM BENJAMIN
KELSOE HUGH
KELSOE JAMES
COLCLAISER DANIEL
ACRES ABRAHAM
WATSON ISAAC
RILEY JAMES
BROWN BOLING
FERGUSON JESSE
McCOY RICE
WESTFALL HENRY
McCLUNG JAMES
McPHETERS JOHN C

WASHINGTON COUNTY

WALKER WILLIAM
McPHETERS JAMES
KING JACOB
DAINIHUE DANIEL
ATKINSON STEPHEN
ATKINSON ELIJAH
MARTIN WILLIAM W
McPHETERS JAMES SR
McPHETERS ALEXANDER
WILLIAMS JAMES
WYBLE ADAM
ORCHARD ISAAC
BLANCHARD EZEKIELS
BENEDICK DAVID S
REDUS JOHN
RIDGEWAY JOHN
MARTIN WILLIAM
PURKISER SAMUEL
PURKISER JOHN
KITE LEWIS
COLCLASIER DAVID
COLCLASIER JOHN
LEE JONATHAN
CAUBLE PHILIP
DRAKE JOHN
RAY DANIEL
CAUBLE DAVID
CLARK SAMUEL
HAUGER JOHN
HAUGER GEORGE
MARTIN JOHN
WADE JAMES
BANKS BURR
SUTHERLAND ROGER
COLCLASIER ABRAHAM
MITCHEL WILLIAM
PAVEY ANDERSON
WRIGHT ASA
RIDERS JAMES
SCOTT DAVID R
KETCHART PIERSON
YOUNG THOMAS
COLLIER WILLIAM
HUTTON JAMES
HUTTON LEONARD
FORD WILLIAM
DAVIS ISAAC
HASLEY JOHN
HARDMAN JACOB
SELLERS ROBERT SR
SELLERS ROBERT JR
RODMAN HUGH

LITTLE AMOS
TROWBRIDGE DAVID
SCOTT JACOB J
TROWBRIDGE JOHN
NEAL SAMUEL
ROGERS PHILIP
HOOZER WILLIAM
SKELTON JOHN
STRUPE PETER
BOND THOMAS
SPURGIN JESSE
ACRES PAUL
SNIDER JOHN
RIPPLE JOHN
RIPPLE HENRY
SNIDER DANIEL
BRASETTON JOHN
LAGENAUR JOHN
HARDMAN HENRY
MOTSINGER MICHAEL
SOUDERS FREDERICK
WILSON JAMES
McCOY JAMES
LANE JESSE
HUME JOHN SR
HUME THOMAS
RODMAN JAMES SR
HUME JOHN JR
HURST JAMES
LAGENNAUER JACOB
PEELER ALLEN
SNIDER HENRY
RUSSEL JOHN
STEWART JOHN
STEWART WESTLEY
CURTIS BENNET
CAMPBELL GEORGE
GRAY JOSEPH
PHELPS WILLIAM
GRAY JEDUTHAN
GRAY LEWIS
HOSEA WILLIAM
WILLIAM ALEXANDER
CRANFORD ISOM
RUSSEL ARCHABALD
CRANFORD MARVEL
SIDES LEONARD
HUST JOHN A
GREEN WILLIAM
GREEN THOMAS
HURST JAMES
WHITE JOHN

HIGHNOTE ALEXANDER
BURK LUCAS
WHITE WILLIAM
WELCH JAMES
FLOWERS THOMAS
DEWESE DAVID
GODFROY ELIJAH
MANNIN JOHN
MANNIN WILLIAM
HALL WILLIAM
MANNIN JOSHUA
MANNIN DAVID
MARRS WILLIAM
MARRS JAMES
WRIGHT PETER
THORNTON THEOPHELUS
McKEE JAMES
THORNTON SAMUEL
THORNTON LEVI
HARDIN JOHN JR
ELLIOTT HENRY
HARDIN ELISHA JR
HARDIN JOHN JR
ARCHER JAMES S
SIMMONS JOHN SR
SIMMONS JOHN JR
McKINNEY ALEXANDER
REDUS JOEL
GALBREATH THOMAS
YOUNG WILLIAM
YOUNG THOMAS
McINTIRE ROBERT
McCRARY JAMES
LYND JAMES
McINTIRE JAMES
CRAIN ISHABOD G
WAGGONER JOHN
GUTHRIE JOHN
TRINKLE FREDERICK
PHILIPS ROBERT
MAGILL WILLIAM
SHEPHERD THOMAS
MATTOCKS NATHANIEL
TRABUE GEORGE S
NOBLET WILLIAM
MARSHAL JESSE
COULTER CHARLES
DOAN TOMAS
TRINKLE JACOB
JONES WILLIAM SR
JONES WILLIAM JR
JONES JONATHAN

WASHINGTON COUNTY

LOWRY JOHN
SHERWOOD DANIEL JR
SHERWOOD HUGH
HALL RICHARD
EVERETT JOHN
EVERETT JAMES
BOLE THOMAS
NOBLET ABRAHAM
HOLLOWELL ROBERT
HALL JOHN
INMAN JOHN
VANDEVEER ARON
VANDEVEER JOHN
RALSTON ALEXANDER
BROWN THOMAS
McKENSTER JAMES
BRADFORD WILLIAM
LANDUO ISAAC
DENNING WILLIAM
VANLANDINGHAM WM
ANDREWS WILLIAM
CURRY WILLIAM
DENNING JOSEPH
YOUNG EWIS
NEWSOM JOEL
RUTHERFORD WILLIAM
ROBY HENRY
THOMAS HOSEA
WALL ROBERT
WALL EPHRAIM
HAUGER SOLOMON
RUTHERFORD DAVID
ASH JOSEPH
DICKS JOSHUA
HARDIN AARON
HARDIN STEPHEN
WOOD WILLIAM
ANSTOTT JOHN
FUNK CHRISTOPHER SR
COCKRELL ALEX'R
TRINKLE ADAM
SARGENT ABSALOM
CLARK JOHN
HAMMER JOHN
TRINKLE JOHN
DEWESE EVIN
BUTLER JOHN
SHERWOOD DANIEL
SAPP GEORGE
KESTER PAUL
JOHNSON FERGUS
MULLINIX PREMENTER
STIPP JACOB

WALLS WILLIAM
JACKSON SAMUEL
WOODRUM ARCHABALD
SCHNUM JOHN
CAMPBELL CHARLES
HARMON LEVI
ELLIOTT WILLIAM
VANMETER JOSEPH
GADBERRY JAMES
GRUBB JACOB
WRIGHT JOSHUA
BISHOP ABRAHAM
SMITH ABRAHAM
HARRAMAN ELISHA
HARRAMAN CHARLES
HARRAMAN SIMON
VOYLES JOHN
LOFTIN THOMAS
LOFTIN WILLIAM
ROBISON WILLIAM
MISONHAMMER JOHN
GARRETT ANTHONY
NORMAN JOHN
ROW PHILIP
ROW HENRY
ALLIS PETER
BOSTON JACOB
ROYCE MARTIN
CROCKET JOHN R
DILLIN DANIEL
McKINNEY JAMES
BENTLEY THOMAS
ROYCE WILLIAM
ZIGLAR JOHN
KENNEDY JOHN
HARRIS THOMAS
HUSTON JOHN
STARK ARCHABALD
HANEY JOHN
STARK ASAATT
STARK SAMUEL
STARK ASA
WEATHERS THOMAS T
BLACKBURN JOSEPH
MAY GEORGE
MAY JOHN
MOORE HENRY H
MOORE THOMAS M
MOORE JOSEPH
LUCE WARREN
McANELTY OLIVER
ROTHWELL KAY

RICHARDSON IRA
SHERWOOD WILLIAM
NEWSOM JOHN
DONE ARCHABALD
COLCLASIER JOHN
COLCLASIER JACOB SR
COLCLASIER JACOB JR
DOAN JACOB
RANEY SAMUEL
McGREW JAMES
CHINWORTH JOHN
CHINWORTH JOSEPH
ROLLINS ARON
DENNIN ANTHONY
DEREMIAH JOHN SR
RUDE THOMPSON
DEREMIAH JOHN JR
ROLLINS WILSON
POWEL LEWIS
SMITH NICHOLAS S
ROLLINS EDWARD
RATLIFF DAVID
KEY CRASSY D
RATLIFF BENJAMIN
SAVARY HENERY
GRAVES ALVIN
EDWARDS ISAAC D
GREEGG JOHN
HAINS DANIEL
HAINS SAMUEL
HORNER WILLIAM
HORNER JACOB
HORNER GEORGE
SANDERS PETER
LAFERTY PETER
LAFERTY THOMAS
DOLTINE JOHN
KING ELISHA
KING GEORGE
POLSON THOMAS
ROYCE JOHN
VANLANDINGHAM GEORGE
BRANDINGBURGH JACOB
VANLANDINGHAM ELIJAH
WARE WILLIAM
VANLANDINGHAM RICHARD
DENNIN JOSEPH
GRAHAM WILLIAM
SEALES SAMUEL
GREEN ENOCH
GREEN JOHN
BUSH DAVID
KELLEY JAMES

WAYNE COUNTY

REDY CHRISTOPHER	BORELAND WILLIAM	GAY JOHN
WRIGHT RALPH	SENA OWEN	FISHER JOHN
MARLIN ISAAC	WALSON ROBERT	BALDWIN JESSE
FLEMMING PETER	DRAKE JOHN	BALDWIN JESSE SR
COLLINS JOHN	McGRUE ARCHABAL	BRATTON REUBIN
WOODS ANDREW	GAINES ARMSTRONG	JACOBS SAMUEL
CANON DAVID	BURK JOHN JR	BOSWELL LEVI
LANCASTER WRIGHT	SWAIN JOB	ALRED WILLIAM
LAWMAN HENRY	LAMB THOMAS	KEESLIN JOHN
HENDERSON SHEDRECK	HILL ROBERT	GALE WILLIAM S
BALL JANES	PIERSON JOHN	McCLAIN GEORGE
BLACK JAMES	BALDWIN JOHN	BAILEY HENRY
MEEK JOSEPH	PEEL MARK	DECKARD JACOB
JENTRY WILLIAM	JONES JAMES	PIERSON NATHAN
WOODS SAMUEL	CANNEDAY ISAAC	FRORKIN DANIEL
SMITH NATHAN	STEWART JOHN	LAMB WILLIAM
JUSTICE WILLIAM	STANLEY JOHN	GRIMES GEORGE
JOHNSON PETER	BOSWELL JOHN	BRENO SAMUEL
GRINSLEY JOSIAH	SMITH JAMES	WHITAKER WILLIAM
GARNY THOMAS	HILL THOMAS JR	TURNER JOHN
WRIGHT JAMES	MANDLIN ENOCH	NANCE RICHARD
SMALL AMOS	CHARLES JOSEPH	COX WILLIAM
VORAS OLAVER	WASSON ARCHABALD	ADDISON THOMAS
SMITH JAMES	BARKER THOMAS	McCAVINS ABRAHAM
MABET BERRY	MORGAN MICAGAH	CAINE ABIJAH
FISHER ELISHA	MOURON RABER	MARTIN AARON
HOGGET JOHN	RYNARD GEORGE	BOON OVID
HAVERTON THOMAS	BLAIN JOHN	RAMBO ISAAC
WALKER SAMUEL JR	HUTTON THOMAS	HIATT JOHN
BOSWELL SAMUEL	SUTTON ALEXANDER	COX THOMAS
LANCASTER CEEA	WRIGHT RALPH	WILLSON THOMAS
JOHNSON GEORGE	BALDWIN DANIEL JR	MARTIN JAMES
JOHNSON STEPHEN	HENDERSON RICHARD	SMALL JOHN
WILCOT CLARK	VORE JAMES	ALBERTSON JOSHUA
HAMPTON DAVID	BUTLER SAMUEL	MAN JESSE
FISHER THOMAS	BUTLER WILLIAM	WILLIS JOHN
MARTINGILL DAVID	WASSON JOSEPH	MOORE JOHN
CLARK WILLIAM	ALBESON HENRY	CRAIG WILLIAM
HIETT ELEAZAR	AULD JOHN S	KEESLIN DANIEL
LEWIS JOSEPH	WOODEY JOSEPH	DAVESON JOHN
WATKINS JOHN	CREGG RODERICK	HOLMES SAMUEL
TEAGAL JOSEPH	WILKESON JOHN	GREY JOHN
DRAKE JOHN	ALEXANDER JAMES	WOOFTER JAMES
MILLER DAVID	JACOBS ELIJAH	COLLE JOHN
SHARK WILLIAM	McCOMBS JOHN	RALLIFF RICHARD
CHANY NATHAN	VESTAL SAMUEL	RANIGS DAVID
BUTLER LEVI	REESE HENRY	FISHER JAMES
DRAKE MOSES	VENRIDGE GEORGE	ANDERSON JOHN
DEVENPORT JESSE	McBROOM WILLIAM	KEESLEY PETER
CLARK THOMAS	MOOR JOEL	CAMMAC SAMUEL
BUTT EDMOND	COONS JEREMIAH	WOODKIR JOSEPH
FOWLER WILLIAM	JOHNSON JAMES	FRIER JOHN H

WAYNE COUNTY

STEVESON GEORGE
BUNDEY THOMAS
HARPER THOMAS
ALL JOHN S
WILLIAMS BURNARD
DWEGGINS JOSEPH
CAMMINT THOMAS
HONLLEY HEZEKAH
THOMAS ELIJAH
PAXTON JOHN
STEWART ABSALOM
CAIN JOHN
THOMAS BENJAMIN
ROSS WILLIAM
FINDER GABRIEL
FISHER SALVANUS
THOMAS DANIEL
CENADAY SAMUEL
JOHNSON JEDIAH
COOK DAVID
STOODY JACOB
KENWORTHY JOHN
FARLOW SAMUEL
ADDINGTON JOHN SR
BOON RANDEL
WRIGHT JONATHAN
LACEY EPHRAIM
LACEY ELIJAH
SMITH SAMSON
STANBUCK WILLIAM
WHITE JAMES
COMPTON NATHAN
BRADLIN WILLIAM
WATTS RICHARD SR
HALL WILLIAM
BEESLEY THOMAS
CHARLEY JOHN
MENDENHALL FRANCIS
FENDER JONATHAN
SPRINGER DEMUR
BEAUCHAMP ALEX.
SIMMONS WILLIAM
SIMMONS JOHN
NORTH DANIEL
MOORE WILLIAM JR
MOORE MALICHI
ENSLEY ABRAHAM
COMMINS ISAAC
CALEY JOHN
PEEL JOHN
EDWARDS JONATHAN
POTTER THOMAS

JEFFERY JOB JR
BUTLER HIRAM
GRIMES JAMES
BUTLER WILLIAM
JACKSON ISAAC
DECHERS EPHRAIM
MORROW ANDREW
STAR JOHN
BROWN JULIAS
FALBERT JACOB
MADEN JOSEPH
HILL JONATHAN
ELLIOT NATHAN
GARNER BRADLEY
CULBERTSON ROBERT
BUNCH RICHARD
JARVIS BENJAMIN
MENDENHALL JOHN
MURPHY JAMES
ASHLEY ABRAHAM
HUNT JONATHAN
WILLIAMS SAMUEL
ALLMAN MATHEW
RATCLIFF JOSEPH
BISHOP BENJAMIN
SPRINGER JOB
WILLOT WILLIAM
WATSON WM
ROOF PETER
NEWMAN THOMAS
CHAFFIN EVAN JR
HOSIER WILLIAM
HERVEY MICHAEL
BLACK JOHN
JAMES ISAAC
EDWARDS JOHN
WATTS RICHARD
CLARK JOHN JR
HAWKINS JOHN
HORNEY WILLIAM
HORNEY JOHN
JARVIS SAMUEL
HOOVER ANDREW
MESSICK ISAAC
MESSICK DAVID
BRATTAIN JOSEPH
FAWCET BENJAMIN
CUSHMAN BENJAMIN
PRICE HENRY
BEALS JONATHAN
MAGUIRE JAMES
ROBERTS DAVID

PEG JOAB
ELSTON JOSEPH
LAUGH JOHN
PASSON WILLIAM
CARMMAC WILLIAM
HACKET NATHAN
JESSUP ISAAC SR
COMBS ELLIOT
NORTON ELIAS
POOL JOSHUA
EVANS JOHN
SMALL NATHAN
MORRIS JESSE
BERRY JOSEPH
ADDINGTON BISHOP
DRAPER JOSIAH
HAWKINS NATHAN
GRAVES NATHAN
DRAPER JOSIAH JR
PERKINS JAMES
FENDER HENRY
DRAPER JESSE
BURGER JOHN
HARREL GABRIEL
BURGER JOHN L
HILL THOMAS SR
HAWKINS AMOS JR
TEAGLE THOMAS
HARLIN VALENTINE
BURGER SAMUEL
ADDINGTON THOMAS
SPRINGER BARNABAS
GORDON WILLIAM
GARR ABRAHAM
DRAPER JOSEPH
TRINBLE DANIEL
MOORE JOSIAH
WASON SAMUEL
ALBERTSON JESSE
TEISE CHARLES
DINKINGS JAMES
WRIGHT ELIJAH
LESLEY GEORGE
VETAN JONATHAN
BURK JOHN
VATTEAN DANIEL
WILEY EDWARD
HOLLOT JOHN
HOLLMAN EDWARD
LOUGH SAMUEL
GERTIN JEREMIAH
RAPER JOHN

WAYNE COUNTY

ALLEN WILLIAM	BOND JOSEPH	ADDINGTON JAMES
ELIOT EDWARD	WILLIAMS JOHN	STARBUCK JAMES
MEEK JOSHUA	McLEER NATHANIEL	LAMB JOHN
VINCENT CHARLES	CORNER ROBERT	HAM HEZEKIAH
DENT EDMUND	JUSTICE PATRICK	QUEEN HAMPTON
BEACHAM RUSS	HOWEL CHARLES	MARINE JONATHAN
TENKLE HENRY	LEE LEVI	JOHNSON JOSIAH
HARRIS JAMES	JUSTIAN BOHAN	ASHLEY BLADEN
STANLEY JOHN JR	THOMAS STEPHEN	CANS ROBERT
HORNEY JACOB B	MOORE JAMES	WHITE JOSEPH
NEWTON HENRY	SMITH DAVID	ALLTERTSON S'M
HAYLEY HUGH	STEPHENSON JOSEPH	ALEXANDER JOHN
NOCHOLSON JOHN	FLAKE PHILIP	THOMAS STEPHEN SR
ELIOT JOB	BOND BENJAMIN	BLAIR THOMAS
PRICE JAMES	CARMMAC JAMES	HALE JOHN
GRAVE ENOS	ADDINGTON JOSEPH	ARETT ISAAC
STEWART JEHU JR	BLACK ROBERT	WALLS MATHEW
THOMAS BENJAMIN JR	THOMSON ROBERT	PARMER DAVID
WHITE JOHN JR	CONNER LEWIS	MASAIR RICHARD
WILLIAMS RICHARD	JAMES DAVID	MEDCAFF ISAAC
WORD DANIEL	HUNT JOHN S	SUFRINS JOHN
GUEVER AARON	COMER JOHN	PERSON AXSOM
McLANE DAVID	PRICE ALEXANDER	PUGH WM
WILEY THOMAS	RUSSEL JOHN	DILL SAMUEL
CULBERSON THOMAS	JAROT ELI	JACKSON WILLIAM
MINOR GEMISON	WESTERFIELD S'M D	SMITH BENJAMIN
HARLAN ELIHU	BEAUCHAMP MATTEW	MILLR HEZEKIAH
BEASON ISAAC	EAVANS JAMES	NELSON WILLIAM
BENBO JOHN	MINOR WILLIAM	COX JOSEPH
BELL JOHN	KING ELSHA	JOHNSTON GEORGE
ANDREW ROBERT	BEAUCHAMP LEVI	CLARK JOHN
MASON THOMAS	LEWIS S'M D	WILIAMS MORGAN
WALKER THOMAS	SENA JACOB	KINADAY EDWARSE
LAMB JOSIAH	RENO RICHARD	ANDREWS WILLIAM
LONGFELLOW JAMES	RUSSEL GEORGE	GRIMES ALEXANDER
WILLIAMS CALEB	HERVEY BENJAMIN	SHEARER PETER
SMITH GEORGE	HARRISON JOSEPH G	CHENNAULT WILLIAM
ZEEK ADAM	HALL JOHN	HAINEY SOLOMAN
WATTS JOHN	WILLIAMS JOSHUA	WARD THOMAS
HARROL JOHN	HALLOT THOMAS	WASSON NATHANIEL
HARLIN JOSHUA	SENOR OEN JR	ROBERTS PHINEAS
NOORE ALEXANDER	HERVEY EVAN	LYMAN SAMUEL
RUSSEL SAMUEL	ESTEP JAMES	WHITE JOHN SR
HENDERSON SAMUEL	DAVENPORT DAVID	WRIGHT DAVID
HORSON THOMAS	HERVEY CALEB	PRIKER MOSES
MILLS JONATHAN	SHELLY WILLIAM	COGGSWEL LAURANCE
KNIGHT THOMAS	CHARLES S'M	RATLIFF CORNELIUS
WALKER JAMES	HUNTER WM	McLAIN JOHN
SOTT JOHN	GAY JOHN	COX JEREMIAH
McBROOM JOHN	JESSOP ISAAC	GRIMES WILLIAM
PRICE JAMES	BARKER ISAAC	FULBRAITH ROBERT
MOORMAN ELI	MAUDLIN JESSE	CHATTAM JONAH

73

WAYNE COUNTY

SHANE DANIEL JR
HARMON ANDREW
KINDELL HIRAM
BISHOP JOHN
ELSTON JOSIAH
STRONG LEWIS R
BANSAY CHRISTOPHER
BANSAY CHRISTOPHER
WALKER JOHN
ROBERTS THOMAS SR
RATLIFF RICHARD
HANT JOSIAH
TECUMSIRA WILLIAM
ADDINGTON JOHN JR
WALKER SAMUEL
MOFFET JEREMIAH
RATLIFF CORNELIUS
BOND JOSHUA
HAWKINS HENRY
BENTLY JOHN
STANLEY THOMAS
BROODE ELI
PIEKES JOSHUA
BATES HEZAKIA
CLARK DANIEL
ADDISON WILLIAM
HENLEY MICAJAH
STEPPORD THO'S
HOOVER DAVID
COODY CURTIS
WHITE JAMES
GRAVE JESSE
MENDENHALL GRIFFITH
BULLA WILLIAM
BULLA ISAAC
SUALLOW WILLIAM
HOUDESTON JOSEPH
CLANTON WILLIAM
BOSSWEL EZRA
HOLLINGSWORTH NATHAN
HARRIS BENJAMIN JR
ADDINGTON JOSHUA
HUGHS JOHN
HALEY JESSE H
HIATT ELI
OGEN SAM'L
EAST WILLIAM
CLAUSON ABNER
PICKET BENJAMIN
GARRISSON GIDEON
JOHNSON CHARLES
BOND EDWARD

RATLIFF JOSEPH JR
STARBUCK DAN'L
SUTHERLAND JOHN
HIATT WILLIAM
MOORE WILLIAM
COOK THOMAS
WAULLS DRURY
LINOTT JOHN
HENRY JAMES
ALDRIA THOMAS
SMITH JOHN
MARINE CHARLES
HOOVER HENRY
SOGG WALTER
HOLMAN GEORGE
PRICE THOMAS
HARENY WILLIAM
SHUTE SAMUEL
POOL JOHN
McWILLIAMS WILLIAM
BETHELL WILLIAM
VOIE JACOB
WILLIAMS HEZEKIAH
SEXTON JAMES
SCOTT WILLIAM
GARRETT HENRY
DAVENPORT JAMES
VOIE JACOB JR
VOIE JOHN
BOLES EPHRAIM
ROBERTS SOLOMON W
JACOBS WILLIAM
CHARLES SAMUEL JR
GRAVES JACOB
HARVEY JOHN
BOYED ADAM
WILLIS ISAAC
JACOBS WILLIAM
EASTRIDGE EPHRAIM
OWENS PLEASANT
HOOVER FREDERICK
KINDILL THOMAS
COOK WILLIAM
WOODKIRK JOHN
LEUELLIN BENJAMIN
COX HARMON
SWAIN PAUL
SKINER JOSEPH
SCARCE WILLIAM
HARVY AMOS
SMITH JOHN
DILHORN ROBERT

OSBOIRN WILLIAM
BALLA THOMAS
BONIGEN ISAAC
STRATTON BENJAMIN
COX BENJAMIN
HENDERSON JOHN
CLARK WILLIAM
HARTER PHILLIP
THOMAS JOHN
THOMAS PIERCE
JAMES JOHN
MOON DAVID
CARTER CHARLES
HILL WILLIAM
LAMB HOZA
SANDERS JACOB
WEAUP WILLIAM
BANINC JAMES
McLOVE NATHANIEL
HUNT IRA
HUNT BARNABAS
WITT ENOCH
McLOVE DAVID
DOOGAN JOHN
McLOOCE THOMAS
HOOVER ANDREW JR
BALDWIND THOMAS
LONG HARRY M
COMPTON JAMES
SHARP FINDLEY
ROBERTS THOMAS JR
SAUNDERS AARON
PEGG JESSE
JACKSON MICAJAH
BROWN WILLIAM
WARNER ITHAMER
TAYLOR JAMES
BERRY WILLIAM
BODEN WILLIAM
SHARON CALEB
CHALFANT EVAN
PALONOR JOSEPH
HOGGET NATHAN
HILL BENJAMIN
HILL THOMAS
HILL JONATHAN
HAUKINS SILAS SR
NIXON WILLIAM
THOMAS BENJAMIN SR
THOMAS JOHN
WILMOTT JOSEPH
SULLIVAN THOMAS

WAYNE COUNTY

CAMMACK AMOS
BROWN JAMES
DRAKE JAMES
BAILEY STANTON
JOHNSTON WILLIAM
WINSLOW JOHN
BAYS JOHN
HOOVER JOB
HOOVER SAMUEL
GIFFORD ICHABOD
HARRIS JONAS
CRAVER THOMAS
McCOY FRANKLIN
SEDWICK RICHARD
HALLA BENJAMIN
HOLLA RICHARD
HUNT JOHN
CROW DAVID
CARROD THOMAS
FROST EDWARD
WHITE JOHN
WALLS JOHN
BARDNOWER GEORGE
FOULTZ LEVI
SCOTT SAMUEL
SELLS SAMUEL
GRAY COUTTANT
LEWIS JOSEPH
HEATH DANIEL
PUCKET DANIEL
PUCKET BENJAMIN
CROWE ABEL
ENSLY ANAVE
MOORE JOHN
ALEXANDER JOSEPH
McCOY JOHN
JEFFREYS ASA
ALEXANDER SAMUEL
WEEKS WILLIAM
SULLIVAN THOMAS
RANETS JACOB
MEEK WILLIAM
ELLIOTT JOHN
PRICE JEDIAH
JESSOP ABRAHAM
HUTCHINS BENJAMIN
BLOOMFIELD ROBERT
GARR JONAS
GOODEN JOHN
MOON BENJAMIN
RANEBS ABRAHAM
CAIN JOHN JR

MILLER JACOBS
GRAVES JAM'S L
ELLIOTT AXEUM
CARTUP JAMES
MILLER JOHN
BOND ORENEN
BROWN DAVID
BEARD ALEX'R
SHAFFER DAVID
CRIGG RODERICK
LAMBETH AARON
GOOR FIELDING
SHAVEN JOSEPH
GRIFFITH GOOKLY
MILLER MICHAEL
THORNBURGH ABEL
ELLIOTT WASHINGTON
KENDLE CHRISTIAN
WOODARD ASAHU
JONES JOHN A
SYMONS JESSE
BANA SAMUEL
BANA SAMUEL
EASTUP JOHN
HOARAN HENRY
THOMAS JOHN
HUNT JOHN
BRATTON WILLIAM
WIATT BRATON
TOMISSIND IAN
ELLIOTT JACOB JR
LAMB JAMES
COX STEPHEN
SPRINGER MATTHEW
BOND WILLIAM
BOND THOMAS
McBROOM EAUDEA
SEDAELL ATTICUS
SMITH CALEB
McLANE HENRY
WITTIAS THOMAS
LONGFELLA JOHN
JONES ANDREW
STEPHENSON VINCENT
POTTER STEPHEN
CACTON JONAH
HURST STEPHEN
CLANTON AMOS
FISHER JOHN
LENA SAMUEL
DAVIS WILLIAM
RUSSELL ROBERT

DALLY JOHN A
DWIGGINS JAMES
ELLOTE JOB
CLLOTT BENJAMIN
HUNT WM JR
HUNT WILLIAM
HUNT EDWARD
STARBUCK EDWARD
JONES MICAJAH
HAMPTON ANDREW
HARRIS BENJAMIN
BOSWELL BARNIBUS
MEEK JOHN
MORTON JAMES
MASON THOMAS
BUNDY SAM'L
WASSON JOHIAL
WILLIAMS WM
WILLIAMS JESSE
McGUIRE JAMES
LEVINGSTON ANDERSON
BROWN JOSEPH
SUGERS GEORGE
STARBUCK WM
MENDENALL FRANCES
THOMPSON ROBERT
THOMPSON JOHN
ELIOTT NATNAN
HARLEN ELIHU
HARLEN VOLINTINE
HARLEN JOSHUA
BUNKED JOHN
BUNKED ABRAM
JOHNSTON WM
ADLEMAN WM
SAWMAN ALFORD
HENLY HEZEKIAH
KIVITY JOHN C
SUTHERLAND WM
MUNSHED JEREMIAH
PEARSON NATHAN
McARTY THOMAS
MORROW JOHN
COGLE CALEB
CRAMPTON SM'L
JESSOP JACOB
KNIGHT SOLOMON
THOMAS ELIJAH
BOND EDWARD SR
PEGG VOLENTINE
GILBERT JOSIAH
GILBERT THOMAS

WAYNE COUNTY

POTTS SM'L
POTTS EDWARDS
WILSON STEPHEN
HUNT ALLIN
MORGAN MICAJAH
HORNED SM'L
WILCUTS THOMAS
SPREY BENJAMIN
CLARK JAMES
HAMMON WM
BURKET GEORGE
STEPHENS ISAAC
BOLDWIN JOHN
DRAKE ISAH
HARRIS OBEDIAH SR
HARRIS OBEDIAH JR
LEVERTON THOMAS
BEALS JONATHAN
MILLS JAMES
MILLS WILLIAM
MILLS THOMAS
WILMOTT JOSEPH
BALDWIN DANIEL SR
JEFFREY JOB
MARINE JESSE
HAUGH ISRAEL

CLARK JESSE
HAUGH JESSE
HAUGH JOHN
CARTER SOLOMON
HOWEL JACOB
CLARK WILLIAM
CURTIS JONATHAN
CHANCE REEDEN
WALKER ISAAC
LEWIS THOMAS T
GILLMORE JAMES
BLOOMFIELD LETT
HEMMING DAVID J P
WILLMOTT JOSEPH SR
REARDON JAMES
CHARLES DANIEL
BARNS JOHN
HARDON JAMES
MACEY CHARLES
LACEY WILLIAM
LACEY JOHN SR
SPRINGER GEORGE
SPRINGER STEPHEN
FRY AMOS
CHAPMAN ROBERT
GARDNER JESSE

TEASE THOMAS
THOMPSON JOHN SR
TOWNSEND JOHN
MORROD JAMES
BEAUCHAM CALOB SR
HAUGH JAMES
THORNBURGH THOMAS
UNTHANK JOHN
BEAUCHAM WILLIAM JR
VANSANT CHARLES
VANSANT JAMES
WHITEMAN WILLIAM
HIATT DAVID
WARREN ABRAHAM
WYLEY EDWARD
WILEY THOMAS
WILLIAMS SAMUEL
ANTONY DANIEL
FILES SM'L
WHITIKER WM
HARIMAN WM
HARIMAN GEORGE
UNTHARK TEMPLE
WILLIAMS ACHILLIS
MARRURGE JOSIAH

INDEX

A

ABBITT NATHAN		50
ABBOT JOHN		18
ABBOTT JOHN		23
ABBOTT MICHAEL		21
ABECRUMLY ALEXANDER		4
ABEL PETER		36
ABELL FRANCES		1
ABERTE WILLIAM		28
ABLE POLLARD		12
ABRAHAM BOSWELL		39
ABRAHAM THOMAS		36
ACKINS REUBEN		19
ACRE THO'S		17
ACRES ABRAHAM		68
ACRES JESSE		64
ACRES PAUL		69
ACRES STEPHEN		64
ACRES THOMAS		64
ACUFF HOGAN		49
ACUFF JOHN		49
ACUFF JOHN D		49
ADAM JOHN		4
ADAM WILLIAM		56
ADAMS ALLEXANDER		24
ADAMS AMOS		34
ADAMS BENJAMIN		63
ADAMS DAVID		24
ADAMS FRANCIS		66
ADAMS GEORGE		36
ADAMS JAMES		4 63
ADAMS JOHN		28 33
ADAMS L		22
ADAMS PRATER		48
ADAMS SAMUEL		4 24 33 34
ADAMS THOMAS		33
ADAMSON ABRAHAM		36
ADAMSON DAVID		36
ADAMSON JONATHAN		39
ADAMSON MORDECAI		36
ADAMSON SIMON		9
ADDAMS CHARLES		50
ADDINGTON BISHOP		72
ADDINGTON JAMES		73
ADDINGTON JOHN JR		74
ADDINGTON JOHN SR		72
ADDINGTON JOSEPH		73
ADDINGTON JOSHUA		74
ADDINGTON THOMAS		72
ADDISON THOMAS		71
ADDISON WILLIAM		74
ADEASON SETH		4
ADLEMAN WM		75
ADMINES JESSE		19
ADYLOTT PARKER		59
AGAN WILLIAM		43
AGANS WILLIAM		42
AGELL JAMES		24
AGINS J		13
AIGNER FREDERICK JR		53
AIGNER FREDERICK SR		53
AKIN DAVID		57
AKIN JAMES		4
AKINS ANDREW		65
AKINS JOSEPH		51
AKINS REUBEN		15
AKINS WILLIAM		15
ALBEERTSON ELIAS		61
ALBERT MARTIN		27
ALBERTSON BENJAMIN		61
ALBERTSON ELIAS		62
ALBERTSON JESSE		72
ALBERTSON JOHN		63
ALBERTSON JOSHUA		61 71
ALBERTSON NATHAN		62
ALBERTSON THO'S		12
ALBESON HENRY		71
ALBRIGHT ADDAM		50
ALBRIGHT JOHN		50
ALBRIGHT WM		50
ALBY PETER		21
ALCORN THOMAS		4
ALDERSON MOSES		40
ALDREDGE JOHN		4
ALDREDGE WM		16
ALDRIA THOMAS		74
ALDRIGE DENNIS		14
ALEXANDER JAMES		14 51 71
ALEXANDER JOHN		4 36 51 73
ALEXANDER JOSEPH		75
ALEXANDER REUBEN		9
ALEXANDER SAMUEL		75
ALEXANDER THOMAS		66
ALEXANDER W R		16
ALEXANDER WALKER		1
ALEXANDER WILLIAM		18
ALEXANDER WM		51
ALEXANDER ZEBULON		36
ALISON JOHN G		36
ALL JOHN S		72
ALLCORN JOHN		15
ALLEN ARCHIBALD		43
ALLEN ARCHIBALD		1
ALLEN BALAS		56
ALLEN CHARLES		35
ALLEN CLEMANT		4

ALLEN	DANIEL				42
ALLEN	DANIEL C				58
ALLEN	DAVID				46
ALLEN	ELKENER				67
ALLEN	ISAAC				59
ALLEN	JAMES				62
ALLEN	JOHN	3	20	23	42
ALLEN	JOSEPH	10	29	44	60
ALLEN	JOSIAH				23
ALLEN	LEWIS				39
ALLEN	MONTGOMERY				56
ALLEN	MOSES				19
ALLEN	ROBERT			49	59
ALLEN	WILLIAM		17	23	73
ALLEN	WM				51
ALLGOOD	PRESLEY				44
ALLIGUE	JILES				43
ALLIN	JOHN				46
ALLIS	PETER				70
ALLISON	JA'S SR				10
ALLISON	JAMES				14
ALLISON	JAMES JR				10
ALLMAN	MATHEW				72
ALLON	GASHAM				4
ALLTERTSON	S'M				73
ALMON	THO'S JR				49
ALMON	THO'S SR				49
ALMY	HUMPHRY				30
ALMY	PHILLIP				29
ALMY	SENICA				28
ALRED	WILLIAM				71
ALREDGE	AARON JR				51
ALREDGE	AARON SR				50
ALREDGE	ELIJAH				50
ALREDGE	EZEKIEL				50
ALREDGE	HENERY				50
ALREDGE	JOHN SR				50
ALREDGE	PASSON				50
ALREDGE	RHEUBEN				50
ALREDGE	SAM'L JR				50
ALREDGE	SAM'L SR				51
ALREDGE	WM				50
ALREDGE	WM JR				50
ALSOP	JOHN				36
ALSOP	REUBIN				4
ALSOP	WILLIAM				4
ALSPAUW	DAVID				40
ALTON	BENJAMIN				32
ALTON	JAMES				32
ALTON	JOHN				32
ALTON	JOHN SR				32
ALTON	JOSEPH				32
ALTSTATT	DANIEL				63
ALTSTATT	JOHN				63

ALUSON	JAMES				48
ALVEY	HENERY				46
ALVEY	JOHN B				46
ALVEY	THOMAS G				46
ALVIS	DAVID				61
ALVORD	JAMES				67
AMBY	JOHN				19
AMES	AARON				16
AMICK	PHILIP				50
AMINON	WILLIAM				63
AMMON	RUPHAS				10
AMMONS	THOMAS				18
AMOS	JOHN				18
AMOUS	WILLIAM				3
AMUEL	JASON				47
ANDERSON	ALEX'R				18
ANDERSON	ALEXANDER				60
ANDERSON	DANIEL				36
ANDERSON	GEORGE			24	36+
ANDERSON	GEORGE JR				36
ANDERSON	ISAAC			36	57
ANDERSON	JA'S				10
ANDERSON	JAMES	4	16	17	18
ANDERSON	JAMES		23	51	54
ANDERSON	JOHN	16+	18	57	71
ANDERSON	NOAH				42
ANDERSON	ROBERT				36
ANDERSON	SAMUEL				46
ANDERSON	SPEAIR				39
ANDERSON	THOMAS			16	58
ANDERSON	WILLIAM	14	16	18	23
ANDERSON	WILLIAM T				36
ANDIE	JOHN				39
ANDREW	JAMES				36
ANDREW	ROBERT				73
ANDREWS	ANSON S				51
ANDREWS	JAMES				34
ANDREWS	JOSIAH				24
ANDREWS	LUMAN				55
ANDREWS	SILAS				67
ANDREWS	STEPHEN				21
ANDREWS	WILLIAM	1	34	70	73
ANIKLE	BARNABAS				50
ANKERMAN	ANDREW				46
ANNABLE	SAMUEL				58
ANNIBLE	BRUMLY				50
ANNICE	JACOB				59
ANSON	MONTGOMERY				46
ANSTOTT	JOHN				70
ANTHIS	FRANCIS				35
ANTHIS	JACOB				35
ANTHIS	JOHN				35
ANTHONY	HIRAM				35
ANTHONY	JAMES				57

Name	Page
ANTHONY JOHN	57
ANTONY DANIEL	76
APPLEGATE HESAKIAH	12
ARBUCCLE JOHN	9
ARBUCCLE THO'S	9
ARBUCKEL MATHAN	24
ARBUCKLE JAMES	67
ARBUCKLE JOHN	16
ARBUCKLE NATHAN	18
ARBURTHNOT JOHN	4
ARCHABALD JOHN	46
ARCHER EDWARD	36
ARCHER JAMES S	69
ARCHER JOHN	36
ARCHER THOMAS	4
ARCHER WILLIAM	4
ARETT ISAAC	73
ARION COPELAND J L	21
ARMFIELD JONATHAN	62
ARMS REUBEN	67
ARMSPAW EACH LEONARD	27
ARMSTRONG ALEXANDER	36
ARMSTRONG ANDREW	29
ARMSTRONG BENONI	63
ARMSTRONG DAVID	36
ARMSTRONG EDWARD	36
ARMSTRONG ELSBURY	52
ARMSTRONG FELIX	41
ARMSTRONG HAWES	36
ARMSTRONG JOHN	36 59
ARMSTRONG JOHN JR	59
ARMSTRONG JOSEPH	65
ARMSTRONG KIRBY	59
ARMSTRONG LANTY F	19
ARMSTRONG ROBERT	58 65
ARMSTRONG THOMAS	20
ARMSTRONG WILLIS	4
ARNALD JOHN	23
ARNETT SAMUEL	17
ARNOLD BENJAMIN	36
ARNOLD JOHN	23 61
ARNOLD JOSEPH	23
ARNOLD WILLIAM	63
ARTHUR - - -	39
ARTHUR ELIAS	10
ARTHUR JOHN	39
ARTHUR JOSEPH	36
ARTMAN JOHN	46
ASBY BARTLETT	31
ASDALE ROBT	16
ASH JAMES	4
ASH JOSEPH	70
ASH PATRICK	28
ASH ROBERT	4
ASH THOMAS L	4
ASHBY NOAH	32
ASHLEY ABRAHAM	72
ASHLEY BLADEN	73
ASHLEY JOHN	49
ASHLEY THO'S	52
ASHTON ELIAKIM	68
ASHWORTH CHRISTOPHER	50
ASHWORTH JOHN	50
ASHWORTH JOHN SR	50
ASHWORTH NATHAN	50
ASKINS EDWARD	46
ASPON WM	11
ATHENS JOSEPH	45
ATHERINGTON HENRY	4
ATHERLON ISRAEL	48
ATHRON JETHREN	23
ATHRON WILLIAM	23
ATKINS ROBERT	67
ATKINSON ELIJAH	69
ATKINSON JAMES	42
ATKINSON JOHN	42
ATKINSON JOSHUA	19
ATKINSON STEPHEN	69
ATKINSON THOMAS JR	40
ATKINSON THOMAS SR	40
ATTIZER ELIAS	51
ATWOOD JAMES B	36
AUBREY THOMAS N	1
AULD JOHN S	71
AULSIK JOHN	8
AUSTIN DANIEL	34
AUSTIN JOSEPH	34
AUSTIN STEPHEN	56
AUSTIN THISON	56
AUSTIN THOMAS	34
AUTERIETH CHRISTIAN	53
AUTERIETH ENGELHARD	53
AUTERIETH FERDINANT	53
AUTRIGHT FERDOMON	36
AVERRY D	58
AVLIGNE LAUREAU	28
AYRES AZERIAH	4
AYRES CHRISTOPHER	4
AYRES HENRY	4
AYRES ISAAC	58
AYRES NATHANIEL	50

B

BABB STEPHEN		1
BABB WILLIAM		1
BABBETT STEPHEN		27
BABBIT CHARLES		8
BABCOCK ORLOW		60
BABCOCK PELAGE		27
BABER HENRY B		27
BACKEY SAMUEL		27
BACKMAN E		20
BACKMAN LEWIS		21
BACKSTER DANIEL		13
BACKSTER JAS		13
BACON AARON		50
BACON EDMON		50
BADGELY ANTHONY		20
BADGER WILLIAM		33
BADGLEY BENJAMIN		20
BADOLOTT JAMES		30
BADOLOTT JOHN		30
BADOLOTT SIDENNY		30
BAILEY AARON		17
BAILEY EDWARD		44
BAILEY HENRY		71
BAILEY HENRY m\o		9
BAILEY J		22
BAILEY JOSEPH		13
BAILEY JUSTICE		45
BAILEY ROBERT		31
BAILEY SETH		16
BAILEY STANTON		75
BAILS WILLIAM		42
BAILY HENRY		9
BAILY JOHN	1	18
BAILY JOHN JR		28
BAILY JOHN SR		28
BAILY SAMUEL		18
BAILY THOMAS		28
BAINER PETTER		35
BAIRD ARCHIBALD		32
BAIRD ROBERT		22
BAIRD THOMAS		32
BAIRD WILLIAM		61
BAITH JOHN		34
BAKEN ELIJAH		51
BAKER DANIEL		42
BAKER E R		58
BAKER ELIGAH		24
BAKER ESRA		21
BAKER FREDRICK		45
BAKER JOEL		24
BAKER JOHN		34 35 50
BAKER JOHN L		53
BAKER JOHN S		58
BAKER JOSIAS		36
BAKER MICHAEL		61
BAKER MORRIS		24
BAKER NATHANIEL		33
BAKER PELEY		24
BAKER RICHARD		10
BAKER ROMELIUS L/S		53
BAKER SAMUEL		66
BAKER THOMAS		56
BAKER VALENTINE		66
BAKER WILLIAM		4 20 24 44
BAKER WM		15
BALDEN WM W		52
BALDIN SAMUEL		16
BALDING JOSEPH		33
BALDWIN ALONSON		59
BALDWIN DANIEL JR		71
BALDWIN DANIEL SR		76
BALDWIN JACOB		12
BALDWIN JAMES		4
BALDWIN JESSE		71
BALDWIN JESSE SR		71
BALDWIN JOHN		12 71
BALDWIN JOSEPH		59
BALDWIN LEMUEL		4
BALDWIN THOMAS		46
BALDWIN WILLIAM		46
BALDWIND THOMAS		74
BALES EDWARD		36
BALES JAMES I		36
BALES JAMES II		36
BALL JANES		71
BALLA THOMAS		74
BALLARD JOHN		24
BALLARD URIAS		24
BALSOVER JA'S		57
BALSOVER JOHN		57
BALTHIS GEORGE		32
BALTHIS JOHN C		32
BAMESBARGER JOHN		53
BAMFORD MOSES		35
BANA SAMUEL		75+
BANDY JOHN		15
BANE SAML		13
BANEE ROBT		13
BANER FREDERICK		57
BANFIELD JOHN		24
BANIER JOHN		35
BANINC JAMES		74
BANKS BURR		69
BANNON JOSEPH		1
BANSAY CHRISTOPHER		74+

BANTA JOHN		15
BANTZ GEOGE W		21
BANTZ WILLIAM		21
BARANY JOHN		24
BARBER HENRY		58
BARBER T		19
BARBO FRANCIS		30
BARBRE ELI		46
BARBRE JESSE		46
BARBRE PETER		46
BARDNOWER GEORGE		75
BARGE WILLIAM		24
BARGER ABRAHAM		46
BARIONS ERICK		29
BARKER AB'N		57
BARKER DAVID		21
BARKER FRANK		59
BARKER HENRY		1
BARKER ISAAC	33	73
BARKER JESSE		4
BARKER MOSES		46
BARKER STEPHEN		60
BARKER THOMAS	36	71
BARKER WILLIAM		4
BARKER WM		15
BARKMAN HENRY		34
BARKMAN JOHN		34
BARLAW SAMUEL		46
BARLOW SAMUEL K		36
BARNARD JOHN		67
BARNARD REWEL		67
BARNARD RICHARD		32
BARNARD SAMUEL JR		67
BARNARD SAMUEL SR		67
BARNES JOHN	24	36
BARNES LEONARD		18
BARNET ADAM		62
BARNET ALEXANDER		1
BARNET HUMPHREY		57
BARNET JACOB		62
BARNET JAMES		1
BARNET JETHRO		62
BARNET JOHN		62
BARNET WILLIAM		1
BARNETT BYRUM		17
BARNETT CHARLES W		22
BARNETT MARK		28
BARNOTT JAMES		4
BARNS DAVID		24
BARNS JOHN		76
BARNS REUBEN		18
BARNS THOMAS		1
BARNUM BARNEY		24
BARR HENRY		24

BARR JOHN	4	15	45
BARR SAMUEL H			28
BARR WILLIAM			4
BARRETT ABRAHAM			24
BARRETT GEORGE			49
BARRETT JONATHAN			24
BARRONS FREDRICK			24
BARROW JOSEPH			28
BARROWS THOMAS			1
BARRY ROBERT			17
BARTEN JOSEPH			1
BARTER RICHARD			50
BARTER WM			50
BARTIN THO'S			51
BARTLE JOHN			15
BARTMAS JOHN			52
BARTON ALEXANDER			51
BARTON DANIEL			51
BARTON DAVID			4
BARTON JOHN			51
BARTON ROBT			14
BARTON ROSWELL			13
BARTON SAM'L			51
BARTON WILLES			51
BARTON WM			51
BASS ARTHUR			62
BASS WILLIAM			33
BASSET WILLIAM			55
BASSETT ELISHA			19
BASSETT THOMAS			55
BASTEN JAMES			1
BATES ALFRED			14
BATES HEZAKIA			74
BATES ISACHOR			35
BATES JACOB			36
BATES JESSE			53
BATSON JONATHAN			29
BATTELL CHARLES J			51
BATTERTON HENRY			36
BATTERTON PETER			36
BATTERTON WILLIAM			36
BATTSMON PETER			51
BAUER CHRIS'N			53
BAUER GEORGE			53
BAUER JACOB			53
BAXTER DANIEL			20
BAXTER JAMES			22
BAYLEY CHESLEY			36
BAYLEY HENRY			36
BAYLEY JAMES			36
BAYLEY S NATHAN			22
BAYLEY THOMAS			36
BAYS JOHN			75
BEACH JOHN			58

Name	Page
BEACHAM RUSS	73
BEACHAMP JOHN	42
BEACHBOARD WM	23
BEACHER ALVA	10
BEACHER THO'S	10
BEALER THOMAS	66
BEALS JONATHAN	72 76
BEAMAN CARTER	28
BEAMEN LYONS	28
BEAN STEPHEN	49
BEAN WM	49
BEAR CHRISTIAN	22
BEAR HENRY	17
BEARD ADAM	43
BEARD ALEX'R	75
BEARD SAMUEL	4
BEARDSLEY JOHN	47
BEARS ANDRUS	3
BEASON ISAAC	73
BEATTY WM A	9
BEAUCHAM CALOB SR	76
BEAUCHAM WILLIAM JR	76
BEAUCHAMP ALEX.	72
BEAUCHAMP LEVI	73
BEAUCHAMP MATTEW	73
BEBBY ALLEN	3
BEBEE DUDLY	22
BEBY ALLEN	2
BECK ANDREW	65
BECK GEORGE JR	65
BECK GEORGE SR	65
BECK JACOB	65
BECK JAMES	43 64
BECK JOHN	65
BECK PHILIP	65
BECK STEPHEN	21
BECKEHAMMER JOHN	9
BECKER JACOB	53
BECKER PHILIP	53
BECKES BENJIMIN V	34
BECKNELL ALFRED	31
BECKNELL JOHN	31
BECKNELL McGAJAH	31
BECKNELL MUMFORD	31
BECKS BENJAMIN V	4
BEDELL ELIAS	33+
BEDELL WILLIAM	33
BEDLE LUTHER	9
BEDSTER JOHN	43
BEDWELL JOHN	3
BEEBE DUDLEY	15
BEEBE FREDERICK	15
BEEBE SYLVESTER	15
BEEBE TIMOTHY	15
BEEM MICHAEL JR	8
BEEM MICHAEL SR	8
BEEM RICHARD	8
BEERS DAVID S	48
BEESLEY THOMAS	72
BEIPER BOSSILIUS	53
BEIPER GEORGE	53
BEIPER ROMANUS	53
BEKER JOHN	66
BELCHER JAMES	39 41
BELCHER JESSE	1
BELCHER JOHN	45
BELDING AARON	12
BELDING AARON O	12
BELDING G H	21
BELL DAVID	49
BELL JOHN	1 73
BELL WILLIAM	27
BELLINGS INCREAS	35
BELT ASBURY	54
BELT HENRY	54
BELT JOHN	54
BENBO JOHN	73
BENDOW JOHN	25
BENEDICK DAVID S	69
BENEDICT JOHN	32
BENEFIELD GEORGE	14
BENEFIELD GEORGE SR	14
BENEFIELD WILLIAM B	20
BENGAMAN CHRISTIAN	40
BENHAM JAMES	54
BENNEFIELD GEORGE	16
BENNEFIELD WILLIAM	14
BENNET JAMES T	3
BENNET JOHN	24
BENNET ROBERT	24
BENNET SAMUEL	24
BENNET WILLIAM	24
BENNETT BROOK	21
BENNETT HEZEKIAH	4
BENNETT JAMES	53
BENNETT JAMES W	32
BENNETT JOESPH	53
BENNETT JOHN	53
BENNETT LEGNO	53
BENNETT LEWIS	4
BENSON DAVID	52
BENSON JOHN	4 20
BENSON NATHAN	42
BENSON SAMUEL	42
BENSON WILLIAM	4
BENSON WM	59
BENSONS CHARLES	57
BENTEL ARNOLD	53

BENTEL GEORGE JR	53	
BENTEL GEORGE SR	53	
BENTEL ISRAEL	53	
BENTLEY BASEL B	21	
BENTLEY JAMES	58	
BENTLEY JOSEPH	55	
BENTLEY THOMAS	70	
BENTLY JOHN	74	
BENTLY WILLIAM	1	
BENTON DAVID	10	
BENTON EDWIN	20	
BENTON HENRY	10	
BENTON WALTER	10	
BENTZ GEORGE	53	
BENUM JOHN	31	
BENZENHEFER JACOB	53	
BENZENHEFER MICHAEL	53	
BENZINGER CONROD	54	
BERDSLEY JOHN	48	
BERGEN CHRISTOPHER	14	
BERGEN GEORGE	14	
BERKEY CHRISTIAN	9	
BERKEY HENRY	9	
BERNETT JOHN	4	
BERON HENRY	27	
BERRY JAMES	14	
BERRY JOHN	36	
BERRY JOSEPH	36 72	
BERRY WILLIAM	36 74	
BERRY WILLIAM G	41	
BESHEARS REASON	16	
BESLEY SAMUEL	1	
BESSON JOHN	53	
BEST JOHN	46	
BETHEL CLOUD T	39	
BETHELL WILLIAM	74	
BICE JOHN	19	
BICKEL ISRAEL	32	
BICKERSON JESSE	16	
BICKERSON LAMBERT W	23	
BIDDEC ALLEN	31	
BIDLEMAN SAMUEL	4	
BIELS DAVID	1	
BIELS JOSEPH	1	
BIGGS JOSEPH	24	
BIGLER DAVID	21	
BILDERBACK DANIEL	65	
BILDERBACK JOHN	34	
BILLOPS ROBERT	66	
BILLUE JAMES	8	
BINDER SAMUEL	21	
BINGAMAN JOHN	44	
BINGAMAN PETER	44	
BINGHAM WILLIAM	4	
BINKET JOHN	59	
BIRD JOHN	50	
BIRD JONATHON	1	
BIRD MASON	1	
BIRD THOS	13	
BIRYEAR FRANCIS	30	
BISHOP ABRAHAM	70	
BISHOP BENJAMIN	72	
BISHOP GEORGE	65 66	
BISHOP JOHN	74	
BISHOP MICHAEL	65	
BISHOP PRESTON	60	
BISHOP SAMUEL	67	
BISHOP WILLIAM	66	
BLACBURN HUGH	4	
BLACK EZEKIL	52	
BLACK JAMES	51 71	
BLACK JOHN	29 50 72	
BLACK RICHARD	1	
BLACK ROBERT	4 7 73	
BLACK SAMUEL	46	
BLACK THO'S	50	
BLACK THO'S P	50	
BLACK WM	50	
BLACK WM JR	49	
BLACKBELL PETTER	34	
BLACKBURN EPHRAIM	1	
BLACKBURN JOSEPH	70	
BLACKFORD ANTHONY	64	
BLACKFORD ISAIAH	16	
BLACKMAN MR	57	
BLACKMAN NATHANIEL	28	
BLACKMAN SAMUEL	66	
BLACKMAN THOMAS	66	
BLACKMORE DAWSON	19	
BLACKWOOD JA'S	9	
BLAIN ABNER	36	
BLAIN JAMES 3	46	
BLAIN JOHN	71	
BLAIN JOHN	48	
BLAIN ROBERT	36	
BLAIR BEVERLY	55	
BLAIR ENOS	36	
BLAIR JA'S	12	
BLAIR JOHN	12	
BLAIR RICHARD	56	
BLAIR THOMAS	73	
BLAKCBURN THOMAS	30	
BLAKE GEORGE	18	
BLAKE KENNETH A	63	
BLAKE LEWIS	18	
BLAKE THOMAS H	28	
BLAKE WILLOBY	43	
BLAN JAMES	13	

BLANCHARD ENOCH	45
BLANCHARD EZEKIELS	69
BLANCHARD ROSWELL	24
BLAND ABEL JR	11
BLAND ABEL SR	11
BLAND BENJAMIN	9
BLAND FRANCIS	43
BLAND HENRY	43
BLAND JOHN	11
BLAND MOSES	11
BLAND THO'S	11
BLAND THOMAS	40
BLAND WILLIAM	43
BLAND WM	11
BLANEY DANIEL T	27
BLANK FRANZ	53
BLANKENBAKER SAMUEL	60
BLANKENSHIP ISOM	18
BLANKENSHIP JAMES	17
BLANKENSHIP LEWIS	24
BLANKENSHIP WILLIAM	23
BLANKINSHIP ISEAH	24
BLEDSOE PTOLEMY	42
BLETHING DANIEL	35
BLEVINS WARREN	41
BLEVINS WM	59
BLISS JA'S	9
BLITHE ANDREW	4
BLIZZARD WM	52
BLOOMER JOHN R	21
BLOOMFIELD LETT	76
BLOOMFIELD ROBERT	75
BLOOMFIELD SAMUEL	36
BLOSS DORMON	12
BLUHM JOHN	54
BLUNT SAMUEL	65
BLUNT THEOFFILUS	49
BLY MESOM	1
BOARDMAN SYLVESTER	58
BOAS GEORGE	11
BOAS HENRY JR	8
BOAS HENRY SR	8
BOATMAN HENRY	56
BOBERTS HARVEY	27
BODDOLETT ALBERT	28
BODEN WILLIAM	74
BOEHM CONROD	53
BOEHM EUSEBUIS	53
BOFFMAN JACOB	11
BOGARD BENJAMIN	1
BOGARD JACOB	49
BOGARD JAMES	1
BOGLE JAMES	68
BOGUE AARON	62

BOGUE JESSE		62
BOGUE MARK		62
BOGUE NATHAN		62
BOHANNON JAMES		51
BOHANNON WILEY		52
BOHANON NATHAN		36
BOICOURT SAMUEL L		4
BOIES JA'S A		58
BOIL WM		51
BOILES CHAS ALLEN		29
BOILES JOHN		4
BOILS SIMON		46
BOLDWIN JOHN		76
BOLE THOMAS		70
BOLES EPHRAIM		74
BOLIN ELET		48
BOLING JAMES		46
BOLING JOHN	48	59
BOLING MICHAEL		58
BOLING WILLIAM		48
BOLO FRANCIS		30
BOLO MABB		29
BOLUE PETTER		28
BOMAN JOHN		51
BOMAN WM		46
BOND BENJAMIN		73
BOND EDWARD		74
BOND EDWARD SR		75
BOND JOHN		64
BOND JOSEPH	33	73
BOND JOSHUA	33	74
BOND ORENEN		75
BOND THOMAS	69	75
BOND WILLIAM		75
BONDURANT NOAH		13
BONER HENRY		21
BONER JOHN		24
BONIGEN ISAAC		74
BONNAR WILLIAM		27
BONNER DAVID		29
BONNER JAMES		33
BONNET FRANZ		53
BONNET JOHN		53
BONO FRANCIS		30
BONO JOHN BT		28
BONTE CORNELIUS		13
BONTEN STEPHEN		28
BONTY HENRY		54
BONTY JACOB	54	64
BOOHAR DANIEL		54
BOON OVID		71
BOON RANDEL		72
BOON WILLIS		14
BOONE HEZEKIAH		42

BOONE JOEL		11
BOONE WANTLEY		1
BOONE WILLIAM		36
BOOTH BEEBEE		61
BOOTH JOHN		14
BOOTHE WADE		40
BOOTHIS WILLIAM		28
BORAN EZEKIEL		52
BORDEN GAIL		17
BORDEN JOHN		54
BORDEN JONATHAN		67
BORELAND EDWARD		36
BORELAND WILLIAM		71
BORER VALINTINE		46
BORING ABSOLAM		4+
BORING GEORGE		4
BORING JOHN		4
BORING JOHN D		4
BORING NICHOLAS		4
BORIOURT THOMAS		21
BORRELL JOHN		24
BORRWAY JOHN MARY		30
BORRWAY LAMBAIR		30
BORWAY JOHN		28
BORWAY LOMBAR		28
BOSLEY ABRAHAM		41
BOSORE GEORGE		41
BOSS FREDERICK		66
BOSS JOHN		24
BOSS PHILIP		66
BOSSWEL EZRA		74
BOSTON JACOB		70
BOSWELL BARNIBUS		75
BOSWELL JOHN	21 57	71
BOSWELL LEVI		71
BOSWELL SAMUEL		71
BOTTINGHOUSE JOSEPH		46
BOTTOMS THO'S		8
BOTTOMS WM		13
BOUDINOTT ELISHUA		28
BOUGH JOSEPH		36
BOULTONHOUSE JOHN		62
BOURDELOW ENIAS		30
BOURDELOW PIERRE		30
BOURDELOW RAME		30
BOURLAND JAMES		36
BOURLAND JOHN		36
BOWEN ISAAC		36
BOWEN J H		13
BOWERS GEORGE		33
BOWERS JOHN		64
BOWERS SHELDRAN		58
BOWERS SOLOMON		60
BOWLES ISAAC		65

BOWLES MATHIAS C		30
BOWLES WILLIAM A		65
BOWMAN GEORGE		4
BOWMAN JAMES		1
BOYCE JAMES		55
BOYCE WILLIAM		55
BOYD ANDREW		48
BOYD ARCHIBALD		43
BOYD BENJAMIN		18
BOYEAU GABRIEL		30
BOYEAU LEWEY		30
BOYED ADAM		74
BOYER TIMOTHY		60
BOYERYON NICHOLAS		29
BOYLE GEORGE		24
BOYLE JOHN	24	52
BOYLS JOHN		35
BOZARD WILLIAM		55
BOZARTH JAMES		51
BRACHEN JOSEPH		36
BRACHNEY ELI		3
BRACKEN JOHN		24
BRACKENRIDGE THOMAS		40
BRACKEY SAMUEL		24
BRACKNEY HUDSON		44
BRADA CHARLES		22
BRADFORD WILLIAM		70
BRADGELEY JOHN		19
BRADING JAMES		4
BRADLEY BURR		61
BRADLEY DAVID		50
BRADLEY ELIJAH		52
BRADLEY ISAAC		22
BRADLEY JOHN		50
BRADLEY WM		11
BRADLIN WILLIAM		72
BRADLY VALENTINE I		28
BRADSHAW PLEASANT	15	20
BRADY CHARLES		14
BRADY JOHN		29
BRADY THORNTON		43
BRALY JOHN		22
BRAMAN GEORGE		61
BRAMAN JA'S		9
BRAMWELL JOHN		13
BRANAMAN CHRISTIAN		62
BRANAMAN JACOB		64
BRANAMON ABRAHAM		11
BRANDINGBURGH JACOB		70
BRANDON EBENZOR		24
BRANDON JOHN		24
BRANDON MOSES		24
BRANETT FELIX		20
BRANFIELD THOMAS		24

BRANHAM EBIN	23	
BRANHAM JOHN	24	
BRANHAM LINSFIELD	19	
BRANHAM ROBERT	19	
BRANSON BRISCO D	63	
BRARETTON JOHN	4	
BRASETTON JOHN	69	
BRASHEARS REASON	22	
BRASS JAMES J	51	
BRATTAIN JOSEPH	72	
BRATTON REUBIN	71	
BRATTON WILLIAM	75	
BRAUGH JOHN	46	
BRAUN FREDERICK	53	
BRAWFORD JOHN	60	
BRAXTON JONATHAN	46	
BRAXTON THOMAS	42	
BRAY ABIJAH	43	
BRAY EDWARD	42	
BRAY HENRY	44	
BRAY JOHN	43	
BRAZELTON DAVID B	4	
BRAZELTON JACOB	7	
BREADING WILLIAM E	28	
BREDON WILLIAM	67	
BREEDER RICHARD	36	
BREEDLOVE JAMES	4	
BREEZE JAMES	50	
BREEZE JOHN	42	
BREEZE ROBERT	42	
BREEZE ROBERT JR	42	
BREMAN JAMES	54	
BREMAN JESSE	54	
BREMAN JONATHAN	54	
BRENER GEORGE	45	
BRENO SAMUEL	71	
BREUNER FREDERICK	4	
BREWER BENJAMIN	62	
BREWER ENOCH	55	
BREWER JOHN	63	
BRIAN ANDERSON	9	
BRIAN JAS'S	11	
BRIAN WILLIAM	68	
BRIANT EDWARD	42	
BRIANT JOHN	41	
BRIANT WILLIAM	40	
BRIARS FRANCIS	49	
BRIDGES JOHN	24	56
BRIDGEWATER DAVID	68	
BRIDGEWATERS ELIAS	44	
BRIDGEWATERS JOSEPH	44	
BRIDGEWATERS LEVI	44	
BRIENT JAMES	36	
BRIGES JOHN	9	

BRIGG WILLIAM	29
BRIGGS GEORGE H	27
BRIGGS IZREAL	29
BRIGHT DAVID G	22
BRIGHT LEWIS	4
BRIGHTMAN GEORGE	12
BRIGHTMAN WM D	46
BRIGS JOHN	21
BRILEY ABSOLOM	1
BRILEY JAMES	1
BRINER PETER	12
BRINER PHILIP	12
BRISBEN JAMES	23
BRISBIN JOHN	19
BRISCE WILLIAM	32
BRISCOE PHILLIP	4
BRISCOW WILLIAM	1
BRISTAW JAMES	48
BRISTOW JOHN	48
BRITON JOHN	40
BRITT NELSON	65
BRITTEN JESSE	49
BRITTEN MARKES	49
BRITTINGHURN WILLIAM	4
BRITTON NATHAN	52
BRITTON WM	52
BRNHUST SELVISTER	32
BROADHEAD THO'S	50
BROADHEAD WM	50
BROADSTREAT THO'S	12
BROADWELL HENRY	39
BROCK GEORGE	62
BROCK GEORGE JR	62
BROCK JESSE	66
BROCK JOHN	67
BROCK LEWIS	66
BROCKAW HENRY	27
BROMWELL WILLIAM C	24
BRONGHER JACOB	24
BRONTON JOSEPH	19
BROOCK JOHN	33
BROODE ELI	74
BROOK JEREMIAH	34
BROOKS ANDERSON	30
BROOKS GEORGE R	42
BROOKS HUMPHREY	15
BROOKS JOHN	16
BROOKS JOSEPH	10
BROOKS M	15
BROOKS MIKAJAH	40
BROOKS NOAH	15
BROOKS NOR	22
BROOKS SAMUEL	16
BROOKS W	13

BROOKS	WILEY		15
BROOKS	WILLIAM		45
BROOKS	WILLIAM JR		30
BROOKS	WILLIAM SR		30
BROOKS	WM		11 13
BROOKS	WM m/o		10
BROOMFIELD	DAVID		59
BROTHER	RANSSEL		11
BROTHERS	ABNER		43
BROTHERS	DAVID		4
BROTHERS	JOSHUA		43
BROTHERS	WILLIAM		4 43
BROTHERS	WILSON		43
BROTHERTON	JOHN		65
BROTHERTON	ZACHAUS		65
BROULLETT	MICHAEL		27
BROULLETT	PIERRE		29
BROWEN	JOHN		11
BROWFIELD	WILLIAM		1
BROWN	ALEXANDER		40
BROWN	BARTLET		56
BROWN	BASEL		4
BROWN	BENJAMIN		4 24 56
BROWN	BOLING		68
BROWN	DAVID		32 75
BROWN	DAVID S		42
BROWN	ELISHUA		29
BROWN	FREDRICK		4
BROWN	GEORGE		4
BROWN	HERMAN J		24
BROWN	HUGH		12
BROWN	ISAIAH		13
BROWN	JA'S		11 12+
BROWN	JAMES		1 3 4 16 20
BROWN	JAMES		21 24 36 75
BROWN	JOEL		62
BROWN	JOHN	4+ 12 15 23 31 45	
BROWN	JOHN	52 57 58 60 62	
BROWN	JOHN K		21
BROWN	JOSEPH		12 65 75
BROWN	JOSEPH R		4
BROWN	JOSHUA		57
BROWN	JULIAS		72
BROWN	MANNUSHA		29
BROWN	MATHEW		36
BROWN	MICHAEL		67
BROWN	MOSES		24
BROWN	NATHANIEL		8
BROWN	PARKER		55
BROWN	PATRICK		20
BROWN	PETTER		29
BROWN	SAM'L		12
BROWN	SAMUEL		29+
BROWN	THO'S H		20
BROWN	THOMAS		67 70
BROWN	WILLIAM		1 19 20 24 36
BROWN	WILLIAM		62 64+ 66 68 74
BROWN	WILLIAM B		36
BROWN	WILLIAM P		19
BROWN	WM		10 49
BROWNING	JOSEPH		35
BROWNING	MARSHALL		35
BROWNLEE	GEORGE		4
BROWNLEE	HUGH		7
BROWNLEE	JAMES		7
BROWNLEE	JOHN		8
BROWNSLON	JACOB		17
BROXKAW	HENRY		30
BROYLES	CHARLES		9
BROYLES	JA'S		9
BROYLES	WM		9
BRUCE	ELIJAH		67
BRUCE	NATHANIEL		67
BRUCE	THOMAS		44
BRUCKLEBANK	JOHN		30
BRUMBARGER	JACOB		15
BRUMBARGER	JOHN		15
BRUMMET	BANNER		36
BRUMMET	GEORGE		36
BRUMMET	JAMES I		36
BRUMMET	JAMES II		36
BRUMMET	JAMES III		36
BRUMMET	PIERSON		36
BRUNER	JOSEPH		36
BRUNNER	ABRAHAM		28
BRUNNER	ISAAC		28
BRUNNER	JOHN		28
BRUNNER	SAMUEL		29
BRUSTER	JAMES		23
BRYANT	JOHN		59
BRYANT	JOHN JR		59
BRYANT	WALTER		59
BRYANT	WM		59
BTEAST	FRANCIS		32
BUBBARD	NICHOLAS		62
BUCHANAN	DAVID		55
BUCHANAN	JOHN		22
BUCHANAN	WILLIAM		55
BUCHANAN	WILLIAM B		55
BUCHANAN	WILLIAM H		55
BUCHANAN	WILSON		55
BUCHANON	JOHN S		4
BUCHMAN	DAVID		22
BUCKANON	ALEXANDER		36
BUCKANON	JAMES		36
BUCKELS	JAMES		24
BUCKELS	WILLIAM		24
BUCKEN	EDMOND		28

BUCKHANNON WILSON	15		BURK JOHN	29	72
BUCKHANNON WM	10 16		BURK JOHN JR		71
BUCKNER HALEY	42		BURK LUCAS		69
BUCKNER HENRY	4		BURKE WILLIAM		55
BUCKSTON E	28		BURKET GEORGE		76
BUHLER FREDERICK	53		BURKET HENRY		36
BULL WILLIAM	67		BURLESON AARON		50
BULLA ISAAC	74		BURLIN JOHN		4
BULLA WILLIAM	74		BURNET JOHN		63
BULLARD BRYANT	4		BURNET WM		57
BULLARD JOHN	4		BURNETT ARMSTED		4
BULLARD PETER	4		BURNETT JAMES		4
BULLINGTON BENGAMIN	43		BURNEY ROBERT		34
BULLINGTON ROBERT	43		BURNHAM CALVIN		19
BULLINGTON WILLIAM	3		BURNHAM JOSIAH		23
BULLOCK JOHN	1		BURNS EDWARD		23
BULLOCK WILLIAM A	24		BURNS JAMES		20
BUMGARDNER GEORGE	24		BURNS JAS		22
BUNCH DAVID	68		BURNS JESSE		36
BUNCH RICHARD	72		BURNS JOHN		24
BUNDEY THOMAS	72		BURNS SOLOMON		46
BUNDIAN LEE	15		BURNSIDES JOHN		23
BUNDON LEANDER	20		BURR DAVID		10
BUNDY ABRAHAM	62		BURROWS JESSE		3
BUNDY CHRISTOPHER	60		BURROWS WILLIAM		1
BUNDY GIDEON	42		BURRUAW JOHN BT		27
BUNDY MILES	24		BURT ASA		40
BUNDY SAM'L	75		BURT JOHN		34
BUNKED ABRAM	75		BURTIS JESSE		59
BUNKED JOHN	75		BURTON GEORGE		19
BUNNEL FRANCISS	8		BURTON JOHN	4	36
BUNNEL JESSE	8		BURTON THOS		24
BUNNEL REUBEN	8		BURTON WILLIAM		36
BUNTIN HUGH	55		BUSEY SAMUEL		65
BUNTIN ROBERT JR	28		BUSH DANIEL		66
BUNTIN ROBERT SR	28		BUSH DAVID		70
BURCH JOHN	36		BUSH JOHN		66
BURCH SELBY	17		BUSH JOSEPH		66
BURCH WILLIAM	24 30		BUSH JOSIAH		11
BURCHEM SAM'L JR	9		BUSH SAMUEL		64
BURCHFIELD JEREMIAH	55		BUSH WARREN		35
BURCHFIELD ROBERT	55		BUSHEY FRANCIS		30
BURCHFIELD THOMAS	55		BUSHEY LAURISH		30
BURCHIM JOHN	8		BUSHEY VITAL		29
BURCHIM SAM'L JR	8		BUSHING JOHN BT		30
BUREY CHARLES	65		BUSHOY JOSEPH		29
BURGE ISAAC	9		BUSICK GABRAEL		40
BURGE ROBERT	10		BUSKIRK ISAAC		39
BURGER JOHN	42 72		BUSKIRK JAMES		39
BURGER JOHN L	72		BUSKIRK JOHN		39
BURGER SAMUEL	72		BUSKIRK MICHAEL		36
BURGESS MASON	41		BUSLINGAME WILLIAM		18
BURGETT GEORGE	11		BUTCHER DANIEL		36
BURGOY FRANCIS	28		BUTCHER DAVID		68

BUTCHER JOHN		68
BUTCHER SOLOMON		36
BUTLER ABEL		46 48
BUTLER ANDREW		21
BUTLER CHANCY		24
BUTLER HIRAM		72
BUTLER JAMES		24 52
BUTLER JOEL		24
BUTLER JOEL SR		24
BUTLER JOHN		11 24 52 70
BUTLER JONATHAN		17
BUTLER LEVI		71
BUTLER NELSON		7 29
BUTLER SAMUEL		71
BUTLER SILAS		46
BUTLER THOMAS		7 24
BUTLER WILLIAM		71 72
BUTLER WILSON		52
BUTNER ISAAC		22
BUTT EDMOND		71
BUTTLER JOHN		29
BUTTON JESSE		8
BYRAM LEWIS		43
BYRELEY JACOB		66

C

CABBASHE PEIRRE		30
CACTON JONAH		75
CADDY JOHN		32
CAFFEE WILLIAM		46
CAHILL ELISON		52
CAHILL WM		52
CAIN CHRISTOPHER		24
CAIN JACOB		17
CAIN JOHN		22 72
CAIN JOHN JR		75
CAIN PETER		19
CAINE ABIJAH		71
CALDWELL JAMES		49
CALDWELL JOHN		7
CALDWELL NATH		58
CALENDAR ISAAC		57
CALEY JOHN		72
CALL JACOB		29
CALL MOSES		34
CALLAHAN THOMAS		66
CALLAWAY MICAJAH		62
CALLEMS GILBERT		43
CALLEMS JOHN		41
CALLICOT WILLIAM		24
CALLIHAM JOHN		24
CALLIHAN JESSE		10
CALVERT M W		20

CALVERT PATRICK		59
CALVIN JAMES		49
CALVIN WILLIAM		4
CAMBERS WM		10
CAMERON STEPHEN		42
CAMMAC SAMUEL		71
CAMMACK AMOS		75
CAMMERN IGNATIOUS		46
CAMMINT THOMAS		72
CAMP CHARLES		1
CAMP REUBEN		1
CAMP SAM'L		1
CAMP WILLIAM		1
CAMPBELL ABNER		51
CAMPBELL AJACKS		51
CAMPBELL ALEX'R		22
CAMPBELL ALLEN		24
CAMPBELL CHARLES		70
CAMPBELL DANIEL		51
CAMPBELL DAVID		24
CAMPBELL ENOS		1
CAMPBELL FRANCES		24
CAMPBELL GEORGE		18 69
CAMPBELL JAMES		14 15 20
CAMPBELL JOHN		15 16+ 23 24 56
CAMPBELL JOHN S		23
CAMPBELL JOSEPH		22
CAMPBELL LAW'E		17
CAMPBELL ROBERT		40
CAMPBELL SAMUEL		40
CAMPBELL WILLIAM		60
CAMPBELL WILLIAM H		3
CAMPBELL WM		15
CAMRON SAMUEL		46
CANBY I T		22
CANDSEY CALEB		17
CANE CORNELIUS		43
CANE JOSIAH		46
CANFIELD SAMUEL		58
CANNEDAY ISAAC		71
CANNON JOHN		1
CANNOR TARRENCE		46
CANON DAVID		71
CANROOD HENRY		3
CANS ROBERT		73
CANTREL WILLIAM		65
CANTRILL ABRAHAM		42
CANTRILL DUKE		39
CANTRILL JOHN		40
CAPEHART THOMAS		7
CAPELEY GEORGE		66
CAPLINGER ADAM		14
CAPLINGER SAMUEL		14
CAR ELI		48

CARBOUGH ABRAM		56
CARDINAL JOSEPH		28
CARDINAL MADORE		30
CARDINAL NICHOLAS		29
CARDNER ANDREW		54
CAREY JACOB		60
CAREY WILLIAM		61
CARIGHT JOHN		29
CARISS SIMON		61
CARLEY ELIGAH		25
CARLEY RICHARD		24
CARLISLE RICHARD		57
CARLTON WILLIAM	5	66
CARMACK ALLEN		62
CARMAN ELIJAH		60
CARMMAC JAMES		73
CARMMAC WILLIAM		72
CARNER DAVID		49
CARNER JOHN		49
CARNES WILLIAM		57
CARNEY WM		49
CARNEY JOHN		24
CARNEY PLEASANT		24
CARNS DAVID		61
CAROD JACOB		1
CARPENTER JACOB		18
CARPENTER MR		57
CARPENTER SAM'L		52
CARPENTER WILLIAM		22
CARR AMES		56
CARR ELIJAH	67	68
CARR ELISHA		67
CARR HENRY		12
CARR JONATHAN		11
CARR SAM'L		12
CARR THOMAS	11	56
CARR WILLIAM		44
CARREL BARTHOLOMEW		18
CARREL HENRY		18
CARREL JOHN		19+
CARROD THOMAS		75
CARSON ABRAHAM		45
CARSON DANIEL		25
CARSON FELIX W		25
CARSON HAMILTON		49
CARSON JAMES		25
CARSON JOHN		51
CARSON WALTER		25
CARSON WALTER JR		25
CARSON WILLIAM		25
CARSONS WILLIAM		27
CART JOHN		46
CARTER BAYLEY		36
CARTER BENJAMIN	12	52

CARTER CHARLES		63	74
CARTER ELDRIDGE			52
CARTER ELEAZER B			28
CARTER HENRY			62
CARTER JAMES		24	64
CARTER JEDDIAH	1	65	67
CARTER JOB			12
CARTER JOHN			52
CARTER JOSHUA			40
CARTER McKINNEY			9
CARTER NATHANIEL			42
CARTER SOLOMON			76
CARTER THOS			17
CARTER TRAVIS			12
CARTOR JOHN			62
CARTRIGHT NEUTON			51
CARTRIGHT PETTER			34
CARTS EDWARD			3
CARTUP JAMES			75
CARTWRIGHT REDDICK			49
CARTWRIGHT SAM'L			49
CARUTHERS SAMUEL			29
CARUTHERS WM			11
CARVIN EDWARD			61
CARY ANTHONY			28
CARY PEIRRE			34
CARY WILLIAM			24
CASCEY JOEL F			5
CASE ABRAHAM			35
CASE JOSEPH			67
CASE WILLIAM			67
CASEY GEORGE			51
CASEY HENREY			51
CASEY JOSEPH			57
CASEY WM JR			51
CASEY WM SR			51
CASH JEREMIAH			39
CASSADAY JOHN			46
CASSELBERY PAUL			49
CASSELBURY THO'S E			49
CASSON TAFFEE			46
CAST GEORGE			57
CASTATOR MICHAEL			55
CASTER ISAAC			13
CASTLE GEORGE			65
CASY JOHN			67
CATER JOSEPH			59
CATER WM			59
CATLAND EBENESAR			23
CATLIN THEODORE			65
CATT GEORGE			34
CATT JOB			34
CATT MICHAEL			34
CATT PHILLIP			34

CATT THOMAS		34
CATTIN DANIEL		59
CATTRON VALENTINE		65
CAUBLE ADAM JR		61
CAUBLE ADAM SR		61
CAUBLE DAVID		69
CAUBLE PETER		61
CAUBLE PHILIP		69
CAULKINS JOEL		67
CAULSTEN JAMES		49
CAUSBEY JOHN		1
CAVATT JOHN		16
CAVE THOMAS		41
CAVENDER JOHN		13
CAVENS JESSEE		51
CAVET THOS		15
CAVINS REZIN		53
CAVITT ANDREW		53
CAWSON JAMES		59
CECHUM WILLIAM		29
CENADAY SAMUEL		72
CERN JOSEPH		24
CERNS WILLIAM		18
CESTER JOHN		9
CETCHIM WILLIAM		27
CHADWELL DUFF		44
CHAFFIN EVAN JR		72
CHALFANT EVAN		74
CHAMBERLEN ASA		33
CHAMBERLEN JONATHON		33
CHAMBERS ALEX'R		18
CHAMBERS ALEXANDER		31
CHAMBERS ALLEXANDER		25
CHAMBERS ANTHONY		14 36
CHAMBERS AVERY		18
CHAMBERS DAVID		31 36+
CHAMBERS GEORGE		4
CHAMBERS ISAAC		22
CHAMBERS JAMES		19 31
CHAMBERS JOHN		8 31 36 61
CHAMBERS JOHN JR		25
CHAMBERS JOSEPH		5 31
CHAMBERS LEVI		31
CHAMBERS NATHANIEL		63
CHAMBERS SAMUEL		31 41
CHAMBERS THOMAS		34 36
CHAMBERS WILLIAM		17 60 63
CHAMNESS AARON		44
CHAMPBELL ADLAI		43
CHAMPBELL JOHN		42
CHANBERS JOHN SR		25
CHANCE DANIEL		36
CHANCE PURNEL		36
CHANCE REEDEN		76
CHANCE TILMAN		36
CHANCEY WILLIAM		36
CHANDLER ALFORD		24
CHANDLER BENJAMIN		36
CHANDLER BRADDOCK		24
CHANDLER DANIEL		24
CHANDLER H B		58
CHANDLER JAMES		36
CHANDLER JOHN G		57
CHANDLER L		58
CHANDLER WILLIS		24
CHANEY CHARLES		45
CHANEY JOHN		68
CHANLER ISAAC		62
CHANLER WILLIAM JR		62
CHANLER WILLIAM SR		62
CHANSLER ISAAC		32
CHANSLER JESSE		32
CHANY NATHAN		71
CHAPEN SAMUEL		1
CHAPLE JOHN		35
CHAPMAN JAMES		25
CHAPMAN JOHN		10 61
CHAPMAN JOSEPH		58
CHAPMAN ROBERT		13 76
CHAPMAN THOMAS		5
CHAPMAN THOMAS F		45
CHAPMAN WILLIAM		66
CHAPMAN WM		58
CHAPMAN WM JR		59
CHAPPEL THOMAS		4
CHAPPORE AUGUST		30
CHARLES AZER		45
CHARLES DANIEL		76
CHARLES JOEL		45
CHARLES JOSEPH		71
CHARLES RISDON		61
CHARLES S'M		73
CHARLES SAMUEL JR		74
CHARLEY JOHN		72
CHASE ISAAC		61
CHASE JAMES		40
CHASE JOSEPH		59
CHASE WILLIAM J		67
CHASTEEN WILLIAM		43
CHATFEY AUSTIN B		28
CHATHAM JOHN		43
CHATTAM JONAH		73
CHATTBURN JOHN		30
CHATTSEY BENJAMIN		27
CHATTSEY JOHN		27
CHECE ASA		24
CHECE SETH		24
CHEEK JAMES		4

CHEEK LEWIS		4
CHEEK WILLIAM		5
CHEIREU ABNER H		25
CHEIVER JOSHUA C		24
CHENNAULT WILLIAM		73
CHENOWETH THOMAS		20
CHERRY WM		49
CHESNUT JACOB		36
CHESSER WILLIAM		46
CHILCOT JOHN		11
CHILD EZRA		67
CHIMLEY JOHN		25
CHINNETH ABRAHAM		10
CHINOUETH JAMES		19
CHINWORTH JOHN		70
CHINWORTH JOSEPH		70
CHISM JOHN		16
CHITTENDEN HOMER		4
CHITTENDEN WILLIAM		5
CHITWOOD AMOS		17
CHITWOOD JAMES		17
CHITWOOD JOSHUA		23
CHOUDOIN SAMUEL		36
CHOWNER JOHN S		12
CHRISE JACOB		29
CHRISENHALL SAMUEL		57
CHRISENHALL WM		57
CHRISTIE - - -		39
CHRISTIE ANDREW		39
CHRISTIE JAMES		55
CHRISTIE JOSEPH		36
CHRISTIE RICHARD		39
CHRISTY ISAAC	13	14
CHUME JOHN		36
CHUTE DANIEL		58
CIBBIT WILLIAM		32
CINDY WM		10
CINNONS SILAS		9
CINNS AARON		9
CLA JAMES m/o		14
CLACOMB JOHN		46
CLANTON AMOS		75
CLANTON WILLIAM		74
CLAREWATERS DAVID		36
CLARK ABSALOM		68
CLARK AMOS		58
CLARK ARCHEY		5
CLARK BANESTER		68
CLARK BANJAMIN W		24
CLARK DANIEL		74
CLARK GEORGE		35
CLARK JACOB		36
CLARK JAMES	45 56	76
CLARK JAMES W		36

CLARK JEREMIAH		62
CLARK JESSE		76
CLARK JOHN	1+ 2 25	70
CLARK JOHN JR		72
CLARK JOHN E		61
CLARK JOHN W		39
CLARK JOSEPH		56
CLARK MASTEN G		65
CLARK NATHANIEL		36
CLARK OBEDIAH		5
CLARK ORINGE		27
CLARK RICHARD		62
CLARK ROBERT	36 44	46
CLARK ROBERT JR		62
CLARK ROBERT SR		62
CLARK SAM'L		10
CLARK SAMUEL		69
CLARK THOMAS		71
CLARK WARNER		52
CLARK WILLARD J		58
CLARK WILLIAM	24 68 71 74	76
CLARK WILLIAM A		31
CLARK WM		50
CLARWATERS JACOB		36
CLARWATERS REUBEN		36
CLATON ROB'T		50
CLAUSON ABNER		74
CLAXON CASSIUS		22
CLAYCOMB ADAM		33
CLAYCOMB FREDERICK		33
CLAYCOMB GEORGE		46
CLAYTON JAMES		41
CLEM CHRISTOPHER		55
CLEMENTS THOMAS		44
CLEMINGS WILLIAM		22
CLENDENIN JOHN G		45
CLEVELAND EZER		41
CLEVELAND JOHN		51
CLINDINEN JOSIAH		36
CLINE JOHN		13
CLINE LEVI		13
CLINES LEVI SR		13
CLINES NICHOLAS		25
CLLOTT BENJAMIN		75
CLOAK JOHN		9
CLOSE SAMUEL		21
CLOUD ISHAM		16
CLOUD JOSEPH		67
CLOVER CURNELUS		25
CLOYAR HENRY		19
CLOYD JAMES	17	23
COAL ROBERT		48
COAPLAND ANDREW		1
COAPLAND CHARLES		1

92

COATS	BENJAMINE			52		COLCLASIER	ABRAHAM			69
COATS	ERASTUS			27		COLCLASIER	DAVID			69
COBB	EBENEZER			28		COLCLASIER	JACOB JR			70
COBB	HENRY			40		COLCLASIER	JACOB SR			70
COBB	SAMUEL			40		COLCLASIER	JOHN		69	70
COBB	THO'S			19		COLE	JEREMIAH			56
COBB	WM			15		COLE	CHARLES			56
COCHRAN	ANDREW			19		COLE	JESSE			56
COCHRAN	BENJAMIN			32		COLE	SAMUEL			56
COCHRAN	FRANCES			19		COLEGROVE	GEORGE			34
COCHRAN	GLASS			32		COLEMAN	ISAAC			29
COCHRAN	JAMES		20	60		COLEMAN	JOHN			17
COCHRAN	JEREMIAH			29		COLIER	HESEKIAH			68
COCHRAN	JOHN		19	33		COLIER	I T			24
COCHRAN	WILLIAM			43		COLIER	JAMES		23	68
COCHREAL	ENODS			33		COLIER	JOHN			68
COCKESHAM	WM			10		COLLARS	JOHN			46
COCKOM	JAMES			4		COLLE	JOHN			71
COCKOM	WILLIAM			4		COLLIER	WILLIAM			69
COCKRAM	JAMES			5		COLLINS	AMOS			17+
COCKRAM	WILLIAM			4		COLLINS	ANDREW			21
COCKRELL	ALEX'R			70		COLLINS	CHARLES			46
CODE	GEORGE			4		COLLINS	DAVID			27
CODY	DAVID			12		COLLINS	GARTER		33	56
CODY	JOHN			58		COLLINS	GEORGE			55
COFFEE	JOHN H			60		COLLINS	JAMES			42
COFFEE	WILLIAM			39		COLLINS	JEREMIAH		30	32
COFFER	HORRATIO			51		COLLINS	JOHN	29 33	36	63
COFFIN	BARNABAS			12		COLLINS	JOHN		68	71
COFFIN	JAMES			62		COLLINS	JOSEPH			33
COFFIN	LIBNI JR			67		COLLINS	SAMUEL		27	30
COFFIN	LIBNI SR			67		COLLINS	THOMAS			56
COFFIN	MARMADUKE			63		COLLINS	WILLIAM		33	56
COFFIN	MATTHEW			63		COLMAN	JEREMIAH			28
COFFIN	NATHANIEL			63		COLMON	NATHANIEL			51
COFFIN	STEPHEN			61		COLT	ARASTUS			10
COFFIN	THOMAS			45		COLVIN	MOSES			51
COFFIN	WILLIAM			64		COLVIN	JOBE			51
COFFMAN	ABRAHAM			36		COLVIN	JOBE JR			51
COFFMAN	GEORGE			22		COLVIN	JOHN			52
COFFMAN	JACOB	14	22	23		COLVIN	LEWIS			43
COFFMAN	JOHN			22		COLVIN	LUTHER			51
COFFMAN	NICHOLAS			36		COLVIN	NATHAN			52
COFFMAN	PHILIP			22		COLWELL	BENJ			21
COFFMAN	SOLOMON			36		COLYER	RICHARD			8
COGGSWEL	LAURANCE			73		COMBS	ELLIOT			72
COGHILL	MATTHEW			16		COMBS	WILLIAM			47
COGLE	CALEB			75		COMBS	WM			57
COGSWELL	WARNER			60		COMER	JOHN		55	73
COGWELL	LEONARD			18		COMLEY	ABSOLOM			19
COLCLAISER	DANIEL			68		COMMINS	ISAAC			72
COLCLASHER	ABRAHAM			44		COMPANIOTTE	JOSEPH			30
COLCLASHER	JACOB			44		COMPANIOTTO	PIERRE			30
COLCLASHER	JOHN			44		COMPOW	ANTOINE			29

COMPOW ENIAC	28	
COMPOW MICHAEL	29 30	
COMPOW NICHOLAS	30	
COMPTON JAMES	74	
COMPTON KENNETH	57	
COMPTON NATHAN	72	
COMSTACK JOHN	24	
COMSTOCK ASA	58	
COMSTOCK BATSFORD	21	
COMSTOCK DANIEL	21	
CONAWAY JOHN	60	
CONAWAY SAMUEL	29	
CONDRA JACOB	44	
CONDRA PHILIP	1	
CONDREY CLABORN	23	
CONDRY JOHN	1	
CONGER LEWIS	4	
CONGER SEBASTON	4	
CONGLETON WM	9	
CONKLIN ZEDEKIAH	44	
CONLEN JAMES	50	
CONLEY HENRY	23	
CONN JOSEPH	43	
CONNELL WILLIAM	39	
CONNELLY ARTHUR	39	
CONNELLY LEMUEL	9	
CONNER JOHN	58	
CONNER JOHN JR	58	
CONNER JONSEY	42	
CONNER LEWIS	14 15 73	
CONNER LEWIS m/o	14	
CONNER PHILLIP	25	
CONNER ROBERT	5	
CONNER WILLIBY	24	
CONNERS MATHEW	36	
CONNOR DADE	46	
CONNOR JOHN	46	
CONNOR SAMUEL	46	
CONNOR TARENCE	46+	
CONNOR TARRENCE	46	
CONNOR WILLIAM	46	
CONROUGH MICHAEL	28	
CONSLEY SAM'L	22	
CONSLEY THOS	17	
CONZELMAN GEORGE	53	
COODY CURTIS	74	
COOK ASHER	60	
COOK DAVID	72	
COOK EMMORY	59	
COOK JACOB	32 44 48	
COOK JOHN	14 34 40	
COOK THOMAS	59 74	
COOK WILLIAM	14 42 74	
COOK WM	51	
COOKSON ANDREW	55
COOLEY ADONIJAH	65
COOLEY ANUNAH	65
COOLEY EDWARD	63
COOLEY JAMES	65
COOLEY JOHN	65+
COOLEY THOMAS	63
COOMBS JOEL	60
COONFIELD JOHN	25
COONS JEREMIAH	71
COONS JOSEPH	30
COONSE JOHN	51
COOPER CHARLES	27
COOPER EDMUND	60
COOPER JACOB	44
COOPER JOEL	60
COOPER JOHN	45 49 61
COOPER JOHN JR	44
COOPER JOHN SR	44
COOPER JOHN G	4
COOPER JONATHAN	40
COOPER ROBERT	60
COOPER WILLIAM	45
COOPER WILSON	65
COOPPER JOHN	46
COPE DAVID	15 19
COPE JESSE	20
COPE JONAHTAN	19
COPE WILLIAM	20
COPELAND HUGH	9
COPELAND JA'S	9
COPELIN JAMES	14
COPELIN JOHN	20
COPELIN SAMUEL	14
COPELIN THOMAS	41
COPELIN THOS	14
COPELIN WM	20
COPES WM	58
COPPLE JOHN	43
CORALE SAMUEL	14
CORBERN NATHANIEL	28
CORD JOHN	9
CORN WM	12
CORNELISON MOSES	17
CORNELUS ELIHU	51
CORNER ROBERT	73
CORNET WILLIAM	64
CORNIA FRANCIS	28
CORNIEA AMBROIS	29
CORNIEA ANTOINE	29
CORNS EDWARD	27
CORNWELL GEORGE	34
CORNWELL JAMES	44
CORR HUGH	36

CORRELL ANDREW		32	COX SAMUEL	15 31
CORY DAVID		34	COX SOLOMON	13
CORY JOSEPH		34	COX STEPHEN	13 75
COSAND BENJAMIN		61	COX THOMAS	39 71
COSSE JESSE		13	COX WILLIAM	46 71
COT JOHN		3	COX WM	12
COTLAND EBENESAR		23	COX WM SR	12
COTNEY ARCHABALD		9	CRABB CHARLES	8
COTNEY JA'S		9	CRABB EDWARD	11
COTNEY PHENEHAS		9	CRABB JA'S S	11
COTTON JAMES C		22	CRABREEE WM	49
COTTON ROBERT		19	CRABTREE JOHN	49
COULD JOHN		42	CRABTREE WILLIAM	43
COULTER CHARLES		69	CRABTREE WM SR	49
COULTER JOHN		29	CRACRAFT JAMES	64
COULTER THOMAS		30	CRAGE JOHN JR	68
COURANITON JAMES		28	CRAGE JOHN SR	68
COURSE WILLIAM		1	CRAGE THOMAS	68
COURTNEY HENRY		33	CRAIG ALEX'R C	8
COVELL JOHN		7	CRAIG JOHN	8
COVERDALE PERRY		36	CRAIG JONATHAN	42
COWAN JAMES		22	CRAIG JOSEPH	56
COWDEN JAMES		21	CRAIG MERIT S	55
COWEN JOHN		24	CRAIG WILLIAM	36 71
COWEN MILES		65	CRAIN ISHABOD G	69
COWHERD HENRY		45	CRALE SAM'L	20
COWHERD THOMAS		40	CRAMPTON SM'L	75
COWHERD WILLIS		40	CRANAHAM ROBERT	54
COX ABSOLOM		52	CRANE ASA	12
COX ALSOLOM		49	CRANE DAVID	12
COX AMOS		36	CRANE EDWARD	54
COX ARON		8	CRANE JABEZ	12
COX ASAS		13	CRANE JABEZ O	12
COX BENJAMIN		9 74	CRANE JAMES	36
COX CHRISTOPHER		14	CRANE JONAS	12
COX ENOCH		12	CRANE JOSEPH	36
COX ER		19	CRANE OBADIAH M	12
COX FURNEYFOLD		49	CRANFORD ISOM	69
COX HARMON		12 74	CRANFORD MARVEL	69
COX HENRY		13	CRANSE WILLIAM	25
COX J		23	CRAVENS BENJAMIN	24
COX JACOB		62	CRAVENS JOHN	18
COX JAMES		58	CRAVENS ROBERT	20
COX JEHU		64	CRAVENS WILLIAM	18
COX JEREMIAH		73	CRAVER THOMAS	75
COX JESSE		9 31	CRAWFORD DAVID	16
COX JESSEY		31	CRAWFORD GEORGE	68
COX JOHN	13 15 16 20	61	CRAWFORD ISAAC	19
COX JOHN JR		49	CRAWFORD JAMES	68
COX JOHN SR		49 51	CRAWFORD JAMES M	19
COX JONATHAN		31 49	CRAWFORD JAS	23
COX JOSEPH	36 58	73	CRAWFORD JOHN	16
COX NATHAN		12	CRAWFORD JOSEPH	44
COX RUSSEL		14 20	CRAWFORD THOMAS	19

CRAWFORD WILLIAM	16 19
CREAMER SIMEON	60
CREEK ISAAC	8
CREEK JACOB	5
CREEK KILLION	4
CREEK KILLON JR	8
CREEK WILLIAM	1
CREELY CHARLES	30
CREELY GEROME	28
CREGG RODERICK	71
CRERY JOHN	24
CRESWELL JOHN	17+
CRETCHELOW JAMES	46
CRETH ROBERT	56
CRIDER JOHN	12
CRIGG RODERICK	75
CRIM JESSE	66
CRISLEY M	56
CRISMAN JACOB	18
CRISS CHRISTIAN	67
CRISS MICHEL	7
CRIST JOHN	46
CRISTY SAMUEL	63
CRITCHELL MOSES	57
CRITS HENRY	22
CRITTENDON HENRY	64
CRIUTOUS PHILIP	1
CROCKET JOHN	65
CROCKET JOHN R	70
CROCKET WILLIAM	65
CROKER JESSE	46
CROOCK DAVID	35
CROOCK GEORGE	35
CROOKS JACOB	31
CROOKS MICHAEL	32
CROSBY JOHN	32
CROSBY LEONARD	32
CROSS CHARLES	7
CROSS CHESTER	9
CROSS ELI	67
CROSS FITHUSON	5
CROSS JAMES	49
CROSS SAMUEL T	20
CROTHERS JOHN	17
CROTTS VALENTINE	67
CROUCH AARON	67
CROUCH JOHN	67
CROUCHER DAVID	11
CROW DAVID	75
CROW JAMES	42
CROW JAMES JR	4
CROW JOHN	5 41 67
CROW JOSHUA	67
CROW LEWIS	62

CROW ROBERT	4
CROW WILLIAM	5
CROWE ABEL	75
CROWLEY JAMES	8
CROWLEY KENELUS	8
CROWLEY MATHEW	23
CROWNOVER DANIEL	41
CROWSMAN JOSIAH	27
CRUM COONROID	35
CRUM HENRY	40
CRUM PHILLIP	32
CRUMB JOHN	36
CRUNK JOHN	49
CRUSAN THOMAS	25
CULBERSON ANDREW	4
CULBERSON BENJAMINE	4
CULBERSON THOMAS	73
CULBERTSON CHARLES	20
CULBERTSON ROBERT	72
CULLY JOSEPH	53
CULLY SAM'L	50
CULLY THO'S	49
CULMARY JAMES	21
CULTON JAMES	45
CUMINGORE DANIEL	16
CUMMINGS ELI	46
CUMMINGS EPHRAIGM	46
CUMMINGS JOHN	46
CUMMINGS JOSIAH	46
CUMMINGS THOMAS	46
CUMMINGS URIAH	46
CUMMINGS WILLIAM	46
CUMMINS MAJOR	11
CUNNARD HENRY	24
CUNNINGHAM ALEXANDER	46
CUNNINGHAM ALXANDER	35
CUNNINGHAM ANDERSON	62
CUNNINGHAM ANDREW	4
CUNNINGHAM ANDREW P	23
CUNNINGHAM ARON	46
CUNNINGHAM ELIJAH	62
CUNNINGHAM FRANCIS	28
CUNNINGHAM GEORGE	5
CUNNINGHAM JAMES D	18
CUNNINGHAM JOHN	28 35
CUNNINGHAM JOSEPH	35
CUNNINGHAM PHILIP	21
CUNNINGHAM STEWART	4
CURL DUDLEY	36
CURL JAMES	36
CURL WILLIAM	36
CURRAN THOMAS	55
CURRELL JOHN	18
CURREY JOHN	61

CURRIE	JAMES		23 55
CURRIE	ROBERT		16
CURRY	ANDREW		34
CURRY	DAVID		18
CURRY	ELIJAH		10
CURRY	HENRY		5
CURRY	JAMES		44
CURRY	JAMES R		5
CURRY	JOHN		35
CURRY	ROBERT		58
CURRY	WILLIAM		35 70
CURRY	WILLIAM R		3
CURRY	WM		10
CURTES	ARNOLD		13
CURTICE	JASHUWAY		50
CURTICE	JOSHUWAY		50
CURTICE	WILLIAM		52
CURTIGHT	RALPH		62
CURTIN	DANIEL		50
CURTIS	BENNET		69
CURTIS	FREDRICK		25
CURTIS	FREDRICK A		25
CURTIS	JONATHAN		76
CURTIS	REUBEN		58
CURTIS	WILLIAM		24
CUSHAW	JOHN		21
CUSHMAN	BENJAMIN		72
CUSTER	RUEL		20
CUSTER	WILLIAM		19
CUSTES	JESSE		13
CUSTES	WILLIAM		13
CUTLER	LENARD		24
CUTSINGER	JACOB		41
CUTSINGER	MARTIN		45
CUTTER	JOHN		36
CYAN	ABRAHAM		29

D

DABYEAN	ANDREW		29
DAINIHUE	DANIEL		69
DAKMAN	FRANCIS XAVIER		30
DALLY	JOHN A		75
DAMPILL	WM		3
DANFORD	JOSIAS		4
DANFORD	WILLIAM		19
DANIEL	JOHN		48
DANIEL	MERCER		28
DANIEL	PETER		48
DANIEL	RICHARD		5
DANIEL	WILLIAM		7 28
DANIELS	CHANEY		35
DANIELS	JOHN		14 50
DANIELS	WM		50
DANIOU	TOUSANT		30
DANNER	D		16
DANNER	JOHN		16
DANNER	JOSEPH		16 40
DANSEY	JOHN		23
DARINGER	JACOB		14
DARLING	WM		10
DARNELL	EPHRAIM		5
DARNIELLE	ISAAC		37
DARROCH	DANIEL		42
DAUGHERTY	GEORGE		42
DAUGHERTY	HENRY		42
DAUGHERTY	JESSE		46
DAUGHERTY	JOHN		42+ 45
DAUGHERTY	ROBERT		45
DAVENPORT	DAVID		73
DAVENPORT	JAMES		74
DAVENPORT	WM		11
DAVESON	JOHN		71
DAVID	ATWELL		55
DAVID	CHARLES		55
DAVIDSON	ALEXANDER		16
DAVIDSON	DANIEL		2 4
DAVIDSON	ELIJAH		5
DAVIDSON	JAMES		37
DAVIDSON	JOSEPH		5
DAVIDSON	THOMAS		1 17
DAVIDSON	THOMAS SR		17
DAVINPORT	JESSE		12
DAVIS	ADAM		42
DAVIS	AMOS		19
DAVIS	ASY		3
DAVIS	BARNABAS		43
DAVIS	BENJAMIN		18 22 58 66
DAVIS	BENJAMINE		5
DAVIS	DANIEL		5 8 43
DAVIS	ELIAS		9
DAVIS	ELIGAH		25
DAVIS	EVIN		1
DAVIS	EZRA		67
DAVIS	GEORGE		29 62
DAVIS	HANDY T		23
DAVIS	HENRY		60
DAVIS	ISAAC		69
DAVIS	JACOB		2 46
DAVIS	JAMES		25 55 62
DAVIS	JESSE		5 35 60
DAVIS	JOEL		42
DAVIS	JOHN		5 12 37 46
DAVIS	JOHN H		43
DAVIS	JONATHAN		25
DAVIS	JOSEPH		2 42
DAVIS	LEVI		65
DAVIS	LOVE		5

DAVIS	NATHANIEL			25		DEFFINDALL	PHILLIP			5
DAVIS	NEWEL			61		DEFURR	LEANDER			53
DAVIS	PENUEL			25		DELELE	CHARLES			30
DAVIS	PETER			1		DELENIA	JOSEPH			30
DAVIS	RANSOM			41		DELENIA	LEWEY JR			30
DAVIS	RICHARD		5	46		DELENIA	LEWEY SR			30
DAVIS	ROBERT C			5		DELENIA	PAINE JR			30
DAVIS	SEPTEMUS			25		DELENIA	PEINE SR			30
DAVIS	SOLOMON		5	18		DELIELE	JOHN			29
DAVIS	THEODORUS			46		DELLENICO	FRANCIS			30
DAVIS	THOMAS	1	17	55		DELLENICO	JOHN BT			30
DAVIS	THOS		14	18		DELLENIEA	LESCAU			30
DAVIS	URIAH			59		DELLINGER	CHRISTOPHER			33
DAVIS	VALENTINE			65		DELLINGER	JOSEPH			33
DAVIS	WILLIAM	5	35	75		DELLINGER	THOMAS			33
DAVIS	WM			49		DELLINGER	WILLIAM			33
DAVIS	ZACHARIAH			12		DELONG	AMASA			22
DAVISON	SAMUEL			27		DELUNIOW	JOSEPH			29
DAWKINS	WILLIAM			56		DEMAREE	DANIEL			20
DAWS	L			21		DEMAREE	SAMUEL			13
DAWSON	DANIEL			42		DEMEN	WM			16
DAWSON	DANIEL JR			42		DEMENT	JOHN			16
DAWSON	JAMES			63		DEMOSS	ANDREW			43
DAY	ELIAS			8		DENBO	JAMES			40
DAY	RICHARD			61		DENFORD	JOHN			3
DAY	ROBERT			5		DENFORD	TOBIUS A			3
DAY	SAMUEL			22		DENION	LEWIS			29
DAYLEY	E O			13		DENISON	JOHN			2
DEALY	JAMES			67		DENLOW	JOHN			25
DEAN	ELIAS			65		DENNEY	ISAAC			63
DEAN	HALLET B			45		DENNEY	THOMAS			63
DEAN	JOSEPH		10	31		DENNEY	WESTLEY			63
DEAN	ROBERT			54		DENNIN	ANTHONY			70
DEARBORN	RICHARD			22		DENNIN	JAMES			25
DECHERS	EPHRAIM			72		DENNIN	JOSEPH			70
DECK	JAMES			15		DENNING	JOSEPH			70
DECKARD	JACOB			71		DENNING	WILLIAM			70
DECKER	ABRAHAM		5	34		DENNIS	DAVID			62
DECKER	DANIEL			35		DENNIS	ROBERT JR			62
DECKER	HIRAM			29		DENNIS	ROBERT SR			62
DECKER	ISAAC			35		DENNISON	TIMOTHY			57
DECKER	ISAAC T			35		DENNY	CHRISTOPHER			13
DECKER	JACOB			5		DENNY	DAVID			61
DECKER	JOHN			5		DENNY	ELISHA			61
DECKER	LUKE		5	34		DENNY	FEILDEN			25
DECKER	NICHOLAS			5		DENNY	HENRY			9
DEDWAIRE	CHARLES			29		DENNY	JAMES		45	61
DEE	DANIEL			9		DENNY	JOHN	35	41	63
DEE	SAMUEL			1		DENNY	MARDICA			45
DEEN	RICHARD			46		DENNY	ROBERT			49
DEEN	STEPHEN			46		DENNY	SAMUEL			61
DEEN	WILLIAM			46		DENNY	SIMON			41
DEEVER	MILES			48		DENNY	WILLIAM			61
DEFFINDALL	JOSEPH			5		DENNY	ZACHARIA			45

DENOE TOUSANT		29
DENSLOW CHAPMAN		25
DENSLOW JOHN		25
DENT EDMUND		73
DePAUW BONAPARTE		63
DePAUW CHARLES		63
DePAUW JOHN		63
DEPEW ELIJAH		46
DEPEW ISAAC		46
DEPOISTER JOHN		49
DEPOSITER JOHN		52
DEPUTY JOSHUA		18
DEREE SAMUEL		13
DEREMIAH JOHN JR		70
DEREMIAH JOHN SR		70
DERINGER JOSEPH		55
DERUMPLE SAM'L		49
DEVENDALL JOHN		30
DEVENDALL SIMON		29
DEVENISH STEPHEN		10
DEVENPORT CHARLES		50
DEVENPORT JESSE		71
DEVEROUGH RICH'D		21
DEVIN ALEXANDER		5
DEVOIR NICHOLAS		37
DEVORE BENJ		13
DEVORE D		14
DEVORE JOHN		34
DEWALT HENRY		61
DEWEBER JOHN		60
DEWESE DAVID		69
DEWESE EVIN		70
DEWEY CHARLES		45
DEWIT BARNET		12
DEWITT ELISHA		46
DEWITT JOHN		60
DEWYER CHARLES		27
DEXON FRANCIS		29
DICK DAVID		5
DICK JAMES		22
DICK JOHN		54
DICKENS JAMES	36	44
DICKENS JOHN		36
DICKENS PEMBERTON		36
DICKENS WILSON		36
DICKENSON JA'S		10
DICKERSON JAMES	46	56
DICKERSON JOHN		17
DICKEY GEORGE		56
DICKEY HAMILTON		56
DICKS JOSHUA		70
DICKSON DAVID		50
DICKSON JAMES	49	50
DICKSON JESSE		9

DICKSON JOHN		50
DICKSON THOMAS		9
DICKSON WM		50
DICKSON WM JR		11
DICKSON WM SR		11
DIETERLE MARTEN		53
DIFFINDALL SIMON		7
DILHORN ROBERT		74
DILL ABNER		37
DILL SAMUEL		73
DILLARD JOHN		42
DILLARD WILLIAM		44
DILLERY RICHARD		43
DILLIMO MICHAEL		1
DILLIN DANIEL		70
DILLING ANDREW		42
DILLON ROBT		22
DILWOURTH SAMUEL		29
DIMICK ADOLPHUS		55
DIMICK CORDIAL		55
DINGLE JEDEDIAH		56
DINGLER JACOB		53
DINKINGS JAMES		72
DINWIDDIE ALEX'R		16
DISHAN JAMES		41
DISHON JACOB		45
DITCH HENRY		54
DITSLER JOHN		17
DITTAMORE ADAM		65
DITTAMORE JOHN		63
DITTAMORE MICHAEL		65
DITTEMORE THOMAS		41
DITTO SHADRACK		43
DIVINE THOMAS		58
DIX ZACKARES		37
DIXON OZEY		66
DIXON CARNTON		41
DIXON HENRY		18
DIXON JACOB		40
DIXON JOHN	23+ 40	45
DIXON SIMON		43
DOAN JACOB		70
DOAN TOMAS		69
DOBBINS JOHN		25
DOBSON JOHN		12
DOCKINGS JESSE		49
DODD SAMUEL		37
DODDS ANDREW		10
DODGE WM		52
DODSON JOHN		46
DOE ZEMEDO		30
DOLF STEPHEN		25
DOLLARHIDE ABSALOM		37
DOLLARHIDE JOHN		37

DOLOHAN DANIEL	35	
DOLOHAN JOHN	35	
DOLOHAN MILES	35	
DOLTAN BRADLEY	41	
DOLTINE JOHN	70	
DOLTON JAMES	41	
DOLTON JOHN	67	
DOLTON SAMUEL	41	
DOLTON WILLIAM R	41	
DONALDS JAMES W	17	
DONE ARCHABALD	70	
DONE DAVID	43	
DONE EBENEZER	41	
DONE EPHRAIM	45	
DONE JOHN	42	
DONE JONATHAN	42	
DONELLY DAVID	30	
DONEY ANTHONY	30	
DONIVAN JEREMIAH	27	
DONLY JOHN	48	
DONNAH GEORGE	19	
DONNALDSON EBENEZER	22	
DONNELL JAMES	43	
DONNELSON DAVID D	50	
DONNELSON JOHN	50+	
DONNER GEORGE	13	
DONNER JACOB	13	
DONNER JOHN	13	20
DONNER TOPIAS	13	
DOOGAN JOHN	74	
DOOLEY THOMPSON	65	
DOOLY JAMES	54	
DOOLY WILLIAM	54	
DORAN JOHN	16	
DORSEY JOHN	22	
DORSEY SAMUEL	20	
DOTY EPHRAIM	17	
DOTY JOHN JR	10	
DOTY JOHN SR	10	
DOTY JONATHAN	28	
DOUCHY SAMUEL	56	
DOUGHERTY JOSEPH	59	
DOUGLAS AMZI	21	
DOUGLAS ASHEL	20	
DOUGLAS CYRUS	12	
DOUGLAS WIILLIAM	35	
DOUGLASS THO'S	21	
DOUGLASS WILLIAM	60	
DOUGLESS MARTIN	9	
DOUGTHERTY HENRY	27	
DOUGTHTY SIMPSON	24	
DOUNS JOHN	31	
DOUT JOHN	53	
DOUTHARD SOLOMON	34	
DOUTHIT JOSE	17	
DOVER THOMAS	3	
DOVER JACOB	4	
DOW JOHN	11	
DOW WILLIAM	15	
DOW WM	15	
DOWDEN JA'S	8	
DOWDEN WM	8	
DOWDEN ZACHARIAH	9	
DOWDEN ZEPHANIAH	9	
DOWER GEORGE	56	
DOWERS AZARIAH	56	
DOWLAND WILLIAM	66	
DOWN EZEKIEL	1	
DOWNEN DAVID	49	
DOWNEN JOSIAH	49	
DOWNEY ALEXANDER	53	
DOWNEY JAMES	52	
DOWNEY JOHN	5	52
DOWNEY PETER	53	
DOWNEY WM	52	
DOWNEY WM SR	51	53
DOWNEY WM R JR	51	
DOWNING JAMES	41	
DOWNING MICHAEL	64	
DOWNING TIMOTHY	49	
DOWNS CHARLES	40	
DOWNS DAVID	37	
DOWNS URLANDOW	49	
DOYLE JACOB G	21	
DRAIN CHARLES	37	
DRAKE ALEXANDER	28	
DRAKE ISAH	76	
DRAKE JAMES	75	
DRAKE JAMES P	51	
DRAKE JOHN	69	71+
DRAKE MOSES	71	
DRAKE SAMUEL	28	
DRAPER BENJAMIN	9	
DRAPER GIDEON	46	
DRAPER JESSE	9	72
DRAPER JOSEPH	61	72
DRAPER JOSIAH	72	
DRAPER JOSIAH JR	72	
DRAPER NATHAN	12	
DRAPER PETER	9	63
DRAPER THOMAS	63	
DRAPER WILLIAM	63	
DREW LANGSTON	53	
DRINKWATER HENERY	46	
DRINKWATER PAUL	46	
DRINKWATER THOMAS	46	
DRISKEL WILLIAM	63	
DRISKILL ELIJAH	64+	

DRUGGAN JOSIAH		16
DRYDEN JOHN		18
DRYDEN THOMAS		23
DUBOIS AKINS		28
DUBOIS MICHAEL		28
DUCKSWORTH GEORGE		51
DUCKWORTH EZEKILL		50
DUCKWORTH JAMES		53
DUCKWORTH JOHN JR		50
DUCKWORTH NATHANIEL		35
DUCKWORTH THO'S		50
DUCKWORTH WILLIAM		35
DUCKWORTH WM JR		50
DUCKWORTH WM SR		50
DUDLEY JA'S		12
DUDLEY JAMES		67
DUDLEY RANSOM		67
DUFF DANIEL		51
DUFF JOSEPH		5
DUFFEY JOSEPH		61
DUFFIELD THOMAS		37
DUFFIELD WILLIAM		61
DUFFY ANDREW		19
DUFFY JAMES		19
DUFFY JOHN		18
DUFIELD WILLIAM	14 15	20
DUGAN SAMUEL	14	20
DUKE EPHRAIM		36
DUKES EZEKIEL		52
DUKES JOHN		57
DUKES ROB'T		52
DUKES ROBERT S		37
DUMMAREE JOHN		55
DUN ROBERT		31
DUNAN ANDREW		4
DUNBAR JAMES		46
DUNBAR JOHN		51
DUNCAN CHARLES		64
DUNCAN FLEMING		42
DUNCAN GEORGE JR		42
DUNCAN GEORGE SR		44
DUNCAN JOHN		40
DUNCAN RUBEN		42
DUNCAN WILLIAM		43
DUNGAN JOHN		17
DUNGAN NATHAN		23
DUNGAN SAMUEL		23
DUNHAM HUXFORD		59
DUNHAM JESSE		8
DUNHAM JOHN M		58
DUNHAM WM		10
DUNICK WILLIAM B		5
DUNK CHARLES		59
DUNK SAMUEL		59
DUNKIN GREEN		5
DUNKIN JOSHUA		5
DUNLAP JOHN		60
DUNLAP STEPHEN S		60
DUNLOPE JOHN		16
DUNN BERRY		49
DUNN JAMES		51
DUNN JOHN	28 46 51	57
DUNN JOSEPH	31	61
DUNN ROB'T		51
DUNN SAMUEL		31
DUNN WILLIAM		16
DUNNING JAMES		37
DUNNING SAMUEL		37
DUNNING THOMAS		36
DUPREE LEWIS		28
DUPREEST WILLIAM		5
DUPRIEST JOHN		5
DUPUY B		22
DURANT CORNELIUS		57
DURBINE AMUS		25
DURELL JOHN		30
DURELL STEPHEN		30
DURELL STEPHEN B		30
DURHAM JOHN		32
DURKEE ASIEL		50
DURLEY ARTHUR JR		49
DURLEY ARTHUR SR		49
DURLEY JAMES		49
DURPHY ELISHA		57
DURR FRAMPERT		53
DURR JACOB JR		53
DURR JACOB SR		53
DURT RICHARD		21
DUSKIN WILLIAM		37
DUTTON JOHN		37
DUTY MATTHEW		53
DUTY RICHARD		31
DUTY WM		52
DUVAUL CHARLES		14
DUVAUL LOT		14
DUVAUL NOAH		14
DWEGGINS JOSEPH		72
DWIGGINS JAMES		75
DYER EZEKIEL		37
DYER JOHN		49
DYER WILLIAM		37

E

EARLEY JOHN		64
EARLY JOHN D		28
EASLY THOMAS		1
EASMAN NATHAN		25
EASMAN NATHANIEL		25
EASMAN SOLOMON R		25
EASON HARMIN 2		48
EAST WILLIAM		74
EASTER GEORGE JR		66
EASTER GEORGE SR		66
EASTRIDGE EPHRAIM		74
EASTRIDGE ISAAC		39
EASTRIDGE JAMES		46
EASTRIDGE JOHN		39
EASTUP JOHN		75
EATON GEORGE		53
EATON JAMES		54
EATON JOHN		52
EATON MORGAN	49	52
EATON SOLOMON		21
EATON STEPHEN		52
EATON T W		21
EATON THOMAS		52
EATON WM		52
EAVANS JAMES		73
EBLEN JOSHUA		22
EBLEN MICHAEL		19
ECCLES BAZEL		13
ECCLES JOHN		13
ECCLES SAMUEL		13
ECHOLS JOSEPH		23
EDDINGTON JOHN		66
EDDINGTON THO'S		17
EDDLEMAN DANIEL		18
EDDY CHARLES		33
EDEN ELIAS		15
EDES JOHN		2
EDES THOMAS		43
EDINGLOW SILAS		5
EDMESTER JOSEPH		25
EDMOND GEORGE		57
EDMOND JOHN		57
EDMOND WILLIAM JR		37
EDMONS HENERY		51
EDSOL DANIEL		1
EDWARDS DAVID		11
EDWARDS ELI		11
EDWARDS GRIFFETH		68
EDWARDS HENRY		37
EDWARDS ISAAC		44
EDWARDS ISAAC D		70
EDWARDS JA'S		11
EDWARDS JAMES		34
EDWARDS JOHN	25	72
EDWARDS JONATHAN		72
EDWARDS LEWIS B		30
EDWARDS MEREDITH		45
EDWARDS NANCY		18
EDWARDS PETER		45
EDWARDS RICHARD	40	50
EDWARDS THOMAS	41	43
EDWARDS WM		11
EDWARDS WRIGHT		37
EENS ENOCH		25
EHMAN JACOB		53
EKINSBARGER FREDERICK		54
ELDER J ELI		29
ELDER WILLIAM		28
ELDRIDG JOHN	47	48
ELDRIDGE LEVI		17
ELDSWORTH JAMES		30
ELEWELL DAVID		23
ELGIN JESSE		68
ELGIN JESSE JR		68
ELGIN JOHN		68
ELIOT EDWARD		73
ELIOT JOB		73
ELIOTT ALLEX'R McCLURE		25
ELIOTT NATNAN		75
ELISON FINLEY		52
ELKENS JOSIAH		51
ELKINS JOSHUWAY		52
ELKINS SHADERICK		51
ELKINS WM		10
ELLESON CHARLES		51
ELLESON HUGH		51
ELLIAS STEPHEN		15
ELLIOT EDWARD		37
ELLIOT ELIJAH		37
ELLIOT NATHAN		72
ELLIOT SAMUEL		37+
ELLIOTT AXEUM		75
ELLIOTT CALIB		9
ELLIOTT DAVID		25
ELLIOTT FRANCISS		10
ELLIOTT HENRY		69
ELLIOTT JACOB JR		75
ELLIOTT JAMES	25 32	58
ELLIOTT JOHN	10 32 33 67	75
ELLIOTT JONSTON		25
ELLIOTT JOSEPH		67
ELLIOTT LEVI		31
ELLIOTT ROBERT	5 20 25 32	64
ELLIOTT WASHINGTON		75
ELLIOTT WILLIAM	22 25 32 63	70

ELLIOTT ZIMRIE		44
ELLIS DANIEL		42
ELLIS JOSEPH		15
ELLIS ROGER		55
ELLIS SETH		10
ELLIS STEPHEN		22
ELLISON JAMES		64
ELLISON JOSEPH		42
ELLISON ROBERT		63
ELLOTE JOB		75
ELOXANDER JOHN		29
ELROD JACOB		41
ELROD JOHN	41+	66
ELROD ROBERT		40
ELROD STEPHEN	40	66
ELSON ISAAC C		31
ELSTON JOSEPH		72
ELSTON JOSIAH		74
ELSWORTH ARON		57
ELY GEORGE		10
EMBREE WILLIAM		5
EMERSON JONATHAN		5
EMMERSON BENJ		15
EMMERSON JESSEE		5
EMMERSON JOHN		32
EMMERSON RUBIN		5
EMMERSON SAMUEL		29
EMMERSON THOMAS		32
EMMONS JESSE		12
EMPSON PETER		13
ENDICOTT AARON		52
ENDICOTT THO'S SR		52
ENDICUTT JESSE		52
ENGLISH JOSEPH		25
ENLELE JOHN		54
ENNIS ARCHABALD E		12
ENNIS JOHN		5
ENOS W C		22
ENSLEY ABRAHAM		72
ENSLY ANAVE		75
EPPERSON JAMES		21
EPPERSON WILLIAM		21
ERLE JACOB		25
ERLE JAMES		25
ERNEA JOSEPH		29
ERNEA LEWIS		29
ERSKINE ANDREW		57
ERSKINE JOHN		57
ERSKINE THOMAS		57
ERVIN JAMES		53
ERVIN ROBERT		60
ERVIN SAM'L		53
ERVIN WM		49
ESK JAMES		56

ESLIH SAMUEL		46
ESLINGER CHRISTIAN		37
ESLINGER JOHN		37
ESLY STEPHEN	1	3
ESSARY JONATHAN		47
ESTEP JAMES		73
ESTES BARTLEY		52
ESTES THO'S		52
ESTES WM		52
ETHERINGTON JOSEPH		14
EVANS ABNER		37
EVANS JAMES		5
EVANS JESSE		9
EVANS JOHN	43	72
EVANS RICHARD		57
EVANS ROBERT	63	66
EVANS ROBERT M		5
EVANS SOLOMON		56
EVANS STROUD		43
EVANS THOMAS		63
EVANS WILLIAM		63
EVANS WILLIAM B		37
EVENS ABRAHAM		3
EVERETT JAMES		70
EVERETT JOHN		70
EVERHART JOHN		22
EVERHART WILLIAM		22
EVERLING GEORGE		25
EVIRAGE ABRAM		1
EWALT JOHN		11
EWING AARON		49
EWING BARTIS		37
EWING GEORGE		29
EWING GEORGE JR		46
EWING GEORGE SR	30	46
EWING HENRY		59
EWING JOHN	29	47
EWING NATHANIEL		29
EWING ROBERT		47
EWING THO'S		8
EWING WM		59
EWING WM H		10
EWINGS MOSES		49

F

FAFOYE LAMBARE	28	
FAIRCHILD ALPHEA J	58	
FAIRCHILD ALPHEAS JR	58	
FAIRCHILD ELAM	58	
FAIRCHILD ISAAC	58	
FAIRCHILD JONATHAN	58	
FAIRCHILD ORMAND	58	
FAIRCHILD SETH	58	
FAIRCHILD THOMAS	45	
FAIRCHILD WALTER	57	
FAIRCHILD ZERA	58	
FAIRHUST JOHN	33	
FAIRHUST SAMUEL	32	
FAIRHUST WILSON	32	
FAIT HENRY	41	
FAITH JOHN	46	47
FALBERT JACOB	72	
FALKINBERRY JAMES	47	
FALLS ROBERT	5	
FANCHER BENJAMIN	43	
FARABEE JOHN	60	
FARES ISAAC	37	
FAREWELL JOHN	51	
FARIS JOSHUA	67	
FARIS THOMAS	33	
FARLOW GEORGE	37	
FARLOW JOSEPH	42	
FARLOW SAMUEL	72	
FARMER FREDERICK	57	
FARMER HILCHAM	57	
FARMER MR SR	57	
FARNAER ISAAC	57	
FARRINGTON JAMES	27	
FARRIS GIDEON	39	
FARRIS JOHN	45	48
FAULKNER WILLIAM	40	
FAVOURS THOS	16	
FAWCET BENJAMIN	72	
FEASLE JOHN	33	
FEATHERS STEPHEN	13	
FEILEY JAMES	27	
FEKHAMNER GEORGE	54	
FELL MAHLON	21	
FELLOW HART	27	
FELLOW WILLIS	27	
FELLOW WILLIS JR	27	
FELLOWS - - -	57	
FELLOWS EDMONS	57	
FELTON JOHN	32	
FENDER HENRY	72	
FENDER JONATHAN	72	

FENNING THOMAS	61	
FENNIR THO'S	54	
FENNY JAMES	5	
FENTON BART.	14	
FENTON BARTHOLOMEW	20	
FENTRESS EDWARD JR	9	
FENTRESS EDWARD SR	9	
FENTRESS JA'S	9	
FENTRESS PHOROAH	9	
FERGERSON JAMES	5	
FERGUSON JAMES	61	
FERGUSON JESSE	68	
FERGUSON JOHN	41	
FERGUSON STEWART	67	
FERGUSON THOMAS	43	
FERGUSON WASHINGTON	24	
FERRARI ANDREW	30	
FERREE ISRAEL	51	
FERREL JOHN	59	
FERRON ISAAC	25	
FERSITHE DENMARK	43	
FEUCHT MICHAEL	53	
FICUS ADAM	66	
FIELD JOHN	16	23
FIELD WILLIAM	16	
FIELDER JOHN	5	
FIELDING LUCAS	6	
FIELDS ABERHAM	5	
FIELDS BENGAMIN	40	
FIELDS JOHN	42	
FIGGINS GEORGE	47	
FILES SM'L	76	
FILLINGIM ENOCH	52	
FIMISE WILLIAM	47	
FIN JACOB	17	
FINCH HADEN	44	
FINCH JAMES	44	
FINCH JAMES JR	44	
FINCH WILLIAM S/L	25	
FINCH YELVINGTON	51	
FINCOAT THO'S	17	
FINDER GABRIEL	72	
FINDLEY JESSE	45	
FINDLEY SAMUEL	41	
FINLEY ABLE JR	10	
FINLEY ABLE SR	10	
FINLEY DAVID	45	
FINLEY HARVEY	68	
FINLEY HUGH	10	
FINLEY HUGH SR	8	
FINLEY JOHN	13	32
FINNEY JOSEPH	11	
FINNEY ROBERT	25	
FINNY ANDREW	5	

Name	Page
FINNY SAMUEL	5
FINTCH ABRAHAM	47
FINTCH PHILIP	46
FINTCH WILLIAM	48
FIPPIN ANDREW	64
FIPS WILLIAM	64
FISCUS FREDERICK SR	66
FISCUS FREDERICK SR	66
FISCUS HENRY	66
FISCUS PETER	66
FISHER ALEXANDER	29
FISHER CHARLES	29
FISHER ELISHA	71
FISHER HENRY	54 68
FISHER JACOB	60
FISHER JAMES	71
FISHER JAMES B	63
FISHER JOHN	68 71 75
FISHER JOHN B	5
FISHER NOAH	43
FISHER PALMER	28
FISHER PERNELL	5
FISHER PETER JR	68
FISHER PETER SR	68
FISHER PHILIP	54
FISHER SALVANUS	72
FISHER STEPHEN	5
FISHER THADEUS	41
FISHER THOMAS	71
FISHER ZELEK	41
FISLER JACOB	12
FISLER JESSE	12
FISLER JOHN	12
FISLER JOSEPH	12
FITCH ELIAS	15
FITCH JOHN	18
FITCH-PATRICK J	14
FITSGERALD ARON	47
FITSPATRICK JAMES	44
FITTSGERALD JOHN	37
FITZGERALD ARCH'B	58
FITZGERALD JOHN	58
FITZGERALD MORRISON	58
FITZGERALD THOMAS	46 47
FITZGERALD WM	58
FITZGERAULD JAMES	5
FITZGERAULD JOHNSON	5
FITZJERAULD JAMES	5
FITZPATRICK HENRY	44
FIX JACOB	22
FIX WILLIAM	22
FLAKE PHILIP	73
FLANERY JOHN	3
FLANNERY JAMES	1
FLANNERY JOHN	1
FLARHERTY PATRICK	24
FLEENER ABRAHAM	62
FLEENER FREDERICK	62
FLEENOR JOHN	62
FLEMING JAMES	66
FLEMING JOHN	18
FLEMING ROBT	22
FLEMMING PETER	71
FLEMMON DAVID	1
FLEMMON THOMAS	1
FLENOR NICHOLAS	37
FLETCHER GEORGE	27
FLETCHER JOHN	66
FLETCHER THO'S	53
FLETCHER VERDAMAN	66
FLETCHER WILLIAM	42
FLICK CHRISTOPHER	39
FLINN AARON	10
FLINN DANIEL	34
FLINN GEORGE	11
FLINN JACOB	11
FLINN JAMES	1
FLINN JOHN	10
FLINN MATHEW	10
FLINN ROBERT	11
FLINN THO'S	49
FLINN WM JR	11
FLINN WM of JACOB	10
FLINN WM SR	11
FLOWER WILLIAM	34
FLOWERS THOMAS	69
FLOYD JONATHAN	39
FOISTER BENJAMINE	52
FOLLER RICHARD	3
FOLLOWELL JOHN	1
FOLLOWELL LINDSEY	3
FOLLOWELL MARTIN	4
FOLLOWELL WILLIAM	1
FONTANY JOHN BT	30
FOOTS WILLIAM	61
FORBUS JOHN	8 23
FORBUSH GEORGE	5
FORD JOHN	47
FORD NOAH	1
FORD NOAH JR	4
FORD ROBERT	18
FORD WILLIAM	31 69
FORDHAM ELIAS H	7
FORDYCE CYRUS	64
FOREUM JOHN	52
FORGERSON JOHN	5
FORSCHNER GEORGE	53
FORSCHNER MICHAEL	53

FORTNER	FORD		9
FOSSEY	JOHN		65
FOSSEY	ROBERT		65
FOSSEY	THOMAS		65
FOSTER	A		22
FOSTER	AMASA D		7
FOSTER	BARTLEY		68
FOSTER	DRURY		40
FOSTER	GABRIEL		18
FOSTER	JOHN		37 63
FOSTER	SAMUEL		52
FOSTER	WILLIAM		63
FOSTER	WILLIAM P		5
FOSTER	WM		52
FOSTER	WM A		58
FOULTZ	LEVI		75
FOUNG	ADAM		53
FOUTS	DAVID		60
FOUTS	NOEL		63
FOWLER	CHESTER		36
FOWLER	DUDLY		3
FOWLER	JACOB		41
FOWLER	JAMES		25
FOWLER	JOSHUA		25
FOWLER	RAWLEY		51
FOWLER	WILLIAM		41 71
FOX	DANIEL A B C		55
FOX	GEORGE		43
FOX	ROBT		23
FOX	SHUBAL		15
FOYLES	JAMES		28
FRABER	HENRY		62
FRAIKES	JOHN		47
FRAKES	ALEXANDER		1
FRAKES	JOHN		68
FRAKES	PETER		1
FRANCE	JOHN		52
FRANCIS	JAMES		35
FRANCIS	JOHN		13
FRANCIS	JOHN SR		13
FRANCIS	WALTER		13
FRANCIS	WILLIAM		25
FRANK	GEORGE		53
FRANKHUSM	- - -		39
FRANKLIN	JOHN		37
FRASIER	ABMEN		66
FREDERICK	DANIEL		7
FREDERICK	MICHAEL		5
FREDERICK	PETER JR		5
FREDERICK	PETTER		34
FREDERICK	PHILIP		5
FREDERICK	SEBASTIAN		34
FREDERICK	SEBASTIN		5
FREED	JOHN		44 67
FREED	JOSEPH		67
FREED	MARTIN		44
FREELAND	BENJAMIN		37
FREEMAN	ABSOLAM		40
FREEMAN	BENJAMIN		40
FREEMAN	DANIEL		40
FREEMAN	DANIEL JR		40
FREEMAN	GARBIAL		35
FREEMAN	JOHN		40 41
FREEMAN	JOSHUA		41
FREEMAN	SAMUEL		43
FREEMAN	STEPEN		25
FREEMAN	THOMPSON		40
FREEMAN	WILLIAM		41
FRENCH	DORRES		50+
FRENCH	FELEN		50
FRENCH	GEORGE		40
FRENCH	HARRIS		25
FRENCH	JAMES		50
FRENCH	RALPH		50
FRENCH	SAMUEL		40
FRENCH	ZEPHNIAH		25
FRESURE	BENGAMIN		25
FRICK	FREDERICK		21
FRIDLEY	JOHN		61
FRIEND	JOSEPH		17
FRIER	JOHN H		72
FRITZ	MICHAEL		54
FROMAN	ABRAHAM		1
FROMAN	JACOB		1
FRORKIN	DANIEL		71
FROST	EDWARD		75
FRY	AMOS		76
FRY	BENJAMIN		37
FUEL	MASON		19
FUEL	NATHANIEL		23
FUEL	SPENCER		18
FUGATE	SAMUEL		33
FUGIT	JESSE		22
FULBRAITH	ROBERT		73
FULCH	ANDREW		66
FULCH	JOSEPH		66
FULCH	LEONARD		66
FULFER	ABRAHAM		45
FULFER	JOSEPH		45
FULK	MARTIN		62
FULLEN	RUEBIN		37
FULLEN	JOHN		37
FULLER	ARCHABALD		48
FULLER	DARLING		37
FULLER	JAMES		37
FULLER	JOHN		37
FULLER	PORTER		58
FULLETION	JOHN		29

FULLINGTON WILLIAM C		29
FULLINGWIDER HENRY		1
FULMER HENRY		61
FUNK CHRISTOPHER SR		70
FUNK JOHN	1	15
FUNK JOSEPH		1
FUNK PETER		1
FURGUSSON JOHN		19

G

GABHARD HENRY	3
GADBERRY JAMES	70
GADDES JAMES	18
GAGEBY JOHN	22
GAGER ADDAM	53
GAGER JACOB	53
GAIL JOHN	51
GAIL REASKIN	54
GAILARD EDWARD	61
GAINES ARMSTRONG	71
GALAHER THOS	17
GALASPY GEORGE	9
GALASPY ROBERT	9
GALAWAY DAVID	5
GALBREATH THOMAS	69
GALDBREATH SAMUEL	68
GALE ELMON	23
GALE ISAAC	20
GALE RUFUS	20
GALE WILLIAM S	71
GALLAGHER ADAM	35
GALLAGHER WILLIAM	35
GALLAND ABLE	31
GALLOWAY ELIHU	25
GALSPIA PATRICK	29
GALUSHA AZABAH	17
GALY DAVID	46
GAMBEN TUCATE	30
GAMBERL DAVID	5
GAMBERL WILLIAM	5
GAMBLE JOSEPH	33
GAMBLE WILLIAM	33
GAMBLIN USTAS	30
GAMBORE HENRY	5
GAMLIN PEIRRE	29
GAMMON JAMES	67
GANTER JACOB	53
GARDENER JOHN I	35
GARDENOR ANDREW	29
GARDINER STEPHN	10
GARDISON JOHN	5
GARDNER EPHRAIM	63
GARDNER JESSE	76

GARDNER JOHN		37
GARDNON RICHARD		5
GARISON DANIEL		51
GARISON ELIJAH		50
GARNER BRADLEY		72
GARNER PHINES		28
GARNER WYATT		12
GARNY THOMAS		71
GARR ABRAHAM		72
GARR JONAS		75
GARRET GIBSON		37
GARRET JAMES		15
GARRETT AMBROSE		60
GARRETT ANTHONY		70
GARRETT CALEB		61
GARRETT HENRY	5 60	74
GARRETT ISAAC		60
GARRETT JACOB		60
GARRETT PRESLY		5
GARRETT WILLIAM		32
GARRIOTT SIMEON		65
GARRIOTT WILLIAM		65
GARRIS JOSEPH JR		52
GARRIS JOSEPH SR		52
GARRISON ABRAHAM		50
GARRISSON GIDEON		74
GARROTT GEORGE		34
GARTON WILLIAM		5
GARVAS ALEXANDER		52
GARVEY JOHN	43	68
GARWOOD JOSEPH		42
GASAWAY THO'S		18
GASKINS JAMES		64
GASKINS SAMUEL		68
GASTON ANSON		37
GASTON THOMAS		37
GATES WILLIAM		19
GATTES JOHN		25
GAULT WILLIAM		29
GAVIT JOHN		21
GAVIT MARCUS		21
GAY JOHN	71	73
GEAR JOHN C		25
GEATER CHRISTIAN		29
GEER J C		23
GEI JOHN		62
GENTLE WILLIAM		63
GEORGE DAVID		62
GEORGE JAMES T		63
GERDON JOSEPH		18
GEREW LEVEY		28
GEROME ANTOINE		30
GERRARD SAMUEL		59
GERTIN JEREMIAH		72

GHARKINS WILLIAM	64	
GHARRIS SHARP	52	
GHASKINS JOHN	62	
GHOLSON FREDERICK	21	
GIBBENS JAMES	67	
GIBBS JAMES	37	
GIBSON BARNEY	37	
GIBSON JOHN	21	59
GIBSON JULIUS	59	
GIBSON ROBERT	57	
GIFFORD ICHABOD	75	
GIFFORD LEVI JR	42	
GIFFORD LEVI BR	42	
GILBERT JOHN	62	
GILBERT JONATHAN	37	
GILBERT JOSEPH	37	
GILBERT JOSIAH	75	
GILBERT SAMPSON	51	
GILBERT THO'S	51	52
GILBERT THOMAS	75	
GILBERT WILLIAM	47	48
GILBREATH ANDREW	49	
GILCREASE JAMES	64	
GILCREASE ROBERT	62	
GILCREASE WILLIAM	62	
GILES JOHN	62	
GILES THOMAS	45	
GILHAM JOHN	55	
GILL JOHN	45	
GILL ROBERT	35	
GILL SAM'L	50	
GILLAM DRURY	37	
GILLESPIE ISAAC	37	
GILLESPIE WILLIAM	65	
GILLETT ARKIMUS	58	
GILLILAND JOHN	46	1
GILLMORE EPHRAIM	33	
GILLMORE JAMES	76	
GILLMORE JOHN W	59	
GILLMORE ROBERT	32	
GILMORE LUTHER	13	14
GILSTRAP DAVID	65	
GILSTRAP PETER	65	
GILSTRAP RICHARD	65	
GILSTRAP WILLIAM	65	
GIVENS ELISHA	42	
GIVENS JOHN A	37	
GIVINS CHARLES C	50	
GIVINS THO'S	51	
GIVINS WM	51	
GLASBROOK WILLIAM	61	
GLASGOW SAMUEL	13	
GLASPEY JOHN	35	
GLASS GEORGE	3	

GLASS THOMAS	34
GLASSEY MICHAEL	28
GLASSON WM	9
GLAZEBROOK CLIFT	63
GLAZEBROOK JULIUS	62
GLEEN JAMES	1
GLEEN SAMUEL JR	1
GLEEN SAMUEL SR	1
GLEEN THOMAS	1
GLEN ISAAC B	43
GLEN SAMUEL	39
GLENN JOHN SR	1
GLORE JACOB	21
GLOSSEN WM	9
GLOSSER FREDERICK	66
GLOVER ASA	10
GLOVER CHARLES	45
GLOVER JAMES	20
GLOVER JOHN	45
GLOVER JONAH	40
GLOVER STEPHEN	41
GLOVER THO'S	19
GLOVER URIAH	40
GLOVER URIAH SR	45
GOAD GALY	48
GODARE ANDREW	29
GODARE FRANCIS	30
GODARE JOHN	28
GODFREY WILLIAM	48
GODFROY ELIJAH	69
GOETZ JOSEPH	53
GOFF JOSHUA	10
GOFF SAMPSON	55
GOFOUTH WM	11
GOLA DAVID	55
GOLD AUSTIN	10
GOLD EDMAN	22
GOLDEN EDWARD	1
GOLDEN JONATHAN	58
GOLDMAN GEORGE	33
GOLDMAN MARTIN	33
GOLDMAN MOSES	3
GOLDSBY BRIGS M	63
GOLDSBY EDWARD	63
GOLDSBY GEORGE	63
GOLDSBY JOHN	63
GOLDSBY WILLIAM	21
GOLDSMITH DANIEL L	58
GOLDY WILLIAM	45
GOLMAN JOHN	1
GOLY DAVID	14
GONZALES SIMON	28
GOOD GEORGE	51
GOOD JOHN	51

Name	Page
GOOD PETER	51
GOOD THO'S	51
GOODALE WILLIAM	14
GOODEN JOHN	75
GOODEN SAMUEL	62
GOODLETT J R E	58
GOODLETT MOSES	50
GOODMAN BARTLETT	31
GOODMAN GEORGE	37
GOODMAN JESSE	1
GOODMAN JOHN	31
GOODMAN JOHN SR	31
GOODMAN JOHN BT	29
GOODMAN WILLIAM	1
GOODRICH CARMY	55
GOODRIDGE SAMUEL E	48
GOODSON JOHN	1
GOODSON JOSEPH	63
GOODWIN ELIAS	37
GOODWIN JOHN	37
GOODWIN SETH	37
GOODWIN WILLIAM	37
GOOLMAN JOHN JR	1
GOOR FIELDING	75
GORDEN GEORGE	30
GORDON AARON	60
GORDON GEORGE	14 58
GORDON GEORGE JR	14
GORDON HOWARD	63
GORDON HUGH	64
GORDON ISAAC	62
GORDON JAMES	14
GORDON JOHN	5
GORDON SAMUEL	5+
GORDON WILLIAM	62 64 72
GORDON WM	14
GORE FREDERICK	10
GORE LEVI	17
GORHAM SILAS F	15
GORMAN PATRICK	57
GORSUCK JOHN	21
GORTNEY THO'S	49
GOSNEL ADAM	37
GOSS EPHRAIM	37
GOSS FREDERICK	11
GOSS GEORGE	37
GOSS JOHN	61
GOSS JONATHAN	59
GOSS JOSEPH	11
GOSSETT JOHN	9
GOSSETT WILLIAMSON	9
GOTHARD ISAAC	59
GOTT GLAYSEN	3
GOTT HASON	4
GOTTERWA JOSEPH	53
GOUCHER SAMUEL	56
GOULD ADOLPHUS	67
GOULD JOHN JR	67
GOULD JOHN SR	67
GOUNT NICHOLAS	20
GOURDAN MOSES	4
GOW PETER	16
GOWEN WALTER	4
GOWENS STEPHEN	56
GOWER WALTER	3
GOYER GEORGE	37
GRACE JESSE	67
GRACE RUSSEL	68
GRACE WILLIAM	67
GRACE WILLIAM JR	68
GRADDEY JOHN	49
GRADY THO'S	50
GRAHAM ANDREW	59
GRAHAM HUGH	65
GRAHAM JA'S	10
GRAHAM JAMES	21 61
GRAHAM JEREMIAH	9
GRAHAM JOHN	64
GRAHAM JONATHAN	9
GRAHAM ROBINSON	37
GRAHAM WILLIAM	70
GRAHAM WM	8
GRANEY THOMAS	5
GRANT CALIN	15
GRANT DAN'L	10
GRANT JA'S	10
GRANT WIAT	52
GRANT WILLIAM	20
GRANT WILLIAM A	25
GRANTHAM JESSE	62
GRANTHAM JOEL	10
GRANTHAM JOSEPH	62
GRANTHAM MOSES	62+
GRATEHOUSE WM	57
GRAVE ENOS	73
GRAVE JESSE	74
GRAVES ALVIN	70
GRAVES JACOB	74
GRAVES JAM'S L	75
GRAVES JAMES C	76
GRAVES JOHN	51
GRAVES NATHAN	72
GRAVES WILLIAM	1+
GRAY COUTTANT	75
GRAY JEDUTHAN	69
GRAY JESSE	19
GRAY JOSEPH	69
GRAY LEWIS	69

GRAY	ROBT			15	GRIFFETH	JOSEPH			66
GRAY	SAMPSON			9	GRIFFETH	LUKE			64
GRAY	SAMUEL			61	GRIFFETH	WILLIAM		44	64
GRAY	WILLIAM			25	GRIFFIN	BENGAMIN			25
GRAY	WILY			10	GRIFFIN	HIRAM			58
GREATER	FREDERICK			28	GRIFFIN	IRA			28
GREATHOUSE	DANIEL			50	GRIFFIN	JOHN		15	24
GREATHOUSE	DAVID			50	GRIFFIN	RALPH			19
GREATHOUSE	JOHN L			50	GRIFFIN	THOMAS			25
GREEGG	JOHN			70	GRIFFITH	GEORGE			10
GREEN	ABRAHAM			19	GRIFFITH	GOOKLY			75
GREEN	ENOCH			70	GRIFFITH	JOHN		37	44
GREEN	GEORGE			21	GRIFFITH	JOHN B			41
GREEN	GRAVENON			40	GRIFFITH	RICHARD			41
GREEN	HENRY			1	GRIFFITH	WILLIAM C			41
GREEN	JAMES	25	37	60	GRIGGS	DAVID			1
GREEN	JOHN	14 32	68	70	GRIGGS	GEORGE			67
GREEN	JOSEPH	25 37	49	66	GRIGGS	HUGH			8
GREEN	LOVREIGN			17	GRIGSBY	DEMPLES			5
GREEN	McCALLEN			9	GRIGSBY	JOHN			44
GREEN	NATHANIEL			9	GRIGSBY	TOLEVER			52
GREEN	PETER			68	GRIGSBY	WILLIAM			42
GREEN	ROBERT			61	GRIMES	ALEXANDER			73
GREEN	SOLOMON			37	GRIMES	D D			48
GREEN	THOMAS		8 64	69	GRIMES	DANIEL			66
GREEN	WILLIAM		66	69	GRIMES	DAVID			37
GREENAUGH	DEVORICK			29	GRIMES	GEORGE			71
GREENAUGH	WILLIAM			27	GRIMES	JAMES			72
GREENAWALT	JOHN			61	GRIMES	JOHN			56
GREENFIELD	JAMES			35	GRIMES	ROBERT		1	4
GREENWOOD	ABRAHAM			52	GRIMES	STEPHEN		15	37
GREER	GEORGE			61	GRIMES	THOMAS			37+
GREER	JAMES		61	66	GRIMES	WILLIAM			73
GREER	JOHN H			66	GRINSLEY	JOSIAH			71
GREGERY	JOHN			50	GRINSTEAD	JOHN			25
GREGORY	JOHN			48	GRISSOM	JOHN			42
GREHAM	JAMES			25	GRISSOM	JOHN W			7
GREHAM	JAMES SR			25	GRISSOM	THOMAS S			5
GREHAM	LEWIS			25	GROMORE	CHARLES			30
GREHAM	SAMUEL S			25	GROSS	HIRAM			44
GREHAM	THOMAS			25	GROSS	JOHN			44
GREHAM	THOMAS JR			25	GROVER	JER.			21
GREHAM	WILLIAM			25	GROVES	BENJAMIN			21
GREIGS	DAVID			4	GROVES	GEORGE			37
GREMORE	FRANCIS			28	GROVES	N D			21
GREY	JOHN			71	GROVES	PETER			64
GREY	JOHN JR			41	GRUBB	JACOB			70
GREY	JOHN SR			41	GRUDGEL	JOHN			18
GREYHAM	BURRELL			42	GUDGEL	NATHAN			17
GRIER	RICHARD			45	GUDGEL	STEPHEN			17
GRIESMIER	HENRY			8	GUDGIL	NATHAN			17
GRIFFETH	BARTLEY			64	GUDGILL	ISAAC			17
GRIFFETH	HORATIO			67	GUEN	ISM			1
GRIFFETH	JAMES			67	GUERKIN	JOHN			42

GUEVER AARON		73
GUIE ABSALOM		68
GUIE ROBERT		65
GUIN JOHN		21
GUINEY CHARLES		25
GULION WILLIAM		23
GULLICK JONATHAN		5
GULLY ELIAS		55
GUN JAMES		23
GUNN JOHN		43
GURLOR JOHN		67
GUTBROADT PETER		54
GUTHRIE HUGH		11
GUTHRIE JOHN		22 69
GUTHRIE RICHARD		19
GUTHRIE WILLIAM		13
GUTRY JOHN		14
GUTRY RICHARD		14
GUYER HENRY		12
GUYER SAM'L		12
GUYNER JAMES		45

H

HACKET EPHRAIM		51
HACKET NATHAN		72
HACKNEY JOHN		42
HADDEN SAMUEL		47
HADEN GEORGE		48
HADLEY JOHN		42
HADLEY JOSHUA		41
HADLEY THOMAS		42
HADLY ELI		42
HADLY JAMES		42
HADON THOMAS		67
HAGAN GEORGE		60
HAGEN THEODORE		31
HAGERMAN JOHN		43
HAGMEIER LEWIS		54
HAINED JONATHAN		39
HAINEY SOLOMAN		73
HAINING JAMES		23
HAINK GEORGE		53
HAINLEE PHILIP		54
HAINS DANIEL		70
HAINS SAMUEL		70
HAIRBACK HENRY		27 30
HALBROOK DANIEL		5
HALE DAN		12
HALE GEORGE		25
HALE JAMES		37+
HALE JOHN		37 73
HALE LEMUEL		27
HALE NATHAN		58

HALE TEMPLE		28
HALEY JESSE H		74
HALEY JOSIAH		27
HALL AARON		53
HALL ABNER		25
HALL CORNELIUS		1
HALL DAVID		19
HALL EDWARD		37
HALL FRANCIS		37
HALL GARRET		3
HALL ISAAC JR		25
HALL ISAAC SR		25
HALL JESSE		47
HALL JOHN		14 70 73
HALL RICHARD		70
HALL ROBERT W		19
HALL SAMUEL		5
HALL SQUIRE		23
HALL WILLIAM		1 3 19 69 72
HALL WM		14 57
HALL ZACHARIAH		14 22
HALLA BENJAMIN		75
HALLBROOKS GEORGE		5
HALLBROOKS WILLIAM		5
HALLOT THOMAS		73
HALY RUIR		3
HAM HEZEKIAH		73
HAMBLIN JOHN		4
HAMDEN JOHN D		17
HAMELL HUGH		30
HAMELTON ADAM		9
HAMELTON JOHN		8
HAMELTON JOSHUA		8
HAMILTON ARCHABALD		66
HAMILTON BENJAMIN		55 63
HAMILTON FRANCIS		50
HAMILTON HENRY		55
HAMILTON JAMES		21 55 63
HAMILTON JOE		8
HAMILTON JOHN		44 50 60
HAMILTON JOHN R		57
HAMILTON ROBERT		37
HAMILTON SAMUEL		21 23
HAMILTON WALKER		20
HAMILTON WILLIAM		56+
HAMILTON WILLIAM		21 22 23 37
HAMMER HUGH		67
HAMMER JOHN		70
HAMMERSLEY ABRAHAM		67
HAMMERSLEY JAMES		66
HAMMERSLY JAMES SR		67
HAMMON ARASTUS		12
HAMMON JOHN		12
HAMMON JONATHAN		16

HAMMON OLIVER		10
HAMMON WM		76
HAMMOND JAMES		24
HAMMONS LEWIS		42
HAMMONWAY JOHN		59
HAMPTON ANDREW		75
HAMPTON DAVID		71
HAMPTON JA'S		12
HAMPTON JAMES		25
HAMPTON JOHN		12
HAMPTON JONATHAN		12
HAMPTON STEPHEN		44
HAMPTON WM		59
HANAWAY AMOS		27
HANCOCK THOMAS		37
HANCOCK WILLIAM		62
HAND AARON		10
HAND CHARLES		30
HANDMAN JOHN		5
HANES SAMUEL		45
HANEY JOHN	21	70
HANING WILLIAM		16
HANKINS WM		15
HANKINS ABSOLEN		15
HANKINS JOSEPH		15
HANKINS LEWIS		9
HANKS JOSEPH		1
HANKS NICHOLAS A		7
HANKS PETTER		35
HANKS WILLIAM		5
HANLEY WILLIAM G		37
HANN EPHRAIM		56
HANNA JOSEPH		11
HANNAH JOHN		25
HANNEN BARTHOLIMIUS		8
HANNEN JOHN		8
HANNON JA'S		10
HANT JOSIAH		74
HARBAND MOSLEY		35
HARBART JOSEPH B		67
HARBEN JOHN		34
HARBER JOSEPH		5
HARBERT ROBERT		20
HARBIN EDWARD V		61
HARBISON JAMES		62
HARBOLT HENRY		65
HARDEN DAVID JR		57
HARDEN DAVID SR		57
HARDEN SION		33
HARDIN AARON		70
HARDIN ABRAHAM		49
HARDIN ELISHA JR		69
HARDIN JOHN JR		69+
HARDIN NICHOLAS		49
HARDIN STEPHEN		70
HARDIN WILLIAM		37
HARDISON - - -		30
HARDISTER SAMUEL		37
HARDMAN HENRY		69
HARDMAN JACOB		69
HARDON JAMES		76
HARDON JOHN		46
HARDWICK THO'S		12
HARDY LUKE		5
HARDY RICHARD		6
HARDY WILLIAM A		5
HARDYSON HARDY		34
HARENY WILLIAM		74
HARGRAVENES THO'S		50
HARGRAVES EZEKIEL		50
HARGUESS JOHN		47
HARIMAN GEORGE		76
HARIMAN WM		76
HARIMON SAMUEL		37
HARISON WISE		51
HARKINS GEORGE		20
HARKINS JOHN		25
HARKMAN DANIEL		41
HARLAN ELIHU		73
HARLAND JAMES		60
HARLAND WILLIAM		20
HARLEN ELIHU		75
HARLEN JOSHUA		75
HARLEN VOLINTINE		75
HARLIN JOSHUA		73
HARLIN VALENTINE		72
HARLOW JOSHUA		12
HARLOW RICHARD		12
HARMAN GEORGE		25
HARMON ANDREW		74
HARMON DANIEL		65
HARMON GEORGE		65
HARMON JOHN		11
HARMON LEVI		70
HARMON LEWIS		5
HARMON MATTHIAS		65
HARMON MOSES		66
HARMON SAM'L		49
HARMON WM		52
HARNARD JOHN		61
HARNED THOMAS		41
HARNED WILLIAM		41
HARNES JOHN		41
HARNES NATHANIEL		47
HARNESS ADAM		35
HARNESS MICHAEL		35
HARNESS NATHANIEL		35
HAROLD ELISHA		10

HARPER	ADAM			5
HARPER	EZEKIEL			56
HARPER	GEORGE		16	35
HARPER	J			16
HARPER	JACOB			32
HARPER	THOMAS		32	72
HARRAMAN	CHARLES			70
HARRAMAN	ELISHA			70
HARRAMAN	SIMON			70
HARREL	GABRIEL			72
HARRES	CHARLES			52
HARRINGTON	CHARLES			5
HARRINGTON	DANIEL			29
HARRINGTON	JOHN			29
HARRINGTON	WILLIAM			5
HARRIS	AUGUSTUS			14
HARRIS	BENJAMIN			75
HARRIS	BENJAMIN	JR		74
HARRIS	DANIEL			13
HARRIS	JACOB			13
HARRIS	JAMES			73
HARRIS	JESSE		55	68
HARRIS	JOAB			58
HARRIS	JOHAH			68
HARRIS	JOHN		11	68
HARRIS	JONAS			75
HARRIS	JOSEPH			55
HARRIS	MICAJAH			67
HARRIS	NATHAN			56
HARRIS	NATHANIEL			67
HARRIS	OBEDIAH	JR		76
HARRIS	OBEDIAH	SR		76
HARRIS	RHOADIS			39
HARRIS	RICHARD			49
HARRIS	THO'S			13
HARRIS	THOMAS		68	70
HARRIS	WILLIAM			68
HARRISON	- - -			34
HARRISON	BAILES			58
HARRISON	CHRISTOPHER			61
HARRISON	DAVID		11	58
HARRISON	ELISHA			58
HARRISON	JOHN			58
HARRISON	JOHN JR			58
HARRISON	JOSEPH G			73
HARRISON	NICHOLAS			61
HARRISON	ROBERT			18
HARRISON	SIMMS C			27
HARRISON	THOMAS			67
HARRISON	WILLIAM JR			31
HARRISON	WILLIAM SR			31
HARRISON	ZEPHANIAH			58
HARRISS	WILLIAM			33
HARROD	THOMAS			60
HARROL	JOHN			73
HART	DAVID		5	29
HART	JOHN		4	42
HART	McKENZIE			42
HART	REGUS			1
HARTER	PHILLIP			74
HARTLEY	JAMES			60
HARTLEY	JOHN		11	34
HARTLEY	JOSEPH			11
HARTLEY	SAMUEL			60
HARTLEY	STILMAN			11
HARTLEY	WILLIAM			60
HARTMAN	HENRY			53
HARTON	GEORGE			5
HARTSOCK	JAMES			19
HARTSOCK	SAMUEL			37
HARTWELL	EPHRAIM		16	20
HARTWELL	WILLIAM			25
HARTWELL	WILLIAN JR			25
HARVEY	ALEXANDER			5
HARVEY	ANDREW			5
HARVEY	JOHN		62	74
HARVEY	MARMADUKE			67
HARVEY	MICHAEL JR			1
HARVEY	MICHAEL SR			1
HARVEY	ROBERT			67
HARVEY	WILLIAM			67
HARVY	AMOS			74
HASETT	JOSEPH			23
HASLEY	JOHN			69
HASTE	WILLIAM			17
HATCHET	PLENA			22
HATFIELD	JAMES			49
HATFIELD	WM			52
HATTABOUGH	GEORGE JR			64
HATTABOUGH	GEORGE SR			64
HATTABOUGH	JACOB			64
HATTABOUGH	MARTIN B			64
HATTABOUGH	PHILIP			64
HATTON	JOHN			11
HAUFLER	MICHAEL			53
HAUFLER	TOBIAS			53
HAUGER	GEORGE			69
HAUGER	JOHN			69
HAUGER	SOLOMON			70
HAUGH	ISRAEL			76
HAUGH	JAMES			76
HAUGH	JESSE			76
HAUGH	JOHN			76
HAUGH	PHILIP			37
HAUGHBOY	JACOB			22
HAUKINS	SILAS SR			74
HAUN	JAMES			37
HAVEN	DAVID			17

HAVENS JOHN		55
HAVENS STEPHEN		37
HAVERTON THOMAS		71
HAWES JAMES		1
HAWKEE ARTHER		47
HAWKINS AMOS JR		72
HAWKINS ARTHER		5
HAWKINS DAVID		1
HAWKINS HENRY		5 74
HAWKINS JOHN		72
HAWKINS NATHAN		72
HAWKINS THOMAS		5
HAWKINS WILLIAM C		18
HAWLEY ZALMON		56
HAWN HENRY		65
HAWN JACOB		62
HAWORTH JOHN		37
HAWS REUBEN		24
HAY JOHN D		10 28
HAY WILLIAM		16
HAYES JOHN		33
HAYLEY HUGH		73
HAYNES ANIEL		66
HAYNS DANIEL		50
HAYNS JOHN		51
HAYS GEORGE		52
HAYS JAMES		19 21
HAYS JOSHUA JR		65
HAYS JOSHUA SR		65
HAYS MOSES		68
HAYS SAMUEL		18 68
HAYS WILLIS		37
HAZELET SAMUEL		37
HAZELET WILLIAM		37
HAZELTON DANIEL		5
HAZELTON JAMES		35
HAZLE RICHARD		48
HAZLEWOOD JOSIAH		40
HAZLEWOOD MEREDITH		45
HAZLEWOOD RUBEN		45
HEAD ANTHONY		64
HEAD GEORGE		41
HEADLEY SAMUEL		67
HEADRICH DAVID		65
HEADY ELIAS		47
HEADY THOMAS		37
HEANING GEORGE		16
HEATH BENJAMIN		20
HEATH DANIEL		75
HEATH JOHN		22+
HEATH MARTIN		22
HEATH SAMUEL		16
HEATH WILLIAM		35
HEATH WM		16

HEATON DAVID		22
HEATON WASHINGTON		61
HEATON WILLIAM		61
HEDDY THO'S		52
HEDESTOOW ALEXANDER		5
HEDGPETH ISAAC		7
HEDRICK ABRAM		25
HEDRICK GEORGE		37
HEDRICK JACOB		66
HEFNER JOSEPH		63
HELBY JOSEPH		1
HELBY RICHARD		1
HELDRITH HENRY		21
HELLER DEWALT		62
HELM JAMES		16
HELMS ABR.		15
HELMS ABRAHAM		22
HELMS G		15
HELMS ISAAC		15
HELMS JOHN		15
HELMS THO'S		2
HELMS THOMAS		4
HELOBY JACOB		1
HEMMING DAVID J P		76
HEMPHILL PETER		21
HENBY JESSE		62
HENBY SILVANIS		62
HENCHELL JOHN		50
HENDERSON - - -		28
HENDERSON ANDREW		22+
HENDERSON C A		16
HENDERSON DAVID		8
HENDERSON JAMES		40 48
HENDERSON JOHN		37 74
HENDERSON JOHN G		61
HENDERSON RICHARD		71
HENDERSON ROBERT		11 67
HENDERSON SAMUEL		62 73
HENDERSON SHEDRECK		71
HENDERSON WILLIAM		17
HENDERSON WM		11
HENDRICKS DANIEL		47
HENDRICKS DAVID		54
HENDRICKS HENRY		45
HENDRICKS ISAAC		45
HENDRICKS JAMES		48
HENDRICKS JOHN		22
HENDRICKS WILLIAM		21 65
HENDRICKSON WM		15
HENDRIX JOHN		12
HENDRY JOHN		51
HENIGAN JOHN		13
HENLEY JORDON		61
HENLEY MICAJAH		74

HENLY DANIEL		44
HENLY HEZEKIAH		75
HENLY WILLIAM		37
HENNING ARNOLD		57
HENNING HILARUS		53
HENRY J		15
HENRY JAMES		74
HENRY JOHN		13
HENRY PETER		54
HENRY PHILIP		68
HENRY WILLIAM		27
HENSHAW HENRY		55
HENSLEY JOSEPH		19
HENSLEY RICHARDSON JR		8
HENSLEY RICHARDSON SR		8
HENSON ABSOLOM		54
HENSON COONROD		37
HENSON DAVID		59
HENSON JEREMIAH		43
HENSON JESSE		59
HENSON JOHN	7 42 54	59
HENSON JONATHAN		54
HENSON SAM'L		50
HENSON THOMAS		5
HERCKABA LEWIS		42
HERENDON ELLIOTT		9
HERKOY PIERRE		30
HERRAL ISAAC		32
HERRELL JOHN		33
HERRELL WILLILAM		33
HERREN EPHRAM		49
HERREN JOHN		49
HERRICK ANSEL		37
HERRING BARTLETT		14
HERRING FIELDING		14
HERRING JOHN		13
HERRING PRESTON		14
HERRINGTON EZEKIEL		64
HERRINGTON JOSEPH		25
HERRMAN GEORGE		53
HERRMAN JOHN		53
HERRON WILLIAM		60
HERSHMAN GEORGE		50
HERVEY BENJAMIN		73
HERVEY CALEB		73
HERVEY EVAN		73
HERVEY MICHAEL		72
HESLEY JOHN		47
HETHER JOSEPH		41
HETHER WILLIAM		41
HEWMAN PETER		59
HIATT DAVID		76
HIATT ELI		74
HIATT JACOB		12

HIATT JOHN		71
HIATT JOSEPH		12
HIATT WILLIAM		74
HIATTE EVEN		41
HIBBARD TRUMAN		21
HIBNER JAMES		20
HIBNER JOSEPH		20
HICK WILLIAM		61
HICKES WILLIAM		29
HICKLEN JONATHAN		35
HICKLIN JOHN		25
HICKLIN JOHN L		25
HICKLIN WILLIAM		25
HICKLON JAMES		35
HICKMAN - - -		54
HICKMAN FRANCIS		37
HICKMAN JOHN		54
HICKS DAVID		23
HICKS DEMSY		43
HICKS ELERY		54
HICKS HIRAM		44
HICKS JAMES		21
HICKS MOSES		37
HICKS WILLIAM		44
HICKS WM		10
HIDE ANSIL		47
HIDE BENGAMIN		44
HIERS - - -		27
HIESTAND JOHN		66
HIETT ELEAZAR		71
HIGGINS ABRAHAM		23
HIGGINS ELI H		59
HIGGINS JAMES R		61
HIGHFIELD WILLIAM		47
HIGHLEY ABRAHAM 2		47
HIGHNOTE ALEXANDER		69
HIGHNOTE HIRAM		66
HIGHNOTE PHILIP		66
HIGHT JOHN		37
HILER JOSEPH		18
HILL ABEL		17
HILL BENJAMIN		74
HILL CHARLES		50
HILL CHRISTOPHER		43
HILL EDWARD		58
HILL HENRY		47
HILL JAMES	21	46
HILL JOAB		47
HILL JOHN	17	35
HILL JONATHAN	72	74
HILL JOSEPH	13 22 23	40
HILL MOSES G		54
HILL ROBERT	47	71
HILL THOMAS	37	74

HILL	THOMAS	JR			25
HILL	THOMAS	JR		25	71
HILL	THOMAS	SR		25	72
HILL	WILLIAM		37	40	74
HILL	WM		9	12	49
HILLIS	DAVID				16
HILLIS	EBENESAR				14
HILLIS	JAMES				19
HILLIS	MATTHEW				19
HILLS	JOHN				19
HILLYAR	ALEXANDER				59
HILLYAR	JAMES				59
HILLYAR	JOHN				59
HILLYAR	WM				59
HILORY	CHAMNESS				4
HILTON	JAMES				25
HIMAN	ALEXANDER				51
HINDELL	JACOB				63
HINDS	FRANCIS				18
HINER	JOHN				54
HINER	THOMAS				56
HINGER	WM				53
HINKLE	ANTHONY				60
HINKLE	NATHAN				63
HINKLE	SAMUEL				63
HINTON	DANIEL				46
HINTON	GEORGE				44
HINTON	THOMAS			14	45
HINTON	THOS				23
HINTON	WALKER				8
HITCHCOCK	WILLIAM				62
HITE	ABRAHAM				20
HITE	THO'S				8
HITT	JESSE				63
HIX	WILLIAM				47
HOADLAND	AARON				18
HOAGLAND	HENRY				16
HOARAN	HENRY				75
HOBACK	ANDREW				1
HOBACK	MARQUES				3
HOBACK	MARQUIS				1
HOBB	ISAAC				1
HOBBS	ABRAHAM				1
HOBBS	ELISHA				61
HOBBS	HIRAM				1
HOBBS	JAMES				25
HOBBS	JOSHUA W				25
HOBBS	NATHAN				1+
HOBBS	NEHEMIAH				49
HOBBS	WILLIAM				61
HOBSON	BALEY				44
HOBSON	JACOB				39
HOBSON	JOHN				40
HOBSON	NATHAN				43
HOBSON	STEPHEN				43
HODGEN	JOSEPH				62
HODGEN	NATHAN				62
HODGEN	WILLIAM				62
HODGENS	JAMES				29
HODGENS	WILLIAM				29
HODGES	ALLEN				60
HODGES	GEORGE				43
HODGES	JOHN				64
HODGES	PHILIP				37
HODGES	RICHARD				56
HODGES	SAMUEL				56
HODGES	THOMAS				60
HODGES	WILLIAM				56
HOERNLY	JOHN				53
HOERNLY	JOSEPH				53
HOFF	ISAAC				28
HOFFERT	JACOB				44
HOGE	JAMES W				5
HOGE	SAMUEL				5
HOGELAN	JOHN				37
HOGER	WILFERD				5
HOGG	JOHN SR				35
HOGGATT	WILLIAM				45
HOGGET	ABNER				65
HOGGET	JOHN				71
HOGGET	JOSEPH				65
HOGGET	NATHAN			65	74
HOGGET	PHILIP				65
HOGGETT	JOSEPH				61
HOGUE	JOHN				32
HOGUE	JOSEPH				32
HOGUE	ZEBULON				32
HOIL	GEORGE				29
HOKE	CORNELIUS				68
HOKE	GEORGE				68
HOKE	HENRY JR				68
HOKE	HENRY SR				68
HOLBERT	SETH				43
HOLCOB	BENJAMIN				52
HOLCOMB	HOSIA				5
HOLCOMB	JOHN				5
HOLDERMAN	JOHN				33
HOLEMAN	AARON				11
HOLEMAN	BENNETT				51
HOLEMAN	ISAAC				12
HOLEMAN	ISAAC JR				11
HOLEMAN	MOSES				12
HOLEMAN	RICHARD				24
HOLEMAN	WM				10
HOLESAPPLE	GEORGE				64
HOLIDAY	ROBERT				42
HOLLA	RICHARD				75
HOLLAND	ANDREW B				10

Name	Page
HOLLAND ANTHONY	1
HOLLAND WILLIAM	68
HOLLENBECK ANDREW	16
HOLLENBECK JOHN	16
HOLLENSHEAD BENNONI	25
HOLLER JOHN	64
HOLLER ZACHARIAH	64
HOLLET SAMUEL	43
HOLLEWELL HENRY	41
HOLLEY TRUEMAN	30
HOLLIDAY ABRAHAM	45
HOLLIDAY HENRY	43
HOLLIDAY JACOB	43
HOLLIDAY SAMUEL	45
HOLLINGSWORTH BARNARD	31
HOLLINGSWORTH DANIEL	32
HOLLINGSWORTH JESSEY	31
HOLLINGSWORTH JOHN	31
HOLLINGSWORTH JOSEPH	32
HOLLINGSWORTH LEVI	31
HOLLINGSWORTH NATHAN	74
HOLLINGSWORTH PETTER	32
HOLLINGSWORTH THOMAS	32+
HOLLINGSWORTH WILLIAM	32
HOLLISTER JOHN W	25
HOLLMAN EDWARD	72
HOLLOT JOHN	72
HOLLOWAY JESSE	58
HOLLOWELL JESSE	39
HOLLOWELL JOHN	40
HOLLOWELL JONATHAN	44
HOLLOWELL LEVI	27
HOLLOWELL NATHAN	44
HOLLOWELL ROBERT	70
HOLLOWELL SMITHSON	44
HOLLOWELL THOMAS	40 62
HOLLSELL REZIN	51
HOLMAN GEORGE	74
HOLMAN RICHARD	30
HOLMAN TANDY	49
HOLMES BENJAMIN	11 13
HOLMES FORGUS	11
HOLMES FRANCISS	13
HOLMES GEORGE	15+
HOLMES HUGH	40
HOLMES JAMES	40
HOLMES JOHN A	32
HOLMES JOSEPH	41
HOLMES ROBERT	9
HOLMES SAMUEL	71
HOLMES SOLOMON	8
HOLMES THOMAS	4
HOLMES WILLIAM	32
HOLMES WM	11
HOLMS JOSIAH L	29
HOLMS S	21
HOLSCAW WILLIAM	30
HOLSCLAW RICHARD	40
HOLSTETLER CHRISTIAN	44
HOLSTETLER DAVID	44
HOLSTETLER JOSEPH	45
HOLT JOSHUA	1
HOLTON ALLEXANDER	25
HONLLEY HEZEKAH	72
HONNAL JOHN	8
HONNALL ISAAC	8
HOOD JACOB	51
HOOKEN WM	57
HOOKER THOMAS	57
HOOKER THOMAS JR	57
HOOP ISAAC	28
HOOPE ISAAC	27
HOOPINGGARNER CONRAD	11
HOOPINGGARNER JACOB	11
HOOPINGGARNER JOHN	9
HOOT JOHN	13
HOOVER ABRAHAM	11
HOOVER ANDREW	72
HOOVER ANDREW JR	74
HOOVER DANIEL	50
HOOVER DAVID	50 62 74
HOOVER FREDERICK	74
HOOVER HENRY	74
HOOVER JACOB JOHN	63
HOOVER JOB	75
HOOVER JOHN	11
HOOVER SAMUEL	75
HOOZER WILLIAM	69
HOPKINS DAVID	25 31
HOPKINS EDWARD	57
HOPKINS FRANCIS	5
HOPKINS HENRY	12
HOPKINS JAMES	31
HOPKINS JAMES	35
HOPKINS JOHN	23 25 31 54
HOPKINS LEMUEL	37
HOPKINS REUBEN	58
HOPKINS RICHARD	17
HOPKINS SAMUEL	25
HOPKINS STEPHEN	43 57
HOPKINS THOMAS	25
HOPPER JAMES	13
HOPPER MOSES	13
HOPPER SMALLWOOD	13
HOPPER WILLIAM	14
HOPSON JESSE	59
HOPSON WM	52
HORMELL FREDERICK	67

HORMELL	JACOB		67
HORN	FREDARICK		12
HORNBACK	NATHAN		33
HORNBROOK	SANDERS		59
HORNBY	WM		57
HORNED	SM'L		76
HORNEDA	ISAIAH		10
HORNER	GEORGE		70
HORNER	JACOB		70
HORNER	JOHN		63
HORNER	WILLIAM		70
HORNEY	JACOB B		73
HORNEY	JOHN		72
HORNEY	WILLIAM		72
HORSON	THOMAS		73
HORTON	ANTHONY		47
HORTON	JAMES	15	20
HORTON	JOHN		13
HORTON	JOHN S		34
HOSEA	WILLIAM		69
HOSIER	WILLIAM		72
HOSKEN	NENUR		1
HOSTON	JA'S		12
HOUDESTON	JOSEPH		74
HOUGLAND	MARY		18
HOUSE	BURKETT		33
HOUSE	JOHN		31
HOUSE	WILLIAM		48
HOUSH	ADAM		63
HOUSH	ANDREW		63
HOUSH	GEORGE		63
HOUSH	THOMAS		63
HOUSTEN	LEONARD JR		11
HOUSTEN	LEONARD SR		11
HOUSTEN	WM		11
HOUSTON	SAMUEL		22
HOUTS	JOHN		37
HOVEY	ABIEL		50
HOW	ROBERT		5
HOWARD	ALEX'D		10
HOWARD	ISAAC		15
HOWARD	JAMES		45
HOWARD	JOHN		32
HOWARD	ROBERT		65
HOWARD	THOMAS		65
HOWARD	WILLIAM	32	35
HOWARD	WILSON		45
HOWCHIN	JESSE		8
HOWCHIN	WILLIAM		8
HOWE	JOSHUA O		37
HOWE	LEVI		15
HOWE	LEVI JR		15
HOWE	WILLIAM		8
HOWEL	CHARLES		73
HOWEL	JACOB		76
HOWEL	JONATHAN		37
HOWEL	JOSIAH		37
HOWEL	WM		9
HOWERD	CHARLES		47
HOWES	JOHN		21
HOWLAND	AMOS N		61
HOWLET	WILLIAM		25
HOYT	WILLIAM		1
HUBBARD	RICHARD		17
HUBBARD	JOHN		64
HUBBARD	PETER		11
HUBBELL	HENRY		54
HUBBELL	JOHN		54
HUBBLE	BENJAMIN		12
HUCKLEBERRY	PETER		65
HUDDLESTON	IRAM		65
HUDDLESTON	JOB		65
HUDDLESTON	SAMUEL		65
HUDELSON	DAVID		43
HUDLIN	DAVID		40
HUDSON	ANNIAS		25
HUDSON	PETER B		24
HUDSON	THOMAS		19
HUETT	JACOB		55
HUEY	BENJAMIN		1
HUFF	ABRAHAM JR		11
HUFF	ABRAHAM SR		11
HUFF	ELIJAH		50
HUFF	GABRIEL		65
HUFF	JESSE		47
HUFF	JOHN		61
HUFF	ORSON E		21
HUFF	RUBEN		47
HUFFMAN	BENJAMIN		9
HUFFMAN	FELIX		63
HUFFMAN	JOHM		34
HUFFORDE	GEORGE		16
HUFMAN	JEROD		3
HUFMAN	PHILIP		65
HUGGINS	ADOLPHUS		54
HUGHES	HENRY		56
HUGHES	PARLEY		51
HUGHES	THO'S		19
HUGHES	WILLIAM	24	56
HUGHEY	JOSEPH		25
HUGHEY	PETER		20
HUGHS	DANISTON		25
HUGHS	ELEPAT		1
HUGHS	JAMES	25	66
HUGHS	JESSE		66
HUGHS	JOHN		25
HUGHS	JOHN		74
HUGHS	PETER		14

HUGHS SAMUEL		25
HULEN AMBROSE		31
HULEN JOHN		31
HULEN THOMAS		31
HULEN WYETT		31
HULICK ABRAHAM		23
HULICK ISAAC		23+
HULICK SAMUEL		17
HUMBLE JOSEPH		15
HUMBLE JOSIAH		20
HUME JOHN JR		69
HUME JOHN SR		69
HUME THOMAS		69
HUMMER WILLIAM		32
HUMPHREY GEORGE		8
HUMPHREY JAMES		66
HUMPHREY JOHN		67
HUMPHREY SAMUEL		19
HUMPHREY WILLIAM		67
HUMPHREYS CORNELIUS		13
HUMPHREYS GEORGE SR		5
HUMPHREYS JOSEPH		5
HUMPHREYS LOVE S		13
HUMPHREYS SAMUEL		13
HUMPHREYS UNAL		5
HUMPHRY HARRIS		37
HUNCUTT WILLIAM		32
HUND AMAYEN		58
HUNGATE JOHN		68
HUNN JOHN		53
HUNT ALLIN		76
HUNT BARNABAS		74
HUNT DANIEL		40
HUNT EDWARD		75
HUNT IRA		74
HUNT ISAIAH		62
HUNT JAMES		40
HUNT JOHN	21	75+
HUNT JOHN S		73
HUNT JONATHAN		72
HUNT NATHANIEL		21
HUNT NOAH		40
HUNT TUNOSS		35
HUNT WILLIAM	45	75
HUNT WM JR		75
HUNTER EDWARDS C		65
HUNTER HARRY		8
HUNTER HENRY		8
HUNTER JOHN	5 7	55
HUNTER ROBERT		28
HUNTER WM		73
HURLBUT CELEP		25
HURLBUT LEWIS		25
HURST JAMES		69+

HURST JOHN		67
HURST STEPHEN		75
HURST WILLIAM JR		60
HURST WILLIAM SR		60
HURTSOCK DANIEL		37
HUSE CALEB		56
HUST JOHN A		69
HUSTED CALIB		47
HUSTON ALEXANDER		60
HUSTON JAMES B		60
HUSTON JOHN	12	70
HUSTON ROBERT		47
HUSTON SAMUEL		60
HUTCHENSON JA'S		8
HUTCHESON WM		51
HUTCHINS BENJAMIN		75
HUTCHINS DANIEL A		25
HUTCHINS WM		58
HUTCHINSON DANIEL		16
HUTCHINSON EBENESOR		24
HUTCHINSON JAMES		59
HUTCHISON EBENEZER		19
HUTCHISON NATHANIEL		18
HUTCHISON SOLOMON		19
HUTTO WM		9
HUTTON JAMES		69
HUTTON LEONARD		69
HUTTON THOMAS		71
HUTTSELL JACOB		17
HUZZY THOMAS		37
HYATT GIDEON		14
HYATT MISHACK		19
HYATT SHADRACH		55
HYND ISRAEL		65
HYNES PETER		21

I

IDINGS DAVID		41
ILIFF RICHARD		37
INDICUTT JOSEPH		52
INDIOUT JOHN H		52
INGALLS ABRAHAM		20
INGALS CHESTER		15+
INGALS EBENEZER		14
INGLE JOHN		59
INGRAM JAMES	21	22
INGRAM RICHARD		5
INGRAM WILLIAM		45
INGRUM ANDREW		44
INGRUM GEORGE		41
INGRUM WILLIAM		41
INLAW JOHN		47

INMAN	JOHN			57 70
INMAN	SANDY			52
INMAN	STEPHEN			57
INMAN	THO'S			51
INMAN	THOMAS			41
INNIS	WM			12
INWOOD	WM			57
INYARD	JOSEPH			56
INYARD	SILAS			37
IRELAND	JOHN			32
IRELAND	JONATHAN			10
IRISH	SMITEN			48
IRVIN	DANIEL			47
IRVIN	JAMES			27 47
IRVIN	JOHN			16 35
IRVIN	ROBERT			47+
IRVIN	ROBT			13
IRVIN	SAMUEL			47
IRVINE	WILLIAM			40
IRWIN	JAMES			13
IRWIN	THOS B			13 22
ISAMINGER	GEORGE	JR		9
ISAMINGER	GEORGE	SR		9
ISGRIGG	DANIEL			56
ISGRIGG	STEPHEN			56
IVA	JAMES			7

J

JACK	SAMUEL			65
JACKERY	SCOTT			28
JACKMAN	DANIEL D			67
JACKMAN	VINCENT			8 45
JACKSON	ALIJAH			23
JACKSON	DRURA			23
JACKSON	GEORGE			17
JACKSON	GIDEON			13
JACKSON	ISAAC			72
JACKSON	JAMES			16+ 18
JACKSON	JAMES R			18
JACKSON	JOHN		15+ 37	57 65
JACKSON	JOSEPH			43
JACKSON	JOSHUA			20
JACKSON	LAMANUEL			12
JACKSON	LEWIS			37
JACKSON	MATHIAS			11
JACKSON	MICAJAH			74
JACKSON	MILLINGTON			8
JACKSON	SAMUEL			16 61 70
JACKSON	THO'S			18
JACKSON	THOMAS			5 16 64
JACKSON	TIMOTHY			58
JACKSON	WILLIAM		20 37	65 73
JACKSON	WILLIAM	JR		37
JACKSON	WILLIAM B			37
JACOBS	DANIEL			29
JACOBS	EDWARD G			8
JACOBS	ELIJAH			71
JACOBS	ELISHA			45
JACOBS	GEORGE W			58
JACOBS	JAMES			29
JACOBS	JOHN			4 10
JACOBS	SAMUEL			29 71
JACOBS	WILLIAM			74+
JACOBUS	JACOB			5
JACOBUS	THOMAS			5
JAESON	ROBERT			4
JAMES	DAVID			73
JAMES	ISAAC			51 72
JAMES	JAMES			35 37
JAMES	JOHN			25 74
JAMES	JOSEPH			37
JAMES	JOSIAH			35
JAMES	RICHARD			43
JAMES	SAM'L			51
JAMES	SAM'L JR			49
JAMES	THOMAS			25
JAMESON	ALEX'R			23
JAMISON	ALEX			14
JAMISON	ALEXANDER			64
JAMISON	GARRETT			64
JAMISON	JAMES			48
JAMISON	ROBERT			20
JAMISON	ROBT			15
JAMISON	SAMUEL			48
JAMISON	THOMAS			13
JAMISON	THOS SR			13
JAQUESH	JONATHAN			54
JAQUESS	GEORGE F			28
JAQUESS	JOHN			22
JAQUESS	JOHN JR			22
JAQUISH	GARISON			54
JARAULD	EDWARD G			7
JARBO	HENRY			47
JARBO	JOHN			47
JARBO	JOSHUA			47
JARBO	PETER			46
JARBO	RICHARD			47
JAROT	ELI			73
JARVIS	BENJAMIN			72
JARVIS	EDWARD			42
JARVIS	HENRY			8
JARVIS	JAMES			23
JARVIS	SAMUEL			72
JASSON	JOHN			47
JEAN	WESTLEY			67
JEANNERETT	P			21
JEARDIN	THO'S			49

JEFFERS	FRANCIS		25
JEFFERS	JAMES S		52
JEFFERY	JOB JR		72
JEFFRES	ELIAS		4
JEFFREY	JOB		76
JEFFREYS	ASA		75
JEFFRIES	C G		22
JELBA	JOHN		27
JENKINGS	JOHN		46
JENKINGS	WESTLEY		46
JENKINS	JOHN M		37
JENKINS	JOSEPH		61
JENKINS	NATHANIEL		67
JENKINS	SAM'L		50
JENKINS	THOMAS		37
JENKS	WELCOME		67
JENNINGS	EDMAN		48
JENNINGS	EDMOND		47
JENNINGS	OSIAH		18
JENNINGS	SHERROD		23
JENTRY	DAVID		52
JENTRY	WILLIAM		71
JERAULD	WILLIAM		5
JERDIN	ELIJAH		54
JERDON	OVER R		8
JERRELL	ELI		31
JERRELL	JAMES		31
JERRELL	WILLIAM		31
JESSOP	ABRAHAM		75
JESSOP	ISAAC		73
JESSOP	JACOB		75
JESSUP	ISAAC SR		72
JEWELL	JAMES		20
JEWELL	JOHN		21
JEWELL	JOHN JR		1
JEWELL	JOHN SR		1
JEWELL	WILLIAM		1
JOHNS	JOHN		25 56
JOHNS	THOMAS		60
JOHNSON	AARON		63
JOHNSON	ALEXANDER		5 37
JOHNSON	ANDREW		11
JOHNSON	ARCHABALD		62
JOHNSON	CHARLES		20 74
JOHNSON	CHARLES M		59
JOHNSON	DANIEL		10
JOHNSON	DAVID		5 10
JOHNSON	ELISHA		15
JOHNSON	FERGUS		70
JOHNSON	FRANCIS		62
JOHNSON	GEORGE		5 56 71
JOHNSON	GEORGE W		37
JOHNSON	HENRY		62 67
JOHNSON	HUGH		19
JOHNSON	JA'S		10
JOHNSON	JACOB		5
JOHNSON	JAMES		18 59 63 71
JOHNSON	JEDIAH		72
JOHNSON	JEHU		60
JOHNSON	JOHN		5+ 39 47 52 55
JOHNSON	JOHN		66
JOHNSON	JOSEPH		5 10+ 49
JOHNSON	JOSEPH J		61
JOHNSON	JOSEPH P		66
JOHNSON	JOSHUA		37
JOHNSON	JOSIAH		73
JOHNSON	L/I		22
JOHNSON	MARK		55
JOHNSON	PETER		10 71
JOHNSON	RANSON		65
JOHNSON	RICHARD		10 51
JOHNSON	ROSWEL		55
JOHNSON	SAMPSON		52
JOHNSON	SAMUEL		20
JOHNSON	STEPHEN		71
JOHNSON	THOMAS		5 8
JOHNSON	WILFORD		63
JOHNSON	WILLIAM		20+ 55
JOHNSON	WM		10 59
JOHNSTON	ALEXANDER		44
JOHNSTON	DAVID		45+
JOHNSTON	GEN. W		28
JOHNSTON	GEORGE		73
JOHNSTON	HOMER		28
JOHNSTON	HUGH		32
JOHNSTON	JAMES		30 45
JOHNSTON	JAMES W		27
JOHNSTON	JOHN		30 45 59
JOHNSTON	JOSEPH		35+
JOHNSTON	JOSUA		33
JOHNSTON	LEVI		41
JOHNSTON	MARTIN		45
JOHNSTON	MICHAEL		42
JOHNSTON	PRESLEY		29
JOHNSTON	ROBERT		32 34
JOHNSTON	RUBEN		33
JOHNSTON	SAMUEL O		32
JOHNSTON	THOMAS		31 34
JOHNSTON	WESTLEY		29
JOHNSTON	WILLIAM		29 32 75
JOHNSTON	WM		75
JOLLY	STEPHEN		58
JOLLY	WILLIAM		56
JONES	ABRAHAM		51
JONES	ALLEN		44
JONES	AMOS J		51
JONES	ANDREW		75
JONES	CADWALLADER		63

JONES	CHARLES		5 50
JONES	DAVID		1 14 19 50 68
JONES	DAVID JR		14
JONES	ENOCH		52
JONES	EVAN		44
JONES	FELIX		5
JONES	GEORGE		4 9
JONES	GOREG		1
JONES	HANBERRY		68
JONES	HENRY		43
JONES	HOMER		1
JONES	ISAAC		18 28 33+ 60
JONES	JA'S		10 11
JONES	JACOB		1
JONES	JAMES		17 41 71
JONES	JAMES W		5
JONES	JEREMIAH		9
JONES	JOHN		5 18
JONES	JOHN A		75
JONES	JOHN S		34
JONES	JONATHAN		41 57 69
JONES	LEVEN		28
JONES	LEVI		8
JONES	LEWIS		25
JONES	MICAJAH		75
JONES	MICHAL		1
JONES	NICHOLAS		50
JONES	PHILIP		60
JONES	ROBERT		63
JONES	SAM'L		50
JONES	SAMUEL		41
JONES	SETH		33
JONES	THOMAS		16 19
JONES	WILLIAM		37 47
JONES	WILLIAM	JR	69
JONES	WILLIAM	SR	69
JONES	WM		12
JONSTON	JESSE		25
JONUR	JAMES R S		2
JORDAN	THOMAS		33
JORDON	LEVI		5
JORDON	LEVI R		5
JOURDAN	THOMAS		34
JOURNEY	WILLIAM		31
JUCTION	JOSEPH		28
JUDA	JOHN J		9
JUDKINS	DAVID		59
JUDKINS	JESSE		59
JUDSON	MICH		20
JULIAN	WILLIAM		37
JUNKINS	JAMES		33
JUNKINS	WILLIAM		33
JUSTIAN	BOHAN		73
JUSTICE	DANIEL		35

JUSTICE	JOHN	1
JUSTICE	PATRICK	73
JUSTICE	PETER	25
JUSTICE	WILLIAM	71
JUSTUS	MOSES	1

K

KANT	DAVID	53
KAPPEL	JOHN	54
KARNS	ADAM	37
KAUSTLER	JOHN	28
KEATH	JACOB	31
KEATH	JOHN	31
KEATH	WILLIAM	31
KEATON	JAMES	22
KEEDY	JOHN	45
KEEL	JOHN	16
KEELEE	THOMAS	55
KEELER	HERMAN	55
KEEN	SAMUEL	22
KEENE	DANIEL	57
KEENE	DAVID	22
KEENE	SAMUEL B	58
KEES	EDWARD E	51
KEESLEY	PETER	71
KEESLIN	DANIEL	71
KEESLIN	JOHN	71
KEETH	JAMES	25
KEETH	SAMUEL A	25
KEIDY	ABRAHAM	41
KEITH	ALEXANDER	40
KEITH	DANIEL	12
KELHORN	THOMAS	59
KELL	ARCHABALD	6
KELL	JOHN	6
KELL	MATHEW	6
KELLER	ABRAHAM	11 12
KELLER	ADAM	25
KELLER	ANDREW	62
KELLER	EDWARD	12
KELLER	GEORGE	12
KELLER	ISAAC	12+
KELLER	JACOB	52
KELLEY	JAMES	70
KELLEY	SAMUEL	59
KELLION	JOHN	25
KELLOR	JOHN	2
KELLY	ABRAHAM	19 65
KELLY	CORNELIUS	22
KELLY	DAVID	11
KELLY	GEORGE	37
KELLY	HENRY	35
KELLY	JACOB	10

KELLY	JOHN	11 19 25		KEY	WILLIAM		5
KELLY	SAMUEL	19		KEY	WILLIAM SR		6
KELLY	THOMAS	35		KEYS	JOHN		22 37
KELMS	ISAAC	1		KEYT	JESSE		65
KELMS	JAMES JR	1		KEYT	JOHN		65
KELMS	JAMES SR	1		KEYTON	JAMES		21
KELSEY	AMBRON	57		KIA	PHILLIP		25
KELSEY	ELIAS	42		KICTLAND	AARON F		27
KELSOE	HUGH	68		KIKENDALL	JOHN		21
KELSOE	JAMES	68		KIKENDALL	SAMUEL		21
KEMIKAEL	WILLIAM	45		KILK	JAMES		37
KEMP	GODLOVE	61		KILLOUGH	DAVID		37
KENDALL	THORNTON	44		KILLYAN	DANIEL		60
KENDALL	WILLIAM	39		KILYEN	MICHAEL		11
KENDELL	YELLY	2		KIMBALL	JESSE		5
KENDLE	CHRISTIAN	75		KIMBALL	NATHAN		57
KENNADA	DAVID	50		KIMBERLY	ZENES		25
KENNADY	SAM'L	50		KIMBLE	NATHANIEL		61
KENNED	JOHN	15		KIMBROE	JAMES		40
KENNEDY	ALEXANDER	21		KINADAY	EDWARSE		73
KENNEDY	ALPHRED	64		KINCAID	JOHN		1
KENNEDY	ELIJAH	61		KINDELL	HIRAM		74
KENNEDY	JAMES	61 65 68		KINDER	DAVID		46 47
KENNEDY	JOHN	22 67 70		KINDER	JOHN		47
KENNEDY	JOSEPH	18		KINDER	PETER		25 47
KENNEDY	NORVAL	61		KINDILL	THOMAS		74
KENNEDY	REUBEN	68		KINDLE	HENRY		9
KENNEDY	ROBT	14		KINDLE	THO'S		9
KENNEDY	WILLIAM	60		KINDRED	BARTHOLEMEW		11
KENNERLEY	EVERTON	59		KINDRED	DAVID		8
KENNET	SAMUEL	55		KINDRED	EDWARD		11
KENOSH	ANTHONY	51		KINDRED	JOHN		11
KENT	CARLTON	22		KING	ALEX'R		22
KENT	DAVID	20 59		KING	ALEXANDER		1
KENWORTHY	JOHN	72		KING	CORNELIUS		44
KEPLER	JACOB	46+		KING	CORNELIUS SR		44
KEPPLER	FLORIAN	53		KING	DANIEL		16
KEPPLER	GEORGE	53		KING	DAVID T		6
KERBY	JOEL	40		KING	ELISHA		70
KEREY	ZADON	29		KING	ELSHA		73
KERR	MICHAEL	44		KING	GEORGE		14 70
KERR	THOMAS J	41		KING	GEORGE SR		14
KERSEY	STEPHEN	42		KING	JA'S		59
KESTER	GEORGE	54		KING	JACOB		69
KESTER	JACOB	12		KING	JAMES		40 56
KESTER	PAUL	70		KING	JOHN	14 22 25 44
KESTER	SOLOMAN	54		KING	JOHN B		39
KESTLER	FREDERICK	17		KING	SAMUEL		6
KETCHART	PIERSON	69		KING	SIDNEY		56
KETCHUM	JOHN	37		KING	SOLOMON D		6
KEY	CRASSY D	70		KING	THO'S		10
KEY	JOHN	7		KING	THOMAS		39
KEY	LANDON	5		KING	VICTOR		21
KEY	THOMAS	6		KING	WILLIAM		37

KINGSBERRY BENJAMIN		59
KINGSBERRY JOHN		61
KINKAD JOSEPH JR		1
KINKADE JAMES		15
KINKAID ANDREW		1
KINKAID WILLIAM		1
KINKAND JOSEPH SR		1
KINNE WILLIAM		57
KINNEAR CAMPBELL		19
KINNEAR JOHN		20
KINNEAR MICHAEL		19
KINNEAR ROBERT		19
KINNER RODIN		6
KINNERLY ISAAC		52
KINNEY HIRAM		16
KINNEY JOHN		40
KINWORTHY THO'S JR		8
KINWORTHY THO'S SR		8
KINYAN JOHN		62
KIPHART CHARLES		55
KIPHART PHILIP		55
KIRBY ALEXANDER		42
KIRBY EDWARD		42
KIRBY JOEL		56
KIRBY JOHN JR		56
KIRBY JOHN SR		56
KIRK ADAM		21
KIRK DANIEL		5
KIRK HENRY D		29
KIRK JOHN	5 41	21
KIRK MOSES		21
KIRK RICHARD M		5
KIRK WILLIAM		34
KIRKENDALE HENRY		37
KIRKHAM HENRY		37
KIRKLAND JAMES		14
KIRKMAN JAMES		6
KIRKMAN JOHN		43
KIRKMAN WILLIAM		41
KIRKPATRICK ANDREW		13
KIRKPATRICK D		58
KIRKPATRICK JOHN		58
KIRKWOOD WILLIAM		6
KIRTLEY ABREHAM		25
KISER JACOB		22
KISTLER JOHN		17
KISTTER MANUEL		23
KITCHELL ASA		12
KITCHEN JOHN S		59
KITCHEN THOMAS		6
KITCHEN WILLIAM		6
KITE EZEKIEL		49
KITE LEWIS		69
KIVIT GEORGE		50

KIVIT HENERY		51
KIVIT PETER		51
KIVITY JOHN C		75
KLEIN JACOB		53
KLEIN MATHEW		53
KLINGENSTEIN ERHARD		53
KLINGENSTEIN FREDERICK		53
KNAP AMUS		25
KNAP DANIEL		25
KNAP JOHN		25
KNAP JOHN W		25
KNAPPER ANTON		54
KNIESS JOHN		47
KNIGHT ANDREW		67
KNIGHT DAVID		57
KNIGHT ISAAC		57
KNIGHT ROBERT		41
KNIGHT SOLOMON		75
KNIGHT THOMAS		73
KNIGHTEN JESSE W		37
KNODEL ALBERT		53
KNODEL CHRISTOPHER		54
KNODEL CONROD		53
KNODEL GEORGE JR		53
KNODEL GEORGE SR		53
KNOLES DAVID		6
KNOLES ELIGAH		6
KNOWLES EDY		5
KNOWLES JAMES		5
KNOWLES JAMES JR		6
KNOWLES JESSE	5	6
KNOWLES PURTYMAN		5
KNOX BENJAMIN		35
KNOX GEORGE		29
KNOX WILLIAM	33	35
KNOX WILLIAM JR		35
KNUCKLES CHARLES		63
KNUCKLES DAVID		37
KNUCKLES ROBERT		62
KOENIG DAVID		53
KOFFMAN SAMUEL		31
KOONS GASPER		37
KOONS JOHN		22
KRAIL JACOB		53
KRANTER DAVID		53
KREHMER MELCHION		53
KRISS GEORGE		10
KRISS HIRAM		10
KRISS NICHOLAS		12
KUIDER GEORGE		47
KUNTZ JOHN		53
KURTZ FREDERICK		53
KURTZ GEORGE JR		54
KURTZ GEORGE SR		54

KURTZ JACOB		53	LAMB THOMAS	71
KUTCH JOHN		37	LAMB WILLIAM	47 48 62 71
KUYKENDALL ABRAHAM		35	LAMBERT DAVID	67
KUYKENDALL GEORGE		35	LAMBETH AARON	75
KUYKENDALL JACOB		29 32	LAME CALEB	13 20
KUYKENDALL JOSEPH		33	LAME JOESPH	13 19 23
KUYKENDALL NATHANIEL		35	LAMMA JAMES	59
KYLE FREDERICK		21	LAMOUNT JOHN HENRY	30
KYLE JAMES		18 32	LAMPHEAR HYNSEN	58
KYLE JOHN		21	LANCASTER CEEA	71
KYSOR JOHN		25	LANCASTER WRIGHT	71
KYTE HOSTA		64	LANDER LEVI	29
KYZER FREDERICK		25	LANDERS WILLIAM	2
KYZER JOHN		25	LANDMAN DANIEL	42
KYZER WILLIAM		25	LANDMAN TRISTRAM	42
			LANDON HUGH	56
			LANDRUM THOMAS	61
			LANDUO ISAAC	70

L

LACEY ELIJAH	72	LANE EDWARD	12
LACEY EPHRAIM	72	LANE JESSE	57 69
LACEY JOHN SR	76	LANE JOHN	12 57
LACEY WILLIAM	76	LANE JOSEPH	57
LACY JOHN	49	LANE SAMUEL	34
LACY NAHAMIAII	11	LANE WILLIAM	64
LACY TIMOTHY	47	LANG CHRIS'T	53
LADERUTE LEWIS	29	LANGDON PHILIP	65
LAFERTY PETER	70	LANGDON THOMAS G	64
LAFERTY THOMAS	70	LANGTON DANIEL	32
LAGENAUR JOHN	69	LANGTON SAMUEL	32
LAGENNAUER JACOB	69	LANHAM JOHN	15
LAGRANGE ARON	6	LANIER J F D	20
LAIKY SIMON	38	LANKFORD MEAN	41
LAIN JAMES	50	LANNAN GEORGE	46
LAKE JESSE	47	LANNEN JEREMIAH	66
LAKE JOEL	38	LANNING JOSEPH	8
LAKE JOHN	38	LANNON JAMES	47
LAKE ROBERT	38	LANNON JAMES JR	47
LAKE WILLIAM	4	LANNON JOHN	47
LAKEN DANIEL	12	LANNON WILLIAM	4
LALYERS J D	13	LANSON STEPHENSON	25
LAMARR ISAAC	20	LANSREANE JOHN	30
LAMASTERS SIMEON	6	LAPLANT JOHN BT	30
LAMB DORASTUS	48	LAPLANT JOHN BT JR	30
LAMB ERIC	61	LAPLANT JOSEPN BONYEA	28
LAMB EZRA	47	LARANCE OLIVER	47
LAMB HOZA	74	LARD SAMUEL	25
LAMB ISRAL	47	LARGEANT WILLIAM	65
LAMB JAMES	75	LARIMORE DANIEL	15
LAMB JOEL	62	LARTERS GEORGE	32
LAMB JOHN	73	LASHBROOKS JOHN	39
LAMB JOHN D	48	LASHER JACOB	48
LAMB JOSIAH	73	LASSELL HYACINTH	29
LAMB ROBERT	62	LASSER THO'S	8
LAMB SIMEON	61	LASTLY JAMES	6

LATHAM JOHN		37
LATHAM JOHN JR		38
LATHOM WILLIAM		6
LATHROP ISAAC		18
LATHROP SAMUEL		3
LATHROP SILAS		24
LATHROP SIMON		24
LATIMORE DANIEL		18
LATIMORE THOMAS		34
LATREMORE BT		28
LATTE WM		21
LATTIMORE ELISHA	47	48
LATTIMORE JOHN		25
LATTY WILLIAM		23
LATURE JOHN BT		27
LATURE PIERRE		30
LAUGH JOHN		72
LAUGHLIN ALEXANDER		62
LAUGHLIN JOHN		62
LAUGHRIDGE GEORGE		14
LAUGHRIDGE JOHN		15
LAUGHRIDGE SAMUEL		14
LAUGHRIDGE WILLIAM		14
LAUGHRIDGE WM		15
LAUPHLE JACOB		53
LAUPPLE DAVID		53
LAUPPLE FREDERICK		53
LAURANCE ALFORD		3
LAURANCE LANDEN		2
LAURANCE WASHINGTON		2
LAW DANIEL		44
LAW JOEL		18
LAW JOHN		31
LAW JOHN SR		33
LAW STEPHEN		16
LAWDEN THOMAS		6
LAWERS JOHN		40
LAWMAN HENRY		71
LAWRENCE JACK H		25
LAWRENCE NATHANIEL		21
LAWRENCE OLIVER		63
LAWSON WILLIAM		6
LAYBOLD JOHN		43
LAYBOLD JOHN SR		43
LAYLON WM		11
LAYMASTER ABRAHAM		44
LAYTON WILLIAM		19
LEACH JOHN		7
LEACH WM		7
LEAT ISAAC		6
LEATHER JONATHAN		41
LEATHERMAN CHRISTIAN		44
LEATHERMAN JOHN		44
LEAVIT B C		15

LEAVIT DAVID			49
LEBO ISAAC			37
LEBO JACOB			37
LEBO JOSIAH			37
LEDGERWOOD SAMUEL			20
LEE A			13
LEE ABRAHAM			2
LEE ANDRE			41
LEE ANDREW		15	22
LEE CLEMENT		41	45
LEE ELI			37
LEE GERSHAM			14
LEE JAMES			65
LEE JESSE			2
LEE JOHN	15	30	45
LEE JOHN JR			2
LEE JOHN SR			2
LEE JONATHAN			69
LEE JOSEPH			15
LEE LEVI			73
LEE MITCHEL			68
LEE NATHAN		15	20
LEE RICHARD			25
LEE SAMUEL			29
LEE SAMUEL JOHN			27
LEE SPENCER			41
LEE THOMAS			37
LEE WILLIAM		42	65
LEE WILLIAM JR			68
LEE WILLIAM SR			68
LEECH FRANCIS			34
LEECH GEORGE JR			34
LEECH GEORGE SR			34
LEFAVE ANTOINE			30
LEFAVE JOSEPH			30
LEFEVER ABRAHAM			62
LEFLER DAVID		44	46
LEGIER GEORGE			35
LEGIER JESSEY			35
LeMEMORE JOHN BT			28
LEMENTON ROBERT			19
LEMMON DAVID			31
LEMMON GABRIAL			31
LEMMON JOHN			31
LEMMON MATTHIAS			67
LEMMON ROBERT		31	60
LEMMON SAMUEL			31
LEMMON THOMAS			67
LEMMON WILLIAM			31
LEMON JAMES			18
LENA SAMUEL			75
LENTZ DANIEL			53
LENZ DAVID			53
LENZ ISRAEL			53

Name	Page
LEONARD G W	21
LEONARD JAMES	45
LEONARD L R	21
LEONARD THOMAS	42
LEPLANT PIERCE	30
LeROY ALEXIS	29
LESLEY GEORGE	72
LESLY JOHN	6
LESTER ANDREW	57
LESTOR EBENEZER	67
LETHERLAND JOHN	47
LETT ISHEM	25
LETZER JOHN JR	33
LETZER JOHN SR	33
LETZER SAMUEL	33
LEUCHT ANDREW	53
LEUCHT CHRIS'T JR	53
LEUCHT CHRIS'T SR	53
LEUELLIN BENJAMIN	74
LEVENWORTH SETH M	2
LEVENWORTH ZEBULON	2
LEVERTON THOMAS	76
LEVESON ANTOINE	28
LEVETT THO'S	52
LEVI SOLOMON	2
LEVINGSTON ANDERSON	75
LEVITT BANJAMIN	22
LEVITT IGNATIOUS	49
LEVITT JAMES	49
LEVITT NOAH	49
LEWALLEN MASHACK	49
LEWELLING SHEDERICK	62
LEWIS - - -	30
LEWIS AARON	52
LEWIS ABRAHAM	14
LEWIS ALLEXANDER	25
LEWIS DAVID F	45
LEWIS EVANS	52
LEWIS HUGHY	55
LEWIS JACOB	18
LEWIS JAMES	2
LEWIS JOHN	41 52 55 61 65
LEWIS JOHN SR	42
LEWIS JOHN M	45
LEWIS JOSEPH	71 75
LEWIS S'M D	73
LEWIS SAMUEL	42
LEWIS SIMON	58
LEWIS SWEAR	23
LEWIS THOMAS	6 55
LEWIS THOMAS T	76
LEWIS THOS	13
LEWIS WILLIAM	39 55 61
LEWIS WM	58
LEZENBY JERY	44
LICKAS JOHN	57
LIGGIT WILLIAM	63
LIGHT JOHN	35
LIKE ADAM	33
LIKINS MARK	2
LILLIE DAVID	35
LILLIE JAMES	33
LILLIE ROBERT	35
LINDER ISAAC	33
LINDLEY DAVID	40 42
LINDLEY JAMES	40 42
LINDLEY JONATHAN	40 41
LINDLEY LEMON	14
LINDLEY OLIVER	14
LINDLEY OWEN	42
LINDLEY OWEN SR	42
LINDLEY RUBEN	40
LINDLEY SAMUEL	61
LINDLEY THOMAS	42+ 53 61
LINDLEY THOMAS Gent	42
LINDLEY THOMAS T	40
LINDLEY WILLIAM	40 61+
LINDLEY WILLIAM JR	40
LINDLEY WILLIAM SR	40
LINDLEY ZACHARIAS	41
LINDSAY JOHN	55
LINDSAY JOSHUA	23
LINDSAY VINCENT	38
LINDSEY JAMES	31
LINDSEY JOHN	3
LINDSEY NATHAN	47
LINDSEY NICHOLAS	37
LINDSEY SAMUEL	31
LINDSEY WILLIAM JR	29
LINDSEY WILLIAM SR	28
LINDSLEY A B	28
LINDY FREDERICK	7
LINE JOAB	42
LINK JOHN	11
LINKWYLER GEORGE	59
LINKWYLER PETER	59
LINN JOSEPH	62
LINOTT JOHN	74
LION STEPHEN	47
LIPPARD HENRY	56
LIPPARD JOHN	56
LIPPARD MOSES	56
LIPPARD WILLIAM	56
LIPPARD WILLIAM JR	56
LISTON JOHN	3
LITCHSINGER LEONARD	51
LITLE JAMES	50
LITSY ANTHONY	47

LITTELL	ABRAHAM		37
LITTELL	JACOB		52
LITTEN	JOHN		9
LITTEREL	THOMAS		37
LITTLE	ADONIJAH		64
LITTLE	ALEXANDER		61
LITTLE	AMOS		69
LITTLE	JEHU SR		64
LITTLE	JOHN		18 47 64
LITTLE	RICHARD		64
LITTLE	SHUBY		48
LITTLEJOHN	JAMES		20
LITTLEJOHN	JOHN		14
LITTLEJOHN	JOSEPH		23 24
LITTLEJOHN	LEMUEL		14
LITTLEJOHN	WILLIAM		15
LITTON	CALIB		9
LITTON	HIRAM		9
LIVINGSTON	GEORGE		55
LIVINGSTON	JOHN		59
LOCK	THOMAS		41
LOCKE	CHRISTOPHER		59
LOCKHART	JOHN		68
LOCKHART	JOSEPH		68
LOCKHART	WALTER		61
LOCKHART	WILLIAM		40 68
LOCKMAN	CHARLES		38
LOCKMAN	JOHN		13
LOCKMAN	THOMAS		37
LOCKWOOD	JAMES		25
LOCKWOOD	JOHN		25
LOCKWOOD	RICHARD		60
LOCKWOOD	SETH		25
LODGE	JOHN		21
LOFTIN	THOMAS		70
LOFTIN	WILLIAM		70
LOGAN	EZEHIEL		18 64
LOGAN	GEORGE		19
LOGAN	WILLIAM		64
LOGO	CALEB		18
LOGSTON	JOHN		46
LOGSTON	THOMAS		55
LOMAX	JONATHAN		41
LOMIS	OLIVER		19
LONCE	JAMES		20
LONDEN	NATHAN		25
LONG	ABRAHAM		19
LONG	HARRY M		74
LONG	HIRAM		38
LONG	JOSEPH		63
LONG	NICHOLAS		57
LONG	REUBEN		57
LONG	URIAH		33
LONG	WILLIAM		19
LONGEST	CALEB		2
LONGEST	JAMES		2
LONGFELLA	JOHN		75
LONGFELLOW	JAMES		73
LONGMIRE	GEORGE		67
LOOMIS	JAMES		54
LOOMY	TAYLOR		37
LORANT	FRANCIS		30
LORING	DAVID		17
LOTT	ABNER		14
LOTT	ELIJAH		14
LOTT	JAS		14
LOTT	JESSE		14
LOTT	JOHN		14
LOTT	JOHN JR		14
LOTT	WILLIAM		3
LOUDER	CALEB		38
LOUDER	JOSEPH		38
LOUGH	SAMUEL		72
LOUGHHUNN	HENRY		67
LOVE	JOHN		9 16 52
LOVE	RICHARD		10
LOVE	WM		49
LOVELESS	RICHARD		68
LOVELL	REUBEN		2
LOW	GEORGE		52
LOW	JACOB		27
LOW	JAMES		60
LOW	SAMUEL		41 67
LOWDEN	JAMES		17
LOWDEN	ROBERT		63
LOWE	ABSOLOM		64
LOWE	FREDERICK		67
LOWE	JACOB B		37
LOWE	THOMAS		64
LOWE	WILLIAM		37
LOWELL	JONATHAN		23+
LOWELL	SAMUEL D		6
LOWREY	JAMES		16
LOWRING	RICHARD		24
LOWRY	JOHN		70
LOWRY	ROBERT		25
LOWRY	THO'S		51
LOWRY	THOS		16
LUCAS	CALIB		12
LUCAS	GEORGE		38
LUCAS	JESSE		67
LUCAS	JOHN		64
LUCAS	JOSHUA		2
LUCAS	JOSHUA H		37
LUCAS	OLIVE		6
LUCAS	SOLOMAN		38
LUCAS	THOMAS		38
LUCAS	ZACHARIAH		6

LUCCAT WILLIAM JR	56	
LUCE WARREN	70	
LUCKENBILL HENRY JR	66	
LUCKENBILL HENRY SR	66	
LUCKENBILL PHILIP	66	
LUDINGTON HARVEY	35	
LUDINGTON HORICE	35	
LUKIN EPHRAIM	42	
LUKIN JOEL	42	
LUMLEY WILLIAM	63	
LUND JOHN	21	
LUNGO FRANCIS	30	
LUNGO LEWEY	28	
LUPER SAMUEL	16	
LUPTON DAVIS	11	
LUSTER JOHN	29	
LUTHER GEORGE	2	
LUTHER PETER	2	
LUTHERIN JOHN	43	
LYMAN SAMUEL	73	
LYNCH CHARLES	2	
LYNCH CLETON	40	
LYNCH EDWARD	6	
LYNCH JACKSON	40	
LYNCH JESSE	2	
LYNCH JOHN	2 43	
LYNCH THOMAS	2 43	
LYNCH WILLIAM	43	
LYND JAMES	44 69	
LYND SAMUEL	44	
LYNN DANIEL	51	
LYNN HUGH	17	
LYNN JAMES	6	
LYON ANDREW	54	
LYON BENJAMIN	3	
LYON JAMES	3	
LYON JOEL	3	
LYON JONATHAN	61	
LYON TIMOTHY	3	
LYON ZACHARIAH	61	
LYSTER CORNELIUS	9	
LYSTER FRANCISS	9	
LYSTER PETER	9	

M

M'CALEB HENRY S	21
M'CALROY ENOS	21
M'CAMMON ARCHIBALD	24
M'CAMMON JAMES	24
M'CARTNEY COY	16
M'CARTNEY ENOCH	14
M'CARTNEY G B	16
M'CARTNEY JONATHAN	14
M'CASLAND WILLIAM D	23
M'CASLON JOHN	16
M'CLELLEN JOHN	23
M'CLELLEN ROBT	14
M'CLELLEN WM	13
M'CLUNG LYLE	23
M'CLURE DAVID	22
M'CLURE JOHN	53
M'CLURE THO'S	53
M'COLLUM DANIEL	52
M'COLLUM ISAAC	52
M'CONNEL ROB'T	52
M'COULAUGH JOHN	29
M'COWN WM	49
M'COY DAVID	49
M'COY GEORGE	13
M'COY JOHN	13
M'COY MOSES	14
M'COY SAMUEL	14
M'CROSKY JOHN L	14
M'CURDY WILLIAM	20
M'CURDY WM	23
M'DANIEL DAVID	50
M'DANIEL JAMES	49
M'DANIEL JOHN	50
M'DONALD ROBERT	16
M'FADIN ANDREW JR	50
M'FADIN ANDREW SR	51
M'FADIN JAMES JR	50
M'FADIN JAMES SR	50
M'FADIN JOHN	50
M'FADIN ROLEY	50
M'FADIN SQUIRE	51
M'GEE JOSEPH	21
M'GREGAR THOS	16
M'INTAUSH JOSEPH	14
M'INTIRE JOHN	21
M'KAY ABRAHAM	15
M'KAY ALLEN	16
M'KAY ANGUS	24
M'KAY DAVID	16
M'KAY GEORGE	16
M'KAY JOHN	16 24

M'KAY ROBERT	16	
M'KAY THOS	24	
M'KAY URIAH	15	
M'KINLEY L	24	
M'KINLEY SAM'L	24	
M'KINLEY SAMUEL	21	
M'KINNES GEORGE	51	
M'KINSEY ALEX'R	23	
M'LAIN JOHN	23	
M'MAHEN MARTIN	50	
M'MILLEN DANIEL	13	
M'MULLEN ARCHIBALD	13	
M'NULTY JOHN	21	
M'QUESTON WM	15	
M'VICKER JAMES E	22	
MABERY JOHN	47	
MABET BERRY	71	
MABOUGH JACOB H	63	
MABOUGH MICHAEL H	63	
MACBEE SAMUEL	67	
MacBRIDE ALLEN	1	
MacCARTY ABNER	1	
MacCARTY NICHOLAS	2 4	
MacCARTY WILLIAM	1	
MacCULLUM JAMES	1	
MacCURRY EDWARD	1	
MACEY CHARLES	76	
MacFARLAND ROBERT	3	
MacGEE JESS	4	
MACINTIRE JOHN	21	
MacINTOSH JAMES	1	
MACMAHAN SAMUEL	2	
MacMICKLE JACOB	2	
MacMICKLE PETER	2	
MacMURTER JAMES	2	
MacMURTER JOHN	2	
MacMURTER WILLIAM	2	
MACOMSON ANDREW	46	
MacRAE ALEXANDER B	2	
MacRAE DANIEL A	2	
MacWILLIAMS JOHN	3	
MACY GAMALIEL	38	
MADDOX JOHN W	6	
MADEN JOSEPH	72	
MADISON OLIVER	6	
MAESWELL JONATHAN	2	
MAESWELL THOMAS	2	
MAGHALL WILLIAM	6	
MAGILL WILLIAM	69	
MAGILL ZACHARIAH	45	
MAGNER JOHN	40	
MAGNESS PERRY G	18	
MAGUIRE JAMES	72	
MAHALA JOHN	38	
MAHAN PETER	45
MAHLE LENARD	53
MAHON ANDREW	63
MAHONNEY JAMES B	63
MAIDEN ANDREW	16
MAIDLOW EDWARD	59
MAIDLOW JAMES	59
MAIDLOW JAMES JR	59
MAIN DAVID	46
MAIN JOHN	48
MAIN MICHA	48
MAIN RILEY	47
MAIN SAMUEL	47
MALEK DAVID	20
MALLARD GEORGE	57
MALLENEY ANTOINE	29
MALLERY HIRAM	29
MALLETT AMBROISE	30
MALLETT FRANCES	30
MALLETT FRANCIS	30
MALLETT LEVEY	30
MALLOTT PEIRCE	30
MALONE JAMES	6
MALONE JOHN	6
MALORY ELEMUEL	47
MALOTT ELI W	61
MALOY MOSES	48
MAMS SAMUEL	66
MAN JESSE	71
MANAGH THOMAS	61
MANAHAN JOHN	68
MANDLIN ENOCH	71
MANEY JACOB	26
MANGNAM HENRY	6
MANIM SYLVESTER	6
MANLY JOHN R	40
MANNERS JAMES	38
MANNIN DAVID	69
MANNIN JAMES	68
MANNIN JOHN	69
MANNIN JOSHUA	69
MANNIN WILLIAM	69
MANNING JOSEPH	8
MANNING SAMUEL	32
MANNING WILLIAM	68
MANS WILLIAM	66
MANSELL SAMUEL	59
MANSFIELD JAMES	2
MANVILLE NICHOLAS	15
MAPES JAMES	14
MAPES JOHN	10
MAPES JOS	23
MARALLEE JOHN	58
MARCUS JAMES	52

Name	Pages
MARCUS WM JR	52
MARCUS WM SR	52
MAREQUART ADAM	57
MARINE CHARLES	74
MARINE JESSE	76
MARINE JONATHAN	73
MARIS AARON	42
MARIS GEORGE	40
MARIS JOHN	43
MARIS THOMAS	42
MARKS WILLIAM	64
MARKS WILLIAM SR	64
MARKWELL JOHN	60
MARLIN ISAAC	71
MARMIN JOSEPH	12
MARMIN THO'S	12
MARMON FRANCESS	9
MARNEY JOHN	30
MARQUES EBENEZER	22
MARQUES GEORGE	17 20
MARQUES JOHN	15 19
MARQUES ROBT	14
MARQUES SAMUEL	22
MARRS CHRISTOPHER	65
MARRS JAMES	65 69
MARRS WILLIAM	69
MARRURGE JOSIAH	76
MARSH CYRUS J	66
MARSH FRANKLIN	57
MARSH JAHU	12
MARSHAL JESSE	69
MARSHALL DANIEL	19
MARSHALL JAMES	66
MARSHALL JOHN	6 14 20
MARSHALL ROBERT	17
MARSHALL THOS	15 23
MARSHELL ISAAC	13
MARSHELL JOHN	13
MARSHELL SIMON	9
MARSHELL WM	9 10
MARTAIN JESSE	47
MARTAIN JOHN	47
MARTAIN WILLIAM N	26
MARTIN AARON	71
MARTIN ABNER	66
MARTIN CHARLES	59
MARTIN EDWARD	2
MARTIN ELEMUEL	47
MARTIN ENOCH	66
MARTIN GEORGE	21
MARTIN GREEN	42
MARTIN HENRY	34 30
MARTIN HIRAM	42
MARTIN HUTSON	56
MARTIN ISAAC	45
MARTIN JAMES	2 6 59 66 71
MARTIN JAMES JR	66
MARTIN JAMES D	2
MARTIN JAMES H	66
MARTIN JESSE	42
MARTIN JOHN	51 56 65 69
MARTIN JOHN JR	66
MARTIN JOHN B	27
MARTIN JOSEPH	66
MARTIN JOSEPH JR	66
MARTIN MARTIN	49
MARTIN NIMOROD	66
MARTIN ROBERT	44
MARTIN RUBEN	43
MARTIN SAMUEL	44 66
MARTIN THOMAS	59
MARTIN THOMAS H	6
MARTIN WILLIAM	16 66 69
MARTIN WILLIAM W	69
MARTINGILL DAVID	71
MARTON JAMES	14
MARTS JACOB	68
MARTS JOHN	40
MARVEL BENJAMINE	6
MARVEL ELISHA	6
MARVEL JOHN	6
MARVEL PANTER	6
MARVEL PURTYMAN	6
MASAIR RICHARD	73
MASEY ISAAC	63
MASH DAVID	48
MASH RITE	48
MASON ANDREW	2
MASON ANSALAM	12
MASON JACOB	41
MASON JAMES	47
MASON THOMAS	38 73 75
MASSEY ALEXANDER	6
MASTERS JAMES	64
MASTERS WILLIAM	64
MATHENY JOSIAH	29
MATHER ABNER	67
MATHERS JOHN	26
MATHIS JA'S	10
MATINGLEY THOMAS	47
MATLEY HUGH	10
MATLOCK DAVID	38
MATLOCK JAMES	38
MATLOCK JOHN	38
MATTHERS MOSES	42
MATTHEW NATHAN	67
MATTHEW SIMON	67
MATTHEWS JAMES	2 16

Name	Page
MATTHEWS JOHN	22
MATTOCK WILLIAM	38
MATTOCKS NATHANIEL	69
MAUDLIN JESSE	73
MAUZEY GEORGE	64
MAVETY MICHAEL	45
MAXBERRY A	57
MAXEDON JOHN	32
MAXEDON ROBERT	42
MAXEDON THOMAS JR	42
MAXWELL B E	22
MAXWELL DAVID H	38
MAXWELL EDWARD	16
MAXWELL JAMES	40+ 45
MAXWELL JOHN	43 16
MAXWELL JOSEPH	40
MAXWELL SAMUEL C	16
MAXWELL THOMAS	45
MAXWELL WILLIAM	17 41 43+ 45
MAY BENJAMINE	6
MAY FRANCIS	44
MAY GEORGE	70
MAY JOHN	11 23 38 55 70
MAY JOHN II	38
MAY REUBEN	64
MAY RICHARD	55
MAY SILVANUS	39
MAY WILLIAM	2 38
MAYES ELIJAH	34
MAYES JAMES	34
MAYES JEREMIAH	34
MAYES WILLIAM	34
MAYFIELD LEROY	38
MAYFIELD SOUTHERLAND	20
MAYFIELD THOMAS	2 3
MAYHALL FOXWORTHY JR	6
MAYHALL TIMOTHY JR	6
MAYHO JOHN	47
McADAMS DANIEL	47
McAFEE JA'S	10
McAFEE JOHN	11
McALLISTER HENRY	38
McALLISTER ZACHARIAH	60
McANELTY OLIVER	70
MCARTY NICHOLAS	26
McARTY THOMAS	75
McASLON GEORGE	26
McBROOM DAVID	43
McBROOM EAUDEA	75
McBROOM EVAN	43
McBROOM JOHN	73
McBROOM WILLIAM	71
McBROWN JOHN	61
McCAFFEE SIMON	44
McCAGG ROBERT	11
McCAIN JOHN	59
McCALISTER ARCHIBALD	57
McCALISTER JESSE	57
McCALISTER JOSEPH	57
McCALL JAMES	19 20
McCALL JAMES B	29
McCALLON WILLIAM	27
McCAMANT JOHN	18
McCAMEL JAMES	68
McCAMON GEORGE	16
McCANE ANDREW	38
McCANE WILLIAM	38
McCARTHY JOHN	35
McCARTNEY ENOCH	22
McCARTNEY JAMES	18
McCARTNEY NICHOLAS	22
McCARTY JOHN	1
McCASLAND WILLIAM	17
McCASLON JOHN	17
McCASLON RICHARD	20
McCAULEY HENREY	59
McCAULEY JOEL	59
McCAVINS ABRAHAM	71
McCLAIN GEORGE	71
McCLAIN MATTHEW	58
McCLANAHAN JAMES	59
McCLANAHAN JOHN	59
McCLANAHAN ROBERT	18
McCLANE CHARLES	55
McCLANE JOHN	55
McCLANE ROBERT	45
McCLARY JOHN	6
McCLASKEY ISAAC	63
McCLASKEY JOHN	64
McCLASKY JAMES	56
McCLELAND SAMUEL	36
McCLELEN JAMES	17+
McCLELEN JOHN	20
McCLELEN RICHARD	17
McCLELEN ROBERT	20
McCLELLAND JAMES	63
McCLINTIC ROBERT	63
McCLUNG JAMES	68
McCLUNG JOHN	17
McCLUNG SAMUEL	17
McCLURE JAMES	6+
McCLURE JOHN	29
McCLURE MATTHEW	66
McCLURE ROBERT	6
McCLURE WILLIAM	54
McCOLLON STEPHEN	52
McCOLLOUGH JAMES B	16
McCOLLOUGH WM D	38

Name	Page
McCOLM GREER	40
McCOMB WILLIAM	33
McCOMBS JOHN	71
McCONAHAY DAVID	31
McCONALD PATRICK	47
McCONNALL JOHN	42
McCONNEL JOHN	52
McCONNELL WILLIAM	17
McCONOLD PATRICK	48
McCORD ASA	31
McCORD GEORGE	31
McCORD WILLIAM	31
McCORD WILLIAM SR	31
McCORMACK JA'S	12
McCORMACK JOHN JR	12
McCORMACK JOHN SR	12
McCORMACK WILLIAM	6
McCOSKEY JAMES	61
McCOTHIN DANIEL	47
McCOY DAN'L JR	9
McCOY DAN'L SR	9
McCOY DAVID	38
McCOY FRANKLIN	75
McCOY GEORGE	19 40
McCOY JAMES	40 58 69
McCOY JOHN	33 41 47 75
McCOY MALACHI	60
McCOY RICE	68
McCOY ROBERT	33
McCOY STEPHEN	13
McCOY THOMAS	55
McCOY WILLIAM	44
McCOY WILLIS	62
McCRACKEN HENRY	62
McCRACKEN JOHN	41
McCRACKEN ROBERT	41
McCRACKEN WILLIAM	42
McCRAKEN ROBERT	41
McCRAREY JAMES	59
McCRARY JAMES	69
McCRARY ROBERT	6
McCRARY THOMAS	7
McCRARY WILLIAM	68
McCRARY WM	9
McCRAVEY JOHN	59
McCRORY JOHN	18
McCRORY SAMUEL	18
McCRUM JOHN	47
McCRUTCHEN JACOB	63
McCULLAUGH JOHN	21
McCULLAUGH THOMAS	21
McCULLOUGH DAVID	38 54
McCULLOUGH JAMES	54
McCULLOUGH JOHN	61
McCULLOUGH JOHN JR	54
McCULLOUGH MOSES	67
McCUMBER LEVI	45
McCUNE JOHN	6 8
McCUNE JOSEPH	16
McCURE ARCHIBALD	30
McCURE CHARLES	30
McCURE JOHN	30
McCURE SAMUEL KY	35
McCURRY ABRAHAM	18
McDADE WILLIAM	66
McDANIEL ALEXANDER	45
McDANIEL DANIEL	56
McDANNEL JAMES	64
McDONALD ALEXANDER	43
McDONALD CLEMENT	39
McDONALD DANIEL	58
McDONALD GEORGE	27
McDONALD JAMES	32
McDONALD JOHN JR	32
McDONALD JOHN SR	32
McDONALD WILLIAM	32 41
McDONELL JOHN A	8
McDOUGLE JAMES	17
McDOWEL JAMES	56
McDOWEL JOHN	56
McDOWEL MARTIN	56
McDOWELL JOSEPH M	57
McFALL BARNABUS	45
McFARLAND PETER	61
McFARLING DANIEL	47
McFETERIDGE SAMUEL	7
McGAREY HUGH	58
McGAREY WM R	58
McGARY HARRISON	6
McGARY HUGH	6
McGARY JOHN	6
McGARY ROBERT	6
McGAUHY ARCHIBALD	44
McGEE ELIJAH	41
McGEE ELISHA	41
McGEE HENRY	41
McGEE JA'S JR	8
McGEE JA'S SR	8
McGEE JOHN	8
McGEE SAMUEL	43
McGEHEE JACOB	6
McGIFFEN JOHN	28
McGILL JAMES	17
McGILL JOHN	60
McGOWEN PATRICK	34
McGRAGER ANDREW	6
McGREGER ALEX'R	15
McGREW CHARLES	68

McGREW JAMES		70	McKNITT WM		58
McGREW JOHN		68+	McKUHAR ALEX'R		35
McGREW JOSEPH		44	McLAIN JOHN		16
McGRIDER EZEKIEL		59	McLAIN JOHN		73
McGRUE ARCHABAL		71	McLAIN SAMUEL		16
McGUIRE CHARLES		34	McLALLEN CHRISTOPHER		60
McGUIRE JAMES		75	McLALLEN MOSES		60
McGUIRE JESSE		56	McLANE HENRY		75
McGUIRE JOHN		6	McLANE DAVID		73
McHOLLAND DAVID		38	McLAUGHLIN JOHN		60
McHONEY WILLIAM		35	McLEER NATHANIEL		73
McHORNEY BERNARD H		62	McLEY DAVID		26
McINTIRE JAMES		69	McLOOCE THOMAS		74
McINTIRE JOHN	6	64	McLOUGHLIN JOHN M		26
McINTIRE ROBERT		69	McLOUGHLIN JOSEPH		26
McINTIRE THOMAS L		61	McLOVE DAVID		74
McINTIRE WILLIAM	6	64	McLOVE NATHANIEL		74
McINTOSH JOSEPH		55	MCLURE CHARLES		32
McKAN WILLIAM		38	MCLURE DANIEL JR		32
McKAY BARBARY		19	MCLURE DANIEL SR		32
McKAY DAVID		19	McLURE GEORGE		32
McKAY JAMES	18	19	MCLURE JOHN		32+
McKAY ROBERT		19	McLURE THOMAS		32
McKAY THOMAS		19	McMAHAN ALEXANDER		47
McKAY URIAH		20	McMAHAN JAMES		40
McKAY WILLIAM		19	McMAHAN JOHN		61
McKEDDY JAMES		6	McMANNAMY HIRAM		26
McKEDDY STEPHEN		6	McMANNIS JOHN		60
McKEE JAMES		69	McMILLAN JOHN		16
McKEE JOHN		32	McMILLEN JAMES		16
McKEE WILLIAM		2	McMURRY JAMES		45
McKEEHAN GEORGE		26	MCNARY ALEXANDER		41
McKEEHAN JOHN		26	MCNARY HUGH		41
McKENSTER JAMES		70	McNEAL DANIEL		7
McKERN LUKE		40	McNEE ELIAS		29
McKETTRICK JOHN		56	McNEELY ALEXANDER		59
McKINGHT CHRISTOPHER		46	McNEELY DAVID	59	64
McKINGHT ROGER		46	McNEELY JEREMIAH		35
McKINLEY JA'S		10	McNEW BENJAMIN		59
McKINLEY JAMES		17	McNEW RICHARD		62
McKINLEY JOHN		17	McNEW ZADOCH		59
McKINLEY SAMUEL	17	20	McNEW ZEDEKIAH		17
McKINNEY ALEXANDER	41 44	69	McNIGHT JOHN		3
McKINNEY ARCHABALD		65	McNIGHT JOHN JR		60
McKINNEY COLLINS		65	McNIGHT JOHN SR		60
McKINNEY DAVID		44	McNIGHT ROBERT R		60
McKINNEY JAMES	38 68	70	McNIGHT WILLIAM JR		60
McKINNEY JOHN	8	38	McNIGHT WILLIAM SR		60
McKINNEY PETER JR		63	McNULTY JOSEPH		20
McKINNEY PETER SR		63	McNUTT ALEX		18
McKINNEY RANE		63	McNUTT ARCHIBALD		33
McKINNY JOHN		44	McOLLISTER DAVID		26
McKINZER MUTNER		58	MCOLLISTER MATHEW		26
McKLLERORY ARCHIBALD		29	McOMMACE GEORGE		30

McPHERSON	ANGOS		10
McPHETERS	ALEXANDER	44	69
McPHETERS	HUGH		61
McPHETERS	JAMES		69
McPHETERS	JAMES SR		69
McPHETERS	JOHN		65
McPHETERS	JOHN C		68
McPHETERS	JOHN W		65
MCPUR	JOHN		38
MCRACKEN	VIRGIL		26
MCRUE	JOHN		38
McTAGERTT	JA'S		9
MCURRY	JACOB		26
McVAY	EDWARD		43
McVAY	WILLILAM		43
McWILLIAMS	WILLIAM		74
MEACHAM	ISAAC		45
MEAD	ISREAL		33
MEAD	JAMES		35
MEAD	JOSIAH		21
MEAL	CHARLES		34
MEAL	FREDERICK		34
MEAL	ISAAC		34
MEANS	WM		51
MEATHERS	JOHN		2
MEATHERS	WILLIAM		2
MEDCAFF	ISAAC		73
MEDDEAK	EMANUEL		19
MEDDER	AARON		53
MEDDERS	THO'S W		49
MEDE	JA'S		9
MEDFORD	LEWIS		30
MEDISK	GERARDUS		16
MEDLEE	JOSEPH M		66
MEDLEY	JAMES		31
MEDLEY	JOHN	23 24	31+
MEDLEY	SAMUEL		31
MEDLY	JAMES		19
MEDLY	JOHN		32
MEEK	BAZEL		25
MEEK	DANIEL		26
MEEK	DAVID		26
MEEK	JEREMIAH		26
MEEK	JEREMIAH JR		26
MEEK	JOHN	20	75
MEEK	JOSEPH	71	26
MEEK	JOSHUA		73
MEEK	NATHAN		26
MEEK	NATHANIEL		26
MEEK	RICHARD		26
MEEK	ROBERT		22
MEEK	SAMUEL	26	68
MEEK	WILLIAM	26	75
MEEL	A A		21

MEIGS	JOHN		35
MEK	SALASTUS		54
MEKIM	NATHANIEL		45
MELBORN	DAVID		6
MELLBOURN	JOHN		6
MELTON	JOHN		23
MELTON	MICHEL		6
MELTON	THOMAS		31
MELVIN	JAMES		58
MELVIN	JOHN		58
MENDENALL	FRANCES		75
MENDENHALL	FRANCIS		72
MENDENHALL	GRIFFITH		74
MENDENHALL	JACOB		64
MENDENHALL	JOHN		72
MENNIS	COLVIN		6
MERCER	JOHN II		38
MEREAW	HENRY		27
MERICA	JACOB		51
MERL	SETH		26
MERRELL	JOAB		60
MERRIDETH	JAMES		64
MERRIDETH	JOHN		64
MERRIMA	LEWIS		9
MERROW	HENRY		28
MERRY	CORNELIOUS		28
MESSICK	DAVID		72
MESSICK	ISAAC		72
MESSINGER	- - -		57
MEWBY	BENJAMIN		63
MEWHERTER	W P		20
MICHAEL	CONSEDDER		27
MICHAEL	FRANCIS		34
MICHAEL	JOHN		34
MICHAEL	JOSEPH		34
MICHAM	ARCHIBALD		35
MIDCAP	JOHN		26
MIDCIF	URIAH		26
MIEURE	JOHN		30
MIEURE	RICHARD		33
MIEURE	WILLIAM		28
MIKESELL	PETER		17
MIKSELL	JACOB		17
MILER	CHARLES		47
MILER	JOHN		48
MILES	EVAN	13	22
MILES	JESSE		13
MILIGAN	JONATHAN		40
MILIGAN	SAMUEL		41
MILLACE	EDWARD		40
MILLACE	NICKERSON		41
MILLARD	BENJAMIN		38
MILLBOURN	ROBERT		6
MILLER	ABRAHAM	10	31+

MILLER	ADAM			11	42 47	MILSAPS	MOSES			64
MILLER	ALEXANDER				47	MILSAPS	ROBERT			64
MILLER	ANTHONY				44	MILTON	ALLEN			14
MILLER	BENJAMIN			16	35	MILTON	JOHN			14
MILLER	BRISON				11	MINARD	SAM'L J			49
MILLER	CHRISTOPHER				53	MINCHINGTON	E H			58
MILLER	DANIEL			48	59	MINELA	JOHN			16
MILLER	DAVID			2 6	71	MINER	THOS			23
MILLER	GEORGE				49	MINGS	AARON			17
MILLER	HENRY			19	36	MINNIS	MITCHEL			7
MILLER	HINEY				2	MINNIS	THOMAS			7
MILLER	JACOB			44	66	MINOR	BEBE O			22
MILLER	JACOBS				75	MINOR	GEMISON			73
MILLER	JOHN	6	15	26 46	47+	MINOR	JAMES			34
MILLER	JOHN			50	75	MINOR	JOHN			14
MILLER	JOHN S				26	MINOR	ROBERT			19
MILLER	JONATHAN				67	MINOR	WILLIAM		34	73
MILLER	JOSEPH				58	MINTON	JACOB			26
MILLER	MACHAEL				42	MINTON	WILLIAM			26
MILLER	MICHAEL				75	MIRE	REUBEN			64
MILLER	MORDICAI				63	MIRES	GEORGE			14
MILLER	NATHANIEL				50	MIRES	JOHN			26
MILLER	PETER			2	58	MIRRIT	EDWARD			8
MILLER	PETER S				6	MISONHAMMER	JOHN			70
MILLER	PHILLIP				33	MITCHEL	ELIJAH			66
MILLER	PRICE				63	MITCHEL	JAMES		26	38
MILLER	ROBERT				18	MITCHEL	JOHN		14	60
MILLER	SAMUEL	15	21	29 48	52	MITCHEL	JONATHAN			68
MILLER	THO'S				50	MITCHEL	ROBERT			68
MILLER	THOMAS SR				51	MITCHEL	THOMAS		60	62
MILLER	WILLIAM			6 20	45	MITCHEL	WILLIAM		47	69
MILLIKIN	JACOB				38	MITCHELL	JAMES B			20
MILLIKIN	WILLIAM				38	MITCHELL	JOHN M			22
MILLIM	RICHARD				26	MITCHELL	R B			14
MILLR	HEZEKIAH				73	MITCHELL	ROBT			14
MILLS	ALEXANDER				49	MITCHELL	SAMUEL			55
MILLS	AMOS				17	MITCHELL	THOS		14	23
MILLS	DAVID A				50	MITCHELL	WILLIAM P			16
MILLS	FELIN				50	MITCHUR	STEPHAN			8
MILLS	JAMES			6	76	MITINGER	GEORGE			61
MILLS	JESSEE				51	MITTE	JOSEPH JR			30
MILLS	JOHN F				10	MITTE	JOSEPH SR			30
MILLS	JONATHAN				73	MITTE	PEIRRE			30
MILLS	REUBEN				3	MITTON	JAMES			40
MILLS	RICHARD				44	MIZE	JOSEPH			63
MILLS	SAMUEL				48	MOBLEY	EDWARD			44
MILLS	THOMAS				76	MOBLEY	ELIAS			45
MILLS	WILLIAM			2	76	MOCK	DANIEL			46
MILLS	WM JR				58	MOCK	GEORGE			43
MILROY	JAMES				60	MOCK	WILLIAM			46
MILROY	SAMUEL				60	MODE	JOHN			43
MILSAP	BILLY				9	MODLIN	JAMES			68
MILSAP	ROBERT				11	MODLIN	MARK			68
MILSAPS	JAMES				38	MODLIN	NATHAN			68

MOESS	GEORGE		54
MOFFET	JEREMIAH		74
MOFFET	SOLOMON		12
MOFFETT	ALEXANDER		50
MOFFETT	WM		50
MOFFITT	JAMES T		27
MOFFITT	WALTER		27
MOLL	ABRAHAM		38
MOLL	ABRAHAM JR		38
MOLLICOTT	JOHN		63
MONACLE	CHRISTOPHER		66
MONACLE	GEORGE		63
MONACLE	JOHN		64
MONACLE	PETER JR		66
MONACLE	PETER SR		63
MONARCH	GEORGE		40
MONAY	JA'S		11
MONCRIEF	ABNER		20
MONCRIEF	CELEPH		26
MONCRIEF	WILSON		20
MONDON	LEVI		62
MONFORD	JOHN		6
MONGER	JEHIEL		55
MONGIN	M		28
MONK	SIMON		28
MONK	MALECHA		2
MONROE	ARTHUR		18
MONROE	AUSBURN		18
MONROE	CHARLES		17
MONROE	FELIX		18
MONROE	GEORGE		17
MONROE	JAMES		41
MONROE	MICHAEL		18
MONROE	RANDALL		18
MONROE	ROBERT		18
MONROE	WILLIAM		23+
MONROE	WM		22
MONSEY	NATHANIEL		50
MONTGOMERY	ALEX		18
MONTGOMERY	ARCHIBALD		18
MONTGOMERY	BENJAMINE		6
MONTGOMERY	HUGH		8
MONTGOMERY	HUSTON		7
MONTGOMERY	JAMES		6+ 54
MONTGOMERY	JESSE		6
MONTGOMERY	JOHN		6+
MONTGOMERY	JOSEPH		6 54
MONTGOMERY	RICHARD		27
MONTGOMERY	ROBERT		6 44
MONTGOMERY	RUSSELL		8
MONTGOMERY	SAMUEL		6+
MONTGOMERY	THOMAS		6
MONTGOMERY	WALKER C		6
MONTGOMERY	WILLIAM		17

MOODY	ALEXANDER		44
MOON	BENJAMIN		75
MOON	DAVID		74
MOONE	BARNETT		52
MOONEY	JA'S		12
MOONEY	WM		12
MOOR	JOEL		71
MOOR	JOHN		56
MOORE	AARON		53
MOORE	ALEXANDER		31
MOORE	ARCHIBALD		38
MOORE	DAVID		44
MOORE	EDWARD	6 27 40	42
MOORE	ELIJAH		38
MOORE	ELISHA		2
MOORE	HENRY		38
MOORE	HENRY H		70
MOORE	HUGH	51	55
MOORE	JAMES	8 50 51	73
MOORE	JAMES SR		53
MOORE	JAMES T		6
MOORE	JESSE		38
MOORE	JOHN	12 16 29 38	42
MOORE	JOHN	43 46 71	75
MOORE	JOHN III		38
MOORE	JOHN JR		67
MOORE	JOHN SR		67
MOORE	JOHN W		51
MOORE	JOSEPH	38 60	70
MOORE	JOSHUA		12
MOORE	JOSIAH		72
MOORE	MALICHI		72
MOORE	NELSON		38
MOORE	SAMUEL	29 31 38	60
MOORE	SILAS		44
MOORE	T		59
MOORE	THOMAS		38
MOORE	THOMAS M		70
MOORE	WILLIAM	20 38 45	74
MOORE	WILLIAM JR		72
MOORE	WM JR		12
MOORE	WM SR		12
MOOREHEAD	- - -		38
MOOREHEAD	JOHN		49
MOORMAN	ELI		73
MORCKERT	GEORGE		66
MORE	ROBERT		2
MOREHOUSE	JAY		58
MOREL	JOHN		47
MORENCE	GARRETT		6
MORENCE	SMITH		6
MORFOND	JOSIAH T		27
MORGAIN	SAMUEL		47
MORGAN	ABSALOM		38

MORGAN	CHARLES		30
MORGAN	DAVID		30
MORGAN	EBENEZER E		2
MORGAN	ELIJAH		38
MORGAN	ISAAC		60
MORGAN	JOSEPH		34
MORGAN	LAMBETH		47
MORGAN	MICAGAH		71
MORGAN	MICAJAH		76
MORGAN	PETALIAH		57
MORGAN	RANDEL		34
MORGAN	SCHLUSS		30
MORGAN	SOLOMON		38
MORGAN	THOMAS		34
MORGAN	WILLIS		63
MORGAN	ZADIOCH		33
MORIN	BARNARD		63
MORIN	WILLIAM		63
MORING	WALTER		9
MORLAND	JOHN		9
MORRES	ELISHA		52
MORRES	THO'S		52
MORRES	WM		52
MORRIS	ALEXANDER		42
MORRIS	ARCHIBALD		23
MORRIS	ARON		60
MORRIS	BENONI		62
MORRIS	DEMPSY		12
MORRIS	JACOB		13
MORRIS	JAMES		42
MORRIS	JEHOSHAPHAT		60
MORRIS	JESSE		72
MORRIS	JOHN	31	61
MORRIS	JOHN G		61
MORRIS	LEWIS S		61
MORRIS	MATTHEW		46
MORRIS	RICHARD		61
MORRIS	ROBERT		20
MORRIS	SAMUEL		62
MORRIS	STEPHIN		63
MORRIS	WALTER B		21
MORRIS	WASHINGTON		42
MORRIS	WILLIAM	31	42
MORRISON	JOHN		27
MORRISON	MATHIAS		29
MORRISON	ROBT		23
MORRISON	WM C		8
MORROD	JAMES		76
MORROW	ANDREW		72
MORROW	JOHN		75
MORROW	SAMUEL		2
MORSE	WILLIAM		56
MORTON	ANDREW		15+
MORTON	JAMES	15	75

MORTON	JOHN		22	15
MORTON	WILLIAM			15
MOSELY	ROBERT		6	46
MOSES	ADAM			43
MOSES	JEREMIAH			44
MOSES	TOBIAS			44
MOSS	BENEIAH			51
MOSS	BENGAMIN		43	45
MOSS	JOHN			26
MOSS	WILLIAM			65
MOTSINGER	DAVID			66
MOTSINGER	GEORGE			66
MOTSINGER	JACOB		66	67
MOTSINGER	MICHAEL			69
MOUNCE	THOMAS			6
MOUNT	THOMAS			65
MOUNTS	AMOS C			16
MOUNTS	JOSEPH			26
MOUNTS	JOSHUA			26
MOUNTS	MATHIAS			64
MOUNTS	WILLIAM			65
MOURNIN	DAVID			63
MOURON	RABER			71
MOUTRY	JAMES			51
MOYERS	JOHN			44
MOYRES	MOSES			41
MUIR	JAMES			55
MULERY	JEREMIAH			8
MULERY	WILLIAM			8
MULL	TOBIAS			60
MULLEN	EDWARD			15
MULLEN	JOHN			41
MULLEN	WM			52
MULLENS	CHARLES			45
MULLENS	JONATHAN			45
MULLENS	WILLIAM			45
MULLER	DAVID			54
MULLINIX	ELISHA			65
MULLINIX	PREMENTER			70
MULLIS	JACOB			11
MULLOY	MALONE			8
MULPHERD	JOSEPH			62
MUND	SAMUEL			2
MUNDEN	LEVI			62
MUNDLE	ANDREW			40
MUNSHED	JEREMIAH			75
MUNSON	ALANSON			19
MUNSON	HIRAM			26
MURFEY	JAMES			51
MURFIN	JOHN			34
MURPHY	ABRAHAM			47
MURPHY	ALEXANDER			38
MURPHY	DANIEL			68
MURPHY	JAMES	44	67	72

MURPHY JOHN			10 21	38
MURPHY SAM'L				10
MURPHY WILLIAM				19
MURRY JOHN				40
MURRY THOMAS				42
MUSELMAN DANIEL				26
MUSICK ASA				7
MUSICK JAMES				6
MUSICK JOHN				6
MUSROVE AQUILER				2
MYERS DAVID			62	63
MYERS GEORGE A				62
MYERS HENRY				55
MYERS JACOB F				68
MYERS LEWIS				55
MYERS NOBLE J				38
MYERS SOLOMON				43
MYRES FREDERICK				33
MYRES JACOB				33
MYRES JOHN				28

N

NABB JAMES				28
NACHTRUL ADDAM				53
NACHTRUL FREDERICK				53
NACHTRUL JOSHEWAY				53
NAGGLE PETER				63
NAIL JOHN				50
NAIL WILLIAM				38
NANCE JAMES R				2
NANCE RICHARD				71
NASH JESSEE				52
NASH JOHN				52
NATION ISAAC				9
NATTE JOHN				59
NAY BENNET				18
NcNEELY ROBERT				64
NEAGLEY DAVID				58
NEAL DANIEL				15
NEAL JAMES			32	66
NEAL JESE				15
NEAL JOHN	15	16	52	66
NEAL MEEKS				49
NEAL SAMUEL				69
NEAL WALTER				33
NEALEY JAMES				62
NEAVILL GEORGE				19
NEEDHAM ISAAC				13
NEEDHAM JOHN				26
NEEDUM WM				13
NEEL JOHN				26
NEEL MOSES				26
NEELY JOHN J				6

NEIL ARCHIBALD		44
NEILL ARTHUR		41
NEILL JAMES		41
NEILL NOBLE		41
NEILY WILLIAM B		42
NELAS GEORGE		56
NELSON CHARLES		55
NELSON DANIEL H		19
NELSON GEORGE		60
NELSON JAMES		19
NELSON JAMES SR		49
NELSON JOSEPH		55
NELSON SAM'L		10
NELSON SAMUEL		55
NELSON WILLIAM		73
NELSON WM		52
NESBITT JAMES		52
NESLER CHRIS'PHR SR		51
NESLER CHRIST'R JR		51
NESLER JOHN		50
NESLER SOLOMON SR		49
NETTLETON ISAAC S		51
NETTLETON WM		51
NEVILLS - - -		54
NEW JOHN B		21
NEWBERRY JOHN		22
NEWBY EDMOND		38
NEWBY FRANCIS		64
NEWBY GABRIEL		9
NEWBY GABRIEL SR		10
NEWBY JOSEPH		9
NEWBY JOSHUA		60
NEWBY MICAH		61
NEWBY NATHAN		13
NEWBY NATHANIEL		13
NEWBY ROBERT		9
NEWBY THO'S		12
NEWCOMB WILLIAM		38
NEWKIRK BENJAMIN		11
NEWKIRK CORNELIUS		2
NEWKIRK HENRY		11
NEWKIRK ISAA		11
NEWKIRK PETER		26
NEWKIRK RICHARD		64
NEWLAND WM		10
NEWLIN JONATHAN		43
NEWLIN WILLIAM		43
NEWLON JOHN		60
NEWMAN ADAM		22
NEWMAN THOMAS	36	72
NEWSOM JOEL		70
NEWSOM JOHN		70
NEWSOME DAVID		42
NEWSOME WILLIS		41

NEWSON	WILLIAM		8
NEWTON	DANIEL		26
NEWTON	HENRY		73
NEWTON	JOHN		66
NEWTON	JOSEPH		26
NEWTON	LEWETHER		26
NEWTON	REUBEN		26
NEWTON	WILLIAM		38 60
NICHALAW	AMBROIS		30
NICHELSON	SAM'L		9
NICHELSON	THO'S		9
NICHISON	ABIJAH		54
NICHOLAS	- - -		28
NICHOLAS	EZRA		28
NICHOLS	JONATHAN		38
NICHOLS	JOSEPH		43
NICHOLS	JOSHUA		44
NICHOLS	MARTIN		45
NICHOLS	NATHAN		41
NICHOLSON	BENJAMIN		62
NICHOLSON	ELIJAH		64
NICHOLSON	JAMES B		63
NICHOLSON	JOHN		2
NICHOLSON	JOSEPH		2
NICHOLSON	LARKIN		63
NICHOLSON	PETER		64
NICHOLSON	SAMUEL		63
NICHOLSON	THO'S		17
NICHOLSON	THOMAS		64
NICHOLSON	WILLIAM		64+
NICHOLSON	ZACHARIA		2
NICHUM	JOSEPH		22
NICKEBOCKER	HENRY		21
NIDEFFER	JOHN		44
NIDIVER	FREDERICK		62
NIE	JACOB		62
NIELD	DANN		63
NIGHT	ROBERT		2
NIGHT	SAMUEL		57
NILES	JOSEPH		15
NILES	MOSES B		47
NILES	ROBERT		47
NIXON	ABERHAM		6
NIXON	ANDREW		6
NIXON	FOSLER		62
NIXON	JOSEPH		61
NIXON	WILLIAM		74
NIXON	ZACHARIAH		62
NOBLE	THOMAS		19
NOBLET	ABRAHAM		70
NOBLET	WILLIAM		69
NOCHOLSON	JOHN		73
NOEL	LEWIS		38
NOGGLE	DAVID		67
NOLEN	HENRY		28 30
NOLTON	EPRAIM		26
NOLTON	JOSHUA		26
NOLTON	STEPHEN		26
NOORE	ALEXANDER		73
NORMAN	JOHN		70
NORMAN	SAMUEL		31
NORO	GABRIAL		30
NORRIS	EDWARD		61
NORRIS	HEZEKIAH		56
NORRIS	SAMUEL		23
NORTH	DANIEL		72
NORTHWAY	JAMES F		26
NORTON	ELIAS		72
NORTON	JOHN		20
NOWEL	JOHN		51
NOWLAND	THOMAS		6
NOX	FACTOR		4
NOYS	JONATHAN		48
NUHAL	BENJAMIN		4
NUSAM	JOSEPH		49
NUTON	CHARLES P		8
NYSWONGER	JOSEPH		29

O

O'BANNION	JOSEPH		3
O'DANIEL	SETEN		26
O'LOCKLEY	JOHN		26
O'NEIL	HENRY		56
O'NEIL	JAMES		56
O'NEIL	JOHN		54 56
OALDS	ELIJAH		12
OBANION	BRYANT		2
OBRIAN	JOHN I		50
OBRINE	JAMES		15
OCHSTREICHER	ANDREW		53
OCHSTREICHER	CHRIST'R		53
OCKLETREE	JOHN		35
OENS	STEPHEN		46
OFFICER	WILLIAM		18
OGEN	SAM'L		74
OGLE	WM		11
OGLESBURY	THO'S		9
OGLESBY	DAVID		7
OGLESBY	JONATHAN		6
OGLESBY	JOSEPH		21
OGLESBY	WM		9
OLDS	DANIEL		57 60
OLDS	JARED		60
OLDS	WILLIAM		67
OLIVER	JOHN JR		52
OLIVER	JOHN SR		52
OLMSTED	WM		58

OLMSTED SAMUEL	21	
OLOUGHLIN PRESILLA	20	
ONEAL HENRY	6	
ONEAL JAMES	15	
ONEAL JOHN	57	
ONEAL WILLIAM	15	
ONLOY BENJAMIN	28	
ONNEAL JOHN	4	
ORCHARD ISAAC	69	
ORNOLD JOSEPH	17	
ORTEN JOHN Z	40	
ORTON JEREMIAH	23	
OSBOIRN WILLIAM	74	
OSBORN ISAAC G	21	
OSBORN JOHN	38	
OSBORN LEMUEL	51	
OSBORN PETER	16	
OSBOURN JOHN W	30	
OSBURN ABRAHAM	44	
OSBURN ENOCH	43	
OSBURN JAMES	2	
OSBURN JOHN	2	
OSBURN JONATHAN	2	40
OSBURN JOSEPH	2	
OSBURN RICHARD	2	
OSBURN ROBERT	2	
OSBURN SAMUEL	2	
OSBURN SOLOMON	2	
OSBURN WILLIAM	2	
OSBURN WILLIS C	6	
OSMEN WILLLAM	43	
OSMORE NATHAN	52	
OSTEN DANIEL	27	
OVERLAIN JOHN	42	
OVERMAN BENJAMIN	62	
OVERMAN ELI	62	
OVERMAN HENRY	63	
OVERMAN JAMES	62	
OVERMAN JOHN	61	
OVERTON BENJAMINE	8	
OVERTON DANDRIDGE	66	
OVERTON JOSHUWAY	53	
OVERTON RICHARD	49	
OVERTURF CONRAD	55	
OVERTURF JACOB	54	
OVERTURF MARTIN	55	
OWEN BENJAMIN	55	
OWEN GEORGE W	12	
OWEN THOMAS	32	
OWEN WM	12	
OWENS ALEXANDER	38	
OWENS DAN'L	8	
OWENS DAVID	65	
OWENS ENOS	66	

OWENS GEORGE C	16	
OWENS JA'S	8	
OWENS JOHN	38	
OWENS JOHN II	38	
OWENS PLEASANT	74	
OWENS RANDOLPH	6	
OWENS THOMAS	18	34
OWENS WALTER	10	
OWNS BRICKET	26	
OXSHEAR M	14	
OYOTTE JOSEPH	28	

P

PACE WILLIAM	31	
PACKER JESSE	56	
PADELFORD JOSEPH	58	
PADGETT JONATHAN	31	
PADGETT NATHAN	64	
PAGE DOMENICE	29	
PAGE WILLIAM	29	
PAGGET WILLIAM	26	
PAIN MILO	62	
PAINE AARON	43	
PAINE ADAM	43	
PAINE PATERICK	7	
PALMER JOSHUA	26	
PALMER NATHANIEL B	21	
PALMER THOMAS	32	56
PALONOR JOSEPH	74	
PAN HIRYM	38	
PANCAKE JACOB	33	
PANTER DAVID	39	
PARISH LEVI	51	
PARISHAW JA'S	13	
PARISHO JOHN	38	
PARK ALEX'R	16	
PARK JAMES	16	
PARK M	22	
PARKE BENJAMIN	27	
PARKER ABSALOM	12	
PARKER BAZEL	32	
PARKER BENJAMIN	62	
PARKER GEORGE	57	
PARKER JESTIS	48	
PARKER JOHN	32	57
PARKER JOSHUA	26	
PARKER SILAS	58	
PARKERSON WILLIAM	47	48
PARKESON JAMES	27	
PARKEY JACOB	65	
PARKS BENJAMIN	38	
PARKS GEORGE	38	
PARKS GEORGE II	38	

PARKS JAMES		38
PARKS JOHN	9	46
PARKS ROBERT		45
PARKS SAM'L		49
PARKS WILLLAM	16 38	45
PARMER DAVID		73
PARMER JOHN		12
PAROIN WILLIAM		6
PARR ARTHUR		60
PARR ENOCH		60
PARR ISAAC		55
PARR JOHN		60
PARR MORGAN		60
PARR SAMUEL		27
PARR THOMAS		2
PARRETT ROBERT		52
PARSON JAMES J		38
PARSON NATHANIEL		19
PARSONS JAMES		38
PARSONS ROBERT		40
PARTLE HENRY		33
PARTLOW WM		10
PARVIN MARK		6
PASSON WILLIAM		72
PASUR WILLIAM		2
PATRICK BRI		2
PATRICK EBENEZAR		61
PATRICK JOHN F		31
PATRICK MASTEN		2
PATRICK MATTHEW		61
PATRICK OBEDIAH F		31
PATRICK WILLIAM		38
PATTEN JAMES		59
PATTERSON ARTHUR		30
PATTERSON DAVID		12
PATTERSON J		21
PATTERSON JAMES		16
PATTERSON JOHN	17 20 27	38
PATTERSON KENNEDY		68
PATTERSON ROBERT		26
PATTERSON SAM'L		53
PATTERSON SAMUEL		16
PATTERSON WILLIAM		33
PATTERSON WM		59
PATTERSON WM JR		12
PATTERSON WM SR		12
PATTON HEZEKIAH E		13
PATTON HOUSTON		20
PATTON HUSTON		56
PATTON JAMES		23+
PATTON JOHN M		19
PATTON MATHEW		22
PATTON WILLIAM G		42
PATTON WM		49

PAUL CYRUS		59
PAUL JOHN		21
PAUL JOHN of P		19
PAUL MARSHFIELD		59
PAUL SAMUEL		59
PAVEY ANDERSON		69
PAVEY SAMUEL		68
PAWLEY ISAAC		38
PAWLY ABRAHAM		38
PAWNELL JOSEPH		9
PAXTON JOHN		72
PAXTON JOHN A		58
PAYBODY EZRA F		26
PAYNE JOHN	16	66
PAYTON JAMES		2
PEA DANIEL		6
PEA JACOB		34
PEA JOHN		34
PEAL JOHN		50
PEAL THO'S		50
PEARCE EARL		58
PEARCE JOHN JR		59
PEARCE THOMAS		59
PEARCY ROBERT		19
PEARSON CHATWELL		35
PEARSON E		22
PEARSON ISAAC		40
PEARSON JAMES	2	45
PEARSON JOHN		35
PEARSON JOSEPH	43	59
PEARSON MOSES B		27
PEARSON NATHAN		75
PEARSON REUBEN		2
PEARSON THOMAS		27
PEARSON WILLIAM		2
PECK DANIEL		8
PECK ISAAC		38
PECK JACOB		38
PECK JAMES		6
PECK JOSEPH H		45
PECK WM		57
PECKANPAW HENRY		2
PECKHAM ARNOLD		54
PECKHAM LEWIS		29
PECKINGPAUGH JOHN		47
PECKINGPAUGH PETER		47
PECKINGPAW JOHN		2
PECKINGPAW PETER		2
PECOR ALEXIS		28
PEDLEY JOHN		59
PEEL JOHN		72
PEEL MARK		71
PEELER ALLEN		69
PEG JOAB		72

PEGG JESSE	74	
PEGG VOLENTINE	75	
PELSOLL BENJAMIN	55	
PELTON JAMES	67	
PENDLETON CHARLES	59	
PENDLETON DAVID	26	
PENDLETON ROBERT	26	
PENETENT JOHN	55	
PENN EPHRAIM	13 19	
PENNIC ALLEXANDER	26	
PENNICK JOHN	45	
PENNINGTON MOSES	2	
PENNINGTON WILLIAM	2	
PENNYPACKER WM	52	
PEOPLES HECTOR	26	
PEOPLES JOHN	35	
PERCE CHARLES	8	
PERDUE RICHARD	26	
PERIGO DANIEL	44	
PERISHO JOSEPH	38	
PERKINS JAMES	72	
PERRY JOHN	10	
PERRY JOSEPH	6	
PERRY RANSOM	26	
PERRY WILLIAM	63	
PERRY WM	12	
PERSON AXSOM	73	
PERSON DAVID	47	
PERSON JOHN	47	
PERSON NEWSON	8	
PERSON WILLIAM	6	
PERSON WM	15	
PERSONS ABLE	61	
PERYEA PAUL	28	
PETER EDWARD G	2	
PETERS GEORGE	42	
PETERS GODFREY	8	
PETERS JOHN	40	
PETERS WILLIAM	6	
PETIT ANTOINE	30	
PETTERSON JOHN	32	
PETTES SAMUEL	26	
PETTET WILLIAM	2	
PETTICE DAVID	34	
PETTICE JOHN	34	
PETTICOURT BOSWELL	38	
PEW JOHN	67	
PEWED THOMAS	60	
PEYTON GILBERT	51	
PEYTON JOHN	2	
PFIEF FREDERICK	54	
PHAR V K	58	
PHAROW WM	9	
PHELPS ARONAH	54	
PHELPS ARONOUS	26	
PHELPS ASAHEL	11	
PHELPS GEORGE A	11	
PHELPS SETH	26 54	
PHELPS WILLIAM	69	
PHILIP ROBERT	48	
PHILIPS ABRAHAM	66	
PHILIPS BENJAMIN	61	
PHILIPS DAVID	45	
PHILIPS EBENEZER	51	
PHILIPS EDMOND	38	
PHILIPS ELBERT	40	
PHILIPS ELISHA	51	
PHILIPS FREDERICK	66	
PHILIPS GEORGE	45	
PHILIPS JOHN	38 51	
PHILIPS JOHN JR	52	
PHILIPS JOHN H	47 48	
PHILIPS JOSEPH	38	
PHILIPS PRESTLEY	14	
PHILIPS ROBERT	69	
PHILIPS ROBT	14	
PHILIPS SOLOMAN	38	
PHILIPS THOMAS	45	
PHILIPS WILLIAM	45	
PHILLIPS CHARLES	6	
PHILLIPS JOHN	7 18	
PHILLIPS JOSHUA	17	
PHILLIPS ROBERT	19	
PHILLIPS RODY	6	
PHILLIPS WILLIAM	6	
PHILLIPS ZEKIEL	18	
PHIPPS SAMPSON	66	
PHIPS JAMES	2	
PIATTA AUSTIN	47	
PICKARD JOHN	40	
PICKENS JAMES	40	
PICKENS JOHN	41	
PICKET BENJAMIN	74	
PICKET JOHN	43	
PICKETT JEREMIAH	63	
PICKLE FREDERICK	41	
PICKLER JAMES	68	
PICKLER JOHN	68	
PICKSTEY JOHN H	61	
PIEATY THOMAS	31	
PIEKES JOSHUA	74	
PIERCE ELEAZER JR	45	
PIERCE ELEAZER SR	45	
PIERCE ELIJAH	42	
PIERCE JAMES	38	
PIERCE PHILIP C	42	
PIERSON JACOB	63	
PIERSON JOHN	71	

PIERSON MOSES B		65
PIERSON NATHAN		71
PIFER MICHAEL		43
PIFER JOHN		43
PIGEON BENJAMIN		63
PIGEON PATRICK		28
PILES PETER		41
PINKLEY BENGAMIN		41
PINNICK ISAAC		42
PINNICK JAMES		42
PINNICK JAMES SR		42
PINNICK NATHAN		39
PINTOX SAMUEL		3
PITCHER JOHN JR		30
PITCHER JOHN SR		30
PITMAN LEWIS		39
PITTS ANDREW		61
PITTS GIDEON		51
PITTS SAMUEL		61
PITTS THOMAS		61
PLATTER HENRY		56
PLESSING MICHAEL		53
PLOUGH ISAAC		35
PLOUGH JACOB		35
PLOUGH NIM		35
PLOUGH SAMUEL		35
PLOUGH SIMON		35
PLOUGHMAN HENRY		64
PLYMET JOHN		26
PLYMET SERVICE		26
POE JEREMIAH		2
POGUE JOHN		24
POGUE WILLIAM		24
POI JAMES		45
POLK CHARLES	47+	48
POLK EDMON		47
POLK THOMAS		47
POLKE CHARLES JR		31
POLKE CHARLES SR		31
POLKE WILLIAM		31
POLLARD ELISHA		68
POLLOCK J D		20
POLSON THOMAS		70
POLSTEWEIGHT SAMUEL		30
POMROY GEORGE		32
POOL EPRAIM		26
POOL JOHN		74
POOL JOSEPH		26
POOL JOSHUA		72
POOL PETTER		29
POPE ELIJAH		2
POPE PILGRAM		2
POPE WILLIAM		68
POPPLE SIMEON		26

PORTER - - -		26
PORTER AARON		17
PORTER ANDREW		59
PORTER BENJAMIN		66
PORTER CHARLES		54
PORTER CHRISTOPHER		43
PORTER GEORGE K		9
PORTER JAMES		43
PORTER JOHN		4
PORTER JOHN R		45
PORTER JOSEPH		65
PORTER NICHOLAS B		44
PORTER WILLIAM		32
POSEY A W G		2
POSEY RICHARD		32
POSTON LEVI		22
POTTER BENGAMIN	43	44
POTTER DUKE		38
POTTER JAMES		3
POTTER JOHN		58
POTTER JOHN B		26
POTTER LEMUEL		13
POTTER STEPHEN		75
POTTER THOMAS	8 38	72
POTTER WILLIAM		2
POTTORFF ANDREW		68
POTTORFF JOHN		62
POTTORFF MARTIN		62
POTTS EDWARDS		76
POTTS GEORGE		59
POTTS RICHARD F L		47
POTTS SM'L		76
POUGH WILLIAM		38
POUGHMAN JOHN		60
POUNDS JOSEPH		44
POUNDS MARTIN		44
POWE BENJAMINE		8
POWEL ABRAHAM		51
POWEL LEWIS		70
POWEL SAMUEL		46
POWEL THOMAS		46
POWELL WILLIAM		22
POWERS GEORGE		26
POWERS JOSHUA		65
POWERS NEHEMIAH		26
PRACE WILLIAM		32
PRATER HENERY		47
PRATHER BASEL		61
PRATHER DAVID		9
PRATHER ELISHA		10
PRATHER JOHN		9
PRATHER THO'S		10
PRATHER THOMAS		11
PREBLE TEPHEN		56

PRESTON GEORGE	63	
PREWITT MOSES	59	
PRICE ALEXANDER	73	
PRICE DAVID	35	
PRICE DERASTUS	63	
PRICE FREDERICK	49	
PRICE GILLESON	49	
PRICE HENRY	72	
PRICE JAMES	73+	
PRICE JEDIAH	75	
PRICE JOHN JR	49	
PRICE JOHN SR	49	
PRICE JOSEPH	51	
PRICE LARKEN	49	
PRICE RICHARD P	27	
PRICE SAMUEL	34	
PRICE THOMAS	74	
PRICE WILLIAM	6 31	
PRICE WM	49	
PRICHARD HERMON	49	
PRICKETT JAMES	30	
PRICKETT JOHN	6	
PRIKER MOSES	73	
PRIME JOHN	9	
PRIME NATHAN	9	
PRINCE DAVID	66	
PRINCE GODFRAY	63	
PRINCE JACOB	61	
PRINCE JOHN	21	
PRINCE WILLIAM	6 29	
PRINGLE JAMES	60	
PRITCHARD JOHN JR	26	
PRITCHARD JOHN SR	26	
PRITCHARD REES	60	
PRITCHET PRESLEY	58	
PROCTER MOSES	18	
PROCTOR AMOS	28	
PROCTOR WILLIAM	28	
PROTHERO WILLIAM	14	
PROW ADAM	64	
PROW CHRISTIAN JR	64	
PROW CHRISTIAN SR	64	
PROW JOHN	64	
PRUETT AMSTED	38	
PRUETT COLEMAN	38	
PRUETT GEORGE	63	
PRUETT WILLIAM	38	
PRUSTON N	52	
PRYOR JOHN A	55	
PRYOR NICHOLAS M	20	
PUCKET BENJAMIN	75	
PUCKET DANIEL	75	
PUGH JOHN	21	
PUGH WM	73	

PULAM ZACHIRAH	28	
PULLIAM BENJAMIN	68	
PULLIAM BLAN B	68	
PULLIAM M J	19	
PULLIUM ROBERT	15	
PURCEL JESSE	40	
PURCELL ADAM	35	
PURCELL ANDREW	32 34	
PURCELL BENJAMIN	55	
PURCELL ISAAC	35	
PURCELL JAMES	32 35	
PURCELL JOHN	32 34 55	
PURCELL JONATHAN	35	
PURCELL MOSES	55	
PURCELL NOAH	32	
PURCELL SAMUEL	55	
PURCELL WILLIAM	32	
PURDEN CHARLES	19	
PURDIE RICHARD	21	
PURDIN JOHN	17	
PURDUE EDWARD	31	
PURDUE FURGAS	31	
PURDUE JESSEY	31	
PURKISER JOHN	69	
PURKISER SAMUEL	69	
PURLEE JACOB	65	
PURSEL REUBEN	63	
PURSEL WILLIAM	63+	
PURSELL CHARLES	49	
PURSINGER BENJAMIN	47	
PURSINGER LUKE	64	
PUTMAN HAZEAL	58	
PUTNAM HOWARD	35	
PUYER GEORGE	45	

Q

QUAKENBUSH PETER	43
QUEEN HAMPTON	73
QUICK DAVID	47
QUICK JESSE	46
QUIER DAVID	18
QUINATT CHARLES	43

R

RACHELS J BOSWELL		49
RACINE ANDREW		30
RACINE JOSEPH	77	30
RACINE PEIRRE		30
RACINE PIERRE		28
RADBURN WILLIAM		6
RADEY JOHN		17
RADLEY JAMES		56
RAE WILLIAM		46
RAGER JACOB		53
RAGSDELL FREDERICK		7
RAINS JONATHAN		38
RALL MARTIN		53
RALLIFF RICHARD		71
RALSTON ALEXANDER		70
RALSTON GAVIN		65
RAMBO ISAAC		71
RAMORE PEIRRE		28
RAMSEY AARON		35
RAMSEY ALEXANDER		46
RAMSEY ALLEN		35
RAMSEY AQUILLA		35
RAMSEY BENJAMIN		17
RAMSEY GEORGE		59
RAMSEY JOHN	17	64
RAMSEY LEVI		17
RAMSEY THO'S		17
RAMSEY THOMAS		21
RAMSEY WILLIAM		26
RAMSEY WILLIAM H		35
RANDALL JOHN		20
RANDLE JOHN		68
RANDLET JOHN		2
RANDOLPH ROBERT		52
RANEBS ABRAHAM		75
RANETS JACOB		75
RANEY JACOB		56
RANEY SAMUEL		70
RANIGS DAVID		71
RANKIN JAMES		52
RANSBARGER GEROGE		62
RANSOM ISAAC		63
RANSOM ROBINS		26
RANSON TIMOTHY JR		57
RANSON ELISHA		57
RANSON TIMOTHY SR		57
RAPER JOHN		72
RAPER WILLIAM		32
RAPP FRED'K		53
RAPP GEORGE		53
RASOR CHRISTIAN		2
RATCLIFF JOSEPH		72
RATLEY GREEN		50
RATLIFF BENJAMIN		70
RATLIFF CORNELIUS	73	74
RATLIFF DAVID		70
RATLIFF JOSEPH JR		74
RATLIFF RICHARD		74
RATTS GODFROY		65
RATTS HENRY		65
RAVERSON JOHN		30
RAVOLETT FRANCIS		30
RAVOLETTE ANTOINE		30
RAVOLETTE LEWEY		30
RAWLEIGH JOHN B		40
RAWLEY EVANS		38
RAWLINS DANIEL		38
RAWLINS RODERICK		38
RAWSON ANSON		67
RAWSON DANIEL		67
RAWSON HORRACE		67
RAY DANIEL		69
RAY DAVID		33
RAY JOHN		56
RAY MATTHEW		56
RAY ROBERT		56
RAY SILAS		56
RAY WILLIAM	17	38
RAYBORN DAVID		38
RAYBURN CORNELIUS		43
RAYHILL MATTHEW		60
RAYMON A		3
RAZOR ABRAHAM		63
REA JAMES		20
READER SIMON		49
REAL CLARK		2
REARDON JAMES		76
REATHERFORD JOHN		15
REATHERFORD SHELTON		15
REATHERFORD STEPHEN		15
REAVIS WILLIAM		6
RECHUM JUSHENE		56
RECINE JOHN		30
RECKETTS WILLIAM		6
RECTOR DANIEL		19
RECTOR FREDERICK C		49
RECTOR H P		19
RECTOR JOHN		19
REDDEN THOS		13
REDDENBAUGH FREDERICK	16	17
REDDENBAUGH GEORGE		16
REDDENBAUGH PHILLIP		17
REDDENBAUGH SAMUEL		17
REDENOUR HENRY		32
REDIX GEORGE		38

Name	Page
REDMAN GEORGE	27
REDUS JOEL	69
REDUS JOHN	69
REDUS SAMUEL	61
REDY CHRISTOPHER	71
REECE JONATHAN	2
REED A G	22
REED DAVID	45
REED ELIAS	45
REED ISAIAH	64
REED JESSE	61
REED JOHN	26 27
REED JOHN M	55
REED JOSEPH	67
REED JOSHUA	45
REED L W	21
REED RICHARD	52
REED ROBERT	45
REED THO'S N	20
REED WILLIAM	44 45
REED WILLIAM G	64
REEDER ELISHUA	30
REEDY JAMES	45
REEL DAVID JR	34
REEL DAVID SR	34
REEL FREDERICK	6
REEL GODFREY	34
REEL HENRY	6
REEL JOHN	6 33
REEL MICHAEL	2
REES EPRAIGM	48
REESE HENRY	71
REEVES ALLEN	31
REEVES JOHN	54
REEVES JOSEPH	38
REIBLE HENRY	29
REID FREDERICK	17
REID THO'S	18
REILEY DAVID B	29
REILEY JOHN C	28
REILEY JOSIAH	30
REILEY MARTIN	28
REILEY OWEN	28
REILEY PHILLIP	35
REIPP JOHN	53
REITHER WILLIAM	26
RENNICK HENRY	68
RENNO JA'S	12
RENNOCK ALLEXANDER	26
RENNY WILLIAM	6
RENO RICHARD	73
RENSHAW AB'M	59
RETHERFORD MARK	39
REUMINGOR JOHN	34
REVES ISAM	6
REVIS DANIEL	6
REYMAN JACOB B	62
REYMAN JOSEPH	62
REYNOLDS JEREMIAH	43
REYNOLDS ROBERT	29
REYNOLDS RUBEN	47
REYNOLDS S L	19
REYNOLDS WILLIAM	40 45
REYNOLS EZEKEL	6
RHOADS JACOB	19
RHOADS LEWIS	38
RHOADS WILSON W	38
RHODES WILLIAM	45
RHODS JOHN	26
RHUE ABRAHAM	64
RIAN DANIEL	47
RIBBLE ADAM	61
RIBBLE JOHN	10 62
RIBBLE JOSEPH	62
RIBBLE SAMUEL	61
RIBBLE WM	13
RICE DINSEY	64
RICE JACOB	2
RICH AMOS	18
RICH ISEAH	26
RICH JOSEPH	10
RICH JUSTICE	26
RICHARD JOHN	53
RICHARDS GABRIEL	11
RICHARDS GEORGE	11
RICHARDS JACOB	67
RICHARDS JOHN	2
RICHARDS MICHAEL	65
RICHARDS ROLAND B	6
RICHARDS WILLIAM	66
RICHARDS ZADOCK	8
RICHARDSON AMOS	47
RICHARDSON ARTHUR	62
RICHARDSON DANIEL	67
RICHARDSON EBENEZER	47
RICHARDSON IRA	70
RICHARDSON IVY	62
RICHARDSON JA'S H	58
RICHARDSON JOHN	16 67
RICHARDSON JONATHAN	46
RICHARDSON JOSEPH	38
RICHARDSON LARKIN	46
RICHARDSON RICHARD	44
RICHARDSON THOMAS	47 67
RICHARDSON THOMAS JR	47
RICHARSON THOMAS	68
RICHEY GIDEON	8
RICHEY JOHN	6 33

Name	Page
RICHEY JOSEPH	8
RICHEY THOMAS	26
RICHMOND WILLIAM	38
RICKET RICHARD	52
RICKS JOHN W	48
RIDDICK OLOMON	13
RIDDLE CHARLES	2
RIDDLE GEORGE	2
RIDDLE J	15
RIDDLE JACOB	14
RIDDLE JAMES	2
RIDDLE JESSE	2
RIDDLE JOHN	2 22
RIDDLES BENJAMIN	2
RIDENOWER DAVID	51
RIDENOWER JOHN	51
RIDER GEORGE	65
RIDERS JAMES	69
RIDGE BENJAMIN	38
RIDGE CHARLES	2
RIDGEWAY JOHN	69
RIDICE AARON	65
RIFE ABRAHAM	68
RIGGS JOHN	47
RIGGS MOSES	41
RIGHT LEVI	20
RIGNEY ISAAC	44
RIGNEY JOHN	40
RIGNEY MARTIN	44
RIGNEY WILLIAM	44
RIGS JOHN	26
RILEY ABRAHAM	39
RILEY EDWARD	39
RILEY EZEKIEL	45
RILEY ISAAC	39
RILEY JAMES	47 68
RILEY WILLIAM	39
RING JAMES	57
RING MICHAEL	63
RING PHILIP	62
RING SOLOMON	63
RINKER GEORGE	64
RINKER LEVI	64
RIPLEY WILLIAM P	22
RIPPLE HENRY	69
RIPPLE JOHN	69
RIPPY WILLIAM	7
RIRKISER CHRISTOPHER	62
RISING ASELL	51
RISLEY DAVID	33
RISLEY JAMES	33+
RISLEY JOHN	33
RISTINE JAMES	22
RITCHIE ADAM	16
RITCHIE ADAM JR	24
RITCHIE JAMES	14 20
RITCHIE JOHN	19 55
RITCHIE SIMPSON	59
RITCHIE WILLIAM	14
RITCHIE WILLIAM P	20
RITCHY GEORGE	38
RITENBACK STEPHEN	43
RITTER MOSES	61
ROACH JOHN	22
ROACH OWEN	32
ROADES HENERY	47
ROADES JOSEPH	30
ROADS SAMUEL	21
ROADS WILLIAM	39
ROB JAMES	14
ROBB DAVID	6 53
ROBB ELI	53
ROBB JAMES	6 14 49
ROBB JAMES SR	6
ROBB WILLIAM	6
ROBBINS ABEL	43
ROBBINS DANIEL	42
ROBBINS JOSHUA	43
ROBBINS NATHANIEL	45
ROBERSON ABNER	33
ROBERSON HARMAN	33
ROBERSON JAMES	49
ROBERTS ALBERT	26
ROBERTS DAVID	72
ROBERTS EDWARD	54
ROBERTS ELIAS	51
ROBERTS GEORGE	56
ROBERTS HARDING	53
ROBERTS JACOB	56
ROBERTS JAMES	6
ROBERTS JOHN	6 16 26 28 44
ROBERTS JOHN	65 67
ROBERTS JOSEPH	6
ROBERTS LEWIS	66
ROBERTS NOAH	32
ROBERTS PHINEAS	73
ROBERTS RANSEM G	27
ROBERTS SHADRACK	41
ROBERTS SOLOMON W	74
ROBERTS THOMAS JR	74
ROBERTS THOMAS SR	74
ROBERTS WILLIAM	2 22
ROBERTSON ANDREW	8
ROBERTSON ANTHONY	59
ROBERTSON BENNETT	8
ROBERTSON GEORGE	8 47
ROBERTSON JAMES	59
ROBERTSON JOHN	6 7 8

ROBERTSON	PETER		47	RODGERS	ROBERT		20
ROBERTSON	STEPHEN		2	RODGERS	WM		59
ROBERTSON	THOMAS		2	RODMAN	HUGH		69
ROBERTSON	WM		8	RODMAN	JAMES		60
ROBESON	ARCHY		50	RODMAN	JAMES SR		69
ROBESON	GEORGE		53	RODMAN	WILLIAM		61
ROBESON	HENERY		50	RODNEY	DAVID		8
ROBESON	ISAAM		52	RODOLPH	MICHAEL		60
ROBESON	JEREMIAH		50	RODROCK	PETER		2
ROBESON	JOHN		49 50	RODROCK	SOLLEN		2
ROBESON	JONATHAN		52	ROE	JOSEPH		47
ROBESON	JOSEPH		50 52	ROGER	BURKET		57
ROBESON	MOSES		50	ROGER	LEWIS		57+
ROBESON	SAMUEL		26	ROGERS	ALEXANDER		49
ROBESON	ZENO		2	ROGERS	AQUILLA JR		9
ROBINS	G R		20	ROGERS	AQUILLA SR		9
ROBINS	JOHN		31	ROGERS	AQUILLA W		9
ROBINS	WILLIAM		14	ROGERS	BENJAMIN		9
ROBINS	WM		13	ROGERS	DAVID		38
ROBINSON	AMOS		38	ROGERS	GEORGE		15
ROBINSON	BERRISFORD		65	ROGERS	HENRY		8
ROBINSON	DANIEL		19 22	ROGERS	ISAAC		38+
ROBINSON	ELIAS		18	ROGERS	JA'S		9
ROBINSON	HUGH		6	ROGERS	JEREMIAH SR		11
ROBINSON	JAMES		58 65	ROGERS	JOHN		23 26+
ROBINSON	JOHN		18	ROGERS	JONATHAN		38
ROBINSON	JOHN JR		60	ROGERS	LEWIS		8
ROBINSON	JOHN SR		60 65	ROGERS	PHILIP		11 69
ROBINSON	MIDDLETON		18	ROGERS	RICHARD		13
ROBINSON	ROBERT		60 65	ROGERS	SAMUEL		38
ROBINSON	RUSSELL		17	ROGERS	WM		51
ROBINSON	SAMUEL		13	ROLENS	MOSES		33
ROBINSON	WILLIAM	6 20	60 65	ROLER	JACOB		35
ROBISON	BOOTHE		64	ROLIN	THOMAS		48
ROBISON	DRURY		64	ROLLAND	ANTHONY		3
ROBISON	FRANCIS		27	ROLLEY	ELIJAH		61
ROBISON	HENRY		26	ROLLINS	ARON		70
ROBISON	JOHN		64	ROLLINS	EDWARD		70
ROBISON	MARTIN		28	ROLLINS	GEORGE		68
ROBISON	MATTHEW		63	ROLLINS	WILSON		70
ROBISON	NATHAN		26 54	ROLLINSON	AARON		20
ROBISON	STEPHEN		26	ROLSTON	ANDREW D		6
ROBISON	THOMAS		29	ROME	A S D		29
ROBISON	WILLIAM		70	ROMINE	ISAAC		31
ROBY	HENRY		70	ROMJUE	JOHN		8
ROCK	ROBERT		60	ROOF	PETER		72
ROD	THOMAS		42	ROOKS	ELIJAH		6
RODARMELL	JOHN		33	ROOS	DAVID		2
RODEN	ALLEN		43	ROQUESS	SAMUEL		30
RODEN	JAMES		45	RORABACK	JOHN		40
RODEROCK	- - -		2	ROSBOROUGH	JOSEPH		6
RODEROCK	HENRY		2	ROSE	BENJAMIN		59
RODESS	THOMAS		47	ROSE	DANIEL		59
RODGERS	RANDOLPH		59	ROSE	EDWARD W		60

ROSE	ELISHA	JR			60
ROSE	ELISHA	SR			60
ROSE	JAMES	S			68
ROSE	JOSEPH				59
ROSE	JOSHUA				59
ROSE	SAMUEL				60
ROSE	THOMAS				59
ROSEBERRY	GEORGE				18
ROSEBERRY	JOHN				23
ROSEBERRY	THOMAS				26
ROSEBERRY	THOS				18
ROSECRANTY	RICHARD				47
ROSEMAN	JOSEPH				29
ROSEMAN	THOMAS				29
ROSS	BRITMAN				29
ROSS	CHARLES				47
ROSS	ISAAC				2
ROSS	JAMES		16	21	26
ROSS	JOHN				28
ROSS	LEWIS				27
ROSS	MARTIN				32
ROSS	MATHIAS				27
ROSS	RUSSELL				29
ROSS	WILLIAM		23	39	72
ROSSDAN	PETER				54
ROTHBUN	S				16
ROTHBURN	THOS				15
ROTHWELL	KAY				70
ROULLE	GEORGE	H			6
ROUNDEN	ABRAHAM				47
ROUSE	JAMES				2
ROUSE	JOHN				2
ROUSE	WILLIAM				2
ROW	GEORGE				50
ROW	HENRY				70
ROW	JACOB				50
ROW	PHILIP				70
ROW	SAM'L				50
ROWAN	JOHN				56
ROWAND	ALEX'R				17
ROWLAND	JEREMIAH				61
ROWLAND	JESSE				9
ROWLAND	JOHN				64
ROWLAND	WILLIAM				61
ROWLEY	MILLER				26
ROWLEY	NATHAN				58
ROWSER	MARTIN				22
ROYAL	WILLIAM				46
ROYCE	FREDERICK				65
ROYCE	GABRIEL				65
ROYCE	JOHN				70
ROYCE	MARTIN				70
ROYCE	WILLIAM				70
RUBISON	COLZA				68
RUBISON	RICHARD				68
RUBOTTOM	JOSEPH				43
RUBURN	WILLIAM				18
RUBY	PETTER			30	32
RUCKER	REUBEN				13
RUCKLE	CHARLES				21
RUDDICK	MORDICA				13
RUDDICK	SOLOMON	SR			12
RUDDICK	THO'S				9
RUDDICK	WM				12
RUDE	NOAH				15
RUDE	THOMPSON				70
RUDOLPH	ALLEN				51
RUFF	ALBRECHT				54
RUFF	DAVID				54
RUFF	REGORI				54
RUGER	DAVID				35
RUGGLES	WM	B			10
RUHLE	GEORGE				53
RUMBLE	FREDERICK				8
RUNALD	JOHN	M			28
RUNION	SAMUEL				20
RUNNELS	EDWARD				63
RUNNELS	RICHARD				63
RUNNER	DAVID				55
RUNO	JOSEPH				30
RUSECOW	FRANCIS				30
RUSH	- - -				39
RUSH	BENJAMIN				67
RUSH	CHRISTIAN				53
RUSH	ELIJAH				45
RUSH	JAMES				2
RUSHERVILL	ANTOINE				28
RUSHERVILLE	JOHN	BT			30
RUSSEL	ARCHABALD				69
RUSSEL	CURTUS				62
RUSSEL	GEORGE				73
RUSSEL	J				21
RUSSEL	JAMES				57
RUSSEL	JOHN		26	69	73
RUSSEL	ROBERT				26
RUSSEL	ROBERT	JR			26
RUSSEL	SAMUEL				73
RUSSEL	THOMAS				62
RUSSEL	WILLIAM				26
RUSSELL	GEORGE				44
RUSSELL	JA'S				12
RUSSELL	JOHN				52
RUSSELL	ROBERT				75
RUSSELL	WILLIAM				43
RUSSELL	WILLIAM	JR			43
RUSSELL	WM			12	52
RUTH	JOHN				2
RUTHERFORD	DAVID				70

RUTHERFORD LARKIN		13
RUTHERFORD WILLIAM		70
RUTLEDGE ABSOLOM		8
RUTLEDGE J		20
RUTLEDGE JACOB		18
RYAN ELIJAH		56
RYAN GEORGE		56
RYAN JOHN		56
RYAN ROBERT		19
RYKER GERARDUS		14
RYKER J G		20
RYKER JACOB S		17
RYKER JOHN	14+	20
RYKER PETER		20
RYKER SAMUEL	14	22
RYKER SAMUEL J		20
RYKER SAMUEL S		18
RYLE WILLIAM		2
RYLEE JOHN		2
RYNARD GEORGE		71
RYNOT JA'S		12

S

SABERN JOHN		17
SADDLER JOHN		39
SADLER J D		7
SAFLY THOMAS		55
SAGE JESSE		18
SAGE JOHN	9	19
SAGE MORGAN		26
SAGE WILLIAM	19	24
SAILOR JACOB		57
SAINT THOMAS		62
SALMON JACOB		12
SALSBERRY THOMAS		59
SALTSMAN ANDREW		52
SALTSMAN DANIEL		52
SALTSMAN JOHN JR		52
SALTSMAN JOHN SR		52
SALTSMAN MICHAEL		52
SALYERD JEREMIAH		55
SALYERD WILLIAM B		55
SALYERS GEORGE	24	55
SALYERS HENRY		15
SAMPLE ROBT		21
SAMPLE THOMAS		7
SAMPLES JACOB		17
SAMPPLES JOHN		49
SAMPSON BENJAMIN		34
SAMPSON CALEB		56
SAMPSON WILLIAM		33
SAMSON DAVID		3

SAMUELS JOHN		3
SAMUELS ROBERT		2
SAMUELS WILLIAM		3
SANDERS BENJAMIN	2	12
SANDERS HENRY		43
SANDERS HENRY SR		43
SANDERS JACOB	41	74
SANDERS JOHN		41
SANDERS JOSEPH		41
SANDERS PETER		70
SANDERS RICHARD		44
SANDERS SIMEON		63
SANDERS THOMAS		40
SANDERS WILLIAM		64
SANDERS WRIGHT		41
SANDERSON ROBERT		41
SANDFORD WILLIAM		26
SANDS ROBERT		3
SANDWITCH THOMAS		48
SANDY HENRY		65
SANDY JEREMIAH		38
SANDY THOMAS		38
SANDY WILLIAM		64
SANFORD GIGION		26
SAP ELIAS		48
SAPELTON FREDERICK		7
SAPP GEORGE		70
SAPP JOHN		68
SAPP THOMAS		68
SARGENT ABSALOM		70
SARGENT NELSON		17
SATTERLEE GIDEON		58
SATTERLIE ABEL		58
SATTERLIE ASA		58
SATTERLIE ELISHA		58
SATTERLY JOHN		35
SAUNDERS AARON		74
SAUNDERS DAVID		59+
SAUNDERS EZEKIEL		59
SAUNDERS JEFFREY		59
SAUNDERS JOHN		56
SAUNDERS JOHN S		58
SAVAGE CHAMNESS		2
SAVARY HENERY		70
SAVIN PETER		3
SAW WILLIS		23
SAWHEBBER JACOB		4
SAWHEBBER JOHN		4
SAWMAN ALFORD		75
SAWYER DAVID		20
SAWYER HIRAM	20	23
SAWYER LEIR		23
SAWYER MOSES		20
SAWYERS HIRAM		26

Name	Page
SAWYERS LEVY	26
SAYERS JOHN m/o	23
SAYRE DEMICE	28
SAYRE JAMES	28
SAYYEARS LEVY	3
SCABHORN JACOB	33
SCABHORN JOHN	33
SCAGGS JOHN	63
SCAGGS ZACHARIAH	63
SCANLAND JOHN	40
SCANTLING JAMES	7
SCARCE WILLIAM	74
SCARLET JOHN	40 41
SCARLET SAMUEL SR	42
SCARLETT SAMUEL JR	42
SCHAAL GEORGE	54
SCHAAL PHILEMON	54
SCHANBACHER JACOB	53
SCHANBACHER MICHAEL	54
SCHEEL FREDARICK	53
SCHEEL LORENZ	53
SCHNABEL JOHN	53
SCHNEKENBURGER GEORGE	54
SCHNUM JOHN	70
SCHOLLE HELPERT	53
SCHOLLE JACOB	53
SCHOLLE MATTHEW	53
SCHOONOVER DAVID	3
SCIDS JOHN	7
SCOMP HENRY S	31
SCOMP SAMUEL	31
SCONCE ROBT	13
SCONEE ROBT	23
SCOTT ANDREW	56
SCOTT ARCHALAUS	61
SCOTT BENJAMIN	62
SCOTT DANIEL	55
SCOTT DAVID	38 66
SCOTT DAVID R	69
SCOTT GEORGE	29
SCOTT HARMON	67
SCOTT ISAAC	12 43
SCOTT JACOB J	69
SCOTT JAMES	16 29
SCOTT JOHN	8 10 29 41 66
SCOTT JOHN SR	68
SCOTT JOHN C	68
SCOTT JOHN R	3
SCOTT JOHN W	3
SCOTT MORT	2
SCOTT MOSES	55
SCOTT OLLEY	61
SCOTT RAWLEY	10
SCOTT ROBERT	3 66+
SCOTT SAMUEL	38+ 57 75
SCOTT SAMUEL T	8 29
SCOTT THOMAS	26 29
SCOTT WILLIAM	3 54 66 74
SCOTT WILLIAM C	3
SCOTT WM	9 51
SCOTT WM L	3
SCRIBNER IRA	58
SCRITCHFIELD ABSALOM	67
SCRITCHFIELD ARTHUR	67
SCRITCHFIELD JAMES	67
SCRITCHFIELD NATHANIEL	67
SCROGGANS JOSEPH	32
SCRUTCHFIELD JESSE	3
SEAK STEPHEN P	38
SEALES SAMUEL	70
SEALY MORRIS	10
SEARLE THOS C	22
SEARS DAVID	39
SEARS JACOB	39
SEARS JOHN	38
SEARS JOHN B	41
SEARS REUBIN	39
SEATON FRANCIS	33
SEATON SAMUEL	60
SEBREE JAMES	17
SEBRISKEY ABRAHAM	67
SECATT PETER	2
SECHAISE JACOB	66
SECRETS BEESON	38
SECRETS MCPUR	38
SEDAELL ATTICUS	75
SEDGWICK JOHN	38
SEDWICK RICHARD	75
SEELEY STEPHEN I	22
SELBY LINGE	35
SELBY WILLIAM	33
SELF BRADLEY	50
SELF THOMAS	40
SELLERS ROBERT JR	69
SELLERS ROBERT SR	69
SELLS JOHN	65
SELLS SAMUEL	75
SELLS WILLIAM	64 65
SELSON MAJOR	59
SENA JACOB	73
SENA OWEN	71
SENOR OEN JR	73
SERANTEN I G	28
SEREBER PETER	54
SERERIBER LEWIS	54
SERIBER ADAM	54
SERIBER JACOB	54
SERIBER JOHN	54

SERING JOHN	21	SHAVEN JOSEPH	75
SERRA VINCENTS	27	SHAVER JOHN	14 58
SETTLE HENRY	23	SHAVER JONATHAN	3
SEVERS GEORGE	50	SHAVER PETER	58
SEVERS JACOB	50	SHAW HAMILTON	56
SEVERS JAMES	52	SHAW HUGH	33
SEVINEA PIERRE	29	SHAW JAMES	56
SEWEL JOHN	41	SHAW JOHN	3 45
SEWEL THOMAS	43	SHAW JOHN W	58
SEWELL PETER	9	SHAW SAMUEL	56
SEXTON JAMES	74	SHAW THOMAS	39
SHABBOTT JOHN BT	30	SHAW WILLIAM	7
SHABLOTT BURNOW	28	SHAW WM	59
SHACKLE ABRAHAM	3	SHEALDS THOMAS	7
SHAFER JOHN	55	SHEARER PETER	73
SHAFER THORNTON	32	SHEARMAN BENNONCE	15
SHAFFER DANIEL	3	SHEARMAN ELISHA	15
SHAFFER DAVID	75	SHEATS JOHN	33
SHAIK ROSS	24	SHED LUTHER	17
SHALLOTT BARNEAU	30	SHEETS ANDREW	66
SHALLOWS DANIEL	64	SHEETS FREDERICK	66
SHANE DANIEL JR	74	SHEETS GEORGE	21
SHANER GEORGE	33	SHEETS JACOB	65
SHANK JACOB	38	SHEETS JAMES	7
SHANNON ALEXANDER	31	SHEETS JOHN	21
SHANNON GEORGE	16 23	SHEETS LEWIS	22
SHANNON HENRY	21	SHEETS MARTAIN	26
SHANNON JOHN	16	SHEGAW JOHN D	59
SHANNON ROBERT	7	SHEIRER ADAM	28
SHANNON SAMUEL	7	SHELBY JOHN	27
SHANNON THOS	23	SHELL HENRY	38
SHANNON WILLIAM	21	SHELL JOHN	39
SHAPAUR AMBROISE	28	SHELLADY EDWARD	26
SHARK WILLIAM	71	SHELLEDY EPRAIM	26
SHARKEY BATEAST	29	SHELLEDY GEORGE	26+
SHARON CALEB	74	SHELLY WILLIAM	73
SHARP ABRAHAM	5	SHEONE WILLIAM	55
SHARP FINDLEY	74	SHEPARD JONAS	55
SHARP GEORGE	7 38	SHEPARD RUSSELL	55
SHARP HORATIO	7	SHEPARD WALTER	55
SHARP JAMES	7	SHEPARD WHEELER	55
SHARP JOHN	7	SHEPARD WILLIAM D	35
SHARP McCAGAH W	7	SHEPERD JAMES	26
SHARP THOMAS	7	SHEPERD JOSHUA	26
SHARP WILLIAM	7	SHEPERD WILLIAM	26
SHARTEEN SAMUEL	20	SHEPHARD H	14
SHASTEEN ABSALOM	68	SHEPHARD MILES	64
SHASTEEN BERNARD	68	SHEPHERD ABRAHAM	9
SHASTEEN DANIEL	68	SHEPHERD ELI	9
SHASTEEN JAMES	68	SHEPHERD JOHN	3 66
SHASTEEN RANEY	68	SHEPHERD PETER	9
SHASTEEN WILLIAM	68	SHEPHERD REUBEN	66
SHATTO NICHOLAS	10	SHEPHERD THOMAS	66 69
SHAUFNER JOHN	57	SHEPHERD WILLIAM SR	66

SHEPPARD WILLIAM			34
SHERER RUBEN			41
SHERK JACOB			35
SHERK JOHN			39
SHERLY WILLIAM			48
SHERMAN NATHANIEL			22
SHERWOOD DANIEL			70
SHERWOOD DANIEL JR			70
SHERWOOD ELI			57
SHERWOOD HUGH			70
SHERWOOD WILLIAM			70
SHICK SAM'L			9
SHIELDS ARCHIBALD			39
SHIELDS JA'S			12
SHIELDS JACOB			40
SHIELDS JAMES		26	40
SHIELDS JAMES SR			40
SHIELDS JOHN		38	44
SHIELDS ROBERT	27	38	44
SHIELDS SAMUEL		26	40
SHIELDS WILLIAM			26
SHIELDS WILLIAM JR			26
SHIELDS WM			12
SHIN JOEL			39
SHIP EASTON			39
SHIPMAN JA'S			8
SHIPMAN JOHN			9
SHIPMAN NICHOLAS			9
SHIPMAN STEPHEN			10
SHIRLE JOHN			15
SHIRLEY CHARLES			41
SHIRLEY HENRY			42
SHIRLEY JACOB			40
SHOCKLEY JOSHUA			56
SHOEMAKER ADAM			48
SHOEMAKER DANIEL			66
SHOEMAKER JAMES			12
SHOEMAKER JOHN		8	48
SHOEMAKER JOHN JR			48
SHOEMAKER LEONARD C			8
SHOEMAKER STEPHEN			48
SHOMON SAM'L			11
SHORES JOSEPH			29
SHORLAND E H			58
SHORT ELISHA			15
SHORT GEORGE		21	63
SHORT ISAAC			15
SHORT JACOB			15
SHORT JOHN			65
SHOULTS GEORGE			57
SHOUS JOHN			11
SHOUS LEWIS			11
SHREWSBERRY BENJAMIN			19
SHRINCLE MICHAEL			46

SHRINGER JOHN				46
SHSHLOR WILLIAM				29
SHULE ADDAM				53
SHULER LAURANCE S				28
SHULL GEORGE				49
SHULL JOSEPH				63
SHULL PHILIP				49
SHULLER PETTER				28
SHULTS CHRISTIAN				66
SHULTS PHILIP				66
SHUTE SAMUEL				74
SICKMAN FREDERICK				28
SIDES LEONARD				69
SIERS ALEX'R				10
SIERS WM				10
SILLERS JOHN F				39
SILMAN BENJAMINE				52
SILSON WILLIAM				55
SILVER TOBIAS				54
SILVESTER LEVI P				20
SIMMONS CHARLES				51
SIMMONS JEHOSHAPHAT				62
SIMMONS JOHN				72
SIMMONS JOHN JR				69
SIMMONS JOHN SR				69
SIMMONS WILLIAM				72
SIMMS ARAD				47
SIMMS JESSE				41
SIMPERS AMOS				14
SIMPSON ALEX'N				21
SIMPSON ARCHIBALLD				7
SIMPSON GEORGE			32	63
SIMPSON JOHN	7	31	52	62
SIMPSON PATRICK				30
SIMPSON WILLIAM			7	8
SIMS JA'S				10
SIMS JOHN				60
SIMSON DAVID S				2
SINK DANIEL				62
SINK JACOB				64
SINK JACOB				66
SINK PETER				65
SINK PETER SR				62
SIPE FREDERICK				19
SIRKLE ANDREW				57
SIRKLE LEWIS				57
SISCOW MICHAEL				28
SISCOW WILLIAM				28
SKEEN JONATHAN				15
SKELTON JACOB				7
SKELTON JOHN				7+ 69
SKELTON WILLIAM				7
SKINER JOSEPH				74
SKINNER ASE				26

SKINNER	DANNIEL		26
SKINNER	S		16
SKIVER	ALEXANDER		52
SLADE	JAMES		9
SLADE	SAM'L		8
SLATER	FREDERICK		16
SLATER	JAMES		50
SLATER	PHILIP		16
SLATER	PHILLIP		19
SLATER	S		16
SLATER	WILLIAM		2
SLAUGHTER	PHILLIP		33
SLEVIN	JOHN		19
SLOAN	ARCHIBALD		3
SLOAN	JAMES K		6
SLOUGHTER	JER		18
SLOUN	JOHN		17
SLOVER	JAMES		59
SLOW	JOHN		57
SLUCOMB	JAMES		38
SLUDER	ISAAC		62
SMALL	AMOS		71
SMALL	JOHN		29 71
SMALL	NATHAN		72
SMALL	SAMUEL		68
SMALL	THOMAS		29
SMALLWOOD	ELIJAH		68
SMALLWOOD	GEORGE		10
SMALLWOOD	SAMUEL		68
SMILEY	DAVID		52
SMILEY	WILLIAM		54
SMILY	HUGH		61
SMILY	JOHN		61
SMITH	- - -		27
SMITH	THOMAS S		45
SMITH	ABRAHAM		3 70
SMITH	ADDISON		38
SMITH	ALLEN		43 49
SMITH	ANDREW		38
SMITH	ARASTUS		10
SMITH	ASA		20
SMITH	ASHFORD		48
SMITH	AUGUST		53
SMITH	BAMA		13
SMITH	BARNE B		13
SMITH	BASTION		29
SMITH	BENJAMIN		16 48 73
SMITH	CALEB		75
SMITH	CHARLES		28
SMITH	CHRISTOPHER		67
SMITH	DANIEL		20 32
SMITH	DAVID		8+ 73
SMITH	DUDLEY C		38
SMITH	ELIHU		22
SMITH	EPHRAIM		61
SMITH	GEORGE		28 52 73
SMITH	GEORGE JR		53
SMITH	GEORGE SR		28 53
SMITH	GEORGE M		26
SMITH	H		58
SMITH	HENRY		10 14 20 24 42
SMITH	HENRY SR		23
SMITH	HUMPHREY		45
SMITH	ISAAC		11 34
SMITH	JA'S		12
SMITH	JACOB		44
SMITH	JAMES		7 17 28 44 55
SMITH	JAMES		66 68 71+
SMITH	JAS		23+
SMITH	JESSE		42 43
SMITH	JOHN		3 8 12 13 21 32
SMITH	JOHN		38 44 59 66 74+
SMITH	JOHN II		38
SMITH	JOHN III		39
SMITH	JOHN A		41
SMITH	JOHN B		17 67
SMITH	JOHN C		38
SMITH	JOSEPH		38
SMITH	JOSEPH W		59
SMITH	L		20
SMITH	MECHAEL		29
SMITH	MINER		32
SMITH	MOSES		2 32
SMITH	NATHAN		63 71
SMITH	NICHOLAS		18 31 48 68
SMITH	NICHOLAS S		70
SMITH	NICHOLAS W		65
SMITH	OSWALD		17
SMITH	PETER		16
SMITH	PHILLIP		29
SMITH	RALPH		7
SMITH	RITCHIE		18
SMITH	ROB'T B		49
SMITH	ROBERT		31
SMITH	SAM'L		23
SMITH	SAMSON		72
SMITH	SAMUEL		24 56
SMITH	SAMUEL S		56
SMITH	SILAS		29
SMITH	SOLOMAN		17 30
SMITH	THO'S		11 49
SMITH	THOMAS		26
SMITH	W M		14
SMITH	WILLIAM		3 26 39 41
SMITH	WILLIAM		59 64
SMITH	WILLIAM C		28
SMITH	WM		11 12 53 57
SMITH	ZEPHANIAH		54

SMITHEE JOHN		20
SMOCK G		14
SMOCK J R		23
SMOCK JACOB		20
SMOCK JEREMIAH		17
SMOCK PETER		18
SMOCK SAMUEL		20
SMOTHERS JOHN		39
SNAPP ABRAHAM		29
SNAPP ABRAHAM F		29
SNAY JOHN		51
SNIDER DANIEL		69
SNIDER DAVID		32
SNIDER DAVID W		32
SNIDER HENRY		69
SNIDER JOHN	17 33 68	69
SNIDER LEONARD		33
SNIDER SIMON		40
SNIDER WILLIAM		32
SNIDOR DAVID		32
SNILLING BENJAMIN		3
SNODDY WILLIAM		38
SNODGRASS HUGH		17
SNODGRASS SAMUEL		16
SNODGRASS WILLIAM		38
SNOVELL FREDERICK K		51
SNOW SAMUEL		16
SNOWDEN DAVID		39
SNYDER MASKET		39
SODEN JACOB		33
SODEN WILLIAM		33
SOGG WALTER		74
SOLOMAN HENRY		9
SOLOMON DAN'L		13
SOLSBURY JOHN		9
SONGER FREDERICK		44
SONGERS ABRAHAM		44
SONNEVILLE WILLIAM		39
SOOPER DAVID		53
SOOPER JACOB		53
SOPHER HENRY L		26
SORIDER JACOB		40
SORRELS REDMAN		43
SOTT JOHN		73
SOUDERS ABRAHAM		18
SOUDERS CHRISTIAN		67
SOUDERS FREDERICK		69
SOUDERS JACOB		67
SOUHEAVER VALENTINE		3
SOUTHARD WILLIAM		48
SOVERNS JOHN JR		7
SOWDER JONATHAN		11
SPADER BERGEN		16
SPAHAM THO'S		13

SPAID DANIEL		34
SPAIN ARCHIBALD		34
SPAIN MOSES		24
SPALDING GEORGE W		40
SPALDING LEWIS		40
SPALDING THO'S		51
SPANN JESSE		19
SPARK HENRY		11
SPARKS JAMES		9
SPARKS JOHN		29
SPARKS MARTIN		29
SPARKS MOSES		11
SPARKS RICHARD		27
SPARKS STEPHEN		11
SPARLAIN ARCHIBALD		40
SPARLAIN EDWARD		40
SPARLAIN GEORGE		40
SPATH JOHN		54
SPAUN JOHN		20
SPEAKS THOMAS		64
SPEAR JOHN		11
SPEAR MOSES		40
SPEARS STEBEN		58
SPEARS STEPHEN		27
SPEER DANIEL		17
SPELLER WILLIAM		16
SPELMAN JAMES		7
SPELMAN JOHN		7
SPELMAN SAMUEL		7
SPENCER C K		15
SPENCER CHARLES R		20
SPENCER JA'S		11
SPENCER JAMES K		64
SPENCER JOHN	7 22	64
SPENCER JOHN SR		7
SPENCER MATTHEW		57
SPENCER MR SR		57
SPENCER RANSOM		57
SPENCER ROBERT		64
SPENCER THOMAS		7
SPENGLER JACOB		53
SPERGEON JOHN		11
SPERS WILLAM		47
SPIDEL MATTHEW		54
SPOLDING JOSPEH		51
SPOON CHRISTIAN		62
SPOONER CALVIN		40
SPOONER FREDERICK		40
SPOONER WILLIAM		45
SPORTSMAN HUGH		7
SPORTSMAN JAMES		59
SPRAGUE HOSEA		19
SPREY BENJAMIN		76
SPRIGGS DAVID S		48

Name	Page(s)
SPRILLER WILLIAM	14
SPRING JOHN	9
SPRING LEVIN	10
SPRINGER BARNABAS	72
SPRINGER CHARLES	2
SPRINGER DEMUR	72
SPRINGER GEORGE	48 76
SPRINGER JOB	72
SPRINGER JOHN H	10
SPRINGER JOSEPH	47 63
SPRINGER MATTHEW	75
SPRINGER STEPHEN	76
SPRINKLE GEORGE	57
SPURGIN JESSE	69
SPURGIN JOSEPH	60
SPURGIN JOSIAH	60
SPURGIN WILLIAM	62
SQUIRE AMOS	36
SREEVES JONATHAN	55
St ANTOINE FRANCIS	28
St ANTOINE PIERRE	30
St ANTOINE VITAL	30
St CLEAR HENRY	26
St CLEAR THOMAS	10
STACKHOUSE STASEA	8
STACY ABRAM	67
STAGLEY JOHN	65
STAHL JOHN	53
STALCUP HENRY	44
STALCUP JOHN	42
STALCUP PETER JR	44
STALCUP PETER SR	44
STALCUP SAMUEL	43
STALCUP STEPHEN	44
STALCUP WILLIAM	43
STALLENS STEPHEN	42
STALLINGS HENERY	49
STALLINGS JOHN	51 52
STALLINGS JULIUS	52
STALLINGS MOSES	49
STALLINGS WILSON	52
STALLINGS WM	52
STALLINGS WRIGHT	49
STANBUCK WILLIAM	72
STANCIL WILLIAM	48
STANDAFORD AQUILLA	66
STANDIFORD WILLIAM	41
STANDLEY JESSE JR	64
STANDLEY JESSE SR	64
STANDLEY ROBERT H	61
STANDLEY THOMAS	61
STANDRIDGE AARON	39
STANFIELD ASHLEY	57
STANFIELD JOHN	12
STANFIELD SAM'L	12
STANLEY JOHN	71
STANLEY JOHN JR	73
STANLEY SAM'L	10
STANLEY THOMAS	58 74
STANLEY WM	11
STANLY EDWARD	35
STAPELTON JOSEPH	7
STAPLES NATHANIEL	18
STAPP MILTON	21
STAPP SILAS	22
STAPSSOX LEWIS	29
STAR JOHN	72
STARBUCK DAN'L	74
STARBUCK EDWARD	75
STARBUCK GEORGE	63
STARBUCK JAMES	73
STARBUCK WM	75
STARK ARCHABALD	70
STARK ASA	70
STARK ASAATT	70
STARK ELISHA	68
STARK JACOB	68
STARK LEONARD	68
STARK SAMUEL	70
STARK STEPHEN	68
STARK WILLIAM	68+
STARKS THOMAS	40
STARNATURE ANDREW	6
STARNER MICHAEL	31
STARR BENJAMIN	66
STARR JOHN	3
STARR JOHN J P	3
STARR SAMUEL	66
STAZER FREDERICK	57
STEALY JACOB	9
STEAR JAMES	11
STEEL ELI	67
STEEL HUGH	13
STEEL JOSEPH	13
STEEL SAMUEL	58
STEEN JAMES	33
STEEN JOHN	33
STEEN RICHARD	33
STEPELLOW JOSHUA	6
STEPENS HORACE	9
STEPHEN JOHN	12
STEPHENS DAVID	9
STEPHENS EDWARD	50
STEPHENS FRANCISS	10
STEPHENS HENRY	45
STEPHENS ISAAC	17 76
STEPHENS JACOB	15
STEPHENS JACOB JR	45

STEPHENS	JACOB SR			45
STEPHENS	JOHN		19	50
STEPHENS	JONATHAN			9
STEPHENS	SAMUEL		15	22
STEPHENS	THO'S M			49
STEPHENS	THO'S W			51
STEPHENS	THOMAS			45
STEPHENS	WM			49
STEPHENSON	BENJAMIN			68
STEPHENSON	GEORGE			11
STEPHENSON	JOHN			48
STEPHENSON	JOSEPH			73
STEPHENSON	STEPHEN			48
STEPHENSON	VINCENT			75
STEPLES	JAMES			17
STEPLETON	ISAM			48
STEPLETON	JOHN			48
STEPPORD	THO'S			74
STERN	ARTHUR			38
STERN	DAVID			58
STERNS	ISAAC			39
STERRITT	JAMES			22
STEVENS	BENJAMIN			55
STEVENS	EMOR			16
STEVENS	ISAAC			55
STEVENS	IZREA			35
STEVENS	JAMES			55
STEVENS	JOHN			2
STEVENS	JOSHUA			59
STEVENS	LEWIS			39
STEVENS	SAMUEL			55
STEVENS	SOLOMON			55
STEVENS	VANCE			58
STEVESON	GEORGE			72
STEWARD	ALEX'R W			55
STEWARD	AMOS			54
STEWARD	DAVID			18
STEWARD	ISAIAH			55
STEWARD	JOHN	40	43	55
STEWART	ABSALOM			72
STEWART	BENJAMIN			2
STEWART	DAVID			2
STEWART	I/J			13
STEWART	JAMES		6	30
STEWART	JEHU JR			73
STEWART	JOHN 8 15 23 52 69			71
STEWART	LASARUS			2
STEWART	SAMUEL			66
STEWART	WESTLEY			69
STEWART	WILLIAM	6 7 55		66
STEWART	WM			23
STIDMAN	JAMES			26
STIGGERWAULT	JOHN			64
STIGGERWAULT	PETER JR			64
STIGGERWAULT	PETER SR			64
STILL	MURPHEY D			64
STILLWELL	JOHN			26
STILTS	MOSES			68
STILWELL	DAVID			8
STILWELL	WESTLEY			11
STILZ	EDWARD			53
STILZ	JACOB			53
STINNETT	WILLIAM			40
STINSON	JAMES			58
STINSON	JOHN B			58
STIPES	JOSEPH			56
STIPP	JACOB			70
STITES	JOHN			26
STOCKER	ELI			63
STOCKER	GEORGE			60
STOCKER	JONATHAN			63
STOCKS	JOHN			48
STOCKWELL	CYRUS			21
STOCKWELL	JOSEPHUS			55
STOCKWELL	ROBERT			7
STOCKWELL	WILLIAM			68
STODDARD	RUSSEL			23
STOGSDILL	DANIEL			19
STONE	CLEON			2
STONE	ELLIS			38
STONE	JOHN			2
STONE	JOHN W			22
STONE	THOMAS			6
STONE	WILLIAM			40
STONE	WILLIAM S			55
STONEMETS	CASPER			48
STONER	JOHN			57
STOODY	JACOB			72
STOOTSMAN	ABRAHAM			65
STORK	ABRAHAM			68
STORK	JACOB			33
STORK	JOHN			33
STORM	DANIEL			31
STORM	JAMES			39
STORM	JOHN			39
STORM	PETER			14
STORM	THO'S			12
STORMONT	ROBERT			6
STORMS	CONRAD			56
STORRY	THOMAS			26
STOTT	JAMES			26
STOTT	RICHART			26
STOTT	WILLIAM F			26
STOUT	AARON			39
STOUT	DANIEL			38
STOUT	ELISHUA			28
STOUT	HEZEKIAH			13
STOUT	JOHN			42

STOUT	JONATHAN		41
STOUT	JOSIAH		34
STOVER	ABRAHAM	7	63
STOVER	JOHN		66
STOVERING	DAVID		3
STRAIN	BARNET		66
STRAIN	ELI		7
STRAIN	JOHN		66
STRAIN	ROBERT		66
STRAIN	THO'S M		12
STRAIN	WM		9
STRANGE	CORNWELL		44
STRANGE	JOHN		40
STRANGE	WILLIAM		40
STRATTON	BENJAMIN		74
STRAUGHN	NATHANIEL		3
STRIBLING	GEORGE		26
STRIBLING	THOMAS T		19
STRIBLING	WILLIS		26
STRICKLAND	ARON		8
STRICKLAND	ELISHA		7
STRICKLAND	ELISHA JR		7
STRICKLAND	JOSEPH		21
STRICKLAND	STEPHEN		7
STROHEKER	CHRISTIAN		53
STROHEKER	CHRISTOPHER		53
STROHEKER	JACOB		54
STRONG	LEWIS R		74
STROUD	ISHAM		43
STROUD	JOHN		43
STROUD	THOMAS		2
STROWDERD	FILON		26
STROYERS	LEWIS		44
STRUPE	PETER		69
STUART	ABEL		7
STUART	ECOBUD		31
STUART	JESSE		31
STUART	WILLIAM M		7
STUBINS	HARRIS		27
STUCKER	ANDREW		23
STUCKER	HENRY		17
STUCKER	JACOB	17	22
STUCKER	JACOB JR		17
STUCKER	JOHN	17+	23
STUCKER	MICHAEL		17
STUCKER	PHILIP		65
STUCKER	SAMUEL		17
STUCKER	WILLIAM		17
STULL	GEORGE		49
STULL	LAWRENCE		49
STUMP	JOHN		53
STURDAVANT	JAMES		67
STURGEON	DAVID		2
STURGEON	JEREMIAH		2
STURGEON	JOHN JR		2
STURGEON	JOHN SR		2
STURGEON	ROLLY		2
STURGES	AUGUSTUS B		7
STURGES	JOSEPH		49
STURSON	NATHAN		3
STUTSMAN	ISAAC		62
SUALLOW	WILLIAM		74
SUFFIELD	EPHRAIM		52
SUFRINS	JOHN		73
SUGERS	GEORGE		75
SULIVAN	ABLE		7
SULLENDER	WALLACE		10
SULLENGER	RUBEN		35
SULLERS	JOHN		48+
SULLINGER	THOMAS		44
SULLIVAN	ANDREW		58
SULLIVAN	ARYAN		22
SULLIVAN	DANIEL		13
SULLIVAN	GEORGE R C		29
SULLIVAN	JA'S		10
SULLIVAN	JER		20
SULLIVAN	JOHN		33
SULLIVAN	NOAH	26	46
SULLIVAN	PATRICK		12
SULLIVAN	THO'S		20
SULLIVAN	THOMAS	74	75
SULLIVAN	WILLIAM C		21
SULLIVAN	WILLIS		19
SULLIVAN	WM		12
SUMMER	CALEB JR		57
SUMMER	CALEB SR		57
SUMMERS	CALEB		35
SUMMERS	ENOCH		39
SUMMERS	JOHN		9
SUMMERS	WM		9
SUMMETT	HENRY		33
SUMMY	PETER		61
SUMNER	WILLIAM		43
SUMNON	JOHN		7
SUMNOR	JOSEPH		7
SUMPTER	ISOM		38
SUTHARD	BURTON		41
SUTHERLAND	JOHN		74
SUTHERLAND	ROGER		69
SUTHERLAND	WM		75
SUTHERLIN	CHARLES		40
SUTHERLIN	FENDEL		41
SUTHERLIN	PHILIP		40
SUTHERLIN	SAMPSON		41
SUTHERLIN	WILLIAM	40	41
SUTTON	ALEXANDER		71
SUTTON	DAVID		19
SUTTON	HENRY		66

SUTTON JAMES				45
SUTTON JOHN				26
SUTTON REUBEN				56
SWAIN ANTHONY				59
SWAIN JOB				71
SWAIN PAUL				74
SWAN ANDREW				23
SWAN JOHN		16	23	35
SWAN THOS				23
SWANGO JOHN				7
SWANK RICHARD				35
SWANK WILLIAM				28
SWARUNGIN THO'S V				10
SWEENEY BENJAMIN				38
SWEET ABRAHAM				18
SWEET ELIAS				18
SWEET GEORGE				26
SWEET ISAAC				18
SWEET JOBE				23
SWENEY MORDECIA				68
SWENEY WILLIAM				65
SWIFT JAMES W				50
SWIFT JOHN				38
SWIFT SETH				27
SWIM ELIJAH				60
SWINDLER SAMUEL				17
SWINNEY JOHN				12
SWINNEY NATHAN				12
SWISS HENRY				38
SWISSER GEORGE				55
SYBERT JOHN				3
SYBERT JOSEPH				3
SYLVESTER GEORGE				14
SYLVESTER LEVI P				22
SYLVESTER SAMUEL				14
SYMMS ALEXANDER				38
SYMMS NICHOLAS				38
SYMONS JESSE				75
SYOUSCE GOEMAS				30
SYPES I				24

T

TABOUR JESSE				8
TABOUR WM				8
TACIEA FRANCIS				28
TADLACK ELISHA				3
TADLOCK ALEXANDER				43
TADLOCK JEREMIAH				3
TAGGERT JA'S				11
TAGUE JACOB				33
TAGUE JOSEPH				15
TALBERT EDWARD				11
TALBOT JOHN				65
TALBOTT ABRAHAM				56
TALBOTT DANIEL				14
TALBOTT JEREMIAH				56
TALBOTT R C				20
TALBOTT RICHARD				56
TALMAN DAVID				54
TALMAN EPHRAIM				54
TALMAN STEPHEN				54
TALTON JOHN				11
TANNAHILL JAMES				24
TANNER MATHEW				11
TANNIHILL ZACHERIAH				18
TARDICE FRANCIS				30
TARKENTON JESSE				39
TARKINTIN SILVANUS				39
TARR JAMES				39
TATE JOHN				15
TATE THOMAS				43
TATLOCK AARON				60
TATLOCK BENJAMIN				60
TATLOCK CHALKLEY				60
TATLOCK DEMSEY				60
TATLOCK JAMES				60
TATLOCK JOSHUA				60
TATLOCK MILES				60
TAYLER JAMES				59
TAYLOR CLETEN				45
TAYLOR CRANSON				23
TAYLOR DANIEL				48
TAYLOR DAVID		3	23	34
TAYLOR DUDLEY				20
TAYLOR GABRIEL				30
TAYLOR GAMALIEL				22
TAYLOR JACOB				49
TAYLOR JAMES			49	74
TAYLOR JOHN	7	10	43	62
TAYLOR JOHUA				23
TAYLOR JOSEPH				21
TAYLOR NOAH				58
TAYLOR ROBERT				16

TAYLOR	ROBT				23	THOMAS	ELIAS				13
TAYLOR	SAMUEL		45	59	62	THOMAS	ELIGAH				27
TAYLOR	SILAS				48	THOMAS	ELIJAH			72	75
TAYLOR	THOMAS			15	16	THOMAS	ENOCH				66
TAYLOR	THOS				23	THOMAS	EVANS	SR			18
TAYLOR	WILLIAM		7+	45	48+	THOMAS	EVEN				26
TAYLOR	WM				38	THOMAS	FREEMAN				27
TEAGAL	JOSEPH				71	THOMAS	GEORGE				55
TEAGARDEN	BAZIL				41	THOMAS	GOLDEN L				1
TEAGLE	THOMAS				72	THOMAS	HENRY				39
TEAGUE	DAVID				39	THOMAS	HENRY	JR			55
TEAGUE	WILLIAM				39	THOMAS	HENRY	SR			55
TEAL	ADAM				7	THOMAS	HOSEA				70
TEASE	THOMAS				76	THOMAS	ISAAC			7	61
TEBITS	EBENZER				39	THOMAS	JA'S				11
TECUMSIRA	WILLIAM				74	THOMAS	JAMES		26	57	61
TEEGARDEN	JOHN				41	THOMAS	JESSE				33
TEEL	WILLIAM				7	THOMAS	JOHN	11+	19	27 74+	75
TEEPLES	JOHN				28	THOMAS	JONATHAN			11	31
TEISE	CHARLES				72	THOMAS	JOSEPH				32
TEMPLETON	JAMES				58	THOMAS	LEWIS				48
TEMPLETON	THO'S				50	THOMAS	LEWIS	JR			42
TENKLE	HENRY				73	THOMAS	LEWIS	SR			42
TEPPERS	ROB'T C				50	THOMAS	MEEKS				49
TERLL	EDMAN				27	THOMAS	MYERS				56
TERPAN	LEWIS				28	THOMAS	PIERCE				74
TERREL	CHARLES				59	THOMAS	SAMUEL				7
TERREL	WILLIAM				24	THOMAS	STEPHEN			42	73
TERRILL	ACHILLES				18	THOMAS	STEPHEN	SR			73
TERRY	ELISHA				48	THOMAS	WILLIAM				48
TERRY	JOHN			7	48	THOMAS	WM F				20
TERRY	THOMAS				46	THOMPSON	ALEX				16
TERRY	WILLIAM				7	THOMPSON	CARY				60
TESH	JACOB				67	THOMPSON	CHARLES				30
TESH	JOHN				67	THOMPSON	ELIHUE				27
TEST	NICHOLAS				7	THOMPSON	ELISHA				18
TEVERBAUGH	JACOB				33	THOMPSON	FRANCIS				30
TEVERBAUGH	NINROD				33	THOMPSON	GEORGE			12	27
TEVERBAUGH	SOLOMON				33	THOMPSON	HENRY				58
THACKER	AUSTIN				39	THOMPSON	IGNATIOUS				48
THACKER	DAVID				39	THOMPSON	JA'S			8	11
THICKSTEN	ISAAC				17	THOMPSON	JAMES	JR			60
THICKSTEN	WILLIAM				17	THOMPSON	JAMES	SR			60
THICKSTON	ABRAHAM				18	THOMPSON	JOHN		8	58	75
THIXTON	JOHN				33	THOMPSON	JOHN	JR			60
THOM	ALLEN D				3	THOMPSON	JOHN	SR		60	76
THOM	SAMUEL				20	THOMPSON	JOSEPH			60	67
THOM	WILLIAM W				22	THOMPSON	JOSHUA				67
THOMAS	BENJAMIN				72	THOMPSON	LARUE				23
THOMAS	BENJAMIN	JR			73	THOMPSON	LEVI				62
THOMAS	BENJAMIN	SR			74	THOMPSON	McKEE				10
THOMAS	BOOTH				26	THOMPSON	MOSES				60
THOMAS	DANIEL				72	THOMPSON	RICHARD				12
THOMAS	DAVID				50	THOMPSON	ROBERT	7	27	60	75

THOMPSON	ROBT		23
THOMPSON	ROGER		60
THOMPSON	SAMUEL		32
THOMPSON	SIRAS		29
THOMPSON	THOMAS		65
THOMPSON	THOMAS JR		60
THOMPSON	THOMAS SR		60
THOMPSON	WILLIAM		62
THOMPSON	WILLIAM		30
THOMPSON	WILLIAM SR		60
THOMPSON	WM		59
THOMPSON	WM		11
THOMSON	GEORGE		23
THOMSON	ISAAC		4
THOMSON	JAMES	39	52
THOMSON	JOHN	39	48
THOMSON	ROBERT		73
THOMSON	THOMAS		3
THORN	ABSOLUM		33
THORN	ASA		33
THORN	CHARLES		34
THORN	JACOB		33
THORN	JAMES		34
THORN	JOSHUA		34
THORN	MICHAEL		34
THORN	SAMUEL		30
THORN	WILLIAM		26
THORNBERRY	JOSEPH		63
THORNBURG	THOMAS		39
THORNBURGH	ABEL		75
THORNBURGH	AMOS		61
THORNBURGH	BENJAMIN		62
THORNBURGH	THOMAS		76
THORNTON	ABNER		13
THORNTON	BENJAMIN		30
THORNTON	HENRY		62
THORNTON	JOBE		22
THORNTON	JOHN		58
THORNTON	JOSEPH		23
THORNTON	LEVI	13	69
THORNTON	SAM'L		13
THORNTON	SAMUEL		69
THORNTON	THEOPHELUS		69
THRAILKILL	JAMES		29
THRASHER	THOMAS		48
THREALKILL	MOSES		27
THRELDKELD	- - -		11
THURMON	JOHNSON F		7
THURMOND	DAVID		44
THURMOND	HIRAM		44
THURSTON	RICHARD		4
TIBB	JOHN		3
TIBB	JOSEPH		3
TIFNEA	JOHN		12

TILFORD ALEX		17
TILFORD ROBERT		62
TILFORD SAMUEL		18
TILFORD WILLIAM		23
TILINGHURST CHARLES H		30
TILLER GEORGE		2
TILLER JOEL		4
TIMMS JAMES		32
TIMMS JOSEPH		31
TINDAL WILLIAM		48
TINDALL THOMAS		45
TINDALL WILLIAM		42
TIPPIN GEORGE		64
TIPPIN GEORGE SR		64
TIPPIN JOHN		64
TIPPIN THOMAS		64
TIPPIN WILLIAM		64
TISA JOHN		56
TITCHNER MOSES		48
TITTETT JOBE		52
TOBIAS TOBIAS		23
TOBIN GEORGE		48
TOBIN JOSEPH		48
TOBIN THOMAS		48
TOBY SAMMUEL		27
TODD HUGH		50
TODD JOHN		43
TODD JOHN N		28
TODD ROBERT		51
TODD WILLIAM		65
TODD WM		51
TOLLER JESSE		3
TOMISSIND IAN		75
TOMKINS RICHARD		7
TOMLINSON JAMES		43
TOMLINSON JOSEPH		43
TOMLINSON SAMUEL		28
TOMPKINS SYLVENIS		27
TONEY ALEXANDER		3
TONEY JOHN		3
TONEY STEPHEN		43
TOOL DANIEL		58
TOOLE LAURENCE		18
TORQUE JAMES		58
TORR JOHN		41
TORREY PATON		43
TOTTEN JAMES		3
TOTTEN LEWIS		3
TOTTON ARCH		15
TOUCKOY FRANCIS		30
TOWEL DANIEL		40
TOWEL JESSE		42
TOWEL JOHN		44
TOWER A BATES		3

Name	Pages
TOWER COTTEN	3
TOWLER ROBERT	26
TOWNER ELIJAH	58
TOWNSEND ABIEL	55
TOWNSEND JOHN	76
TOWNSEND ROBERT	55
TOWNSEND SILAS	65
TOWNSEND WILLIAM	33 65
TOWNSON ELI	7
TOWNSON ERASTUS	7
TOWNSON WINTON	7
TOWNSOND JOHN	27
TRABUE GEORGE S	69
TRAFFORD EDWARD	51
TRAFTON WM	58
TRANCEWAY ABRAM	57
TRANCEWAY JOSEPH	57
TRAVES J	15
TRAVIS JAMES	16 19
TREADO ROBERT	35
TREECE DANIEL	33
TRENARY BENJAMIN	48
TRIBBY JOHN	7
TRIBITT WARTMON	7
TRIGER SOLOMON	48
TRIMBLE MOSES	40
TRIMBLE ROBERT	16
TRIMBLE WM	9
TRINBLE DANIEL	72
TRINDLE ALEXANDER	67
TRINKLE ADAM	70
TRINKLE FREDERICK	69
TRINKLE JACOB	69
TRINKLE JOHN	70
TROMBLEY STEPHEN	29
TROMPETER GILBERT	54
TROMPETER JOHN	54
TROOP JOHN	42
TROOT ABRAHAM	48
TROTTER JAMES	39
TROUTMAN ADAM	18
TROW GEORGE D	63
TROWBRIDGE DAVID	69
TROWBRIDGE JOHN	69
TROWBRIDGE WM	49
TROXELL JOSEPH	19
TRUEBLOOD ABLE	60
TRUEBLOOD CALEB	62
TRUEBLOOD JAMES JR	61
TRUEBLOOD JAMES SR	61
TRUEBLOOD JOSEPH	41 61
TRUEBLOOD JOSHUA	61
TRUEBLOOD JOSIAH	41
TRUEBLOOD MARK	45
TRUEBLOOD NATHAN	61
TRUEBLOOD WILLIAM	28 41 60
TRUESDELL JOHN N	7
TRULOCK THOMAS	35
TRUMAN HOMER	15
TRUMAN JOSEPH	27
TRUMBO JACOB	18
TRUSDALL FRANCIS	28
TRUSDELL SAMUEL	7
TRUSTER GEORGE	59
TRUSTY WILLIAM	39
TUCKER CHARLES	27
TUCKER DAVID	3
TUCKER JOSHUA	21
TUCKER MARTIN H	3
TUCKER THOMAS L	45
TUCKER WILLIAM	3
TUELL JESSE	9
TUELL REASON	12
TULL JOSEPH	23
TULLES JOHN	8
TULLEY RICHARD	65
TULLIS IZRA	10
TULLIS JOHN	10
TULLIS JONATHAN	10
TUNGATE DENNIS	40
TUNGATE JOHN	45
TUNGATE WILLIAM	45
TURGATE JEREMIAH	45
TURK THO'S	10
TURKIHISOR LEONARD	27
TURNER JESSEY	34
TURNER JOHN	71
TURNER JOSEPH	48
TURNER JULIUS	41
TUTTLE WILLIAM	19
TWADDLE JAMES	16
TWADDLE JOHN	18
TWEEDLE ISAAC	7
TWEEDY PATRICK	27
TYLER ASEY	50
TYLER GEORGE	58
TYLER JOHN	58
TYLER JOSEPH	58
TYLER OLIVER	3
TYLER THOMAS	58

U

UMPHRY WILLIAM		48
UNDERHILL JAMES		3
UNDERHILL JOHN		3
UNDERHILL WILLIAM		3
UNDERSWOOD BENJAMIN		24
UNDERWOOD BENGAMIN		42
UNDERWOOD COLBY		23
UNDERWOOD JACOB		19
UNDERWOOD JAMES	23	40
UNDERWOOD JAMES JR		23
UNDERWOOD JOHN		19
UNDERWOOD JOSIAH		51
UNDERWOOD SALENA		19
UNO JOSEPH		29
UNTHANK JOHN		76
UNTHARK TEMPLE		76
URMY JACOB		66
USURY JOHN		52

V

VAIHENGER ANGULIUS		54
VAIHENGER JACOB		54
VAIHENGER SEBASTIAN		54
VAIL JENNINGS		22
VAIL THOS		21
VAINHAM NEHEMIAH	15	16
VALELY ROBERT		20
VALLALEE ROBT		14
VAN ABSOLOM		57
VANARCLE EB		26
VANARSDALL CHRISTOPHER		7
VANCE CHRISTOPHER		39
VANCE DAVID		68
VANCE JOHN		26
VANCLEAVE BENGAMINE		44
VANCLEAVE JOHN		44
VANCLEAVE PETER		20
VANCLEAVE SQUIRE		68
VANDAVEAR CHARLES		8
VANDAVER JACOB		24
VANDAVIER NICHOLAS		20
VANDENBURGH JOHN		15
VANDERVER CHARLES		49
VANDERVORT JOHN		11
VANDEVEER ARON		70
VANDEVEER GEORGE		44
VANDEVEER JOEL		44
VANDEVEER JOHN		70
VANDEVENTER WILLIAM C		28
VANDEVIER JOHN		44
VANDEVIER JOHN SR		44
VANDIKE JOSEPH		8
VANDIVEER THOMAS		45
VANDIVER THOMAS		48
VANDOREN JABIS		26
VANDUSON JACOB		7
VANGORDEN FOFARINE		35
VANGORDEN JAMES		35
VANHORN B		15
VANHORN BANJAMIN		19
VANHORN RALPH		58
VANKIRK JOHN		32
VANKIRK JOSEPH		32
VANLANDINGHAM ELIJAH		70
VANLANDINGHAM GEORGE		70
VANLANDINGHAM RICHARD		70
VANLANDINGHAM WM		70
VANMETER JOSEPH		70
VANMETER WILLIAM		60
VANMETTER JOHN		3
VANNORMAN AARON		17
VANNORMAN D		22
VANNORMAN DANIEL		17
VANPETT THOMAS P		48
VANSANT CHARLES		76
VANSANT JAMES		76
VANSIL JOHN		26
VANTER JAMES		19
VANTER JESSE		19
VANVRANKEN JOHN		44
VANWINCLE ALEXANDER		48
VANWINCLE ISAAC		48
VANWINCLE JAMES		48
VANWINKLE ABRAHAM		3
VANWINKLE JAMES		3
VANWINKLER JOSEPH		3
VANZEL WILLIAM		57
VARNER JACOB		49
VARVILL ABRAHAM		17
VATTEAN DANIEL		72
VAUGHAN WAIT		48
VAUGHN BENJAMIN		47
VAUGHN ISAAC		64
VAUGHN JAMES		3
VAUGHN OBADIAH		3
VAWTER ACHILLIS		26
VAWTER JOHN		26
VEACH BENGAMIN		44
VEARS JOHN		41
VEIHMEIER JOHN		54
VEIHMEIER MICHAEL		54
VENRIDGE GEORGE		71
VENTIONER JAS		13
VERMILLION JAMES		43

VEST JOHN J	64	
VEST NATHANIEL	42	
VEST SAMUEL	64	
VEST SAMUEL SR	66	
VEST WILLIAM JR	67	
VEST WILLIAM SR	66	
VESTAL SAMUEL	71	
VESTER GEORGE	54	
VETAN JONATHAN	72	
VETTE PHILO	54	
VICKERS BENJ	22	
VICKERS EDWARD	42	
VIGO FRANCIS	29	
VILES JOSEPH	23	
VILNAVE JOHN BT	29	
VINCENT CHARLES	73	
VINCENT RICHARD	26	
VINEYARD JESSE	64	
VINSON JESSE	3	
VOIE JACOB	74	
VOIE JACOB JR	74	
VOIE JOHN	74	
VON THOS	16	
VONTREASE JACOB	43	
VONTREASE WILLIAM	43	
VORAS OLAVER	71	
VORE JAMES	71	
VORIS ABRAHAM	41	
VORIS GARRETT	41	
VORIS JACOB	45	
VOSHELL WM	10	
VOYLES ABLE	65	
VOYLES DANIEL	65	
VOYLES DAVID	65	
VOYLES JOHN	70	
VOYLES JOSEPH	65	
VOYLES MOSES	65	
VOYLES ROLEN	65	
VOYLES THOMAS	65	
VOYLES WILLIAM	55	

W

WADE JAMES	69	
WADE JOSHUWAY	51	
WADE MERREDA	62	
WADKINS JESSE	68	
WADKINS JONATHAN	12	
WADSWORTH THOMAS	40	
WAERS THOMAS	67	
WAGENER GEORGE	54	
WAGGONER GEORGE	66	
WAGGONER HENRY	59	
WAGGONER JOHN	69	

WAGGONER JOHN H	27	
WAGNER GEORGE	22	
WAGNOR WM	58	
WAGONER LEWIS	27	
WAID ZACHARIAH	49	
WAKELAND WILLIAM C	23	
WALDEN ABEDNNGA	39	
WALDEN DAVID	51	
WALDEN JAMES	7	
WALDEN JESSE	39	
WALDEN LEWIS	39	
WALDMAN CHRISTIAN	54	
WALDRON DANIEL	10	
WALKER AARON	67	
WALKER ALFRED	16	
WALKER ANDREW	44	
WALKER BENGAMIN B	46	
WALKER DAVID	11	
WALKER EDWARD	11	
WALKER ELISHA	48	
WALKER HUGH	51	
WALKER ISAAC	29 31 76	
WALKER J	23	
WALKER JA'S	19	
WALKER JAMES	51 73	
WALKER JOHN	16 17 22 27 50	
WALKER JOHN	51 74	
WALKER JOHN JR	16	
WALKER LEWALLEN F	22	
WALKER OBADIAH	9	
WALKER PHILIP	48	
WALKER ROBERT	3 67	
WALKER SAMUEL	74	
WALKER SAMUEL JR	71	
WALKER THOMAS	73	
WALKER VINCE	50	
WALKER WILLIAM	27 69	
WALKER WILLIAM W	29	
WALKER WM	23	
WALL EPHRAIM	70	
WALL RICHARD	68	
WALL ROBERT	70	
WALLACE ALEXANDER	40	
WALLACE DAVID	3 56	
WALLACE FLOWRY	64	
WALLACE JAMES	21	
WALLACE JAMES	21	
WALLACE JOHN	15	
WALLACE NATHANIEL	20	
WALLACE WILLIAM	21	
WALLER JOHN	49	
WALLS ARTHER	17	
WALLS EBENEZZER	51	
WALLS HEZEKIAH	63	

Name	Col1	Col2
WALLS JOHN		75
WALLS MANLOW		45
WALLS MATHEW		73
WALLS WILLIAM	40	70
WALSON ROBERT		71
WALTERS ABNER		9
WALTERS ENOCH		7
WALTERS STEPHEN		7
WALTERS WILLIAM		7
WALTON ABRAHAM		18
WALTON COMFORT		24
WALTON DANIEL		24
WALTON EUPHRATES		24
WALTON ISAAC		18
WALTON JOHN		18
WAMPLER HENRY		39
WARD DANIEL		14
WARD GRANVILLE		39
WARD HIRAM		32
WARD SAMUEL		20
WARD THOMAS	57	73
WARDEN SAMUEL		48
WARDEN WILLIAM		44
WARE THOMAS		68
WARE WILLIAM		70
WARFIELD HENRY ESQ		3
WARFIELD JERARD		14
WARFIELD JOHN		14
WARNER ALAIRSON		57
WARNER ALFRED O		58
WARNER GEORGE		39
WARNER ITHAMER		74
WARNER JACOB		32
WARNER SAMUEL		27
WARNER WM		57
WARNER WM W		57
WARNOCK JAMES		39
WARRELL JOSHUA		17
WARRELL ROBERT		45
WARRELL SAMUEL		40
WARREN ABRAHAM		76
WARREN ALEXANDER		59
WARREN JOHN		59
WARREN LEVY		59
WARREN MATTHEW		59
WARREN STEPHEN		34
WARREN WM		59
WARRICK MONTGOMERY		7
WARSON JOHN		45
WARTH ROBERT		35
WASHER ALEX'R		15
WASHER SOLOMON		15
WASHER SOLOMON JR		15
WASHER STEPHEN		15
WASHER STEPHEN JR		15
WASON SAMUEL		72
WASSON ARCHABALD		71
WASSON HIRAM		7
WASSON JOHIAL		75
WASSON JOSEPH		71
WASSON NATHANIEL		73
WASTNER JACOB		44
WATERMAN JOHN		14
WATERS ELIJAH		58
WATERS JAMES R		7
WATERS JOHN		16
WATERS THOMAS	7	55
WATHERTON DAVID		18
WATKINS JAMES E		58
WATKINS JOHN		71
WATKINS STEPHEN		29
WATSON ANDREW		18
WATSON BENJAMIN		3
WATSON EBER	55	57
WATSON FREDERICK		29
WATSON ISAAC		68
WATSON JACOB		63
WATSON JAMES	18	35
WATSON JEREMIAH		55
WATSON JOHN		3
WATSON JULIAS		27
WATSON PEDIGO		41
WATSON ROBERT		27
WATSON ROBERT SR		27
WATSON SOLOMON		63
WATSON THOMAS		35
WATSON WILLIAM	3	16
WATSON WM		72
WATTS ALEXANDER		66
WATTS BENJAMIN		66
WATTS HOWARD		22
WATTS JOHN	66	73
WATTS MASON		56
WATTS RICHARD		72
WATTS RICHARD SR		72
WATTS WILLIAM		66
WAUGHTEL FREDERICK		61
WAULLS DRURY		74
WAUMAN CHRISTOPHER		55
WAUMAN ELIJAH		55
WAY ABEL		43
WAY ANTHONY		40
WAY JAMES		49
WAY JOSEPH		43
WAY MARTIN		20
WAY ORA		20
WAY SAMUEL		3
WAYMAN EDMUND		66

WEAR	ARCHABALD			60	WEEKS	WILLIAM				75
WEAR	DAVID			60	WEET	ISAAC				15
WEAR	GEORGE			60	WEIDENBACH	MATTHEW				54
WEAR	JOHN			50	WEINGASTNER	CLEMENTS				54
WEAR	JOHN			60	WEINGASTNER	FREDERICK				54
WEAR	WILLIAM			68	WEINGASTNER	GEORGE				54
WEAR	WM			50	WEINGASTNER	MICHAEL				54
WEASE	JOHN			33	WEINGASTNER	WALRATH				54
WEASE	PHILLIP			33	WEIR	ANDREW				62
WEATHEMAN	SIMON			11	WEIR	LINDSEY				45
WEATHERBY	JAMES			55	WELBORN	JOHN				50
WEATHERFORD	HARDEN			22	WELCH	GEORGE				67
WEATHERFORD	HARDIN			14	WELCH	JAMES				69
WEATHERFORD	JAMES			14	WELCH	SAMUEL				15
WEATHERFORD	JOHN			14	WELCH	WILLIAM				66
WEATHERHOLT	HENERY			47	WELL	AUGUST				29
WEATHERHOLT	JACOB			48	WELLER	MATTHIAS				60
WEATHERHOLT	JOHN			48	WELLMAN	BARNABUS				27
WEATHERHOLT	WILLIAM			47	WELLMAN	JOHN				45
WEATHERS	BENJAMIN			3	WELLS	ABRAHAM				7
WEATHERS	ISAAC			10	WELLS	ASA				19
WEATHERS	JOHN		10	43	WELLS	ASA C				6
WEATHERS	JOSEPH			43	WELLS	BENJAMIN				66
WEATHERS	ROBERT			10	WELLS	DAVID				68
WEATHERS	SAMUEL			3	WELLS	ISAAC				40
WEATHERS	THOMAS T			70	WELLS	JACOB				11
WEATHERS	WILLIAM			28	WELLS	JAMES				8
WEATHERSPOON	- - -			15	WELLS	JESSE				7
WEATHERSPOON	DAVID			15	WELLS	JOHN			8	18
WEATHERSPOON	WILLIAM			15	WELLS	JONATHAN			7	42
WEAUP	WILLIAM			74	WELLS	JOSEPH				66
WEAVER	ADAM			17	WELLS	JOSEPH SR				42
WEAVER	JEREMIAH			68	WELLS	LEVI				18
WEAVER	JOHN		32	62	WELLS	NATHAN				42
WEAVER	MICHAEL		43	18	WELLS	PETER				40
WEAVER	PETER			23	WELLS	RICHARD				68
WEBB	ASA			47	WELLS	SAMUEL				16
WEBB	BENGAMIN			41	WELLS	SAMUEL				24
WEBB	DAVID			33	WELLS	STEPHEN				40
WEBB	EZRA			27	WELLS	WILLIAM	7	16	41 66	68
WEBB	JOHN			58	WELLS	WILLIAM				7
WEBER	CHRISTOPHER			54	WELLS	ZACHARIAS				42
WEBSTER	CYRUS			55	WELLUM	SAMUEL				34
WEBSTER	GEORGE B			55	WELSH	STEPHEN S SR				11
WEBSTER	NATHANIEL			55	WELTON	DAVID				33
WEBSTER	NICHOLAS			64	WELTON	JAMES				32
WEBSTER	SAMUEL			55	WELTON	JOHN				32
WEBSTER (HOGAN)	SAMUEL			56	WELTON	JONATHAN				32
WEDDEL	JOHN			11	WELTON	WILLIAM				33
WEDDLE	DAN'L			11	WERE	HUGH				21
WEDDLE	EDWARD			11	WERT	JACOB				15
WEDMAN	JACOB			3	WERT	JER				15
WEED	STEPHEN P			19	WERT	REUBEN				15
WEEKS	JOSEPH			41	WESLEY	JAMES				56

WEST DANIEL	22 52	
WEST JACOB	22	
WEST JAMES	7 17	
WEST JOHN	14 17 36	
WEST JOHN T	17	
WEST NATHANIEL	7	
WEST REUBEN	20	
WEST STEPHEN D	3	
WEST THO'S	50	
WEST THOMAS L	7	
WEST WILLIAM	19	
WESTERFIELD S'M D	73	
WESTFALL ABRAHAM	33+	
WESTFALL ALI	68	
WESTFALL HENRY	68	
WESTFALL HIRAM	7	
WESTFALL ISAAC	32	
WESTFALL JACOB	68	
WESTFALL SAMUEL	3	
WESTFALL THOMAS	33	
WESTFALL VINSON	3	
WESTFALL WILLIAM	4	
WESTGATE J B	21	
WESTNER DAVID	33	
WESTON JOSEPH	64	
WESTON THOMAS	64	
WHALER JOSEPH	57	
WHEALTEY ARTHER	48	
WHEAT ABRAHAM	18	
WHEAT DAVID	18	
WHEATLEY WILLIAM	23	
WHEATLY JOSEPH	17	
WHEDEN SAM'L	12	
WHEEDEN STEPHEN	21	
WHEELER CHAS	7	
WHEELER CLAYTON	7	
WHEELER DAYTON	7	
WHEELER EBENEZER	45	
WHEELER EBENEZER S	67	
WHEELER ELANTHAN	11	
WHEELER HENRY D	27	
WHEELER HEZAKIAH	12	
WHEELER JA'S	12	
WHEELER JAMES	7 47 51 64	
WHEELER JAMES B	7	
WHEELER JESSE	64	
WHEELER JOHN	39	
WHEELER RICHARD	57	
WHEELER ROBERT	7	
WHEELER SAMUEL	7	
WHEELER THOMAS	47	
WHELKEL JOHN	20	
WHELPLOY DAVID	27	
WHETSTONE DAVID	57	

WHETSTONE HENRY	57	
WHETSTONE MATTHIAS	59	
WHICHER STEPHEN	55	
WHICUM JESSE	32	
WHILKELL WILLIAM	20	
WHINNAND GEORGE	39	
WHISNAND JOHN	39	
WHITACKER JACOB	49	
WHITAKER EDWARD	32	
WHITAKER WILLIAM	71	
WHITCONACK JOHN	11	
WHITE ABROSE	19	
WHITE CALEB	12	
WHITE CHARLES	28	
WHITE CRIDEN	9	
WHITE CYRUS	61	
WHITE DAVID	11	
WHITE DAVID SR	10	
WHITE EDWARD	27	
WHITE GEORGE	52	
WHITE GEORGE L	52	
WHITE JAMES	22 54 61+ 72 74	
WHITE JOHN	10 39 69 75	
WHITE JOHN JR	73	
WHITE JOHN SR	73	
WHITE JONATHAN D	10	
WHITE JOSEPH	11 44 47 73	
WHITE JOSIAH	9	
WHITE LEONARD M	44	
WHITE RICHARD	3	
WHITE SAM'L	51	
WHITE SAMUEL	18 61	
WHITE THOMAS	28	
WHITE WILLIAM	44 69	
WHITE WM	57	
WHITEHEAD AMOS	10	
WHITEHEAD ARTHUR	3	
WHITEHEAD JOHN	44	
WHITEHILL DAVIS	3	
WHITEHILL WILLIAM W	3	
WHITEMAN WILLIAM	76	
WHITES RICHARD	21	
WHITES THO'S	21	
WHITESETT JAMES	7	
WHITESETT JOHN	7	
WHITESETT JOSEPH	7	
WHITESETT WILLIAM	18	
WHITESIDE JOHN	27	
WHITESIDES WILLIAM	17	
WHITESITT SAMUEL	18	
WHITHAM BENJAMIN	55	
WHITHAM JAMES	55	
WHITHAM JOHN	55	
WHITIKER WM	76	

WHITING	CHARLES		52
WHITMAN	JOHN		39
WHITNEY	JACOB		21
WHITNEY	JAMES		27
WHITSEY	ISAAC N		28
WHITSON	JOHN		9
WHITSON	THO'S		10
WHITSON	WESLEY		39
WHITTICHKER	ANDREW		55
WHITTICHKER	JAMES		55
WHITTICHKER	JOHN		55
WHITTICHKER	THOMAS		55
WHITTIN	JOB		27
WHITWORTH	JOSEPH S		52
WHORTON	WILLIAM		21
WIATT	ALLEN		67
WIATT	BRATON		75
WIBLE	SAMUEL		44
WICHARD	JOSEPH		56
WICOFF	JAMES		27
WIDDLE	THO'S		10
WIDENER	JOHN		31
WIGGINS	THERON		49
WILBER	WILLIAM P		3
WILBORN	J Y		49
WILCAL	FRANCIS		15
WILCAL	JNO		15
WILCAL	JOHN JR		15
WILCAL	WM		15
WILCOT	CLARK		71
WILCOX	AARON		65
WILCOX	ASHER		67
WILCOX	DAVID		65
WILCOX	ISAAC		65
WILCUTS	THOMAS		76
WILDMAN	BENJAMIN		19
WILDMAN	JAMES		13
WILDMAN	JOHN		13
WILDMAN	JOSEPH		18
WILEY	AQUILLA		56
WILEY	EDWARD		72
WILEY	JOHN		61
WILEY	JOSEPH		17
WILEY	THOMAS	73	76
WILEY	WILLIAM		56
WILEY	ZECHARIAH JR		56
WILEY	ZECHARIAH SR		56
WILGAND	GEORGE		56
WILIAMS	MORGAN		73
WILKASON	SAMUEL		61
WILKENSON	JOHN		18
WILKESON	JOHN		71
WILKEY	SAMUEL		20
WILKING	JAMES		19

WILKINS	JER		16
WILKINSON	JOSHUA		19
WILKISON	BENAJAH		54
WILKISON	BENNIGAH		27
WILKISON	JOHN	55	57
WILKISON	ROBERT		27
WILKS	GEORGE H		3
WILKS	HENRY		3
WILKS	JOSEPH		7
WILKS	SAMUEL		3
WILKY	HIRAM		27
WILLARD	HENERY		48
WILLARD	PETTER		27
WILLARD	TITUS B		27
WILLCOX	ISAAC		46
WILLES	JOSEPH		31
WILLETT	JAMES		59
WILLFONG	MICHAEL		67
WILLHAITE	POSHUA		16
WILLHITE	ECHILLOS		14
WILLHITE	JOHN		14
WILLHOITE	JOHN H		22
WILLIAM	ALEXANDER		69
WILLIAM	JOHN		52
WILLIAMS	- - -		28
WILLIAMS	ABSOLAM		39
WILLIAMS	ACHILLIS		76
WILLIAMS	AMOS		56
WILLIAMS	ANDERSON		10
WILLIAMS	BURNARD		72
WILLIAMS	CALEB		73
WILLIAMS	CHARLES		68
WILLIAMS	CONSTANT		3
WILLIAMS	DANIEL		49
WILLIAMS	DANIEL		56
WILLIAMS	DANN		52
WILLIAMS	DAVID		42
WILLIAMS	EDWARD		14
WILLIAMS	ELU		56
WILLIAMS	ENOCH		52
WILLIAMS	GARRET		13
WILLIAMS	GEORGE	32	52
WILLIAMS	HARVEY		58
WILLIAMS	HEZEKIAH		74
WILLIAMS	ISAAC	3	39
WILLIAMS	J		14
WILLIAMS	JAMES	48 63	69
WILLIAMS	JASPER JR		56
WILLIAMS	JASPER SR		56
WILLIAMS	JESSE	3	75
WILLIAMS	JESSEE		49
WILLIAMS	JOHN	42 48 49+ 56	59
WILLIAMS	JOHN	64	73
WILLIAMS	JOHN R		44

WILLIAMS	JONATHAN				39
WILLIAMS	JOSEPH			23	33
WILLIAMS	JOSHUA				73
WILLIAMS	LEWIS			42	59
WILLIAMS	MICAJAH				63
WILLIAMS	MOSES		14	23	39
WILLIAMS	NOTLEY				11
WILLIAMS	OTHO				56
WILLIAMS	PHILIP				14
WILLIAMS	REMEMBRANCE				13
WILLIAMS	RICHARD		3	56	73
WILLIAMS	ROBERT				7
WILLIAMS	ROBT				13
WILLIAMS	RUFUS				52
WILLIAMS	SAMUEL		27	72	76
WILLIAMS	SAWYER				49
WILLIAMS	THOMAS			20	42
WILLIAMS	WILEY				67
WILLIAMS	WILLIAM	44	49	56	64
WILLIAMS	WILLIAM				68
WILLIAMS	WM		11	49	75
WILLIAMS	ZACHARIAH				39
WILLIAMSON	JOHN				7
WILLIAMSON	JOSEPH				46
WILLIAMSON	THOMAS				3+
WILLIAMSON	W				15
WILLILAMS	HENRY				50
WILLINGTON	JOHN P				24
WILLIS	ISAAC				74
WILLIS	JACOB				63
WILLIS	JAMES ABRAHAM				27
WILLIS	JOHN				71
WILLIS	JOSEPH				31
WILLIS	NOAH C				11
WILLIS	WM				59
WILLLIAMS	ELEANAH				49
WILLMORE	JACOB				33
WILLMORE	JOSEPH				33
WILLMOTT	JOSEPH SR				76
WILLOT	WILLIAM				72
WILLS	ANTHONY				3
WILLSON	ANDREW				24
WILLSON	THOMAS				71
WILMOTT	JOSEPH			74	76
WILSON	ALEX'R				18
WILSON	ABRAHAM				34
WILSON	ALEX'R				18
WILSON	ALEXANDER				64
WILSON	ALLEXANDER				27
WILSON	ANDREW				41
WILSON	BENJAMIN			10	17
WILSON	CHARLES				64
WILSON	DAVID		21	49	58
WILSON	EDWARD				34

WILSON	EPHRAIM					56
WILSON	GEORGE					18
WILSON	HARMON					64
WILSON	HENRY				56	62
WILSON	JACOB					21
WILSON	JAMES	21	40	43	48	54
WILSON	JAMES		55	56	64	69
WILSON	JAMES S					60
WILSON	JAS					19
WILSON	JASPER					41
WILSON	JEREMIAH					44
WILSON	JESSE					56
WILSON	JOB					54
WILSON	JOHN	3	14	20	27+	34
WILSON	JOHN	39+	41	44	50	
WILSON	JOHN				60+	64
WILSON	JOHN A					13
WILSON	JOHN F					10
WILSON	JOSEPH					21
WILSON	JOSEPH					23
WILSON	JOSEPH JR					43
WILSON	JOSEPH SR					43
WILSON	LEWIS					49
WILSON	MOSES				17	18
WILSON	MOSES					27
WILSON	NATHANIEL				19	45
WILSON	PATON					41
WILSON	PATRICK					18
WILSON	RICHARD					14
WILSON	ROBERT				27	49
WILSON	SAMUEL			20	27	41
WILSON	SAMUEL JR					27
WILSON	SAMUEL N					34
WILSON	SOLOMON					19
WILSON	STEPHEN					76
WILSON	STEVEN					3
WILSON	STEWART				3	4
WILSON	THOMAS					67
WILSON	THOMAS					39
WILSON	WALTER					7
WILSON	WASHINGTON					64
WILSON	WILLIAM	18	20	23+	31	
WILSON	WILLIAM			40	54	64
WILSON	WILLIAM L					31
WILSON	WM					58
WILY	JA'S					10
WINCHEL	JOHN					27
WINCHESTER	JOHN					18
WINCLES	JEREMIAH					10
WINDER	DANIEL					51
WINDSOR	THOS					15
WINDSOR	WM					15
WINEMILLER	CONROD					52
WINEMILLER	JACOB JR					52

Name	Page
WINEMILLER JACOB SR	52
WINEMILLER JAMES	49
WININGH MOSES	58
WINKLER JOHN	10
WINKLER THO'S	12
WINN JAMES	11
WINSLOW JAMES	63
WINSLOW JOHN	75
WINSLOW JOHN W	63
WINTERS TIMOTHY	67
WIRE JOHN	67
WIRE THO'S	22
WIRE THOMAS	67
WISE JACOB	45
WISE JAS	13
WISE SAMUEL	28
WISE HART JOHN	48
WISEMEN JOHN	4
WISEMON ROBERT	7
WISMAN ABRAHAM	3
WISMAN FREDERICK	35
WIT B	22
WITHAM GIDEON	22
WITMAN WILLIAM	3
WITSMAN JACOB	43
WITT ENOCH	74
WITTIAS THOMAS	75
WITTY WILLIAM	44
WOEHRLY JACOB	54
WOEHRLY THO'S	54
WOHLGEMUTH JACOB	54
WOLBERTON JOHN D	28
WOLF HENRY	41
WOLF JOHN	44
WOLF PETER	40
WOLF SOLOMON	54
WOLFINGTON ABRAHAM	45
WOLFINGTON JAMES	45
WOLFINTON GEORGE	45
WOLFINTON JOHN	42
WOOD A	57
WOOD ABRAHAM	65
WOOD ANSEL	58
WOOD DANIEL	8 65
WOOD EARL	28
WOOD ELIAS	27
WOOD FRANCIS	41
WOOD GEORGE	60
WOOD HENRY	39
WOOD JEREMIAH	28
WOOD JOHN	17
WOOD JOHN	39 61 63
WOOD JOSEPH	34
WOOD LUKE	58
WOOD MARTAIN M	27
WOOD MATTHEW	61
WOOD MOSES G	11
WOOD VINCENT	7
WOOD WILLIAM	70
WOODARD ASAHU	75
WOODARD BARDET	39
WOODARD JAMES	68
WOODARD JONAH	67
WOODARD SILAS	39
WOODBURN ROBERT	18
WOODEN AMOS	35
WOODEN SOMOMON	39
WOODEN WM	10
WOODEY JOSEPH	71
WOODFILL ANDREW	20
WOODFILL DANIEL	14 23
WOODFILL DANIEL JR	14
WOODFILL GABRIEL	23
WOODFILL GRABRIEL	14
WOODFILL JOHN	19 20 23
WOODFILL SAMUEL	14
WOODFORD JULIS	3
WOODHOUSE HENRY	35
WOODKIR JOSEPH	72
WOODKIRK JOHN	74
WOODMANSEE GABRIEL	10
WOODMANSEE JA'S	10 11
WOODRUFF ANDREW	43
WOODRUFF GAD	67
WOODRUM ARCHABALD	70
WOODS ANDREW	71
WOODS DAVID	7
WOODS ISAAC	7
WOODS JAMES	17 39
WOODS JOHN	3 7
WOODS JOSEPH	7+
WOODS JOSEPH L	7
WOODS MARK D	39
WOODS NATHAN	43
WOODS PATTERICK	7
WOODS SAMUEL	7 43 71
WOODS WILLIAM	27
WOODS WILLIAM P	7
WOODWARD CHARLES	22
WOODWARD CHESLEY	27
WOODWARD HENRY	22
WOODWORTH CALEB	55
WOODY LEWIS	62
WOOFTER JAMES	71
WOOLEY DANIEL	56
WOOLF PETER	7
WOOLFINGTON JOHN	61
WORD DANIEL	73

WORLEY	FREDERICK		64
WORMON	WILSON		11
WORREL	ISAAC		60
WORRELL	JOHN C		67
WORREN	GABRIEL L		9
WORREN	JOEL		9
WORREN	MOSES		12
WORSHAM	DANIEL		59
WREIGHT	JACOB		30
WREIGHT	WILLIAM		30
WREN	WILLIAM		56
WRIGHT	AMOS		65
WRIGHT	ASA		69
WRIGHT	CALEB		39
WRIGHT	CHRISTOPHER		3
WRIGHT	DARLING		55
WRIGHT	DAVID		73
WRIGHT	ELI		63
WRIGHT	ELIJAH		65 72
WRIGHT	EVINS		63
WRIGHT	HORACE		23
WRIGHT	JAMES		39 71
WRIGHT	JESSE		39
WRIGHT	JOHN		39 58 65
WRIGHT	JOHN II		39
WRIGHT	JONATHAN		41 72
WRIGHT	JONATHAN L		12
WRIGHT	JOSEPH 6		48
WRIGHT	JOSHUA		70
WRIGHT	JOSIAH		39
WRIGHT	LEVI		19 62 65
WRIGHT	NOAH		60
WRIGHT	PETER		39 69
WRIGHT	PHILBERT		39 63
WRIGHT	RALPH		71+
WRIGHT	RICHARD		39
WRIGHT	SMITH		9
WRIGHT	THESON		12
WRIGHT	WILLIAM		39 61
WYATT	JONATHAN		39
WYBLE	ADAM		69
WYLEY	EDWARD		76
WYMAN	FREDERICK		66
WYMAN	GEORGE		3
WYMAN	HENRY JR		66
WYMAN	HENRY SR		66
WYMAN	LEONARD		66
WYMAN	LEWIS		3
WYMER	WM		10
WYMN	WILLIAM		39
WYNN	ISAAC		65

Y

YATES	ABRHAM		56
YATES	BENJAMIN		3
YATES	JOHN		3 56
YATES	ROBERT		3
YATES	WILLIAM		56 63
YEARNS	JOHN		57
YEARY	HENRY O		12
YEOMAN	PETTER		27
YORK	ELI		51
YORK	JOHN		48
YORK	JONES		50
YORK	JOSHUA		68
YORK	SAM'L SR		51
YORK	SHUBEL		50
YORK	WM		50
YOST	ISAAC		13
YOUCE	JOSEPH		28
YOUMANS	JOHN		21
YOUNG	ANDREW		18
YOUNG	DAVID		56
YOUNG	EWIS		70
YOUNG	GEORGE		56
YOUNG	HENRY		63
YOUNG	HEZEKIAH		14
YOUNG	IRA		55
YOUNG	JACOB JR		66
YOUNG	JACOB SR		66
YOUNG	JAMES		62
YOUNG	JOHN		32
YOUNG	JOSEPH		39 62
YOUNG	MOSES		16
YOUNG	NATHAN		57
YOUNG	NICHOLAS		63
YOUNG	PETER JR		56
YOUNG	PETER SR		56
YOUNG	REUBEN		10
YOUNG	SAMPOSON		42
YOUNG	SAMUEL		59
YOUNG	THO'S		11
YOUNG	THOMAS		69+
YOUNG	WHITTER		42
YOUNG	WILLIAM		69
YOUNGMAN	JOHN		7

Z

ZARING PHILIP	64
ZEABRISKY HENRY	41
ZEDOR AUGUST	30
ZEEK ADAM	73
ZELLER FREDERICK	54
ZIGLAR JOHN	70
ZIGLER PHILIP	61
ZIMMERMAN JACOB	58
ZIMMERMAN SAMUEL	7
ZIMMERMON JACOB	54
ZIMMERMON NATHAN	54
ZINK DAVID	39
ZINK JACOB	39
ZOLMAN ADAM	10
ZUNDEL JACOB	54
ZUNDEL PINODUS	54